Wissenschaftliche Untersuchungen
zum Neuen Testament · 2. Reihe

Herausgeber / Editor
Jörg Frey (Zürich)

Mitherausgeber / Associate Editors
Friedrich Avemarie (Marburg)
Markus Bockmuehl (Oxford)
Hans-Josef Klauck (Chicago, IL)

287

John C. Poirier

The Tongues of Angels

The Concept of Angelic Languages
in Classical Jewish and Christian Texts

Mohr Siebeck

JOHN C. POIRIER, born 1963; 1993 ThM in New Testament at Duke University; 2005 DHL in Ancient Judaism at the Jewish Theological Seminary (NY); named Chair of Biblical Studies at the newly forming Kingswell Theological Seminary (OH).

ISBN 978-3-16-150569-0
ISSN 0340-9570 (Wissenschaftliche Untersuchungen zum Neuen Testament, 2. Reihe)

Die Deutsche Nationalbibliothek lists this publication in the Deutsche Nationalbiblio-graphie; detailed bibliographic data are available on the Internet at *http://dnb.d-nb.de*.

For Nick and Natalie

Preface

I wish to thank the editors of WUNT, especially Professor Dr. Jörg Frey, for accepting my manuscript and for including it in the second series. Their enthusiasm for the project was inspiring. I particularly want to thank my production editor, Ms. Tanja Mix, for always getting back to me so quickly. Her guidance made the task of reformatting my study to WUNT style much less of a chore.

Franklin, 25 May 2010   John C. Poirier

Table of Contents

Abbreviations

Abbreviations and citation conventions for ancient literature and modern scholarship follow *OCD*³ (1996) and *SBL* (1999) wherever possible. In addition, the following abbreviations are used, with full bibliographical details in the Bibliography:

CMC	*Cologne Mani Codex*
Corp. herm.	*Corpus hermeticum*
Dis	Philodemos, *De dis*
Hist. laus.	Palladius, *Historia lausiaca*
JSJSup	Supplements to the Journal for the Study of Judaism
J&CP	Jewish and Christian Perspectives
London MS Or.	London Oriental Manuscript (British Museum)
Mart. Perp.	*Martyrdom of Perpetua and Felicitas*
NHMS	Nag Hammadi and Manichaean Studies
*OCD*³	S. Hornblower and A. Spawforth (eds.), *Oxford Classical Dictionary* (3d ed.)
SBL	P. H. Alexander et al. (eds.), *The SBL Handbook of Style: for Ancient Near Eastern, Biblical, and Early Christian Studies*
Synopse	P. Schäfer, *Synopse zur Hekhalot-Literatur*
T.-S. K	Taylor-Schechter Cairo Geniza text
VCSup	Supplements to Vígiliae Christianae

Chapter 1

Introduction

What language do angels speak? For the historian of religion, this question connects with questions about early Jewish and Christian beliefs about angels, prophecy, and mystical ascents. The following pages attempt to make the most of this arrangement. The principal burden of this study is to describe the main views of angelic languages in late antiquity, and to classify and discuss the writings that present evidence for these views.

Among Jews in late antiquity, there were two main views about which language angels spoke. It is not clear what the majority view was during the Second Temple period, but, during the rabbinic era, the view that angels spoke Hebrew appears to have been in the ascendency. This goes hand in hand with the heightened importance of Torah during the late tannaitic/early amoraic period. I call this view "hebraeophone". The other major view is that the angels spoke an esoteric heavenly language, normally unintelligible to humans. In the investigation of primary sources that occupies chapters two, four, and five, the esoteric-language view occupies several times as much space as the hebraeophone view, but the reader should not take that to indicate the degree to which this view might have dominated ancient Judaism and early Christianity. It merely represents the difficulty of discerning the esoteric-language view in certain cases.

"Angeloglossy" is the term that I use to denote the language of angels, irrespective of whether that language is also native to humans or not. I also use "angeloglossy" to denote the phenomenon of humans speaking in esoteric angelic languages. The question of which view of angelic languages is the earlier is difficult, and I do not attempt to answer it. I begin with the hebraeophone view simply because the evidence for it is more straightforward. Although we cannot confidently state that the hebraeophone view of angels is older than the esoteric-language view, the earliest extant source attesting this view (*viz. Jubilees*) is undoubtedly older than any of the sources attesting an esoteric angelic language. In discussing the notion of a specifically *angelic* language, I should mention that there is a wealth of speculation about the language of heaven in Jewish tradition in general, including a widespread tradition that Hebrew is the language of creation and/or heaven, thereby implicitly denying that the heavenly language is esoteric. In these sources, it is often assumed that the earliest human tongue was also the heavenly tongue.[1]

A. Purpose and Organization of this Study

The topic of angelic languages has never before received a book-length treatment. To make up for this neglect, I seek first to establish a few basic facts, *viz.* the nature, extent, and durability of the two principal views concerning what language angels speak.[2] The chronological bounds of this study are far flung. I begin with *Jubilees* (mid-2nd cent. B.C.E.) – the earliest text to touch upon the issue of angeloglossy.[3] As a lower bound, this study uses the main redaction of the Babylonian Talmud (ca. 550–650 C.E.), which I take to mark the end of the "classical" period of rabbinic Judaism. These bounds mark off a period of 700 or 800 years.[4]

This study is organized in the following way: chapter two surveys the documentary evidence for the hebraeophone view, found primarily in *Jubilees*, 4Q464, various rabbinic and targumic texts, and in a tiny minority of Christian texts. Chapter three shows a connection between the linguistic situation and the Palestinian rabbinic view, exploring how third-century rabbis used their linguistic circumstances to their advantage. It begins by trying to establish that Hebrew was a minority language in third-century Jewish Palestine, and argues that the hebraic underpinning of rabbinic theology and ideology, combined with the privilege of being able to read Hebrew in a largely non-hebraeophone and illiterate society, culminated in R. Yochanan's attempt to proscribe the practice of praying outside the synagogue, and that the bare fact of the aforementioned privilege empowered the rabbis within their society. Chapters four and five look at a number of

---

[1] See Rubio 1977:40–1; Paul 1987:esp. 235–43.

[2] The question of whether the mental-communication understanding of angelic "speech" (represented sometime later by Thomas Aquinas and Dante) is a third view, or only a subspecies of the esoteric-language view, is immaterial to this study. It is worth noting, however, that Ephrem Syrus's gradation of languages according to their rarefication suggests the latter.

[3] The frequent claim that *1 En.* 61.11–12 or 71.11 refers to angeloglossy fails of demonstration.

[4] I use the term "classical" strictly in a chronological sense. For Jewish antiquity, the "classical period" is usually thought to end with the main redaction of the Babylonian Talmud, around 650 C.E. (perhaps earlier). For Christian antiquity, the "classical period" is often thought to end earlier: with the death of Augustine of Hippo, in 430 C.E. While this study uses "classical period" in the first sense, it should be noted that the Christian sources that are named in section headings all happen to fall into the period defined by the latter sense, with the exception of parts of the *Coptic Wizard's Hoard*, said to have been written in five hands dating from the fourth to seventh centuries C.E.

Jewish and Christian writings that may refer to an esoteric angelic language. Chapter four treats the more certain references at length, including those found in 1 and 2 Corinthians, the *Testament of Job*, the *Apocalypse of Zephaniah*, the *Ascension of Isaiah*, the *Apocalypse of Abraham*, *Genesis Rabbah*, and the Coptic *Book of the Resurrection of Jesus Christ* (hereafter *Book of the Resurrection*) attributed to Bartholomew. Chapter five turns to the cases which are more difficult to decide, including possible references to angeloglossy in the *Songs of the Sabbath Sacrifice*, the Babylonian Talmud, a fourth-century Christian inscription from Kotiaeion (Asia Minor), and the jubilus from the Christian liturgical tradition. These sources represent a wide variety of movements within Judaism and Christianity, which shows the pervasiveness of the esoteric-language view.

The study ends with a summary conclusion (chapter six).

B. Methodological Preface

1. Should Pseudepigrapha be Presumed Jewish or Christian?

Several of the works we will be examining are pseudepigraphic. One of the main concerns of any study comparing elements from pseudepigrapha is that it is often difficult to tell whether a given writing should be classified as (primarily) Jewish or Christian. An earlier generation of scholars was quick to assume that every Jewish-sounding pseudepigraphon with no distinctively Christian elements was bound to be Jewish in origin, but scholarship has recently come to terms with the fact that even those works that contain no distinctively Christian elements may, in fact, be largely or entirely the products of a Christian writer. As William Adler notes, most of the works we are discussing are often ascribed to ancient figures, so that "Semitisms and content seemingly incompatible with a Christian religious outlook may only be antiquarian touches designed to enhance the work's credibility."[5] The tide of opinion of late has been to reverse the burden of proof set up by an earlier generation. According to the new emerging consensus, if a given writing was preserved solely by the church, then, barring clear indications to the contrary, it should be assumed to be Christian.

Robert Kraft addressed these issues in two important essays. He notes that, prior to the eighth century C.E., almost all of the texts that we possess, "[a]part from the DSS and some early Rabbinic materials," were transmitted through Christian channels.[6] These pseudepigrapha "are, first of all,

---

[5] Adler 1996:27.

[6] R. A. Kraft 2001:384. See R. A. Kraft 1994, and the articles now collected in R. A. Kraft 2009. The present trend to take the Christian propagation of the pseudepigrapha more seriously as a clue to its provenance was anticipated in Sparks 1984:xiii–xvii.

'Christian' materials, and recognition of that fact is a necessary step in using them appropriately in the quest to throw light on early Judaism. [This
is] the 'default' position – sources transmitted by way of Christian communities are 'Christian,' whatever else they may also prove to be."[7] To a
bygone generation, such a position might have sounded hypercritical, but
scholars today recognize that Christians and Jews often wrote in the same
styles, and drew from the same material. Kraft writes that he *"expect[s]*
that there were self-consciously Christian authors who wrote new works
that focused on Jewish persons or traditions and contained no uniquely
Christian passages," listing "the rather innocent homily on the heroic life
of a Job or a Joseph" as a prime example.[8] Kraft does not think it impossible for the church to have faithfully transmitted a Jewish writing[9] – but the
burden of proof regarding the church's handling of such writings, as well
as the presumption that a given writing is Jewish, is (he argues) to be assigned differently than once assumed. This stance was recently bolstered
through a book by James R. Davila.[10] Davila supports the use of Kraft's
rule with a case-by-case demonstration of the internal consistency of assigning a number of pseudepigrapha preserved by the Church to Christian
hands. This recognition that a Jewish-sounding pseudepigraphon may actually be Christian is both the product and the spur of recent attempts to
rethink the so-called "parting of the ways" between the two religions. Yet
it is important to note that these are two separate issues: (1) How does one
tell the difference between a Jewish writing and a Christian writing? and
(2) Is there really a solid dividing line between Judaism and Christianity?[11]

---

[7] R. A. Kraft 2001:372.

[8] R. A. Kraft 2001:375. See Kaestli 1995.

[9] R. A. Kraft 2001:379. R. A. Kraft (2001:382–3) notes a famous case (Philo's discussion of the Therapeutae in *De vita contemplativa*) in which the Jewish origin of a writing
has been rehabilitated.

[10] Davila 2005.

[11] Scholars have become more sensitive to the problem of separating Christianity from
Judaism. As Tomson (1999:193) writes, "Christianity developed as a separate religious
community out of Judaism not so much by adhering to a specific messianic confession –
which could have kept its place among other Jewish dissenters – but by integrating
masses of non-Jews who in the course of history quickly ended up setting themselves off
from the mother religion." See J. Taylor 1990; Saldarini 1994:3; Kimelman 1999. Boyarin (1999:10–11) suggests that the border between Judaism and Christianity "was so
fuzzy that one could hardly say precisely at what point one stopped and the other began."
As R. A. Kraft notes, Boyarin comes close to totalizing the lack of distinction between
many forms of Judaism and of Christianity. In some ways, Lieu (1994:esp. 117) has been
programmatic for the current flurry of revisionist studies, but she is more interested in
showing that many early Jews and Christians viewed the separation in more caustic terms
than is implied by the ecumenical-sounding "parting of the ways". The Christians that
she names in connection with this are those that were subsequently canonized as the
voice of orthodoxy. In this respect, Lieu seems to be arguing that "the parting of the

But do the drawbacks of putting all one's egg in a particular basket justify putting them *all* in a different basket? And how does the fact that a given writing was preserved by the church make it more likely that it was originally Christian? William Gruen III writes that the "practical result" of assigning a Christian provenance to a pseudepigraphon as a matter of default is that the only texts that could be excluded on the basis of their textual tradition would be those found at Qumran. "It would be naïve," Gruen writes, "... to imagine that the community of the Dead Sea Scrolls possessed every text that circulated within Judaism of the Hellenistic and Early Roman period."[12] To be fair, the proponents of the "Christian provenance" default position do *not* state the matter in terms that are open to Gruen's *reductio ad absurdum* – to lobby for a default position is not nearly the same as saying that all the writings assigned a provenance on the basis of that position assuredly belong to that default group. There is room to wonder, however, whether the terms of the Kraft/Davila approach are really the most reasonable.

My purpose in these few paragraphs is to register my (at least) partial dissent from the view argued by Kraft and others. It is far from clear that the church preserved *more* Jewish-sounding pseudepigrapha of Christian origin than of Jewish origin, therefore it is not at all clear that a Christian origin is a safer assumption than a Jewish origin. The safest procedure is to leave the question *non liquet*. In my view, after we have expended every effort to determine whether a given writing is Jewish or Christian, the safest position is to discuss the writing without referring at all to its religious provenance, and to give a slight, tentative, and qualified favor to a position of *Jewish* provenance with respect to those questions where it might make a difference. The Christian-until-proven-otherwise position

---

ways" model is not violent enough. She questions whether NT scholars are correct in appealing to the Aphrodisias inscription pertaining to God-fearers: "They need the God-fearers both to establish continuities leading into the Christian church – it was from this group of synagogue adherents that the earliest Christians were drawn – and to demonstrate the fuzziness of first-century ideas of being a Jew – thus Christian redefinition falls within this internal debate" (Lieu 1994:107). Her point is the precise opposite of that of some more recent revisionists, who emphasize the "fuzziness of first-century ideas of being a Jew" *vis-à-vis being a Christian*. For an example of a non-violent revisionist account, based on Justin Martyr's *Dialogue with Trypho* and the (now lost) *Controversy between Jason and Papiscus regarding Christ* (mentioned by Origen), see Watson 1997:310. According to Watson (1997:311), "The real 'parting of the ways' occurs not between Justin and Trypho but between Trypho and Maricon. Justin rejects the programme of a radical de-judaizing of Christianity, and it is precisely because he and Trypho have not gone their separate ways but still appeal to the same texts that the disagreement can be so fundamental." See now the papers collected in Becker and Yoshiko Reed (eds.) 2003.

[12] Gruen 2009:164.

cashes in on some good points, but ultimately it probably is not a real advance on the way things used to be done.

2 Rabbinic Writings as Historiography

There are two basic problems with using rabbinic writings as historiography: (1) there is no guarantee that a saying attributed to a rabbi was really said by him, and (2) sayings do not transparently reveal the social reality behind them: one must grapple with the ideological content of a saying before accepting what it says about the situation in Jewish Palestine at a given time.[13] My approach to rabbinic writings is a mediating position between the "hermeneutic of good-will" of Zionist and Israeli scholarship[14] and the documentary approach associated with Jacob Neusner. It is mainly in response to the former approach that Neusner has turned rabbinic documents in upon their own editorial "voices", and it is mainly in response to the latter that scholars have honed useful and responsible approaches to the rabbinic writings.

In the 1980s and 1990s, Neusner made the editorial voice of any given rabbinic document so deafening that the contents of that document could not be used to determine the prior shape of any traditions taken up into that document.[15] His overcompensation for the role of the editor has resulted in an uncontrolled multiplication of "Judaisms" (his term): since each document is but an expression of its editor's own thoughts, each constitutes a carefully constructed form and distinctive expression of Judaism.[16] This

---

[13] Cf. Boccaccini 1994:255: "rabbinic documents are not chaotic collections of ancient material and parallels; they are consistent ideological documents".

[14] For this description, see Schwartz 2002.

[15] Neusner's approach to constructing history from rabbinic writings can be divided into three distinct stages: (1) in the 1950s and 1960s, Neusner used rabbinic literature to write rabbinic biography, (2) in the 1970s, he denounced his earlier biographical studies, and honed a method whereby attributions to a particular figure were to be assumed as accurate attributions only at the level of that figure's circle of influence (i.e. to that figure's generation), and (3) in the 1980s and 1990s, he attributed so much to the editors of the rabbinic writings that a form-critical study of the rabbinic corpus became a vain gesture. The fact that Neusner believes so strongly in absorbing his earlier writings into new books (*verbatim!*) sometimes plays havoc with the attempt to write Neusner's intellectual biography. When what is essentially a rearrangement of paragraphs from the 1970s is published as a "new" book by Neusner in the 1980s, it becomes difficult to discern what Neusner really believed in the 1980s. Ironically, one might even say that the editorial voice in many of Neusner's *own books* is not nearly as powerful as he assumes the editorial voice to be within rabbinic works, even though the former corpus is not advertised as a compilation of earlier material, while the latter is!

[16] In Neusner's words (1993b:301): "Each of the score of documents that make up the canon of Judaism in late antiquity exhibits distinctive traits in logic, rhetoric, and topic, so that we may identify the purposes and traits of form and intellect of the authorship of

takes things way too far: the claim that there are multiple forms of Judaism is of course one that should be accepted and applied intuitively as an explanatory grid for much that we find, but the claim that each rabbinic document represents its own narrow "Judaism" goes far beyond a judicial use of such a grid.

To be sure, Neusner's infusion of historical skepticism has served well: the credulity of an earlier day has been replaced by an awareness that much of the rabbinic tradition is tendentious. But scholars today are moving beyond the extreme and restrictive premises upon which Neusner built his system. It is now widely realized that careful methods, based on reasonable assumptions about form history (the type of form history that Neusner himself honed in the early 1970s), can often separate the different strata of rabbinic material. The trademark of this mediating position is the caveat that, while rabbinic history is a possibility, biography always lies beyond our reach.[17] The possibility of writing rabbinic history, no matter how gapped that history might end up, provides the methodological underpinning for my own use of rabbinic writings.

David Goodblatt contends that the "debiographization of rabbinic literature"[18] has had a liberating effect on the task of history. He argues that the amoraic stratum of the Talmud is not hopelessly lost in the medley of voices: "the final editors of the Babylonian Talmud did not attempt to 'homogenize' the two strata [i.e., amoraic and saboraic], but rather left the amoraic material essentially intact."[19] It is this unhomogenized state of the rabbinic sources that allows the possibility of getting behind whatever editorial agendas may be operating. Richard Kalmin has also wrestled with the problem of writing rabbinic history. He argues for what we referred to

---

that document. It follows that documents possess integrity and are not merely scrapbooks, compilations made with no clear purpose or aesthetic plan."

[17] The move away from biography is traced in Saldarini 1986:451–4. In light of the now general warning that rabbinic biography cannot be done, many of the old introductions stand in need of rewriting. Green 1978:87 notes that the biographical approach "is evident in virtually every article on an early rabbinic figure in the recent Encyclopedia Judaica".

[18] Goodblatt 1980:35.

[19] Goodblatt 1980:37. Similarly, Kraemer 1989 contends that the "superficial" characteristics of the amoraic stratum can help the historian of rabbinics determine which attributions are authentic. In this connection, the discussion in Wills 1995:215 of the ancient author's lack of concern for editorial inconcinnities is instructive: "Scribal culture is usually the subculture of literate professionals in an illiterate society who reflect so-called craft literacy. Their drive to eliminate clumsy transitions and repetitions was probably less exercised than that of, say, the letter writers of eighteenth-century England who were part of an emerging literate culture. … Scribes in oral culture are often content to conflate texts and insertions without being overly concerned for transitions and narrative flow."

above as the "mediating position": "[T]he Talmud is comprised of diverse sources which were not completely homogenized in the process of editing."[20] Redaction criticism has traditionally relied upon the extreme difficulty posed to an editor who tries to make a document thoroughly tendentious in a direction different from its sources. Kalmin uses this principle to good effect: "Early material bears the stamp of tradition and is difficult to systematically expunge, even when considered inappropriate from the standpoint of later generations."[21] The principle of applying leverage to an unhomogenized text involves paying attention to instances in which the Babylonian Talmud has not completely "Babylonianized" Palestinian tradition.[22]

C. Conclusion

Bearing these methodologems in mind, I turn first to the book of *Jubilees*, the first and perhaps clearest writing to assert that Hebrew was the primordial language, and to imply that Hebrew was also the native language of the angels. The texts that we will study in connection with that position are fewer in number than those that (either certainly or possibly) posit an esoteric angelic tongue, but they are in no way less important. Indeed, they preserve the earliest traces of a view that would become dominant in Judaism.

---

[20] Kalmin 1994:10.

[21] Kalmin 1994:57. Kalmin (1994:53) notes that "it is unlikely that a document as variegated as the Babylonian Talmud was subjected to the tightly controlled and consistent editorial manipulation" that would result in the characteristic distinctions that one finds between strata.

[22] Kalmin 1994:166–7 notes that hostility between rabbis inheres mostly in *attributed* sources. Anonymous commentary has a tendency to make peace between hostile parties, to ameliorate the amount of insult that an attributed source might contain. Kalmin suggests that the amoraim tended to be less insulting to their forbears and colleagues when editing in the guise of the anonymous voice. He compares the situation to that of the modern journal editor, whose duties extend to a neutral presentation.

Chapter 2

Hebrew as the Language of the Angels

As noted in the Introduction, Jewish and Christian writings from late antiquity give witness to two different views concerning what language angels speak. Some writings promoted the understanding that angels speak Hebrew,[1] while others claimed or implied that angels speak an esoteric heavenly language. In this chapter, I introduce the former of these two views.

That a dominant stream within Judaism attached special religious significance to Hebrew should cause no surprise for the student of religion. Many religions attach a religious significance to a foundational language: John F. A. Sawyer lists Arabic, Sanskrit, Latin, and Avestan as examples of languages holding religious significance in modern times.[2] The motivation for such a view, or for the renewed strength that it might receive at a particular juncture, is often transparently sociological.[3] The special status of the sacred language was often represented by attributing that language to the angels or gods, and it was widely held that the most ancient human tongue was also necessarily divine. A much-cited passage of the neoplatonist Iamblichus (ca. 240–ca. 325 C.E.) makes this reasoning nearly explicit, although it stops short of attributing a special language to the gods: "[S]ince the gods have shown that the entire dialect of the sacred peoples such as the Assyrians and the Egyptians is appropriate for religious ceremonies, for this reason we must understand that our communication with the gods should be in an appropriate tongue [κοινολογίας]."[4] Philodemos argues, on similar grounds, that Zeus speaks Greek (*Dis.* 3).[5]

---

[1] This of set writings also contains claims that the angels speak Aramaic, but that view appears to be a reaction to the view that the angels speak Hebrew.

[2] Sawyer 1999:24. See Coseriu 1988:78–9.

[3] Sawyer 1999:25 lists communal isolation, bilingualism, nationalism, literacy, and political infrastructure as contributing factors in the development of a sacred-language ideology.

[4] Clarke, Dillon, and Hershbell (trans.) 2003:297. Cf. the rendering of T. Taylor (trans.) 1968:293, in which κοινολογίας is rendered "language allied to them". See Assmann 1995:37–46.

[5] See Diels 1917:37. See also Borst 1957–63:1.140.

(For some reason, few of the Greek gods ever *wrote* anything.)[6] As we will see, a number of rabbis had their own form of this argument.[7] It is as Johann Reuchlin once wrote in a letter: "the mediator between God and man was language" – specifically Hebrew.[8] Within various streams of Judaism, the pairing of Hebrew-speaking angels with the use of Hebrew at creation seems to have been undertaken as a matter of course, although there was a potential conflict with the view, also widely held, that each of the 70 (or 72) heathen nations speaks the language of its representative angel.[9]

The hebraeophone view of angeloglossy is most explicitly propounded in *Jubilees* and in a saying attributed to R. Yochanan. The ideology driving this view was also apparently embraced by the Qumran community, as demonstrated by 4Q464, although one searches in vain for an explicit reference to angels speaking Hebrew among the Qumran scrolls. The attaching of religious significance to Hebrew goes back at least to the time of Nehemiah and Ezra, but we do not know how early the specific belief in hebraeophone angeloglossy is. For chronological reasons, I discuss *Jubilees* first (together with 4Q464), then the talmudic references, and finally a few stray references from Christian writings.

A. *Jubilees* (and 4Q464)

The church fathers referred to the book of *Jubilees* as the "Little Genesis", because it retells the biblical narrative from Genesis 1 through Exodus 15. It was probably written in Palestine (in Hebrew) in the second century B.C.E., but a few fragments from Qumran cave four are all that survive of the Hebrew original.[10] For the entire book, we are dependent on an Ethiopic version, which in turn was probably based on a Greek version, and is fragmentarily supported by Greek, Latin, and Syriac versions.

Because *Jubilees* exalts the Torah, R. H. Charles thought that the book was written by a Pharisee.[11] The discovery of the Qumran scrolls has made

---

[6] The exceptions are Athena (as shown on a single vase) and the Muses (as in a set scene). See Henrichs 2003.

[7] See Rubio 1977:40–1; Paul 1987:235–43.

[8] Quoted and translated in G. L. Jones 1999:245.

[9] See Borst 1957–63:1.19–5.

[10] VanderKam 1977: 207–85 argues for a date between 161 and 152 B.C.E. See VanderKam 1992:2.635–48.

[11] Charles 1913:2.1.

that view untenable. The book's many affinities with Qumran beliefs have been the subject of many several studies.[12] James C. VanderKam writes,

[I]t can be said with confidence that Jub. and the specifically sectarian texts from Qumran show an extraordinary similarity in their teachings on predestination, the two moral ways, and the future state of the righteous. ... Since Jub. and, in most cases, the Qumran texts date from approximately the same time, one is almost required to see them as products of a common and unique theological tradition. ... [T]he fact that they adhered to a unique calendar makes the case overwhelming.[13]

Fragments of *Jubilees* were found in Qumran caves 1, 2, 3, 4, and 11, and clear echoes from it are found in the sectarian writings.[14] Ben Zion Wacholder even suggests that *Jubilees* and some other works should "be reclassified as sectarian documents."[15] Although Wacholder's suggestion exaggerates the amount of sectarian *distinctiveness* that *Jubilees* evinces, the point that it was a centrally important text at Qumran needs to be taken seriously. The book obviously has some connection to Qumran, although scholars are divided on whether it was written there[16] or whether it was a product of the community's prehistory. Gene L. Davenport sees two stages in the writing of the book: it was first composed before Qumran came into existence, and then a "second edition" was produced at Qumran (ca. 140–104 B.C.E.).[17] Joseph Fitzmyer has shown that the Qumran *Genesis Apocryphon* is dependent on *Jubilees*, and Gershon Brin has recently argued

---

[12] For a bibliography of studies drawing parallels between *Jubilees* and the Qumran scrolls, see VanderKam 1977:259 n. 95. VanderKam 1977:260 compares the two corpora in respect to "their theological doctrines of predestination, the two moral ways, and the postmortem state of the righteous; their calendar; and their exegesis of Gen.". On *Jubilees*'s presence and literary influence at Qumran, see Hogeterp 2009:34. Compare also the Qumran self-title "plant of righteousness" (from 1QS) with *Jub.* 1.16; 7.34; 16.26; 21.24; 36.6. See Tiller 1997; Tyloch 1988.

[13] VanderKam 1977:270.

[14] *Jubilees* is almost certainly mentioned in CD 16.2–4. See VanderKam 1977:255–6. On the influence of *Jubilees* at Qumran, see Boccaccini 1998:86–98.

[15] Wacholder 1997:210.

[16] For a bibliography of studies arguing that *Jubilees* was written at Qumran, see VanderKam 1977:258 n. 94. See also Eissfeldt 1966:607–8. VanderKam 1977:280–1 disagrees with the Qumran-authorship view: "There are ... some noteworthy differences which require that one not assign Jub. to the pen of a Qumran exile. For example, while the sectarians awaited two messiahs, one from Aaron and one from Israel, one looks in vain for a messianic hope in Jub. ... Another example is that Jub. requires the death penalty for sabbath violations (2:25–27; 50:13) in harmony with biblical law (Exod. 31:14–15; 35:2; Num. 15:32–36), but CD explicitly rejects capital punishment for such offences (12:3–6). ... There is an unmistakable awareness in Jub. that within Israel there is a chosen group (23:16; 26), but there is absolutely no evidence in the book that the author and his party have gone into a Qumran-like exile."

[17] Davenport 1971:16. For a similar two-edition view of *Jubilees*, see Gmirkin 2000. On possible Qumranic authorship, see also Cross 1995:44; Ringgren 1963:225–6.

that the *Temple Scroll* (11QTemple) and *Jubilees* are connected in some way.[18] *Jubilees* also bears some relationship to Enochic literature (see the treatment of Enoch in *Jub.* 4.16–9; 10.17), parts of which presuppose the Jubilean/Qumranic solar calendar (*1 En.* 72–82).[19]

Jubilees gives a historical and theological defense of some distinctive views on the solar calendar, predestination, and other issues. Many of these distinctive views bear some relation to *Jubilees*'s hostility toward the Gentiles. John J. Collins emphasizes that *Jubilees*'s Abraham warns Jacob to separate from the gentiles (22.16), that the text strongly condemns intermarriage between Jews and gentiles (30.7–17), and that God blesses Levi and his sons for their acts of vengeance against Israel's enemies (30.18).[20] According to *Jubilees*, God has appointed an angel over every nation (except Israel) in order "to lead them astray from him."[21] The motif of the angels' governance over the nations is widespread within Jewish writings, but it is usually not explained in terms of God's hostility toward the nations.

Among the things that *Jubilees* has in common with Qumran is a connection between piety and the Hebrew language. This Hebrew-centered ideology is not surprising, given the Jubilean view of Israel's place among the nations. A Hebrew-speaking heaven comes into view when Abraham receives the ability to speak and understand Hebrew (*Jub.* 12.25–7):[22]

And the LORD God said to me, "Open his mouth and his ears so that he might hear and speak with his mouth in the language which is revealed because it ceased from the mouth of all of the sons of men from the day of the Fall." And I opened his mouth and his ears and his lips and I began to speak with him in Hebrew, in the tongue of creation. And he took his father's books – and they were written in Hebrew – and he copied them. And he began studying them thereafter. And I cause him to know everything which he was unable (to understand). And he studied them (in) the six months of rain.[23]

---

[18] See Fitzmyer 1971:16–17; Brin 1993:108–9. The *Temple Scroll* (11QTemple) is almost certainly not a Qumran composition. Lignée 1988 had seen the same connection before Brin, but he complicated it by attributing both writings to the pre-Qumranic career of the Teacher of Righteousness.

[19] The Qumran reception of *Jubilees* is evidenced in other texts from the Qumran cache besides *Jubilees* itself: e.g., Milik classified 4Q225–7 as "Pseudo-Jubilees" (VanderKam and Milik, 1995:142), and the fragmentary text 4Q464 (see below) appears to be a sort of *pesher* on *Jubilees*.

[20] Collins 1997b:175. See Kugel 1996; Frey 1998.

[21] See D. S. Russell 1964:246.

[22] Borst 1957–63:1.149 understands the recovery of Hebrew to be an epoch event for the author of *Jubilees*: "Mit diesem Satz tritt eine neue Vorstellung in die Geistesgeschichte ein." Müller 1996a:254 compares Abraham's recovery of his father's writings with the discovery of the Law in the time of Josiah's reform.

[23] Trans. Wintermute 1985:82.

"Day of the Fall" refers to the fall of the tower of Babel (see 10.26).[24] Hebrew had been the universal language until that point. According to 3.28, all the animals in the primeval garden spoke the same language.[25] The text does not specify that the language was Hebrew, but the later indication that the first couple spoke Hebrew (12.25) and the fact that Eve conversed with the serpent make it likely that the term "tongue of creation" implies not only that God used Hebrew to call the universe into existence, but also that every living creature originally spoke Hebrew.[26] As Charles notes, the tradition that Abraham reintroduced the lost language of Hebrew was also known to the author of the Pseudo-Clementine *Recognitiones.*[27]

A number of aspects of the Jubilean view are worth investigating. First, although it is related that Hebrew is the heavenly language, that connection is made only to establish the primacy of Hebrew (and probably also of Israel), rather than to speculate on the nature of angels. However, this devaluation of all other languages may also have implied something about human interaction with God – *viz.* that the heathen nations do not have access to God, or that Jews must preserve Hebrew for religious purposes. The angels in *Jubilees* are presented as Israel's coreligionists. As Steven Weitzman writes, "In *Jubilees* Hebrew is ... said to connect those who use it to the heavenly community."[28] This is expressed in the fact that the highest order of angels in *Jubilees* keep the Sabbath (2.21, 30) and Sukkoth (6.18) and bear the mark of circumcision (15.27), so that, in the words of

---

[24] Park 2008:112 writes, "It seems likely that the confusion of languages in the aftermath of the Tower of Babel had something to do with the cessation of observance of the Noachic covenant. In *Jub.* 6.18–19, the angel of the presence tells Moses that there was a lapse in observance between the death of Noah and Abraham's time."

[25] See Borst 1957–63:1.147–8.

[26] Stone and Eshel 1995:220 take it as established that *Jub.* 3.28 refers to Hebrew as "the primordial language". See Rubin 1998:309–10. The linguisticality of animals was a regular feature of Greek golden age accounts. See Gera 2003:29–32, 61–7. The closest parallel with *Jubilees* is that found in Babrius' introduction to Aesop's fables, since it depicts animals, humans, and gods all speaking the same language. (See Luzzatto and Penna 1986.) Cornford 1957:201 compares the linguisticality of animals in the golden age of Kronos (Plato, *Pol.* 272b) with preaching to the animals, as purportedly practiced by Pythagoras and Francis of Assisi. On the *non*-linguisticality of animals in Greek accounts of the difference between humans and animals, see Renehan 1981:244–5. Speech is often taken as the defining characteristic of being human. See Dierauer 1977:12, 33–4; Baldry 1965:15. Apollonius claimed to know the languages of all humans and all animals, which led Eusebius to ask why he then needed the services of a translator on his travels. See Eusebius, *Hier.* 8, 14; Kofsky 2002:68–9.

[27] See Charles 1913:2.32 (note *ad Jub.* 12.25–6). VanderKam 1989:73 mentions more Byzantine chronographers. Hultgård 1977:267 argues that the idea of an eschatological return to a universal language is derived from an Iranian myth. See Plutarch, *Moralia* 370A–C (= *De Iside et Osiride* 47).

[28] Weitzman 1999:41.

Carol Newsom, "at least those laws that regulate the calendar and holy days appear to be binding on the angels as well as on Israel."[29]

It is also possible that *Jubilees*'s hebraeophone view of heaven was meant to displace the notion that the angels spoke an esoteric language. Weitzman spells out the implications of comparing *Jubilees* with works evidencing a wholly different view of angeloglossy: "the significance of the angel from *Jubilees* having revealed the Hebrew language to Abraham is sharpened by the widespread belief, found in many Jewish and Christian texts, that angelic language is different from ordinary language and is, in fact, beyond human linguistic capacities."[30] He cites *Apoc. Ab.* 15.7, *2 En.* 17.1, and 2 Cor 12.4 as examples of the esoteric nature of angelic speech, and *T. Job* 48–50, *Apoc. Zeph.* 8, and *b. B. Bat.* 134a as examples of privileged human acquisition of this language. It should be noted, however, that all of the works that Weitzman cites as evidence for a competing view are later than *Jubilees*, and the (probably) earliest passage among them (2 Cor 12.4) is not as clear an example of esoteric angeloglossy as Weitzman (and many others) think. Although *Jubilees* apparently rejects the idea of angels speaking esoteric languages, it does not do so for reasons intrinsic to this alternative view. Its enthusiastic embrace of Hebrew as an angelic language seems to be driven by its author's self-understanding as part of a "holy remnant" rather than by a fear of the sort of enthusiastic piety associated with esoteric languages. This understanding fits with the reception of *Jubilees* at Qumran.

We should also discuss 4Q464 in this section, since it appears to hold the same view of Hebrew as *Jubilees*. It would seem to present a false account of the evidence to give the fragmentary text 4Q464 a completely separate discussion, apart from the discussion of *Jubilees*, as the features of this text are best explained as a part of *Jubilees*'s reception history.[31] The Hebrew-first ideology displayed in 4Q464 is particularly significant for understanding why the Qumranites depended so much upon the Hebrew language, at a time when Aramaic was the dominant tongue of Palestinian

---

[29] Newsom 1998:180.

[30] Weitzman 1999:41–2. Recension A of *2 Enoch* seems to locate the origin of Hebrew in heaven: according to *2 En.* 23.2 (ver. A), Enoch's angelic guide revealed "the Hebrew language, every kind of language of the new song of the armed troops, and everything that it is appropriate to learn" (trans. Andersen 1983:140).

[31] I have argued elsewhere (Poirier 2002) that 4Q464 is not an eschatological text, as Michael Stone and Esther Eshel would have it, but that it is essentially a *pesher* on *Jubilees* (cf. Eshel and Stone 1992; 1992–3; Stone and Eshel 1995:215–30). Stone and Eshel's eschatological interpretation is followed by J. M. Scott 2002:213 n. 132.

Jewry.[32] The relevant section of 4Q464, as restored by Michael Stone and Esther Eshel, is as follows:

3.1.1–11

עד [...] 7 ‏ם{ר}לאברה‎ ם[...] 6 נבלת .[...] 5 באחד ‏ש[...] 4 עבד .[...] 3 ‏ים[...] 2 [...] 1
vacat [...] 10 ‏שפה ברורה‏ אל עמים ‏אהפך] ... 9 ‏הקודש לשון ‏רא[...] 8 ‏הואה ‏כיא עולם
[...]...[...] 11

1 [...] 2 [...]... 3 [...] servant 4 [...] in one 5 [...] confused 6 [...] to Abrah{ra}m 7 [...] for ever, for he 8 [...]... the holy language 9 [... Zeph 3.9 Then I will turn] to the peoples a pure language 10 [...] Blank 11 [...]...[...]

Steven Weitzman, pointing out that 4Q464 contains the first known use of the phrase "holy tongue" to refer to Hebrew, contrasts the view of 4Q464 with that of Philo, who rejects Babel as the origin of the earthly languages and accordingly accepts the validity of other languages for Jewish expression (cf. *Conf.* 191).[33] Here I would simply point out that 4Q464 is not the eschatological text that others have supposed it to be, and that its use of Zeph 3.9 is not intended to invoke the promise of the world's eventual return to a "pure language" in the sense in which that biblical passage originally conveyed (and as conveyed in *Test. Jud.* 25.3). Rather, the fact that the next episode in 4Q464 refers to an event in Abraham's life suggests that Zeph 3.9 is being used here merely as a *pesher*-type prooftext to give scriptural backing to the Jubilean account of Abraham's recovery of Hebrew. This interpretation is in keeping, not only with the principles of Qumranic exegesis, but also with the Qumranic understanding of Hebrew. Although the term "eschatological" is relevant for understanding the Qumranites' historical self-understanding, it is *not* a necessary term in that community's ideology of Hebrew. Rather, the eschatological and the hebraeophone aspects of Qumran thought appear to be independent facets of the Qumranic remnant theology.[34]

B. R. Yochanan's Dictum: "The Ministering Angels do not Understand Aramaic" (*b. Soṭah* 33a *b. Šabb.* 12b)

One of the more celebrated examples of a claim the angels speak Hebrew is found in a saying attributed to the third-century C.E. Amora R. Yocha-

---

[32] See Lim 2000:67–8. J. P. Brown (2001:170) suggests that most Jews "[I]n the Hellenistic period, . . . must have thought the Aramaic they spoke simply a vernacular form of the Hebrew they heard in the synagogue without full understanding; only an occasional Rabbi and Jerome understood the true situation."

[33] Weitzman 1999:40. On the importance of Hebrew for the Qumranites, see Schniedewind 1999.

[34] For a more detailed argument, see Poirier 2002.

nan. Although R. Yochanan does not say in so many words that Hebrew is the language of angels, he seems to imply this view when he proscribes praying in Aramaic on the basis of angels' ignorance of that language. The tradition is found at two places in the Babylonian Talmud:

b. Soṭah 33a

תפלה : רחמי היא כל היכי דבעי מצלי ותפלה בכל לשון והאמר רב יהודה לעולם אל ישאל
אדם צרכיו בלשון ארמית דאמר רבי יוחנן כל השואל צרכיו בלשון ארמי אין מלאכי השרת
נזקקין לו לפי שאין מלאכי השרת מכירין בלשון ארמי לא קשיא הא ביחיד הא בצבור ואין
מלאכי השרת מכירין בלשון ארמי והתניא יוחנן כהן גדול שמע ב״ק מבית קדש הקדשים
שהוא אומר נצחו טליא דאזלו לאגחא קרבא לאנטוכיא ושוב מעשה בשמעון הצדיק ששמע בת
קול מבית קדש הקדשים שהוא אומר בטילת עבירתא דאמר שנאה לאייתאהאל היכלא ונהרג
נסקלגם ובטלו גזירותיו וכתבו אותה שעה וכיוונו ובלשון ארמי היה אומראי בעית אימא
בתקול שאני דלאשמועי עבידא ואי בעית אימא גבריאל הוה דאמר מר בא גבריאל ולימדו
שבעים לשון :

The *Tefillah*: It is supplication, and may be said however one wishes. But may the *Tefillah* be recited in any language? Rab Judah has said, "A man should not pray for his needs in Aramaic. For R. Yochanan said, 'If [he] prays for his needs in Aramaic, the ministering angels will not attend to him, because the ministering angels do not understand Aramaic!' There is no difficulty: one pertains to an individual and the other to a community. And do not the ministering angels understand Aramaic? It has been taught: Yochanan, the high priest, heard a heavenly voice from the Holy of Holies, that it said "The young men that went up to fight against Antiochus have returned [victorious]." It happened with Simeon the Righteous that he heard a heavenly voice from the Holy of Holies, that it said, "Void is the decree that the enemy said to put upon the Temple," and Caligula was slain and his decrees annulled. And they wrote down the time [of the heavenly voice] and it agreed. And it was in Aramaic. You may say that a heavenly voice [speaks] so that I will understand, or you may say that it was Gabriel: that as a master said, Gabriel came and taught seventy languages.

b. Šabb. 12b

אמר רבה בר בר חנה כי הוה אזלינן בתריה דרבי אלעזר לשיולי בתפיחה זימנין אמר המקום
יפקדך לשלום וזימנין אמר (ליה) רחמנא ידכרינך לשלם היכי עביד הכי והאמר רב יהודה
לעולם אל ישאל אדם צרכיו בלשון ארמי ואמר רבי יוחנן כל השואל צרכיו בלשון ארמי אין
מלאכי השרת נזקקין לו שאין מלאכי השרת מכירין בלשון ארמי שאני חולה דשכינה עמו דאמר
רב ענן אמר רב מנין שהשכינה סועד את התולה שנאמר ה׳ יסעדנו על ערש דוי תניאנמי הכי
הנכנס לבקר את התולה לא ישב לאעל גבי מטה ולא על גבי כסא אלא מתעסף ויושב לפניו
מפני שהשכינה למעלה מראשותיו של הולה שנאמר ה׳ יסעדנו על ערש דוי ואמר רבא אמר רבין
מנין שהקב״ה זן את התולה שנאמר ה׳ יסעדנו על ערש דוי :

Rabbah b. Bar Hanah said, "When we went out after R. Eleazar to inquire after a sick person, sometimes he said, 'May the Omnipresent visit you for health' (לשלום) [Hebrew], and sometimes he said (to him), 'May the Omnipresent decree for you to be whole' [Aramaic]. How did he do this, for did not Rab Judah say, 'A man should never petition for his needs in Aramaic?', and [did not] R. Yochanan say, 'Everyone who petitions for his needs in Aramaic, the ministering angels will not attend to him, because the ministering angels do not understand Aramaic!'? It is different for an invalid, for the *shekinah* is with him. For R. Anan said in Rab's name, "How do we know that the *shekinah* sustains the invalid? As it says, *The LORD sustains them on their sickbed* (Ps 4:4[3]). It was also taught: the one who enters to visit the invalid does not sit on a bed or on a seat, but must wrap himself and sit in front of him, for the *shekinah* is above the pillow of an invalid, as it says, *The LORD sustains them on their sickbed.* And Raba said in Rabin's name, "How do we know that the Holy One, blessed be He, sustains the sick? As it says, *The LORD sustains them on their sickbed.*"

The two pages leading up to the passage in *b. Sotah* deal with whether one may say various blessings and invocations in any language one pleases, or only in Hebrew.[35] The context therefore implies that angels understand Hebrew. It should be pointed out, however, that, *unless* one has already ruled out prayer in Greek, etc., R. Yochanan's dictum (which mentions on-ly Aramaic) appears to be assymetrical with its talmudic context. This makes it likely that the situation to which R. Yochanan originally respond-ed (if we can trust the attribution) was concrete rather than theoretical: Jews were praying in Aramaic, and R. Yochanan was trying to put a stop to that.[36] Perhaps he would have put a stop to praying in Greek as well, if that were also common in his community, but we cannot know for certain. Overall, the rabbis are less concerned about Greek, but it is not clear whether that reflects greater openness toward that language or simply less contact with it.

The notion that angels take an active role in prayer was widespread in late antiquity. The classic example of this notion is found in Tob 12.6–15:

> [v. 6] Then Raphael called the two of them privately and said to them, "Bless God and acknowledge him in the presence of all the living for the good things he has done for you. Bless and sing praise to his name. With fitting honor declare to all people the deeds of God. Do not be slow to acknowledge him. ...
>
> [v. 12] So now when you and Sarah prayed, it was I who brought and read the record of your prayer before the glory of the Lord, and likewise whenever you would bury the dead. ...
>
> [v. 15] I am Raphael, one of the seven angels who stand ready and enter before the glory of the Lord."

This role is also illustrated in Rev 8.1–5, where angels mediate the prayers of human intercessors.[37] Angels also present the prayers of humans to God

---

[35] See Neusner 1968:158–9. A competing doctrine ascribes first place to Aramaic: see *t. Ber.* 3a; *t. Šabb.* 12b; *Synopse* §348. Petuchowski 1972:43–55 surveys the history of Hebrew as the language of Jewish prayer. On the acceptability of Greek for Jewish prayer, see *y. Meg.* 1.8; *b. Meg.* 9b; *Gen. Rab.* 36.8; *Deut. Rab.* 1.1. On the heavenly voice to the high priest Yochanan, see VanderKam 2004:296–7.

[36] R. Yochanan is mentioned as having spent thirteen (*y. 'Erub.* 5.1; *y. Sanh.* 11.6) or eighteen (*b. 'Erub.* 53a) years in Caesarea, a largely Greek-speaking community. He could not therefore have been oblivious to the use of Greek for the *Shema* and other blessings. And yet he only makes the ministering angels ignorant of Aramaic. This would seem to detract from any attempt to generalize R. Yochanan's motivation: more likely, it was a specific practice that he had in mind to proscribe.

[37] As Wick 1998:512–14 argues, following Knohl 1996, the enigmatic half hour of si-lence, the offering of incense, and the prayers of the people all combine to identify the

in *1 Enoch* (9.2–3; 99.3) and *3 Baruch* (11.3–4). Perhaps this notion also holds the key to 1 Cor 11.10, in which women are commanded to cover their heads while praying and prophesying *because of the angels*. The idea is also found in *Exod. Rab.* 21.4, and is known to Origen, who identifies Michael (rather than Gabriel or Sandalfon) as the angel who mediates prayer (*Princ.* 1.8.1). The connection between incense and prayer in many of these passages (see *T. Levi* 3.5–6) may be based upon Ps 141.2 : "Let my prayer be counted as incense before you, and the lifting up of my hands as an evening sacrifice."[38] Daimons mediate the prayers of men to the gods within the Platonic corpus and its accompanying commentary.[39] It should be pointed out that, by combining the notion that angels mediate prayers with the widespread idea that angels are assigned to the nations of the world, we are met with a scheme not unlike that of R. Yochanan: if we suppose that the angels assigned to the nations speak the languages respective to their geopolitical "assignments", and if we suppose that the "ministering angels" that R. Yochanan mentions are none other than those angels who have been assigned to Israel, then it would make sense that the ministering angels speak only Hebrew (*viz.* Israel's *proper* language). Yet, in airing this possibility, it must be pointed out that not only do the rabbinic writings fail to make these connections for us, but they even evince a contrary tradition: *viz.* each of the seventy nations is assigned to an angel, while Israel is under the direct jurisdiction of God.[40] There are other factors mitigating against this scheme as well, such as the fact that the tradition of angelic jurisdiction over the nations implies that one angel is given to each nation, while R. Yochanan's dictum refers to a plurality of ministering angels.

Louis Ginzberg apparently thought that the saying ascribed to R. Yochanan reflected an idea found among the Babylonian rabbis, but not among the Palestinian rabbis. According to Ginzberg, the Palestinian rab-

---

scene in Revelation 8 with practices surrounding the propitiatory offerings of the Temple. See Briggs 1999:74–85. On angels as mediators generally, see de Lacey 1987:105–7.

[38] See Briggs 1999:77–8.

[39] See Soury 1942:20–7.

[40] See *Deut. Rab.* 2.34; *Pirqe R. El.* 24. According to *b. Hag.* 16a (‖ *'Abot R. Nat.* 37.2 [rec. A]), humans resemble the ministering angels in three respects: they possess understanding, walk upright, and speak the holy language. Stern 1994:41 points out that "[r]eference to Hebrew *may* indicate that this passage refers exclusively to Israel", and that the parallel passage in *Gen. Rab.* 8.11, which finds parallels in human standing, speaking, understanding, and seeing, omits any mention of Hebrew. Given its close parallelism with a formulation found in Ovid (*Metam.* 1.76–86), the *Genesis Rabbah* passage is more likely to represent the original form of the tradition. On the seventy nations, see the in-depth discussion of the table of nations in biblical and Jewish sources in J. M. Scott 1995:5–56. On the association of angels with nations, see Mach 1992:257–62. On the Ovid passage, see Rosati, Villa and Corti 1994:48–51; Bömer 1969:42–47.

bis did not hold to the notion that angels mediate prayer. That view belonged in a Babylonian *milieu*, populated more conspicuously by an intrusive lot of angels and demons, and it conflicted (Ginzberg thought) with the Palestinian proscription of prayer addressed to angels:

The chief difference between the two Talmuds in the field of theology is to be found in the fact that the Palestinian authors of the Talmud excluded, almost entirely, the popular fancies about angels and demons, while in Babylonia angelology and demonology, under popular pressure influenced by Zoroastrianism, gained scholastic recognition and with it entrance into the Talmud. Contrast these two sayings: The first, in the Palestinian Talmud, reads: "Cry not to Michael or Gabriel but to Me says the Lord.' The second, found in the Babylonian Talmud, recommends: "One should never pray in Aramaic because the angels do not attend to him." An intermidiary [*sic*] rôle for the angels is obviously assumed in the latter statement.[41]

A moment's reflection reveals that the two views that Ginzberg set in opposition are not in fact logical opposites: one can easily believe that angels mediate prayer without holding that one should address angels in prayer. (Such an arrangement of views found a home in the Apostle Paul, among

---

[41] Ginzberg 1955:22. See *y. Ber.* 9.13a. It should not be assumed that the contrast between the Palestinian and Babylonian rabbis' position on angelology and demonology was always so stark. As Kasher 1996 argues, the lack of angelological speculation in *Pseudo-Jonathan* may have been the product more of expurgating unwanted material from an existing tradition than of suppressing ideas that were in the air. Kasher 1996:189 connects the need for this work of expurgation with a change in attitudes occurring after the Mishnah was compiled: "It is not inconceivable that TJ [= Targum Jonathan] reflects rabbinical views of the period following the end of the 2nd century C.E., which tended to restrict the powers of angels as far as possible, objecting to angelic cults and to prayers directed toward angels. Where TJ nevertheless introduces angels, it is careful to call them specifically 'angels *of the Lord*,' never assigning them too independent a position. It seems very probable, therefore, that the recension of TJ in our possession represents the greatest possible consideration of the Sages' overall attitude to the angelic world." The evidence is patient of different explanations, however, and it is difficult to know whether the change in the Palestinian rabbinic view to which Kasher refers is a real change, brought about perhaps by an increase in rabbinic power in the generations following the publication of the Mishnah, or whether such a stark contrast between Palestine and Babylonia had always existed (but that the early Palestinian targums do not reflect the views of the [proto-]rabbis). Although Kasher is correct in stating that the scenario he favors "is not inconceivable," it is not more likely than the alternative view–*viz.* that the Rabbis of Palestine and of Babylonia had always seen things differently. Scholars are now keenly aware of how little power the early rabbis actually wielded within the early synagogue, a factor that makes the alternative to Kasher's view somewhat attractive because it ties the targumic tradition's shift of attitude to the rise of the rabbinic power. Shinan's frequent claim that *Pseudo-Jonathan*'s preoccupation with angels is an illustration of that work's connection to folk culture is best understood in this light. According to Shinan 1977:iv, "There is no doubt that [*Pseudo-Jonathan*] is at base a Targum similar to the rest of the Palestinian Targumim and only at a later and secondary stage was expanded with late and 'non-targumic' additions in written form." Cf. Shinan 1983:196–7; 1992:127.

others.)[42] If Palestinian rabbis strongly objected to the practice of praying *to* angels (as in *addressing* angels through prayer, e.g. in the later "ushers of mercy" *piyyut*),[43] this did not mean that they dismissed angels from having any role in prayer.[44] The popular view that angels carried one's prayers to God's throne could well have been widespread among the rabbis, despite their opposition to any sort of cult of angels. The angelologies of the two talmuds do not conflict as fundamentally as Ginzberg thought. All things considered, one should not imagine the Babylonian rabbinic tradition and the early Palestinian targumic tradition joining in common cause against the vague and inactive angelology of the Palestinian rabbis, and, as far as I can tell, there is nothing in R. Yochanan's dictum that was not perfectly at home in a Palestinian setting.

Solomon Freehof, noting the widespread existence of Aramaic prayers from gaonic and earlier times (esp. the *kaddish*), suggests that R. Yochanan's dictum "was more academic than practical."[45] There are real problems with this view. For one thing, it seems to generalize R. Yochanan's dictum, which, while given in a generalized form, was probably aimed at the specific practice of praying outside the synagogue. At the other end of the spectrum, Joseph Yahalom writes that R. Yochanan's statement about the ministering angels' inability to understand Aramaic "surely won credence among the simpler folk."[46] It probably won credence among many of the sages as well (at least the gemara takes it seriously),[47] but Yahalom's implication that this dictum was aimed at the non-scholarly is certainly on target. What better way to discourage prayers in the vernacular, i.e. extrasynagogal prayers, than by theorizing that those who pray in Aramaic are at best only speaking into the air? If putting it this way implies disingenuousness on the part of R. Yochanan, it would only be fair to call attention to that part of the theory that he and most others in his circle appear to have agreed on with utter seriousness: that the angels understood Hebrew,

---

[42] That is, if Paul wrote Colossians: Paul's instructions for the Corinthian women to veil themselves "because of the angels" whenever they "pray or prophesy" (see 1 Corinthians 11) is best understood in terms of the mediating role of angels, yet Colossians does not represent a diminishing of these views when it censures "the worship of angels."

[43] See Malkiel 2003. (I am loath to cite internet sources, but Malkiel's study is too important to ignore. Hopefully it will appear in print somewhere.)

[44] See *y. Ber.* 9.1; *b. Ber.* 60b (a baraita); Bar-Ilan 2004.

[45] Freehof 1923:381 n. 3.

[46] Yahalom 1996:33. Yahalom writes that R. Yochanan's dictum "must apparently be seen as part of the ongoing battle which the sages of Eretz Israel waged against the informal prayers of the simpler Jews, who used their own heartfelt words to speak to the Lord rather than the formally prescribed Hebrew prayers of the scholars."

[47] Some later medieval authorities were perhaps too sophisticated for such a view: they claimed that angels understand Aramaic but ignore it out of reverence for the holy tongue. See the sources listed in Malkiel 2003:178 n. 25.

presumably because it was their native language. That others outside of rabbinic circles took R. Yochanan's words seriously, however, does not imply that private Aramaic prayer disappeared. As Milka Rubin notes, Jews continued to pray for their needs in Aramaic until the end of the Byzantine era.[48]

The rabbis' exaltation of Hebrew affected a constellation of ideas: not only was Hebrew considered the language of angels, but it was also the language by which God created the world.[49] That Hebrew was a potent enough medium for the work of creation gave it mystical properties, so that permutations of the Hebrew alphabet would become forceful exercises in mysticism and magic.[50] As in *Jubilees*, rabbinic tradition often considered Hebrew to be the language of Adam, and of the generations preceding the tower of Babel. This idea also surfaces at the relevant targumic passages: according to *Tg. Neof.* Gen 11.1, "[A]ll the inhabitants of the earth were (of) one language and (of) just one speech, and they spoke in the language of the Temple, for through it the world was created, in the beginning."[51] A similar wording is found in *Pseudo-Jonathan*'s rendering of Gen 11.1.[52] (See also *y. Meg.* 1.2; *Tanḥ.* 1.55; *Gen. Rab.* 18.) *Gen. Rab.* 18.4 concludes that Hebrew must be the language of creation, for otherwise the derivation of "woman" (אישה) from "man" (איש) would not be linguistically possible.[53] As Rubin notes, the idea that all the world once

---

[48] Rubin 1998:315.

[49] Rubin 1998:308 notes that the belief that language played a role in creation was widespread in the ancient Near East.

[50] See Scholem 1972.

[51] Quoted in Sáenz-Badillos 1993:2, based on the Spanish translation of A. Díez Macho. It should be noted that the rabbinic writings also record competing ideas. The belief that Hebrew was the universal language before the fall of Babel did not go unchallenged. Borst 1957–63:1.191 writes, "Rabbi Eliezer stritt sich mit Rabbi Jochanan um die Ursprache. 'Nach dem einen (Eliezer) redete man in 70 Sprachen die alle verstanden, nach dem andern in der Sprache des Einzigen der Welt, das ist in der heiligen Sprache'. Hier ist die Idee von 70 Weltsprachen, die Eliezer sicher nicht erfunden hat, ausgesprochen und in scharfe Antithese gesetzt zu dem zuerst vom Jubiläenbuch formulierten Glauben an die heilige hebräische Ursprache." See Rubin 1998:311–12. Some later Jewish writers, like Maimonides, even denied the divine origin of Hebrew. See Halbertal 1997:35–6. The later fortunes of the Hebrew-first view, especially within early reconstructions of the proliferation of European languages, have been traced in Borst 1957–63 and in Eco 1995:7–24, 73–116. Cf. the wider variety of interpretations of the Babel story at this time, discussed in Williams 1996:74–5. On the original ideology of the Babel story, see Swiggers 1999, and the bibliography cited there.

[52] See Bowker 1969:182–3; Schwartz 1995:32; Rubin 1998.

[53] Sáenz-Badillos 1993:2 n. 4 notes that this view of Hebrew as a special language often "created conflicts in the realm of philology, so that certain medieval linguists, for example Menahem b. Saruq, refrained from comparing it with other languages". Cf. Maimonides, *Guide of the Perplexed* 3.8 (12th cent.); Judah Ha-Levi, *Sefer ha-Kuzari*

spoke the same language, and that that language was revealed by God, leads naturally to the preferment of whichever culture continued to speak that language:

[W]hoever holds onto this unique divine language is in consequence the 'favourite son', closest and most intimate to God, and therefore superior. It is the language itself, not the message or revelation conveyed by it, that decides this question, the winner claiming first and formost linguistic and cultural superiority over all other languages and cultures. The question of the 'language of creation' or the 'primordial language' serves therefore as a cultural yardstick of different cultural identities.[54]

To some degree, this use of Hebrew as a means of securing cultural ascendancy (at least in one's own eyes) probably operates in the background during most of the history of Judaism. It may have been more of concern during the Hasmonaean period, when the threat of hellenization called forth the need for national symbols, but it remained a fairly active concern during the next century or two.[55] For the third century C.E., when R. Yochanan supposedly proscribed the use of Aramaic in petitionary prayer, the ideological use of Hebrew was probably different. It is often said that the ancients did not separate life into religious and secular components, but that is not entirely accurate.[56] Certainly, the distinction between sacred and mundane activity was already a handy one (thanks especially to the concept of ritual purity), and it makes perfect sense to ask whether the ideological use of Hebrew in rabbinic times, in contradistinction to what Rubin theorizes for the Hasmonaean period, fell along the lines of this division of activity. (That question will occupy us later in the next chapter.) That is not to say that the same proofs of Hebrew's exalted status are not to be found in rabbinic literature. They certainly are. (Note that Rab's ascription of Aramaic to Adam [*b. Sanh.* 38b] is *not* an exception to the rabbis' sanc-

---

2.66; 4.25 (12th cent.). Abraham b. Hananiah's 16th-century discourse on "the Mother of All Languages" (trans. Ruderman 1990:297–313) can be read almost as a bibliographic essay upon the Hebrew-first tradition. See Shinan 1975–6; Winston 1991:120–2 n. 30; Eco 1995:7–24, 73–116. On the place of the Hebrew-first tradition in the Protestant Reformation, see Laplanche 1986:465. For an overview of the role of Hebrew in Christian tradition up to the twelfth century, see Goodwin 2006:73–94.

[54] Rubin 1998:308.

[55] Cf. *Tg. Ps.-Jon.* Gen 11.1–8; *Pirqe R. El.* 24. On Hebrew as a national symbol, see Schwartz 1995. Rubin (1998:314) writes, "National identity and language were so closely linked that 'Nation and Language' – *umma velashon* – became a hendiadys meaning 'nation'. … It may be suggested, therefore, that the concept of the primordial language was a direct consequence of the new national ideology which developed during the Second Temple period, or more specifically, during the early part of the Hasmonean era."

[56] Cf. the famous opening quip of Milbank 1990:9: "Once, there was no 'secular'." That claim makes for gritty rhetoric and a handy support for recent trends in Anglo-American theology, but as a purported reflection of biblical sentiments it is little more than an ambitious bluff.

tification of Hebrew [as is commonly held], but rather functions merely as a proof that Adam was outside the covenant of promise.)[57] It should also be pointed out that, notwithstanding the Mishnah's preference for Hebrew, R. Yochanan appears to have been somewhat more insistent on the necessity of that language for proper piety. Sacha Stern observes that "the religious significance of language ... is remarkably limited" in "early rabbinic sources" (*viz.* the Mishnah).[58]

These third-century rabbinic uses and understandings of the importance of Hebrew became staples within rabbinic Judaism. Certain nuances to this understanding represent developments from earlier understandings, which in turn were developed further in later centuries. The fact that individual figures probably had different understandings as well makes it risky to attempt an account of "the" rabbinic understanding. Nevertheless, R. Yochanan's attitude and strategy can be regarded as emblematic of third-century

---

[57] Rubin 1998:316 (with n. 58) cites Rab's belief as an exception to the "promotion of the concept of *Leshon Haqodesh*," noting that "Rav is a Babylonian *amora*, while his opponent Resh Laqish is Palestinian". (A similar view is implied in Chomsky 1951–52:206.) The context of Rab's saying (*b. Sanh.* 38b), however, tells against this interpretation:

אמר רב יהודה א״ר בשעה שבקש הקב״ה לבראות את האדם ברא כת אחת של מלאכי השרת
אמר להם רצונכם נעשה אדם בצלמנו אמרו לפניו רבש״ע מה מעשיו אמר להן כך וכך מעשיו
... אמר רב יהודה אמר רב אדם הראשון מסוף העולם ועד סופו היה שנאמר למן היום אשר
ברא אלהים אדם על הארץ ולמקצה השמים ועד קצה השמים כיון שסרח הניח הקדוש ברוך
הוא ידו עליו ומיעטו שנאמר אחור וקדם צרתני ותשת עלי כפך ... ואמר רב יהודה אמר רב
אדם הראשון בלשון ארמי ספר שנאמר ולי מה יקרו ר עיך אל והיינו ... ואמר רב יהודה אמר
רב אדם הראשון מין היה שנאמר ויקראה׳ אלהים אל האדם ויאמר לו איכה אן נטה לבך

[Translation: Rab Judah said in Rab's name, "When the Holy One, blessed be He, sought to create man, He created a company of ministering angels and said to them: Is it your will that we make a man in our image? They said before Him: Sovereign of the Universe, what will be his deeds? He said to them, Such and such will be his deeds." ... Rab Judah said in Rab's name, "The first man reached from one end of the world to the other end, as it is written, *Since the day that God created human beings on the earth; from one end of heaven to the other* (Deut 4.32). But when he sinned, the Holy One, blessed be He, put His hand upon him and diminished him, as it is written, *You hem me in, behind and before, and lay your hand upon me* (Ps 139.5)." ... Rab Judah also said in Rab's name: "The first man spoke in Aramaic, for it is written, *How weighty to me are your thoughts, O God!* (Ps 139.17). ... And Rab Judah said in Rab's name: "The first man was a Min, as it is written, *But the LORD God called to the man, and said to him, "Where are you?"* (Gen 3.9), that is, where have your turned your heart?]

Note that Rab's portrait of Adam is unstintingly negative throughout this passage. It would seem to follow that Adam's use of Aramaic instead of Hebrew is intended to deprecate Adam rather than the Hebrew language. Far from demoting Hebrew from its status as the holy language, this passage rescues Hebrew from the sinful *min* "Adam".

[58] Stern 1994:80.

Palestinian rabbinism in general,[59] if only because of his tremendous influence.

C. Christian Writings

1. The Vision of Paul

As far as we know, there was no Hebrew-only party in early Christianity. A hebraeophone angelology therefore appears very sparingly within Christian sources. Yet a couple of stray references to Hebrew-speaking angels can be found.

In the (fourth-century?) *Vision of Paul*, a book that Sozomen tells us was "commended by most monks" (*Hist. eccl.* 7.19), we read that Hebrew is "the language of God and angels":

> And I said unto the angel: Lord, what is Alleluia? And the angel answered and said unto me: Thou dost examine and inquire of all things. And he said unto me: Alleluia is spoken in the Hebrew, that is the speech of God and of the angels: now the interpretation of Alleluia is this: *tecel . cat . marith . macha* (Gr. thĕbel marēmatha). And I said: Lord, what is *tecel cat marith macha*? And the angel answered and said unto me: This is *tecel cat marith macha*: Let us bless him all together.[60]

The liturgical concern here is evident: in the immediate sequel to this passage, it is related that anyone who does not participate in the *alleluia*, but is physically able to do so, is guilty of a grave sin. The value of saying "alleluia" is that one thereby speaks in the very language of God and the angels. Even those who do not understand what "alleluia" means bless God by saying it. It should be noted, however, that the different versions of this passage vary considerably. For example, while the Syriac version also refers to "alleluia" as being Hebrew, it does not say that Hebrew is the language of God and the angels.[61]

2. The Coptic Wizard's Hoard

Another reference to Hebrew as the language of heaven deserves to be mentioned here, although there is a question as to whether the writing is Christian or Gnostic. The writing is a magical text, published by William H. Worrell as a "Coptic wizard's hoard," and recently discussed by Paul

---

[59] But see my discussion of R. Hama b. Hanina in the next chapter for a possible exception.

[60] *Vis. Paul* 30 (trans. M. R. James 1924:541).

[61] See Ricciotti 1932:64.

Mirecki under the same terminological rubric.[62] According to Mirecki, the "hoard" was written during the fourth through seventh centuries (by five different hands), somewhere in Egypt, and "appears to be a compilation of traditional materials from a variety of sources."[63] In 1921, it was restored at the British Museum and brought to the University of Michigan. In a passage from 2.15b to 3.10, we read,

Hear our / authority which is over you, all of his ministrants [3.1] who are called (by name) by / those above them, even you great archangels / who are strong in your power, you whose / names were first given to you, [3.5] that is, (you) angels who call all of the special names / which are written (here) in Hebrew, / the language of heaven, in order that they might hear the / one who will activate this prayer / (and that) they might bring to pass for him everything which he will perform [3.10] in purity and chastity of ritual.[64]

This passage illustrates the belief, prominent among practitioners of magic in the ancient world, that Hebrew was an especially potent language for use in magical recipes. This belief was undoubtedly rooted in the antiquity of the language, but may also have had something to do with the attraction of Jewish rites. In this text, we see an example of what we noted above: frank acknowledgement of Hebrew as the language of creation, which drove some Jewish groups to make Hebrew the language of all religious activity, had a completely different effect on at least some Christian groups. Presumably, this Coptic magician has no plans to learn Hebrew: when he encounters a strange-sounding word in the magical tradition, "pure hocus-pocus to the magician," as Worrell writes, "he calls it Hebrew."[65]

It should be noted that these two examples of a Hebrew-speaking angels are rare exceptions to the understanding of angelic languages found in Christian writings. The works in which these two examples appear were not influential in any way. This contrasts with the Jewish works discussed in this chapter, which were central self-definitional texts within major streams of Jewish expression.

---

[62] Worrell 1929–30); Mirecki 1994b. A treatment nearly identical to the latter can be found in Mirecki 1994a.

[63] Mirecki 1994b:451. The translation given in Mirecki 1994a:304 is identical, except that "that" appears (3×) in place of "which".

[64] Trans. Mirecki 1994b:441–2.

[65] Mirecki 1994b:255 n. 2.

Excursus: The Relative Lack of Hebrew-Speaking Angels in Early Christian Sources

Seth Schwartz interprets the lack of an active role for Hebrew in Christian tradition as evidence that "Hebrew was part of an ideological package."[66] The *Epistle to Diognetus* perhaps best expresses Christianity's aloofness to linguistic ideologies: "For the distinction between Christians and other men, is neither in country nor language nor customs. For they do not dwell cities in some place of their own, nor do they use any strange variety of dialect, nor practice an extraordinary kind of life" (*Diogn.* 5.1–2).[67]

This probably represents only one of two major forces in play, however, as the question of what one did with Hebrew also hinged on how one viewed the scriptures written in that language, and what role the inspiration of those scriptures played within one's religion. The difference between the synagogue and the early church in their respective understandings of the ground of scriptural authority appears to have led to different views of the continuing importance of Hebrew. For many streams of Judaism, the fact that Hebrew was the language of *revelation* makes the role of Hebrew extremely important. For Christians, on the other hand, theology was much more about an act of redemption than about an act of revelation, and the act of affirming the divine acts of redemption (i.e., accepting the *kerygma*) occupied the same position within early Christian theology as the act of accepting the scriptures as divinely given occupied within most forms of Jewish theology.[68] When Christians affirmed that Hebrew was the language of creation, therefore, they did so either out of an antiquarian interest, or to vouch for the trustworthiness of the Old Testament (which had been mined for prooftextual supports for the New Testament *kerygma*).[69] We do not find them concluding from the protological nature of Hebrew that that language should play an active role in the church.

Why did Christianity not attach the same significance to the language of its scriptures (whether Greek, Hebrew, Latin, or otherwise) that rabbinic

---

[66] Schwartz 1995:46. Rubin 1998:320 notes that Christianity had no interest "in supporting any issue on a separatist linguistic or cultural ticket".

[67] Trans. Lake 1985–92:2.359.

[68] Christian scholars who cut their teeth on Barthianism's inflated doctrine of revelation are not wont to agree with this description of early Christianity, but the doctrine of revelation was at most a side issue for the early church, and had no direct connection to the doctrine of redemption. See Downing 1964; Barr, 1966:83–4; 1999:484; Wingren 1989:53; Braaten 1990:65–6.

[69] The term "Old Testament" is best in this context, as it best conveys the role of Israel's scriptures within the church's canon. On the early church's use of the Hebrew Bible, see Simon 1984:110; Müller 1996:78–83. There were always important voices in the church urging that more attention be paid to the Hebrew form of the Old Testament – see Hailperin 1963; Goodwin 2006:73–94.

Judaism, Islam, and other faiths have traditionally attached to the language of their scriptures?[70] The answer is that early Christianity did not consider the New Testament to be *inspired* scripture in the same way in which the Hebrew Bible was scripture for rabbinic Jews. Because Christian theology of the last 500 years has seen an unprecedented concentration on the so-called "scripture principle" of the Protestant Reformation, it often comes as a surprise to learn that the early church had a very different conception of the authority behind Christian scripture. Christians are so used to thinking of the concepts of "Old Testament" and "New Testament" in terms of conceptual parity that they are often ill prepared for the facts of the matter: the early church did *not* regard the New Testament as inspired scripture in the same sense that rabbinic, Qumranic, and other streams of Judaism regarded the Hebrew Bible as inspired scripture.[71] This is usually stated in terms of Christianity's failure to answer to the term "book religion": while rabbinic Judaism linked the authority of the Hebrew Bible to the principle of revelation, early Christianity linked the authority of the New Testament to the trustworthiness of the apostles as eyewitnesses.[72] As Guy Stroumsa succinctly puts the matter, "Christianity was from the beginning, rather than a religion of the book, one of the 'paperback'."[73]

The relative lack of references to Hebrew-speaking angels in Christian sources[74] does not mean that the church automatically rejected the claim that Hebrew was the first language. It is true, as Deborah Levine Gera notes, that "[t]he lack of explicit information in the Bible on the language spoken in the Garden of Eden" would eventually lead to competition for the primordiality of Hebrew, including "Greek, Latin, Syriac, [and even] Flemish, French, [and] Swedish,"[75] but, within the period I am discussing, the claim for the primordiality of Hebrew was challenged only by a claim for the primordiality of Aramaic, and that only by a number of Syriac-speaking fathers who were fighting a rearguard action against the Greek-

---

[70] Fishman 1985:13 marks the difference between Judaism and Christianity on this score by discussing the sociolinguistics of Jewish languages, and then observing that "[t]he case for an international sociology of *Catholic languages* [and] *Protestant languages* ... would seem to be exceedingly slight".

[71] See Ritter 1987; Dohmen and Oeming 1992:46–7; Poirier 2008.

[72] See Harnack 1904–5:1.353; Campenhausen 1972:1; Barr 1980:116–17; 1983:19; E. P. Sanders 1985:1431; Lang 1988–2002; Stroumsa 2003.

[73] Stroumsa 2003:173.

[74] But Hebrew-speaking angels would appear in Christian sources well beyond the chronological bounds of this study. E.g., see Hugh of St. Victor, *Miscellanea* 3.34 : bad men speak Egyptian, good men speak Canaanite, and angels speak Hebrew (Migne 1879:655).

[75] Gera 2003:21.

speaking church.[76] Jerome, echoing the rabbis, wrote that Hebrew was the language of creation and "the mother of all languages."[77] Origen said much the same thing, and it has been argued that his understanding of Hebrew as a "natural language" (in the sense of constituting a "nonarbitrary" connection between words and what they signify) left its imprint on the structure of the *Hexapla*.[78] This view can also be counted extensively among the great majority of church fathers who could not read Hebrew.[79] As Rubin writes, "It is clear that [the church fathers] are familiar with many of the Jewish sources and traditions, and that they concur with them."[80] There also seems to be broad agreement among the church fathers that the whole earth spoke Hebrew before God confused the languages at Babel.[81] This view goes back at least to the second- or third-century Pseudo-Clementine *Recognitiones* (1.30), which mentions fifteen generations of Hebrew but not the tower of Babel. Augustine's view is representative:

Hence, just as when all men spoke one language, the sons of pestilence were not lacking on that account – for there was only one language before the flood, and yet all men except the single family of the righteous Noah were justly destroyed by the flood – so also when the peoples were deservedly punished for their presumptuous wickedness by diversity of languages, and the city of the wicked received its name 'Confusion,' that is, when it was named Babylon, one house was still found, that of Heber, in which the language formerly spoken by all men might persist. This accounts for the fact ... that in the enumeration of the sons of Shem who individually founded separate tribes, Heber was mentioned first though he was Shem's great-great-grandson; in other words, he is found in the fifth generation after Shem. Since, then, this language remained in use among his family when the other tribes were divided by various tongues, the language that, not without good reason, is believed to have served previously as the common speech of all mankind was thereafter called Hebrew on this account.[82]

---

[76] They were joined by at least one Greek writer: Theodoret of Cyrrhus (393–466). See Rubin 1998:321–8; Hilhorst 2007:782.

[77] *Comm. Soph.* 541–42 (*ad* Zeph 3.14): "... linguam Hebraicam omnium linguarum esse matricem" (Hieronymus 1970:708). See Borst 1957–63:1.195; Kedar 1990:315; D. Brown 1992:74–5. On Jerome's activity with and embrace of the *hebraica veritas*, see Rebenich 1993; Markschies 1994; Müller 1996:83–9. More generally on Jerome, see Sparks 1970.

[78] See Origen, *Cels.* 30; Borst 1957–63:1.238; Rubin 1998:317–18. On Origen's view of Hebrew as a factor in the *Hexapla*, see the speculations of M. J. Martin 2004. Martin's argument builds on the discussion of Origen's view of language in Janowitz 1991. Janowitz's use of "natural language" (which is adopted by Martin) seems to correspond to the use of "Adamic language" in Gera 2003:24–6.

[79] See Hilhorst 2007.

[80] Rubin 1998:317.

[81] Eusebius of Caesarea and Gregory of Nyssa are important exceptions – see Rubin 1998:320–1. See Hilhorst 2007:780–2.

[82] *Civ.* 16.11 (trans. Sanford 1965:61–3). Augustine's attitude toward the value of studying Hebrew had improved markedly due to his exchange of letters with Jerome,

Despite their usual agreement that Hebrew was the language of creation, the church fathers did not translate their conviction that the scriptures were written in Hebrew into any sort of concern to preserve Hebrew within the church, although the fact that Hebrew was one of three languages used in the superscription on the cross (along with Greek and Latin) eventually earned it a special privilege as a language appropriate for liturgy.[83] Jerome is an exception, but his concern is motivated at least partially by a Stoic use of the science of etymology as a means of returning to the God who gave the original language.[84]

D. Conclusion

The texts that support a hebraeophone angelology are fewer in number than those that seem to indicate a belief in an esoteric angelic language (discussed in the next two chapters), but this does not necessarily mean that the hebraeophone view was only sparingly held. To the contrary, it appears to have been much more widespread, at least within Palestinian forms of Jewish piety. Indeed, within the rabbinic understanding, Hebrew came to be closely tied to Jewish expression in general. As antiquity gave way to the Middle Ages, the rabbis gained more power, and this view became more and more representative of the mainstream.

The contrast between the centripetal force of Palestinian rabbinic Judaism's strongly conservative (and ideologically loaded) approach to Hebrew, on the one hand, that the centrifugal force of the early church's liberal, expansionist embrace of the world's languages is due to a variety of factors. A variety of forms of Palestinian Judaism (Jubilean, Qumranic, third-century rabbinism) embraced Hebrew as the language of either true Jewish religious identity or of a pure and effective expression of piety,

---

which began in 394 C.E. On Augustine's changing views on the origins of language, see Rist 1994:37–8; Goodwin 2006:81–91.

[83] Thomson 1992 has shown that most of the charges leveled against the Latin church's supposed censuring of the use of other languages within the liturgy are baseless. According to Thomson (1992:73–4), the "theory of trilinguism" does not begin with Hilary of Poitiers (c. 310/320–367), or with Isidore of Seville (c. 560–636) – two common allegations – but rather much later. Yet he admits (1992:80), "Already in the fourth century, ... the idea that the three languages of the superscription on the Cross had special merit had been growing in the West."

[84] See Goodwin 2006:80. Mention should also be made of an early Hebrew gospel which the church fathers attributed to Matthew. This gospel was apparently preserved only for a brief while in its original language, and seems to have circulated most widely in Greek translation, before disappearing altogether. For a defense of the claim that it was really written in Hebrew (not Aramaic), see Edwards 2009.

whether for purposes of a sectarian ideology or for corralling popular piety and empowering an establishment. Although some prominent forms of Christianity were sectarian in the same sense, the fact that the early church had little connection with those groups that used Hebrew as a religious marker led to a different role for language in general within Christian self-definition. The missionary impulse also led to a proliferation of languages within the church.

To appreciate the idea that angels speak Hebrew within a historical perspective, we need to look at it alongside the belief that angels spoke an unearthly language. This view is found mostly in Christian writings, but it can also be found in a few Jewish writings. We examine the evidence for this view in chapters 4 and 5.

Chapter 3

Hebrew-speaking Angels and Linguistic Ideology in Tannaitic Tradition

In the preceding chapter, we visited a well known dictum attributed to the third-century C.E. sage R. Yochanan, which states that one should not pray in Aramaic. The reason, we are told, is that praying in Aramaic is a waste of time, for the angels do not understand that language. This saying is found in a nearly identical form in two places in the Babylonian Talmud: "For R. Yochanan said, 'If [he] prays for his needs in Aramaic, the ministering angels will not attend to him, because the ministering angels do not understand Aramaic!'" (*b. Soṭah* 33a; cf. *b. Šabb.* 12b).

What was the motivation for R. Yochanan's insistence that angels do not understand Aramaic? Was it merely the adumbration of a timeless element of rabbinic thought, or is it better understood within the specific setting of third-century Galilee (assuming, that is, that it really represents the sentiments of either R. Yochanan or his contemporaries)? To anticipate the argument of this chapter, it should be noted that a possible answer may incorporate both lines of explanation: perhaps something about the linguistic situation of third-century Jewish Palestine energized the linguistic component of a timeless element of rabbinic thinking. The "something" implied in this suggestion is the vernacular status of Aramaic, and the "timeless element", of course, would be the divine revelation to Israel (Torah) and the associated liturgy. In combination with this straightforward and benign solution, however, one should also admit the possibility that a Hebrew-only policy helped the rabbis achieve something of a political end. That is, the proscription of Aramaic prayer beyond the synagogue was calculated to proscribe extemporaneous prayer beyond the synagogue in general *in order to* restrict the highest exercise of Jewish piety to rabbinic-controlled contexts, and/or it may have amounted to a more direct empowering of the rabbis through their ability to read and speak Hebrew (i.e., by making society more dependent on them).[1] These three items (the hebraic setting of rabbinic piety, the proscription of extra-synagogal prayer, and the direct

---

[1] Goodman (2007:79–90) has argued that the ability to *write* was more empowering than the ability to read, but his reconstruction of the structure of power does not involve any design on the role of Hebrew *vis-à-vis* Aramaic or Greek.

empowerment of the hebraeophone *literati*) will occupy us for the re-
mainder of this chapter.

A. The Hebraic Setting of Rabbinic Piety

There are a number of ways in which language usage can be an expression
of an ideology, most of which seem to be tied to recurring patterns in the
history of any people. As Bernard Lewis writes,

> Jewish history shows two contrasting patterns of cultural relations between Jews and
> their neighbors. In one the Jews are culturally integrated into the society in which they
> live, using the same language and to a large extent sharing the same cultural values as the
> surrounding majority. ... The other pattern is one in which the Jews are linguistically and
> therefore culturally separated, using either Hebrew or, more commonly, some other lan-
> guage they brought from elsewhere and transformed into a Jewish language used exclu-
> sively by Jews. ... These two situations produce different types of Jewish life.[2]

The spectrum laid out in Lewis's remarks is an almost sufficient introduction to the mixture of language and politics, especially *religious* politics.
The point is made in a humorous way by Yigael Yadin's recollection of
David Ben Gurion's response to being shown a cache of Aramaic documents connected with the Bar Kokhba revolt: "'Why did they write in
Aramaic and not in Hebrew?' was his immediate angry reaction," Yadin
writes, "as if the scribes had been members of his staff."[3]

In a number of cases, rabbinic Judaism emphasized the priority or the
exclusive propriety of using Hebrew in religious contexts. For contemporary Jews, the association of Hebrew with both the Temple and the Torah
gave two reasons for identifying the language as the holy language. Seth
Schwartz identifies Temple and Torah as "repositories of power" around
which "related classes of curators" gathered: "These men used Hebrew to
distinguish themselves from the rest of the population."[4] The rabbis
represent, for their time, one of the main groups claiming to be the official
custodians (and interpreters) of the Torah. As we will see below, the im-
plementation of the rabbis' linguistic ideology also benefited from those
who thought of Hebrew more in terms of its Temple associations. I should
stress from the outset, of course, that the rabbis were not all uniform on
this matter. While some apparently insisted that Hebrew should be the exclusive language of liturgy (including all forms of prayer) and Bible reading, others emphasized the need for an Aramaic-speaking populace to understand at least certain parts of the liturgy and the words of the Bible. As

---

[2] Lewis 1984:77.
[3] Yadin 1971:124.
[4] Schwartz 1995:4. See Poirier:2007.

Stefan C. Reif writes, "The status of the language of the Hebrew Bible as against the practical advantage of a widely understood vernacular was destined to become a recurrent theme in the halakhic discussions of the rabbis concerning the precise form in which various prayers were to be recited."[5] This shows just how divided the rabbis could be on issues that some considered gravely important.

Before outlining the elements of the Hebrew-only camp, I should point out that, while these diverging views were in some sense institutionalized by opposing parties in the Second Temple period, with the Qumranites propounding the necessity of Hebrew for proper piety, and the Pharisees promoting the greater need for meeting the people on their own linguistic level,[6] it is not generally helpful to think of the rabbis' linguistic ideology as a precise parallel to that of the Qumranites. (I avoid using the label "Essene" in this connection simply because there is some indication that extra-Qumranic Essenes did not embrace the same strict linguistic policy as the Qumranites.) The similarities are sociologically telling, but so are the differences. Briefly looking at the Qumranites' and Pharisees' respective approaches to language will help us find our bearing when we consider the linguistic issues visited by the rabbis, but it will also be important to note how the rabbinic approach is different still.

Our knowledge of the rise of the rabbinic movement is both scanty and circumstantial. Direct statements in rabbinic sources concerning the tannaitic movement tend to misrepresent things for the sake of later politics, and it is not until our sources refer to the amoraic era that we can trust some of what they say regarding the rabbis' influence in Jewish society, and even then the sources cannot be read uncritically. Steven Fraade refers to a "tannaitic tunnel":[7] although we can speak with a measure of certainty about events and circumstances before and after the tannaim, we cannot speak about the tannaim themselves at the same level of detail or with same degree of certainty. Fortunately, scholars have been attending to this problem ever since Goodenough shook the guild's confidence in an early rabbi-controlled society (what Schwartz calls the "Alon- and Avi-Yonah-derived rabbinocentric historical narrative"),[8] and a judicious use of mirror-reading and a hermeneutic of suspicion has begun to penetrate the darkness. What has emerged from the sources is a cacophony of competing voices, all of them vying for power. What little we can gather about the

---

[5] Reif 1993:76.

[6] Alon's claim (1980:22) that the Pharisees "left behind" a "durable Torah ... accessible to everyman" is therefore true in more ways than he intended. Hengel 1994:172 characterizes the opposing approaches of the Qumranites ("Essenes") and Pharisees as a "family conflict", the two groups developing "in opposite directions".

[7] Fraade 1991:72.

[8] Schwartz 1998b:56 n. 4.

fortunes of the different linguistic approaches shows little agreement among the rabbis.

The Mishnah (*m. Soṭah* 7.1–4) lists a set of blessings and invocations that may be said in any language, as well as a set that may only be said in Hebrew:

1 אלו נאמרין בכל לשון, פרשת סוטה, וידוי מעשר, קריאת שמע, ותפלה, וברכת המזון, ושבועות העדות, ושבועות הפקדון.

2 ואלו נאמרין בלשון הקודש, מקרא בכורים, וחליצה, ברכות וקללות, ברכת כהנים, וברכת כהן גדול, ופרשת המלך, ופרשת עגלה ערופה, ומשוח מלחמה בשעה שהוא מדבר אל־העם.

3 מקרא בכורים כיצד? וענית ואמרת לפני ה' אלהיך, ולהלן הוא אומר, וענו הלוים ואמרו, מה עניה האמורה להלן בלשון הקודש אף כאן בלשון הקודש.

4 חליצה כיצד? וענתה ואמרה, ולהלן הוא אומר, וענו הלוים ואמרו; מה עניה האמורה להלן בלשון הקודש אף כאן בלשון הקודש. רבי יהודה אומר, וענתה ואמרה ככה, עד שתאמר בלשון הזה.

1. These may be said in any language: the paragraph of the Suspected Adulteress (Num 5.19–21), the Avowal concerning the [Second] Tithe (Deut 26.13–15), the recital of the *Shema* (Deut 6.4), the *Tefillah*, the Benediction over food, the oath of testimony (Lev 5.1–3), and the oath concerning a deposit.

2. These must be said in the Holy Language: the paragraph of the First-fruits, the words of *halitzah*, the Blessings and the Cursings, the Blessings of the Priests, and the blessings of the High Priest, the paragraph of the king, the paragraph of the heifer whose neck is to be broken, and [the words of] the Anointed for Battle when he speaks unto the people.

3. Why does this apply to the paragraph of the First-fruits? [Here it is written,] *And thou shalt answer and say before the Lord thy God* (Deut 26.5), and there it is written, *And the Levites shall answer and say* (Deut 27.14); as there the answering must be in the Holy Language, so here the answering must be in the Holy Language.

4. Why does this apply to the words of *halitzah*? [Here it is written,] *And she shall answer and say* (Deut 25.9), and there it is written, *And the Levites shall answer and say*; as there the answering must be in the Holy Language, so here the answering must be in the Holy Language. R. Judah says: *And she shall answer and say thus*; [therefore it is not valid] unless she speaks according to this very language.[9]

There is no discernible principle for determining which items may be said in Aramaic (or Greek, etc.) and which must be said in Hebrew. Scriptural grounding does not appear to be a deciding factor in favor of Hebrew: of the seven items that one may say in Aramaic, only three (the *Tefillah*, the blessing over food, and the oath of testimony) are not directly prescribed or commanded by Scripture. Given the importance of Hebrew within the Temple liturgy, it is not surprising to find a number of items connected with the priesthood in the latter group. (The first item in the first group is spoken by a priest [see Num 5.19–21], but it only makes sense to address

---

[9] Trans. Danby 1933:300 (references added).

the suspected adulteress in a language she understands.)[10] The revised
Schürer suggests some schematization along the lines of writing *versus* reciting: orally, certain blessings may be said in any language, but writing
was a different matter, as *tefillin* and *mezuzot* could only be written in Hebrew.[11]

The Babylonian Talmud records the highlights of debates surrounding
these two lists. Most of what is said in *b. Soṭah* 32a–33a (where these lists
are discussed) merely gives exegetical support for the placement of these
items on one list rather than the other,[12] but we are also told of real differences of opinion among the rabbis, especially when it came to the language
in which one may recite the *Shema* (Deut 6.4), certainly a central symbol
of Jewish expression. We read, in *b. Soṭah* 32b–33a:

קרית שמע: מנלן דכתיב שמע ישראל בכל לשון שאתה שומע תנו רבנן קרית שמע ככתבה
דברי רבי והחכמים אומרים בכל לשון מאי טעמא דרבי אמר קרא והיו בהוייתן יהו ורבנן
קרא שמע בכל לשון שאתה שומע ורבנן נמי הא כתיב והיו ההוא שלא יקראנה למפרע ורבי
שלא יקראנה למפרע מנליה נפקא ליה מדברים הדברים ורבנן דברים הדברים לא משמע
להו ורבי נמי הכתיב שמע ההוא מיבעי ליה להשמיע לאזניך מה שאתה מוציא מפיך ורבנן
סברי לה כמאן דאמר הקורא את שמע ולא השמיע לאזנו יצא לימא קסבר רבי [33a] כל
התורה בכל לשון נאמרה דאי סלקא דעתך בלשון הקודש נאמרה והיו דכתב רחמנא למה
לי איצטריך משום דכתיב שמע לימא קסברי רבנן כל התורה כולה בלשון קודש נאמרה
דאי סלקא דעתך בכל לשון שמע דכתב רחמנא למה לי איצטריך משום דכתיב והיו

Reciting the *Shema*: How do we know [that it may be recited in any language]? As it is
written: *Hear, O Israel* (Deut 6:4), *viz.* in any language that you understand (שומע). The
Rabbis taught, "The *Shema* must be recited as it is written [*viz.* in Hebrew]." These are
[also] the words of Rabbi but the Sages say, "In any language." What is Rabbi's reason?
One reads, *And [these words] shall be* (Deut 6.6), they must remain in their state. And
[what is the reason of] the Rabbis? One reads, *Hear*, *viz.* in any language that you understand. But for the Rabbis is it not written, *And [these words] shall be*? This means that
one may not read it in the wrong order (למפרע). And whence does Rabbi learn that one
may not read it in the wrong order? From the fact that the text uses *these words*. And the
Rabbis do not derive anything from *these words*. But for Rabbi is it not written *Hear*?
This implies for him: Make audible to your ears what you pronounce with your mouth.
But the Rabbis agree with the one who said that if one recites the *Shema* but not audibly
to his ears, he is released from his obligation. Hypothetically the Rabbis could hold [33a]
that the whole Torah may be read in any language, for if your opinion is that it may be
read only in the holy tongue, why did the Merciful One write *And [these words] shall be*?
It is necessary because it is written *Hear*. Hypothetically the Rabbis could hold that all
the Torah must be read in the holy tongue, for if your opinion is that every language [is

---

[10] *b. Soṭah* 32b also adds that the woman who was coerced into adultery should be told
about both the discerning powers of the "water of bitterness", so as not to discredit its
killing powers when she survives the trial.

[11] Schürer 1973–87:2.22 n. 78. Writs of divorce were usually in Aramaic: see *m. Giṭ.*
9.3.

[12] See Freehof 1923:380–1.

permissible], why did the Merciful One write *Hear*? It is necessary because it is written *And [these words] shall be.*

As Hezser observes, "The texts suggest that for the rabbis the Hebrew language was one of the core values of Jewish religious life."[13] Although the hebraicity of the synagogue liturgy served the rabbis' agenda, it would be a mistake to credit the rabbis with the fact that the liturgy emerged from this period with only select portions of Aramaic incorporated into it.[14] At least one other group (probably)[15] vying for control of the synagogue would have felt compelled to guard the hebraicity of the liturgy: the priests. It should also be noted, in this connection, that the popular way of regarding the synagogue as a sort of mini-temple or as a surrogate for the Temple was another factor favoring the conservation of a Hebrew liturgy, but it was one that the rabbis did not support.[16] (According to a *baraita* in *b. Šabb.* 32a, R. Ishmael b. Eleazar taught, "For two reasons the *'amei ha-aretz* die: for calling the holy ark a 'chest' and for calling the synagogue a 'house of the people'.") This progressive "templization"[17] of the synagogue (which may or may not be connected with priestly groups) would have

---

[13] Hezser 2001:241. According to Joshua A. Fishman 1985:12, the view that "ethno-cultural loyalties ... first required, then fostered and finally preserved differences in language vis-a-vis the usage of co-territorial populations ... is so sensible that its validity can certainly not be entirely rejected". In my view, the fact that certain groups might exploit the latency of this principle does not compromise its usefulness, but only gives it depth.

[14] In light of what I wrote above concerning the Pharisees, I think it is not unlikely that they were responsible for some of the early Aramaic elements in the liturgy. Breuer 2006:459–60 argues that "the linguistic awareness of the Tannaim was Aramaic even when they were speaking Hebrew".

[15] Cohen 1999a:973 writes that "there is no indication that any organized groups competed with the rabbis for power in the synagogues and the religious life of Jewry in the second-century", but whether or not the priests were "organized", it is a safe bet that they sought some measure of control of Jewish piety, and that this would have extended to their dealings with the local synagogue. I am not claiming that their bid for control was anywhere overwhelming. On the role of priests in synagogues in the rabbinic period, see Kraemer 2006:310–11; Kimelman 2006:599. J. E. Taylor 1997:186 writes "it would be rash to imagine that, after 70 CE, priests suddenly and completely lost all importance and power in the multifarious synagogues of the Jewish world". Cohen's words should not be taken to mean that the rabbis (according to Cohen) controlled the synagogues in the second century. See Cohen 1999c.

[16] See Schwartz 2001:238. The fact that the Severus inscription (early 4th cent.) from the Hammath-Tiberias synagogue combines a reference to the synagogue as ἁγίος τόπος with allegiance to the patriarch only goes to show that the patriarch was not universally thought of as a symbol of rabbinic power.

[17] The term is Steven Fine's, and is used throughout Fine 1997. See also Fine 1996; Hruby 1971:72–9; Schubert 1992:161–70; Branham 1995; Binder 1997:122–51; Cohen 1999b; Rajak 2002; F. Schmidt 2001:259–63.

helped to fix the propriety of Hebrew within the popular view.[18] It would thus appear that the rabbis benefited from the linguistic programs of other groups vying for control of the synagogue, and they may even have benefited from the linguistic implications of a view of the synagogue that they did not accept. We should not assume that the rabbis stood behind all the developments that played into their hands, or that the stability of Hebrew's role in the synagogue implies that the rabbis were in control of most synagogues at an early date. Nor should we understand the rabbis' bid to replace the priests as the custodians of the Law, and their concomitant bid to control the synagogue, within the framework of the "templization" of the synagogue. Jack N. Lightstone correctly notes that "with the demise of the Jerusalem cult, rabbis presented themselves through Mishnah as priest-like or priestly-scribe-like and, therefore, as the direct inheritors of priestly knowledge and priestly authority."[19] (Unfortunately, Lightstone goes on to identify the rabbis *with* the fallen Temple administration *simpliciter*, which he sets in contrast to the more usual conclusion that early rabbinism was a hodge podge of priestly *and pharisaic* elements.)[20] The rabbis sought to replace the priests as power brokers, and in third and fourth century they even argued that Torah scholars were the rightful beneficiaries of the tithe system,[21] but they did not seek to become the priesthood of a new era.

B. The Proscription of Extra-Synagogal Prayer

How intrusive of life in general did the rabbis intend their promulgation of Hebrew to be? More specifically, how did the rabbinic insistence on using Hebrew within the synagogue translate into halakhic rules governing other (extra-synagogal) aspects of piety? In the following pages, I look at one well known and centrally relevant proscription of Aramaic: R. Yochanan's

---

[18] J. Z. Smith 1978:187–8, commenting on the change from a permanent holy place to a more mobile concept of locative holiness, writes that the "archaic language and ideology of the cult will be revalorized".

[19] Lightstone 2002:69.

[20] Lightstone appears to think that every methodology not anchored in the strongest type of structuralism is circular by definition, and it is mainly from that working assumption that he tries to make the belief that the Mishnah inscribes many long held tenets of "halakic sagism" appear naive and uncritical. Such thinking, of course, is problematic. E.g., the "self-contradictory propositions" that Lightstone finds (2002:13) in Lester Grabbe's work are not at all contradictory by historical standards. They are only "contradictory" as defined by a straitjacket brand of structuralist analysis. On the putative rabbinic links with the Pharisees, see Jaffee 2001:52–60.

[21] See Levine 1989:71. On the priests as holders of "scribal authority" in Second Temple times, see Fraade 1991:73; Lightstone 2002:68.

insistence that prayer cannot be said in Aramaic because the angels do not understand that language (*b. Sotah* 33a; *b. Šabb.* 12b).

The relevant portions of the talmudic passages are as follows:

b. Sotah 33a
Rab Judah has said, "A man should not pray for his needs in Aramaic. For R. Yochanan said, 'If [he] prays for his needs in Aramaic, the ministering angels will not attend to him, because the ministering angels do not understand Aramaic!'

b. Šabb. 12b
[D]id not Rab Judah say, 'A man should never petition for his needs in Aramaic?', and [did not] R. Yochanan say, 'Everyone who petitions for his needs in Aramaic, the ministering angels will not attend to him, because the ministering angels do not understand Aramaic!'?

Gustaf Dalman thinks that the fact that "the objection to praying in Aramaic referred only to private prayers of individuals" means that "Aramaic prayers must have been used in the Synagogue worship."[22] As a direct inference, this seems too strong: the conclusion that Aramaic was used in the synagogue does not follow from the fact that R. Yochanan refers to private prayers. Nevertheless, the Aramaic elements of the synagogue liturgy are often judged to be very old, and it would appear that R. Yochanan's view of the angels' linguistic abilities cannot easily accomodate *all* of the liturgy as it has come down to us. On the face of it, allowing corporate prayer but not private prayer in Aramaic would appear to provide a flimsy base for the explanation that the angels do not understand Aramaic. But would the flimsiness of a broader, systemic application of R. Yochanan's words have been a serious detriment to the sort of *rhetorical* solution that he had in mind? It is in fact possible to save the broader system on the grounds of R. Yochanan's view – e.g., perhaps he objected to the use of all Aramaic in religious contexts, or perhaps he thought that angelic mediation of prayer did not apply to the corporate liturgy (so that God listened directly to the liturgy, but employed angels to mediate "outside" prayers).[23] The latter solution has the advantage of making room, within R. Yochanan's overarching scheme, for the Palestinian Talmud's insistence on reciting the *tefillah* in the vernacular so that one may add one's own personal petitions (*y. Sota* 21b), a scheme that would appear to be necessitated by R. Yochanan's scheme anyway, since it seems to presume that the would-be supplicant

---

[22] Dalman 1929:19.

[23] The latter solution would be consistent with the way in which apocalyptic and mystical texts sometimes depict God descending to his throne in the seventh heaven at prayer time, for which see *3 En.* 48.1 (ver. A); *Hekhalot Rabbati* 11.2 (= *Synopse* §172). Gruenwald 1988:162 refers to this theme as "one of the more original ideas of early mystical literature". See Fujita 1986:181. I have elsewhere argued that this scheme obtains in the *Apocalypse of Abraham*: see Poirier 2004b.

will end up praying in Aramaic within the synagogue. But it is perhaps best to take the *intent* of R. Yochanan's dictum seriously: he identified a problem and honed a brilliant rhetorical solution, and he perhaps neither sought nor cared about the systemic limitations of the worldview that it rendered. With this consideration in mind, I will limit the application of R. Yochanan's dictum to the practice it was directly aimed at stopping: extra-synagogal prayer.

R. Yochanan lived in the third century. He was, in fact, a towering figure in that century, so much so that Levine explains the increase in Babylonian sages living in Palestine as due to R. Yochanan's influence, and suggests that his "longevity and stature attracted students to his academy in Tiberias, swell[ing] the ranks of the subsequent generation of Palestinian sages."[24] In speaking of developments during R. Yochanan's lifetime, we are still in the long period leading up to rabbinic ascendancy over Palestinian Jewish culture. At first blush, this fact would seem to place a question mark over the very idea of R. Yochanan curbing extra-synagogal prayer in order to increase rabbinic control over popular Jewish piety. But the third century represents the beginning of a transition, and that transition was probably established in some locales long before it was established in others. In other words, the well rehearsed warning that the rabbis did not control the "synagogue" does not mean that, by the third century, they did not control *some* local synagogues, and if the rabbinic movement located its headquarters in Tiberias, it is reasonable to assume that at least a few of the numerous synagogues attested in that city were in fact controlled by the rabbis. As Schwartz notes, the Palestinian Talmud implies that the synagogues in certain locales were controlled by the rabbis, while those in other locales were not. His point is to show that many synagogues were not under (some level of) rabbinic control, but the text he cites also shows unequivocally that some *were*:

Though many passages in the Palestinian Talmud unambiguously – indeed, perhaps a bit too insistently – regard the synagogue as the most appropriate place for prayer (e.g., Y. Berakhot 5:1, 8d–9a), others remind us that the synagogues the rabbis had in mind were not the standard local synagogues, but their own. How else are we to understand the law forbidding Jews from Haifa, Beth Shean, and Tivon to lead the prayers (because of what the rabbis regarded as their imprecise pronunciation of Hebrew), obviously not an option in the synagogues of Haifa, Beth Shean, and Tivon (Y. Berakhot 2:4, 4d)?[25]

---

[24] Levine 1989:67. Levine offers these suggestions in partial explanation for placing the zenith of rabbinic activity in the years 280–310 C.E. (= the third generation in Chanoch Albeck's classification – see Albeck 1969:669–81).

[25] Schwartz 2001:238–9. Hezser (2001:250) writes, "If the synagogue was one of the few realms where Hebrew was still used at that time, the strong rabbinic opposition against its replacement by another language becomes understandable."

If R. Yochanan really said that "the townspeople are commanded to do the work of sages" (בני העיר מצווים לעשות מלאכתן של תלמידי חכמים), as *b. Yoma* 72b claims, and if we may assume that this saying had its desired effect, then presumably R. Yochanan's control of the "townspeople" was great enough to allow him at least a hope of proscribing their private prayer habits. (R. Yochanan may have had a gift for diplomacy, as suggested by the story of his successful buffering of the conflict between the Patriarch R. Judah II and Resh Laqish over the issue of taxing the scholars.)[26]

There is another factor that suggests the rabbis held greater control over the synagogues in third-century Tiberias than elsewhere: there may have been less competition with priestly groups in Tiberias. Antipas had built Tiberias on the site of graves (Josephus, *A.J.* XVIII.38), and although R. Simeon bar Yochai had annulled the burden of purity issues related to life in Tiberias in the middle of the second century C.E., we cannot simply assume that priestly groups accepted his ruling.[27] Not only did his ruling fly in the face of priestly sensibilities, but priestly acceptance of a ruling by R. Simeon bar Yochai, especially on so visible and defining an issue, would have amounted to their recognition of rabbinic authority. While some priests had already thrown their lot in with the rabbis by this time, and therefore may have judged themselves free to settle in Tiberias, the threat of priestly opposition to the rabbis presumably did not obtain within the synagogues of Tiberias proper. This could be a contributing factor to the success of the rabbinic program at Tiberias, culminating in the advent of the Palestinian Talmud.

While there is clear evidence that not all the synagogues at Hammath-Tiberias (to name the larger metropolis) were under rabbinic control,[28] there are good reasons, as we have seen, for supposing that the rabbis effectively controlled some of the synagogues there, especially within Tiberias proper, where many priests presumably would not go. This scenario provides a ready context for interpreting R. Yochanan's proscription of extra-synagogal prayer as a sort of corralling of popular piety: in an area where the rabbis ran the synagogue, limiting expressions of piety to the

---

[26] See Kimelman 1981.

[27] Contra Dothan 1983:4, who assumes that the priests who lived in Hammath (*viz.* the Ma'aziah course) accepted R. Simeon bar Yochai's ruling. On Tiberias in rabbinic times, see Alon 1980:8. Tiberias and Hammath were separated by only a mile and were already a unified city by the first century C.E. Kalmin 2006:90–2 discusses a few rabbinic traditions on the purification of Tiberias.

[28] See Goodenough 1953–68:12.185–6. Goodenough writes, "We have obviously no more right to assert that all the Jews at Tiberias were living by the halacha of the rabbis there than that all Jews in Alexandria at Philo's time thought of Judaism as did Philo." See the links between the zodiac mosaic and the priestly courses as discussed in Dothan 1983:48–9.

synagogue was perhaps calculated to increase the rabbis' control of religious life itself.

R. Yochanan's dictum was probably originally received mainly by certain synagogues in Tiberias, but R. Yochanan had a strong influence on succeeding generations of rabbis. In the words of Levine, "in many respects the world of the later third- and early fourth-century sages appears to be an extension of [R. Yochanan's] circle of colleagues and students."[29] Through these developing lines of influence, R. Yochanan's proscription of extra-synagogal prayer may have taken on more significance. (Although it was aimed at proscribing extra-synagogal prayer, R. Yochanan's dictum presumably allowed prayer in the *academy* to continue, as long as it was in Hebrew.)[30] Although it resonated with rabbinic ideology from pre-mishnaic times, its formulation as a saying of R. Yochanan suddenly became emblematic of the community's increasing need for the rabbis. The loss of Judaism's cultic center could have resulted in a fractured, over-democratized culture of popular Jewish piety, but the rabbis took it upon themselves (opportunistically?) to pick up the slack created by the loss of the Temple. Their way of doing it was presumably not something they invented: it was likely the strategy of other groups as well, including priestly groups. (I am not implying that Torah devotion was entirely a post-Destruction development, as some overstructuralizing accounts would have it.) Fraade discusses the rabbis' claim that Torah study now "constitutes the central religious act of Jewish life": "Implied in this claim is the *concomitant* claim of the sages to be that class which, through its dedication to such study practice within Israel, now constitute the sole legitimate leadership – both religious and social – of the people of Israel."[31] The fact that the community's need for the rabbis was fostered by the ideology inscribed within a saying that expressed that need is not a bit of irony: that development was every bit intentional.

C. The Empowerment of the Hebraeophone *Literati*

The pro-Hebrew outlook of third-century rabbinism, whether couched in terms of religious contexts or daily life, is patient of an alternative explanation: the exaltation of Hebrew may have been calculated to increase the power of those who already knew how to speak, read, and (possibly) write Hebrew. That is, rather than being intended as an encouragement for others to learn Hebrew, the pro-Hebrew view might have been aimed at increas-

---

[29] Levine 1989:67 n. 118.
[30] On rabbis praying in the academy, see Levine 1975:224 n. 477.
[31] Fraade 1991:118–19.

ing the community's dependence upon those who *already* understood Hebrew, a scheme corresponding to one that appears regularly in sociological discussions of reading skills as empowerment. Jack Goody writes, "[U]nder Christianity, Islam and Judaism teaching (at least the promotion of advanced literate skills) continued to be dominated by religious specialists until the advent of modern secular education, a position that it was obviously in their interests to preserve in order to maintain their role as gatekeepers of ideas."[32] For the powers that be to make this latter scheme work might have required a certain policing of personal prayers and blessings, but, as we have seen, some rabbis seem to have made an effort to restrict prayer to the synagogue.

The corralling of religious piety through the proscription of extra-synagogal prayer fits hand in glove with another development: tying piety to the Hebrew language (see *b. Ber.* 13a; *Sipre* 32.43)[33] served to increase the community's reliance on the rabbis by setting up the rabbis as the tradents and arbiters of Torah, including but not limited to the halakha of daily life. Although many of the rabbis' halakhic discussions are idealistic, intent upon the proper way of doing things in imaginary situations, there came a point when the rabbis came to be recognized as halakhic authorities in daily activities.[34] Beginning with a knowledge of Bible and the Mishnah, of course, taking part in halakhic deliberations entailed the ability to read and speak Hebrew. As Goodenough observes, "[T]here is no evidence … that the rabbis had any interest in making their Mishnah available to outsiders."[35] Exclusive knowledge of a hallowed or privileged language

---

[32] Goody 1986:17. See Hezser 2001:39.

[33] See Grözinger 1998:75–90, esp. 80. In connection with Grözinger's larger argument: Stern (1994:192) notes a number of rabbinic passages that list Israel's maintenance of its ancestral language as one of the things that merited redemption from Egypt.

[34] Fraade 1991:102 discusses the relationship between study for its own sake and service to the community within rabbinic thinking. On the absence of the rabbis' influence with regard to daily halakha before the third century, Cohen (1999a:969) writes, "If the topic profile fairly represents rabbinic activity, we can clearly see the development of rabbinic authority. The rabbis before Judah the Patriarch were acknowledged experts in the laws of purity and personal status, legal relics of the sectarian past of the rabbinic movement. The rabbis also were sufficiently expert and holy to be able to cancel oaths and vows. But in matters of personal piety, e.g. shabbat, holidays, kosher food, prayer, and synagogue rituals, and in civil matters, the people apparently did not need the rabbis." See Levine 1989:24. In discussing the "growing importance of Hebrew for the Jews" at the time of Justinian novella 146 (in the year 553), Schwartz (1998b:67) writes, "There is, to be sure, nothing inherently rabbinic about the liturgical use of Hebrew – but [in] looking … for a complex of subtle changes which may then serve as tracers of the early stages of the process [of rabbinic ascendancy in the Middle Ages], … it certainly seems reasonable to regard the spread of Hebrew as one such change."

[35] Goodenough 1953–68:12.185. Cohen 1992:211 makes a similar point.

held the key to social power. Hezser writes (citing Hamers and Blanc), "In societies where a number of different languages are spoken, power relationships amongst social groups also tend to be transferred to the languages which these groups represent."[36] Those presented with the opportunity to learn Hebrew had much to gain, at least within the world imagined by the rabbis and which, with the help of the patriarch, began to materialize in third-century Galilee. As Schwartz puts it: "The openness of the curatorial class meant that mastery of Hebrew was not only a social marker, but also an important path to prestige."[37] In the instance at hand, however, specific formulations tended to magnify the social boundaries set up by the privilege of linguistic access, turning the rabbis as a group into a new wellspring of revelation for Israel (replacing priests and prophets). Gabriele Boccaccini writes,

In the Mishnah the legitimacy and consistency of unwritten laws relies only on the unifying authority of the sages. They are acknowledged as the living trustees of Israelite religion. Nobody but themselves may question their decisions; in halakhic discussions they always have the last word. Their self-sufficient authority affects scripture, too. The sages lay down the rules of how to read, interpret, and translate the scripture. If they cannot change a written law, they have the power to suspend its effects (*m. Hor.* 1.3). 'Greater stringency applies to the (observance of) the words of the Scribes, than to (the observance of) the words of the (written) law' (*m. Sanh.* 11.3). People were to obey the sages even if the decisions of the sages were against scripture; people would not be guilty for that (*m. Hor.* 1.1).[38]

In the light of such an elitist self-definition, the teaching of Hebrew may have served a political end (although it would be unwise to dismiss the motivation of piety altogether). This does not necessarily mean that they sought to keep knowledge of Hebrew away from the populace: with certain controls, actually *teaching* Hebrew could have served these same political ends.[39] As Hezser suggests, in connection with the more widespread appearance of schools in the third century, the rabbis may have "promoted Torah-reading skills in order to create a support base for themselves."[40]

---

[36] Hezser 2001:238.

[37] Schwartz 1995:43. See the discussion of "text-brokering" in Snyder 2000:165–88; Keith 2009:99–102.

[38] Boccaccini 1994:257. See also Lightstone 2002:184. But note the limited acceptance of the Mishnah, as discussed in Halivni 1981:209. The rabbis would soon lean on the theory of oral torah to legitimate the Mishnah's view of their authority. See Avery-Peck 1992:35.

[39] Davies (1998:11) writes, "Cultures and societies may resist canons, or even ignore canons, but while canons remain mechanisms of control, and their definition and transmission in the hands of the elite, they will exercise an attraction on any who seek admission to that elite."

[40] Hezser 2001:39. In some societies, literacy *per se* carries religious clout. J. E. Taylor (1997:224 n. 18) writes, "In some traditional societies where literacy is poor, the man

None of this is meant to imply that the rabbis deliberately schemed these designs: religionists have a way of fooling themselves into thinking that their ideological compromises are really in line with a higher form of piety.

The empowerment of the rabbis through their exegetical and halakhic energies represented a shift from earlier times, when authority and expertise in the Law belonged almost exclusively to the priesthood.[41] Concomitant with this shift from priestly power to (real or imagined) rabbinic power was the rabbis' claim to priestly privilege. Jacob Neusner sees a sort of priestly claim implicit within the Mishnah, which he calls a "priestly document ... without priestly sponsorship": "Mishnah points toward a group of people who take over everything of the priestly legacy but the priesthood itself."[42] The rabbis' usurpation of quasi-priestly status brought important privileges: in the third and fourth centuries, ordination as a rabbi meant exemption from taxes, although "usurpation" in that case consists of laying hold of religious-political power and not necessarily of *specifically* priestly status.[43] This displacement of the priests as the curatorial class both served and was served by the growth of the patriarch's power, especially in the person of Rabbi Judah, whose line was apparently not priestly

---

who can read is considered to possess spiritual or magical power. For example, the Marabouts of the Gambia and Senegal sometimes write out passages from the Koran to be eaten in certain remedies. The ability to read the Koran in itself provides the Marabout with considerable prestige, and his ability to know what passage might 'fit' the requirements of the situation is tantamount to a spiritual power." On the paucity of schools in the Second Temple era, see Jaffee 2001:20–5.

[41] Maier (1993:143) writes, "Torah reading was perhaps one of the means to demonstrate power, both by groups/institutions and in front of groups or factions, as far as both sides pretended to have the obligatory Torah traditions at their exclusive disposal. As long as the temple existed, the reading from the 'holy' Torah scrolls proper remained restricted to the respective sacred area, not accessible to laymen. Each reading of this kind represented a demonstration of the privilege to dispose of the sacred master exemplars of the Torah. After the destruction of the temple, this effect lost its persuasive power to the extent that it had been dependent on the quality of the holy space during the temple period. The lay rabbinical authorities transposed the practice later definitively from sacred space to sacred times." As Fraade 2002:317 notes, the rabbinic usurpation of priestly political privilege is symbolized in the disagreement between *m. Sanh.* 2.4 and the *Temple Scroll* on the apparatus of divine approval on a king's declaration of war, with the former identifying that apparatus with a court of 71 sages, and the latter identifying it with the priestly oracles (urim and thummim). See Fraade 1999.

[42] Neusner 1979–80:120. In Lightstone's words (2002:28), the Mishnah "model[s] ... a priestly-scribal virtuosity of comprehensively mapping 'the world'". See Kimelman 1983. See now Alexander 2009.

[43] See Levine 1979:672–4. Lieberman 1945–6:360–1 suggests that the number of scholars that the Patriarch could ordain to the rabbinate was limited. The priests naturally dissented to the patriarch's power (see Alon 1980:1.100–3).

and who is frequently credited with bringing the rabbinic movement into relative prominence.[44] Although certain privileges of the priestly office still obtained throughout tannaitic times and beyond,[45] the fact that some priests would seek power through rabbinic channels probably tells us something about the displacement of the priestly guild by the rabbis.[46] As is commonly noted, the chain of tradition in *m. 'Abot* 1 passes over the priests as custodians of the oral law, a striking and undoubtedly ideological omission.[47] Yet the frequent intensity of the rabbinic polemic against the priestly notion of genetic privilege, and of the displacement of the genetic principle by knowledge of the Law (so that "even the bastard sage has preference over the ignorant high priest"),[48] suggests that some priests were still vying for power, as does the mishnaic account of the priests setting the calendar (*m. Roš Haš.* 1.7). Fraade argues that the Mishnah, "with its privileging of the king over the high priest, [might] be an argument against contemporary priestly circles that surely would have also resisted patriarchal claims to supreme authority."[49] According to Levine, in spite of the continuing presence of the priests as a group, "we have no evidence that they constituted a significant pressure group in Jewish society at the time,"[50] but in light of the limited significance of the rabbis themselves at this time, their pressure may have been felt by some.[51] As I suggested above, the success of using Tiberias as a rabbinic headquarters in the third century may have been partially due to priestly strictures against visiting that city.

---

[44] On R. Judah's nonpriestly line, see the discussion in Goodblatt 1994:132. Cohen 1992:217–19 enumerates a number of ways by which Rabbi Judah "sought to bring the rabbis into Jewish society at large": he (1) sought to increase the power of his office, which would also increase the power of the rabbinate; (2) increased the rabbis' jurisdiction in the courts; (3) opened the rabbinate to the poorer class; and (4) he made the rabbinic movement more urbanized. On the Rabbis' praise for R. Judah, see Levine 1989:33–4. On urbanization, cf. Schwartz 1998a:205: "The rabbis probably gravitated to the cities because their conviction that they constituted the true leadership of Israel made them not sectarian but expansionist." On the number of individuals within the rabbinic movement, see the minimalist argument of Lapin 2006:221–2.

[45] On the continuation of the tithe, see Alon 1980:1.254–60.

[46] See the list of priestly rabbis in Schwartz 1990:100–1. See also Cohen 1999a:943 n. 88; Sivertsev 2005:242–50. Against the view that priests regained a measure of power *vis-à-vis* the Rabbis, see Fine 2005:1–9.

[47] See Herr 1979; Himmelfarb 1997; Rubenstein 1999:176–211; A. Baumgarten 2001:33.

[48] See Levine 1979:659; Cohen 1999a:950.

[49] Fraade 2002:332. On "the priests of the third and fourth centuries", see S. Miller 1984:116–27; Levine 1989:171–2; Schwartz 1990:105–6.

[50] Levine 1989:172.

[51] See Schwartz 1990:99–100.

D. Conclusion

The particular use to which R. Yochanan put the motif of Hebrew-speaking angels was borne of the sort of political jockeying that helped spread rabbinic influence in the third and fourth centuries. To say that the two developments described above (R. Yochanan's corraling of piety to synagogue contexts and the community's dependence on Hebrew experts) fit together hand in glove implies that they are not mutually exclusive, but I would not want us to lose sight of how much of the above reconstruction relies upon a hermeneutic of suspicion, and may or may not correspond to what actually happened. Perhaps the reality of the situation is found in one or the other development rather than in both.

Chapter 4

The Esoteric Heavenly Language:
Fairly Certain Cases

In the ancient world, it was widely believed that the gods, angels, demons, etc., spoke *divine* languages – that is, languages that were *not* also spoken by humans (except in magical recipes or ecstatic rapture).[1] This view competed with the view we encountered in the preceding chapter, in which a given human language was also spoken by the god(s) of a particular nation. In this chapter and the next, I discuss Jewish and Christian texts that claim or imply that angels speak an esoteric language, that is, a language not normally spoken by humans. With regard to the clarity of their allusion to an esoteric angeloglossy, the examples in this chapter and the next fill a spectrum, ranging from "almost certain" to "dimly possible". In this chapter, I discuss those texts that contain relatively certain references (*viz.* 1 Cor 13.1, 2 Cor 12.1–7, *Testament of Job*, *Apocalypse of Zephaniah*, *Ascension of Isaiah*, *Apocalypse of Abraham*, a saying attributed to R. Hama b. Hanina [in *Gen. Rab.* 74.7], Ephrem Syrus' *Hymn* 11, and the *Book of the Resurrection* [attributed to Bartholomew]). In most of the pseudepigraphic texts in this list, reference to an esoteric angelic language is connected to the protagonist's participation in that language, often as a mark of achieving "isangelic status" (*viz.* of being temporarily imbued with angelic qualitites).[2] One must wonder to what degree the authors of other pseudepigraphic works (*viz.* those devoid of any such descriptions of humans joining in angelic praise) might have accepted the view that angels spoke an esoteric language.

A. New Testament (1 Cor 13.1)

The poetic timbre of 1 Cor 13.1, as much as 1 Corinthian 13's visibility within Christian piety, has made it by far the most recognizable reference

---

[1] See Güntert 1921; West 1966:386–8 n. 831. Demons are also often depicted as able to speak various human languages (e.g., in Palladius, *Hist. laus.* 32.1; Jerome, *Life of St. Hilarion* 22 [= chap. 13 in the Sources Chrétiennes edition [Morales and Leclerc 2007:248–53]).

[2] The term "isangelic status" is taken from Golitzin 2001:131.

to angelic languages: "If I speak in the tongues of humans and of angels, but I do not have love, I am a sounding gong or a clanging cymbal" (Ἐὰν ταῖς γλώσσαις τῶν ἀνθρώπων λαλῶ καὶ τῶν ἀγγέλων, ἀγάπην δὲ μὴ ἔχω, γέγονα χαλκὸς ἠχῶν ἢ κύμβαλον ἀλαλάζον). The question before us is "What does Paul mean by 'tongues of angels?'" There is little chance, of course, that Paul refers here to angels speaking human languages. As Ceslas Spicq argues, the construction of 1 Cor 13.1 implies a belief in angeloglossy of some sort: the fact that λαλῶ interposes τῶν ἀνθρώπων and καὶ τῶν ἀγγέλων "invites us to read 'and even (*kai*) of angels' and to consider angelic language as real a language as human speech, but of a higher order."[3]

Many scholars confidently associate Paul's reference to "the tongues ... of angels" with glossolalia. Jean Héring calls the wording of 1 Cor 13.1 "a fuller and more correct expression" (than λαλεῖν γλώσσαις) for glossolalia.[4] But this view also has its detractors – Hans Conzelmann and Nils Engelsen both think that the fact that tongues "will cease" (13.8) controverts any attempt to identify "the tongues of angels" with glossolalia. They maintain that if the eschatological benefits include the translation of the believer to the celestial realm, then speaking in angelic tongues would not "cease" but rather multiply.[5] But this can hardly be right: given that 13.8 also says that prophecies "will fail" and knowledge "will vanish", it is evident that Paul construes these charisms as "ceasing" by token of their being absorbed into the higher order of existence that they signify. Tongues *will* cease, but only because the charism will one day give way to a natural (rather than charismatic) mode of speaking the same mysteries.

Christopher Forbes argues that the angeloglossic understanding of glossolalia is based on an unjustified reification of 1 Cor 13.1, suggesting that the *Acts of Paul* and (possibly) the *Testament of Job* inherited the concept from this verse.[6] There is something strange about this tactic, however, in that it mirrors the practice of explaining the patristic equation of glossolalia with xenoglossy as a reflex of having wrongly universalized the miracle in Acts 2, a practice that Forbes very much opposes. If we should bracket the angeloglossic understanding of glossolalia found in the *Acts of Paul* and the *Testament of Job*, based upon their presumed dependence upon 1 Cor 13.1, why should we not also bracket the xenoglossic understanding of glossolalia found in the second-century church fathers (which Forbes ac-

---

[3] Spicq 1965:145. See also Klauck 2000.

[4] Héring 1962:135.

[5] Conzelmann 1975:225 n. 73 comments on 1 Cor 13.8, "Paul is accordingly not thinking of these [γλῶσσαι] as the language of heaven." Engelsen (1970:202–3) writes, "[T]here is the indirect Pauline understanding that glossolalia is not a heavenly language. It belongs to what is going to cease (I Cor. 13:8)." See also Turner 1998a:228.

[6] Forbes 1995:71–2.

cepts as authoritative), based upon their presumed dependence upon Acts 2? We are directed back to the account in Acts, and to Forbes's attempt to trace the xenoglossic aspect of the Pentecost miracle back to a pre-Lukan source (rather than to Luke's hand, as most commentators argue).[7] Forbes's argument is not a little confused.

Another question is "Whose understanding of angeloglossy does 1 Cor 13.1 reflect?" Some scholars identify the term "tongues of angels" with the view of the Corinthian pneumatics, while others identify it with Paul's own view. Gerhard Dautzenberg believes that 1 Cor 13.1 reflects the earliest Jewish-Christian understanding of glossolalia, and that Paul's citation of Isa 28.11 in 1 Cor 14.21 reflects the *Pauline* understanding, *displacing* the angeloglossic view.[8] M. Eugene Boring holds a view similar to Dautzenberg's: he writes that the Corinthians "thought of glossolalia as the 'language of angels'", but that "Paul ... inverts this valuation."[9] But it should be noted that the angeloglossic and the "Isaian" understanding of glossolalia are not logically exclusive. Even if they were, it would not prove that they could not be concurrently held by the same person.

The possibility that Paul is relying on a source makes the thicket even thicker. Nils Dahl points to a number of non-Pauline features in the so-called "love hymn" in 1 Corinthians 13, which can be explained through his adaptation of a source.[10] If Dahl and others are correct about Paul's use of a source, then perhaps the terminology of 1 Cor 13.1 does not reflect

---

[7] Forbes's objection (1995:155) to the usual reading of Acts 2 is rather strange: "Why Luke should consider a 'human language' miracle more noteworthy than one of divine languages, and hence re-interpret Pentecost in this light is not explained." It is "not explained", of course, because it scarcely *needs* explaining: a glossolalic community that understands glossolalia as speaking in an angelic language would naturally hold the xenoglossic miracle of Acts 2 in higher regard, due to the evidentiary value it holds for skeptics. From a thaumaturgical standpoint, there is no question that a human language miracle is much more valuable than a divine language miracle: the xenoglossy in Acts 2 functions as a proof for converts, and Paul explicitly denies that mass glossolalia leads to conversion: "Will they not say that you are mad?" (1 Cor 14.23).

[8] Dautzenberg 1979:cols. 235, 237. L. T. Johnson 1992:600 refers to the identification of the "tongues of angels" with glossolalia as a "rather odd hypothesis," but does not explain why. On the face of it, I see nothing odd about it, and neither does Klauck: "Warum ... verstehe ich nicht" (2000:278 n. 8). Johnson's article contains a lot of strange and unexplained claims about glossolalia. E.g., his claim (1992:600) that "Paul sees tongues as an optional mode of prayer ... which may need to be outgrown" is a distinctive mark of the most outworn fundamentalist misreading of 1 Corinthians 13.

[9] Boring 1991:126.

[10] Dahl 1936. See Sandnes 1991:100–2. For the arguments against Pauline authorship, see Titus 1959. For a broader view of the debate, see Corley 2004, and the works cited there. Literary parallels to 1 Corinthians 13 are collected in Conzelmann 1975:219–20. J. T. Sanders 1966 argues against the hymnic nature of 1 Corinthians 13.

Paul's preferred choice of words.[11] It might then be possible that "the tongues of angels" originally referred to a pagan ideal, reflecting a pagan understanding of (non-Christian) glossolalia.[12] This suggestion is supported by the possible pagan origins of the references to gongs and cymbals in v. 1, and the possible pagan character of the hypothetical feats that Paul lists in v. 3. [13] Most commentators seem to think that Paul's reference to burning the body refers to cremating the body after death – in fact, the possibility of misinterpreting the verse in this way provides a likely explanation for the origin of the variant reading, in which "burning" (καυθήσωμαι) is replaced by "boasting" (καυχήσωμαι)[14] – but, as Oda Wischmeyer points out, Iamblichus tells of neoplatonists (or perhaps Egyptians or "Chaldeans" in whom he sees neoplatonism's forebears) who are able, by the energizing of true enthusiasm, to withstand the most torturous abuses to their bodies, including setting them on fire, without the slightest sensation of what is happening (*Myst.* 3.4).[15] This interpretation of "give my body to be burned" perhaps makes more sense than the view that "burning" refers to a martyr's death, as burning is not known to have been a form of punishment for Christians at the time of Paul's writing.[16] (It is also perhaps unlikely that Paul's understanding of the believer's resurrection could have made room for cremation.) On this account, the purpose of 1 Cor 13.3 is to refer to pagan spirituality-markers as an improper index of what really counts. No matter how Jewish or Christian the concept of speaking in angelic tongues may appear, we cannot exclude the possibility that the reference to this concept in 1 Cor 13.1 was taken over from a tradition that was neither Jewish nor Christian. (In this connection, it is worth noting that angelic languages are mentioned in *Corp. herm.* 1.26.) The middle section of 1 Corinthians 13 contains several verses that could only have been written by Paul or another Christian – given its perfect alignment with the list of charismata in 1 Corinthians 12 – but that does not implicate the suggestion that the feats listed at the beginning of the chapter are primarily pagan. The question of whether Paul has adapted a preexisting hymn is hardly a question of whether he *would* do such a thing: he evidently cares little about whose terms and formulas he borrows, as long as they help make his point.

---

[11] The judgment that some of the words in 1 Corinthians 13 are pre-Pauline in no way minimizes the importance of this chapter for Paul's argument – Enslin 1938:251 suggests that "Knowledge puffeth up, but love edifieth" is "the key to the whole epistle".

[12] On non-Christian glossolalia, see May 1956; Bunn 1986; Klauck 1999; and the studies cited by Klauck.

[13] On the pagan character of the gongs and cymbals, see Sweet 1966–7:246.

[14] See Westcott and Hort 1882:2.116–17.

[15] Wischmeyer 1981:83.

[16] See Wischmeyer 1981:81–4; Fee 1987:43. Cremation of martyrs is found in Eusebius, *Hist. eccl.* 5.1.62–3.

Most scholars, however, think that Paul composed *all* of 1 Corinthians 13, whether he did so some time prior to inserting it within 1 Corinthians, or during the actual writing of the letter.[17] But this view does not necessarily imply that Paul identified glossolalia with angeloglossy, for, as already mentioned, he may simply be borrowing the terminology of the *Corinthians*. The "if" at the beginning of 1 Cor 13.1 provides the rhetorical space in which Paul can speak of angeloglossy without signaling his agreement with an angeloglossic understanding of glossolalia. Throughout the rest of 1 Corinthians, Paul prefers to identify glossolalia with the divine Spirit (or with the human spirit) rather than with angels.

J. F. M. Smit and James G. Sigountos suggest that the reference to angels has a "hyperbolic function" in this passage. Smit notes that angels fulfill such a function in 1 Cor 4.9, Gal 1.8; 4.14,[18] while Sigountos argues that "[t]he fact that Paul does not elsewhere describe glossolalia in angelic or heavenly terms also tells against the 'realist' understanding."[19] Here we must be cautious: Paul's failure to describe glossolalia elsewhere in these terms tells only against this being *his* view of glossolalia – it does not tell against it being the Corinthians' view.[20] While Paul seems to oppose the idea that believers share in some sort of angelic existence, the Corinthians themselves might have been quite sold on such a view. Gordon D. Fee argues that "tongues is associated with angels" in 13.1:

---

[17] To this end, see the argument of Johansson 1964. See also Holladay 1990.

[18] Smit 1993:254 n. 20.

[19] Sigountos 1994. Forbes (1995:61–2) writes that the phrase "and angels" in 1 Cor 13.1 "does look like a rhetorical flourish": "'Or even those of angels' may well be the sense Paul intended here: clearly his [*sic*] is not really claiming 'all mysteries and all knowledge', or to have sold all that he has." It is not clear, however, that understanding "all mysteries and knowledge" is meant to be hyperbole, and there are other ways of understanding the pairing of "tongues of men" with "tongues of angels". See below.

[20] Paul's question "Do all speak with tongues?" is probably meant to limit glossolalic outbursts to those that are interpretable, by associating glossolalia with other gifts that are given only to a select few. Dale Martin's otherwise exemplary study of the Corinthian glossolalia suffers for supposing that a significant portion of the community was not glossolalic: according to D. B. Martin 1991:578–79, Paul "points out that he will give up speaking in tongues in the assembly out of respect for the interests of the nonglossolalists (14:18–19)". Unfortunately for Martin, there are no "nonglossolalists" mentioned or implied in this passage. (Does he assume that all the glossolalists *understood* their encoded messages?) Rather, Paul refrains from uninterpreted glossolalia because it does not benefit the understandings of those present. Stendahl 1976:110 comes to a much more correct understanding: "To Paul [glossolalia] is just an obvious part of the Christian experience." Stendahl's argument depends in part on taking Rom 8.26 as a reference to glossolalia (a view I accept but which there is not presently space to defend). On the basis of Romans 8, Stendahl 1976:111 concludes, "[I]n Paul's mind, the gift of glossolalia is not a sign of spiritual accomplishment, it is not the graduation with high honors into the category of the truly spiritual. To him glossolalia is the gift that fits into his experience of weakness."

[T]he Corinthians seem to have considered themselves to be already like the angels, thus truly "spiritual," needing neither sex in the present (7:1–7) nor a body in the future (15:1–58). Speaking angelic dialects by the Spirit was evidence enough for them of their participation in the new spirituality, hence their singular enthusiasm for this gift.[21]

If speaking in the tongues of angels were a prized experience in Corinth, its function within 1 Cor 13.1 would not be any less rhetorically effective than if that verse had contained a hyperbolic reference. A. C. Thiselton gives a weak objection to this reconstruction, based on a gross misunderstanding of Paul's argument: "[I]n what sense, if any, could the use of the language of heaven be described as childish?" (cf. 1 Cor 13.11).[22] Thiselton's objection floats on a serious misreading of Paul's argument: the childishness that Paul remonstrates is that of a showy display, not motivated by love.[23] It is not something inherent within the *charismata* as properly employed. As Forbes notes, Paul could hardly call glossolalia a childish practice if he also thanks God that he practices it more than all the Corinthians.[24] It should further be noted that Paul speaks of having left behind his childish way of talking, while also telling the reader that he *continues* to speak in tongues.

In the end, the likeliest view is that Paul *does* identify angeloglossy with glossolalia.[25] The fact that he refers to angeloglossy in the midst of a dis-

---

[21] Fee 1987:573, also 630–1. (This passage also appears verbatim, with the exception of one word, in Fee:1990:150.) See also D. B. Martin 1991; Martyn 1997:98–9. J. T. Sanders 1966:170 apparently disagrees with this reconstruction, as does Thiselton 1979:32: "The suggestion is purely speculative, since with the possible exception of xiii. 1 there seem to be no traces in these chapters of any explicit claim by the Corinthians that they were actually speaking the language of heaven itself." Turner 1998b:236 thinks that Fee's interpretation "perhaps allows too much place for the 'tongues of angels'". Holladay 1990:92 makes the unlikely suggestion that "speaking with the tongues of men and of angels" refers hyperbolically to speaking with "rhetorical flourishes".

[22] Thiselton 1979:32. Hurd 1983:112–13 holds the same view.

[23] Despite the absurdity of Thiselton's reading, the same view can be found in a few other scholars. E.g., L. T. Johnson (1992:600) writes that "Paul clearly suggests that [glossolalia] is among the 'childish' things that must be put aside if maturity is to be reached", and Dunn 1975:243 supposes that Paul regards glossolalia "as a somewhat childish gift". As Tugwell 1973:139 correctly notes, glossolalia, for Paul, "is not simply God's kindergarten". On Dunn's tendency to ignore 1 Cor 14.18 and turn Paul into an anti-glossolalist, see M. Smith 1976:726.

[24] Forbes 1995:70. Similarly, Ellis 1989:115: "[Glossolalia] is a gift much used by the Apostle, and he can hardly have regarded it as a 'consolation prize' for immature Christians." In connection with interpretations that pit love against spiritual gifts, Fee 1987:626 rightly notes, "Paul would wince."

[25] See esp. Klauck 2000. Luz (2004:137–38) argues that Paul would not have agreed with an angeloglossic view of tongues: "above all [Paul] does not raise [glossolalia] to the 'angelic' heights, but to the earthly depths." He argues this on the basis of Rom 8.26–27, in which glossolalia is described (so Luz) in terms of "the inarticulate sighing of unredeemed human

cussion about prophecy and λαλεῖν γλώσσαις supports this view. But then why is Paul so reticent about invoking the angeloglossic understanding of glossolalia elsewhere? One possible solution lies in the somewhat denigrating effect that his christology has upon his angelology. Scholars have long noted that his attitude toward angels is not uncritically positive.[26] Some even find in him an unalloyed aversion to angels. Wilhelm Bousset compares Paul's angelology to the Gnostic denigration of the sidereal powers:

It is extraordinarily characteristic that on the whole, apart from some few passages in which he is operating within the framework of customary language usage, Paul really knows no good angelic powers. For him the angelic powers, whose various categories he is accustomed to enumerating in the well-known stereotyped manner, are intermediate-echelon beings, in part of a pernicious kind. The archons of this aeon brought Christ to the cross, at the cross he battled with the angels and powers and wrested from them their weapons. Angels and men watch the drama which the apostle, despised and scorned by all, offers with his life (I Cor. 4:9). Lascivious angels are a danger for unveiled women (I Cor. 11:10). Paul is buffeted by an angel of Satan (II Cor. 12:7). ... It is especially characteristic how Paul employs the tradition of the proclamation of the law through angels, which the Jewish tradition had framed in order to glorify the law, without hesitation and as though it were obviously in order to degrade the law: The law is given "only" through angels (Gal. 3:19).[27]

---

beings": "Thus it is not the case that human language rises to the level of the divine Spirit or of angels; rather, the divine Spirit stoops to the lowest depths of human creatureliness and turns the call of the unredeemed into his own language." While Luz is correct to identify the wordless groanings of Rom 8.26 with glossolalia – against the judgment of many scholars – Paul's use of the word "groanings" is driven by the preceding verses, and does not serve as a literal description of what he thought glossolalia is.

[26] Kittel 1964–76:85 notes a "tendency, particularly in Paul, to emphasise the comparative unimportance of angelology". Boring 1991:181 rightly remarks that Paul "hardly ever has a good word to say about angels", but his statement that Paul "never refers to angels as the vehicle of prophetic revelation" must be qualified, as Paul seems to imply this very thing in his instructions (in 1 Corinthians 11) for women to cover their heads while praying or prophesying. On Paul's angelology, see Dibelius 1909:7–37; M. Jones 1918; Heiligenthal 1992:97–103; Reid 1993. See also the discussion of "Paul and the demonic" in Twelftree 2007:58–60.

[27] Bousset 1970:257. Mach (1992:285–6) similarly writes, "Die Aussagen des Paulus, die die Engel erwähnen, sind überwiegend in negative Kontexte eingebunden. Weder Engel noch Fürstentümer werden ihn von der Liebe Gottes trennen (Röm 8, 38); ohne Liebe nützt auch das Reden in Engels-Zungen nichts (1Kor 13, 1). Die Christen sollen sich nicht an heidnische Gerichte wenden, denn sie werden eines Tages die Engel selbst richten (1Kor 6, 3). Besonders deutlich sind die drei angelologischen Stellen des Galaterbriefs: Ein Engel vom Himmel, der den Galatern ein anderes Evangelium verkündigte, sei verflucht (1, 8); der νόμος ist durch die Engel angeordnet und durch die Hand eines Mittlers gegeben (3, 19) – im Gegensatz zur Verheißung Gottes an Abraham, die direkt erging. Doch Paulus selbst, der Verkünder des auf dieser Verheißung aufbauenden Evangeliums, wurde von den Galatern ursprünglich aufgenommen wie ein Engel Gottes

Certain items in Bousset's list are not necessarily as he reconstructs them. In particular, his interpretation of 1 Cor 11.10 as a warning against "lascivious angels" is dubious, at best, and should be rejected in the light of the Qumran finds.[28] While the remaining items in Bousset's list impress upon the reader the negativity of Paul's angelology, it should be noted that not every negative aspect of Paul's angelology is absolute: he indeed knows of evil angels, but he also seems to know of angels present within the worshipping community, whose holiness must be guarded from symbols of impurity. It would be bizarre if *these* angels were also evil.[29] Paul is fond of using angels as foils for the surpassing glory of Christ, and he uses the notion of humans standing in angelic stations as a foil for the heights to which the Christian redeemed are raised. His injunction that women cover their heads "because of the angels" (1 Cor 11.10) is evidence enough that he does not *disbelieve* the angelology of his day. It is not that he considers the angels to be, as Martin Luther put it, "useless human ideas ... [and] hodge-podge,"[30] but rather that he dismisses their importance for conceptualizing Christian existence. (Philo held a similar view: as Lala Kalyan Kumar Dey notes, "Being in touch with the angels ... is in Philo a lack of immediacy to God and hence an inferior status.")[31] Thus Paul's view of the angels is not *absolutely* negative. Héring writes,

[T]he rough and ready distinction between good and bad angels does not take into account the complexity of the Pauline angelology. Nothing permits us to believe, indeed, that the angel descending from heaven to announce another Gospel (Gal 1[:]8) is a bad

---

selbst (4, 14). Mit einer Ausnahme sind die anderen von Paulus genannten Engel 'Engel des Satans' (2Kor 11, 14; 12, 7)."

[28] Fitzmyer 1957–8 is credited with pointing out the similarity between 1 Cor 11.10 and the views of Qumran concerning purity and angels. See Newton 1985:106–9. Paul envisions the praying and prophesying Christian to be in the company of angels (cf. 1 Cor 4.9) – and all uncleanness must be avoided in such a setting. See Newton 1985:49–51, 106–9; Swartz 1994; Cothenet 1971–2:1295; Sullivan 2004:167–71. D. B. Martin 1995:299 n. 65 continues to interpret the angelic threat as sexually based, but his attempt to head off Fitzmyer's argument is strained at best: "The main problem with Fitzmyer's argument in my opinion is his insistence that *if* the mention of angels refers to their role as enforcers of proper worship, *then* the other interpretation (that they pose a sexual threat) is necessarily excluded."

[29] Ellis 1993:41 notes that "Jesus represents [for Paul] the presence of God on a level qualitatively different from the angels", and that this "accounts for the reticence with which Paul mentions the activity of angels, especially of good angels". Franklin 1994:70 notes that "Paul so stresses the originality of the work of Christ ... that everything else is seen as contrasted with it". Fee 2007:231 notes that, in Galatians, "Christ is a full rung higher than the angelic theophanies of the OT."

[30] From Martin Luther, *The Babylonian Captivity*, quoted in Chase 2000:138.

[31] Dey 1975:93. See also the role of angels in Hebrews, discussed in Schenck 2001. On angels as mediators in Jewish and Christian texts, see de Lacey 1987:105–7.

angel. On the contrary, it is because he is good in principle, although not infallible, that his teaching runs the risk of leading men into error. Similarly it is not said that the powers called '*archai*' and '*stoicheia*' are powers of darkness; they are angels in the process of falling because they oppose the Gospel.[32]

For Paul, the concept of existence in Christ bursts the soteriological categories of his opponents.[33] It is not surprising, therefore, that he should avoid the idea of humans becoming angels (or *like* angels) in his attempts to describe existence in Christ. His demotion of (originally positive) angelic associations is also apparent in his critique of the Law, in which he turns the tradition of its dispensation through angels into evidence of its inferiority.[34]

A side-glance at a well known passage in Colossians might help make the point about Paul's reticence to use the language of "speaking in the tongues of angels" as a tag for glossolalia. Despite doubts about the authorship of Colossians, the letter appears to reflect Paul's view of angels.[35] Col 2.18–19 has been the subject of much debate:

Let no one disqualify you, insisting on self-abasement and worship of angels [ἐν ταπεινοφροσύνῃ καὶ θρησκείᾳ τῶν ἀγγέλων], taking his stand on visions, puffed up without reason by his sensuous mind, and not holding fast to the Head, from whom the whole body, nourished and knit together through its joints and ligaments, grows with a growth that is from God.

The question of what θρησκεία τῶν ἀγγέλων denotes has brought to bear three widely subscribed solutions, none of which can be dismissed out of hand: (1) τῶν ἀγγέλων is an objective genitive, and "the worship of angels" refers to humans worshipping angels, as found in the pagan angel cults of Asia Minor,[36] (2) τῶν ἀγγέλων is a subjective genitive, and "the

---

[32] Héring 1962:108. Further evidence of the demotion of angels in the New Testament, apparently unconnected with christological safeguards, has been turned up by those tracing the lines of transmission of the biblical text. Leaney (1976:297) writes, "The most usual [septuagintal translation of יהוה צבאות] is κύριος παντοκράτωρ (in Isaiah κύριος σαβαώθ). In the Psalms we meet κύριος τῶν δυνάμεων which is adopted by the καίγε text. ... In the NT κύριος παντοκράτωρ occurs in 2 Cor 6:18 which is a conglomerate of LXX passages, and otherwise only in Revelation; the δυνάμεις are often the astral powers but κύριος τῶν δυνάμεων does not occur, so that God is never closely associated with the 'powers' which in some OT passages are such that he appears as *primus inter pares* among them." If there is any significance to be attached to this phenomenon, it is likely to hold a negative value for NT angelology in general.

[33] See Hengel 1995:155.

[34] Some scholars deny that Paul's use of angels in the *matan torah* tradition is meant to be denigrating. E.g., see Davenport 1971:12 n. 1.

[35] For the arguments against Pauline authorship, see the commentaries, and also E. P. Sanders 1966; Perrin and Duling 1984:210–12; Kiley 1986.

[36] This is the most time-honored of the three views. Its staunchest defender today is Clinton E. Arnold: see Arnold 1995:8–89.

worship of angels" refers to angels worshipping God, so that the misguided spirituality-marker that Colossians censures is a striving after or reveling in mystical ascent experiences that bring the believer within earshot of the angelic hymnody,[37] or (3) θρησκεία τῶν ἀγγέλων refers to the angelic *institution* of the Mosaic covenant, i.e. a substantially, and polemically, reformulated version of the tradition of the angelic *mediation* of the Law.[38] This is not the place to solve the debate over the meaning of θρησκεία τῶν ἀγγέλων. I would simply note that all of these interpretations could contribute to one's suspicion of angelological speculation.

There is also another reason for Paul's reticence to adopt the "tongues of angels" as his preferred terminology for discussing glossolalia: the angeloglossic model had already, independently of Paul, given way to a conceptualization centered upon the technical term λαλεῖν γλώσσαις (derived from proto-Aquila Isa 28.11–12), and Paul's avoidance of the angeloglossic model might be explained by the currency of another model.[39]

The permutations of ways of reading 1 Cor 13.1 go on and on. In lieu of tracing them all, I will simply draw attention to a line of thought that I think has not received its due, and which I believe holds a great deal of promise. Dale Martin has suggested that speaking in angelic tongues functioned somewhat like a status symbol among the Corinthians – that those who participated in this special dispensation were marked as superior in some way.[40] In response to this suggestion, I would point out that it depends in part on the supposition that many believers in the Corinthian church were not so blessed. Such a supposition has almost always been assumed rather than actually argued. Paul's argument in 1 Corinthians 12–14 does not in fact presuppose that glossolalia/angeloglossy was experienced by only a few in Corinth: his rhetorical question "Do all speak with tongues?" (12.30) anticipates a negative response, but it is apparently asked of

---

[37] See esp. Francis 1962; 1967. Francis lists others who had interpreted θρησκεία τῶν ἀγγέλων as a subjective genitive before him: "Ephraem, Luther, Melanchthon, Wolf, Dalmer, Hofmann, Zahn, Ewald." For lists of those accepting Francis's view, see Stuckenbruck 1995:116 n. 177; Arnold 1995:9 n. 7. See also Barth and Blanke 1994:345; Dunn 1995; 1996:136.

[38] See esp. Simon 1971. On the third view, τῶν ἀγγέλων can be *either* a subjective or an objective genitive. As a subjective genitive, τῶν ἀγγέλων would refer to the act of the angels' institution of the Mosaic covenant. As an objective genitive, τῶν ἀγγέλων would refer to the homage paid to angels by dint of the Colossians' obeisance to the angelically instituted covenant.

[39] See Schmithals 1971:175; Harrisville 1976; Richardson 1986:148–9. Klauck (2000:292) writes, "Als Gottesrede verstanden und eschatologisch interpretiert, diente die Verheißung der fremden Zungen in Jes 28 als Schriftgrundlage für die Legitimierung prophetischer, ekstatischer Phänomene, die in Kreisen der Jesusanhänger kurz nach Ostern aufbrachen."

[40] D. B. Martin 1991; 1995:87–103.

tongues as it functions *interpersonally* within the context of a worship gathering.[41] Paul's desiring that all should speak in tongues (1 Cor 14.5) may have either a public or private use of glossolalia in mind, but his generalizing of private glossolalic prayer with the terminology of "praying with the spirit" (14.14–15) is scarcely comprehensible as an elitist or episodic enablement, and such a construal would imply a virtual disconnect with the terminology of "praying in the Holy Spirit" in another NT writer (*viz.*, in Jude 20).[42] "He who speaks in a tongue", Paul tells us, "edifies himself" quite apart from the charism of interpretation (1 Cor 14.4). 1 Cor 12.30 has a public use of tongues in mind, and does not necessarily imply anything about the universality of access to that gift within the sphere of personal communication with God. In this light, there are no grounds for supposing that the divisiveness of glossolalia was related to a split between "haves" and "have nots". That is, there really is no reason to assume that the problem with the gift of tongues at Corinth was related to glossolalists flaunting their gifts before non-glossolalists.

A large part of the fight over 1 Cor 13.1 turns on enlisting the reference to "the tongues of angels" without due consideration of "the tongues of men", and *vice versa*. A more promising approach would be to combine the significance of both references within a single model of understanding. This has occasionally been attempted, as when "tongues of men" is taken to refer to intelligible speech and "tongues of angels" to refer to glossolalic speech, or when "tongues of men" is taken to refer to glossolalic speech and "tongues of angels" to refer to an impossible height of spiritual achievement. But when we give up the idea that speaking in "the tongues of angels" is a status symbol, another model of understanding emerges: "tongues of men" and "tongues of angels" can then be seen to represent the two complementary halves of the earthly-heavenly community of "saints", expressed in terms of the pneumatic-linguistic sign that the new believer receives as a token of his/her newfound citizenship in that community.[43]

---

[41] Turner 1998b:238–42 resists the gesture of exempting private glossolalia from the rhetoric of 1 Cor 12.30. He argues against it by showing that the congregational/non-congregational dividing line between public and private glossolalia cannot be used to categorize all the charisms listed in 1 Cor 12.28–30, thus showing that some of the charisms listed do not presuppose a congregational setting for their primary setting. But it appears to me that that is to judge the list by a wrong denominator. What all the gifts in the list have in common (esp. in view of their representing parts of the body of Christ) is not a congregational setting but rather an *interpersonal function*, and *that* would appear to be what distinguishes a public exercise of tongues (*viz.* tongues for interpretation) from a private exercise. See Hovenden 2002:152–9.

[42] As R. P. Martin 1992:1017 notes, Pauline glossolalia "is to be understood as 'speaking' and 'praying' when the mind is inactive".

[43] Alternatively, "of men and of angels" might refer to the complementary populations of "the world", as in 1 Cor 4.9, but this would hardly affect the idea that glossolalia

(A hellenistic parallel to this idea probably underlies the wording of *PGM* 13.139–40: "I call on you ... in every language and in every dialect", an apparent reference to the *nomina barbara* interspersed in the adjoining lines.)[44] Glossolalia, in this case, functions as a sign that ecclesiology includes the host of heaven.[45] On this interpretation, speaking "in the tongues of angels" is not a high achievement at all (at least not in the sense that would lead to boasting), but rather just a token of one's membership in the "household of God" (Eph 2.19). That is, it represents the betokened status, not of an adept, but rather of a tenderfoot.[46] That is why, I suggest, it is listed first in Paul's paean to love's loveliness. By comparison, the other "achievements" that Paul lists in 1 Cor 13.1–3 – *viz.* prophesying, understanding mysteries, possessing mountain-moving faith, giving away all one's possessions, and finally giving one's own body to be burned – can be seen to climb a certain grade of spiritual achievement, the point of this sustained climb being that, in terms of what really counts, one can never overcome the deficit of not having love. "Speaking in angelic tongues", then, might refer to glossolalia in the preferred terms of that gift's function as a token of conversion.[47] This interpretation has the benefit of allowing the xenoglossy of Acts 2 to share the same functional category as

---

represents participation in a human-angelic community. On the presence of angels within the communion of "saints", see Schlier 1958:140–1; Gutierrez 1968:160 n. 2. Barth 1974:320, on the other hand, denies that Ephesians gives quarter to such a view: "All members of the church are humans according to Eph 2:22. Angels are not built into her." On angels and the communion of the saints, see Heb 12.22–3. The idea behind my interpretation of 1 Cor 13.1 closely parallels the view that Kugel 1996 traces as an ideology operating within *Jubilees*: "Israel's holiness means first and foremost that Israel belongs to an order of being different from the order of being of other humans so that Israel is, in effect, wholly different, the earthly correspondent to God's heavenly hosts." One difference between the idea of human-angelic community in *Jubilees* and that lying behind my interpretation of 1 Cor 13.1, of course, is that *Jubilees* envisions the angels as native speakers of Hebrew.

[44] M. Smith 1986:175. This line constitutes weighty counterevidence to Forbes's claim that the purported hellenistic parallels to glossolalia are not conceived as heavenly languages.

[45] This commonplace is expressed well in the opening sentence of Peterson 1935:13: "Der Weg der Kirche führt aus dem irdischen Jerusalem in das himmlische, aus der Stadt der Juden in die Stadt der Engel und der Heiligen."

[46] That is not to say, of course, that speaking in tongues is less characteristic of the mature believer: Paul himself claims to speak in tongues more than all the Corinthians (1 Cor 14.18).

[47] It might be objected that this makes the reference to "tongues" in 1 Cor 13.1 artificial – that is, that Paul would not mention tongues in this context if he were using it merely as a synonym for being a Christian – but the echoes of that reference to "tongues" a few verses later, and then again more widely throughout chaps. 12–14, bring out the poignancy that this objection demands to see.

an angeloglossic understanding of tongues: that of comfirming member-ship in the household of God – a household in which both human and an-gelic languages are spoken.

B. New Testament Continued (2 Cor 12.1–7)

In response to certain "superapostles" (2 Cor 11.5; 12.11), who apparently predicated their own authority upon visionary experiences,[48] Paul wrote of one who ascended into the "third heaven" (= "Paradise") and heard ἄρρητα ῥήματα: "[Such a man] was caught up into Paradise and heard un-utterable words that no human can speak" (ὅτι ἡρπάγη εἰς τὸν παράδεισον καὶ ἤκουσεν ἄρρητα ῥήματα ἃ οὐκ ἐξὸν ἀνθρώπῳ λαλῆσαι).[49] These ἄρρητα ῥήματα are presumably those of the angels worshipping God.[50] As for the meaning of ἄρρητος, we are confronted with two basic possibili-ties: (1) that which, for reasons of human physiology, is verbally inarticul-able, and (2) that which is too sacred to mention.[51]

There is no shortage of documentation for the philological aspect of the meaning of ἄρρητος: the word is a commonplace in the texts of all the Greek-speaking mystical schools, and has accordingly become a common-place in scholars' efforts to understand mysticism. Perhaps something of what this word means for Paul can be retrieved from what we find in the

---

[48] Lightstone's description (1984:43) of theurgists' authority markers perfectly cap-tures the conception of authority that Paul combats in 2 Cor 12.1–7: "to seek 'mystical' experiences grounds the authority of the theurgist and provides the measure of the extent of that authority".

[49] See Saake 1973; Hurtado 2000. Paul's uncertainty as to whether this experience oc-curred "in the body or out of the body" recalls Philo's discussion of Moses' rapture dur-ing his forty days upon Mt. Sinai (*Somn.* I.33–7), in which Moses' hearing of the heaven-ly hymns is connected with existence ἀσώματος. There have been many fine studies of the merkabah associations within 2 Cor 12.1–7, of which I mention only one of the most complete: Morray-Jones 1993.

[50] Paul's testimony of one hearing the angelic host worshipping God, only to relativ-ize the value of such an experience in light of the importance of the apostolic vocation, calls to mind the similar interpretation of θρησκείᾳ τῶν ἀγγέλων in Col 2.18 as an en-counter with the angelic worship of God in Francis 1962, where glorying in such an ex-perience is relativized in the light of Christ's exalted station. In fact, the parallel is strik-ing enough to serve as a support for Francis's interpretation of Colossians.

[51] The same choice is put by Ruiz 2006:101. Cf. Lincoln 1981:82. Lincoln gives sev-eral examples of the latter meaning. Forbes 1995:62 n. 40 also supports the latter mean-ing, claiming that "nothing [in the text] suggests a special angelic language". Cf. Keener 1997:22, 42–3 n. 199. As I hope to show, that claim is open to doubt. Widdicombe 2000:56 argues against Mortley's claim that Origen understood Paul's use of ἄρρητος in the latter sense. (See Mortley 1986:2.68.) To Widdicombe, the former is both the natural meaning and the one adopted by Origen.

neoplatonists' writings and in the magical papyri. Despite the frequency with which the neoplatonists use this word, it is not clear that they use it as a technical term. It is often linked with a whole series of α-privatives strung together in their description of the highest heaven.[52]

In connection with *Gen. Rab.* 74.7 (below), we will discuss Hans Dieter Betz's interpretation of ἄρρητος (in the Greek magical papyri) as that which "the human mouth is not capable of articulating."[53] We shall see that, for a general understanding of the *voces magicae*, there is much to commend Betz's understanding: humans can only approximate the divine language.[54] This interpretation does not rule out the use of divine language, as there is nothing inherent within the idea of physical inexpressibility to prevent humans from *attempting* to pronounce divine words. For example, appearing in response to a theurgical invocation, Hecate states, "After day-break, boundless, full of stars, I left the great undefiled house of God and descended to life-nourishing earth at your request, and by the persuasion of ineffable words [τ' ἀρρήτων] with which a mortal man delights in glad-dening the hearts of immortals."[55] *Voces magicae* that are described as ἄρρητος are manifestly not unvocalized marks on a page (or amulet). Ra-ther, they are unintelligible but *spoken*.[56] If the transcription of these words in neoplatonic, Gnostic, and magical texts is any indication, they are made up mostly (often exclusively) of vowels – the idea behind their power in-volving a harnessing of the power of the seven vowels as primordial ele-ments (στοιχεῖα).[57]

---

[52] Horn (1992:214 n. 42) writes, "Ἄρρητος in 2. Kor 12, 4 reflektiert die Distanz zu Gott, die Pl in der Entrückung überwunden hat, die aber für den Nicht-Entrückten bestehen bleibt." See Caragounis 1977:11. These strings of α-privatives epitomize the forms of apophatic theology produced by the platonizing impulse. See Carabine 1995. See also the discussion of the (Coptic) α-privatives in the *Gospel of the Egyptians* in Böhlig 1967:23.

[53] H. D. Betz 1995:163.

[54] Forbes (1995:153) asserts that the *nomina barbara* found in the magical papyri "are not conceived as language", but he provides no support for this view, which is certainly not self-evident. There is, in fact, evidence to the contrary: we have already noted, in connection with our interpretation of 1 Cor 13.1 (see above), that the Greek magical pa-pyri refer to the *nomina barbara* as languages.

[55] *Chaldean Oracles* frag. 219 (quoted in Majercik 1989:134–5).

[56] On the relation between *voces magicae* and glossolalia, see Behm 1964–76:723; Aune 2006:412–14.

[57] On the *voces mysticae* in the neoplatonists, see Dornseiff 1925; Speyer 1967:265–7; Hirschle 1979; P. C. Miller 1986; Majercik 1989:25; H. D. Betz 1995; Pearson 1992. On the "naming" aspect of language, see further Winston 1991. A σύμβολον in the ancient world was often not merely referential, but also *efficacious* in and through that referen-tiality.

The idea of words physically impossible for humans to pronounce is found in a wooden translation of the last words in the verse (ἃ οὐκ ἐξὸν ἀνθρώπῳ λαλῆσαι): *Young's Literal Translation* renders them as "that it is not possible for man to speak".[58] This way of translating ἃ οὐκ ἐξὸν ἀνθρώπῳ λαλῆσαι, however, supports an altogether different meaning for ἄρρητα ῥήματα, as the redundancy of Paul's phrase would be too severe if we assigned the same meaning to both modifiers of ῥήματα.[59] Although ἄρρητος is probably not a technical term, some standardization of its use nevertheless seems to have taken place. This standardization brought the more general meaning of "unearthly" to the fore, so that something described as ἄρρητος was not necessarily *physically* inexpressible. Thus the word can denote the type of "ineffability" that William James associated with mysticism in general: "This incommunicableness of the transport is the keynote of all mysticism."[60] Theodore of Mopsuestia seems to have understood the word in this sense: "By ecstasy all of the prophets were receiving the knowledge of the most unutterable things."[61] The ῥήματα are ἄρρητα because they are too wonderful to repeat. They are inexpressible, either because their referential aspects lack an earthly analogue or because they are prohibited.[62] The episode in 2 Cor 12.1–7, in fact, is reminiscent of the preface to *2 Enoch* (rec. A): "From the secret book(s) about the taking away of Enoch the just, a wise man, a great scholar, whom the LORD took away. ... to see the variegated appearance and indescribable singing of the army of the cherubim".[63] This is also the interpretation of 2 Cor

---

[58] Ruiz 2006:101 fails to recognize that the words ἃ οὐκ ἐξὸν ἀνθρώπῳ λαλῆσαι can express the idea of incapacity, taking them instead to indicate words that are "neither ineffable nor unintelligible, since they are the object of a prohibition".

[59] See Saake 1973; Hurtado 2000.

[60] W. James 1982:405 (see also 380–1). Cf. Alston 1956.

[61] *In Nahum* 1.1, quoted in Zaharopoulos 1989:95.

[62] See Krämer 1959:124–5. For the meaning of ἄρρητος in Jewish writings, see Dean-Otting 1984:102–3. The term ἄρρητα ῥήματα also recalls mystery religions (see Lührmann 1965:57–8; Boers 2006:84 n. 163). Cf. the differing use of this term in Clement of Alexandria, discussed in Roberts 1991:212. As Rohrbacher-Sticker (1996:33) writes, "the motif of the secret, unspeakable name belongs to the basic repertory of magical traditions of the most varied provenances". Pulleyn 1997:111 urges that it is wrong to assume that this magical understanding of the power of names characterizes classical Greek religion in general: "The idea that names are powerful is really a phenomenon of post-classical syncretism." Howard (1929:1205) writes, "The 'unutterable utterances' (v. 4) are not the 'voiceless groanings' of Rom. 8[:]26, but transcendent and incommunicable revelations which left on Paul's mind a sense of assurance. In accordance with all ancient mysticism it was regarded as irreverent to report such sacred sensations to the unsympathetic." Howard's translation of Rom 8.26's στεναγμοῖς ἀλαλήτοις as "voiceless groanings" is problematic.

[63] Trans. Andersen 1983:103–5. As Altmann 1946:2 notes, "There is no viewing of the merkabah without singing." See Grözinger 1980.

12.1–7 incorporated within the *Vision of Paul*, which is based on Paul's wording.[64]

Riemer Roukema recently discussed a number of early interpretations of Paul's rapture to paradise, and gives a sidelight to what these interpretations considered the "unutterable words that no human can speak" to be. Interestingly, these interpretations differ as to the correct referent of Paul's phrase. For example, Hippolytus' report on the Naassenes claimed that the latter connected the "ineffable words" of 2 Cor 12.7 with Paul's discussion of "words [not] taught by human wisdom, but in those taught by the Spirit, comparing spiritual things with spiritual. But the psychic man does not receive the things of the Spirit of God, for they are folly to him" (Hippolytus, *Haer.* 5.8.26).[65] At the level of the Naassene's association, this seems to be a reference to something like glossolalia – Paul heard spiritual words, which he (as a spiritual man) was able to "receive". But when Hippolytus discusses Basilides, he reports a different use of Paul's reference to "unutterable words that no human can speak" (*Haer.* 7.20.1–3). There the reference is to a realm that was "above every name that is named", even (apparently) above ineffability, and that the Ogdoad represents that which is "ineffable".[66] Roukema also points out that Origen thought that the ineffable words constituted cosmological knowledge – *viz.* details about the passing of seasons, position of stars, etc. (*Comm. Gen., ad* Gen 1.14).[67] In his response to Celsus, however, Origen uses Paul's words in a very different way: he asserts that there are beings inferior to God which, like God, are ineffable, and he refers to Paul's use of the plural expression ἄρρητα ῥήματα to prove this (*Cels.* 7.42–3).[68] Origen famously connected the sense of 2 Cor 12.4 with the prohibition in Rev 10.4 to write down "what the seven thunders have said" (*Cels.* 6.6).[69]

Another factor is more important for our immediate discussion, however, than the precise meaning of ἄρρητος. I have already mentioned the redundancy that results from translating ἄρρητα ῥήματα and ἃ οὐκ ἐξὸν ἀνθρώπῳ λαλῆσαι in the same way. (I assume that apposition and syn-

---

[64] See Robbins 2003:334–36.

[65] Roukema 2005:271.

[66] Roukema 2005:272.

[67] Roukema 2005:276. In this sense, ἄρρητος may be synonymous with ἀπόρρητος, as used in *Jos. Asen.* 16.14, where the angel calls Aseneth "happy" ("blessed") because "the ineffable mysteries of the Most High have been revealed to you (ἀπεκαλύφθη σοι τὰ ἀπόρρητα μυστήρια τοῦ ὑψίστου)" (Burchard 1985:228–9). See the in-depth philological study of ἀπόρρητα in van der Burg 1939:3-51. Van der Burg divides his study between the use of ἀπόρρητα prior to Alexander, and its use after Alexander. In both periods, the meanings "forbidden" and "secret" predominate. See Caragounis 1977:11.

[68] See Roukema 2005:277.

[69] See Ruiz 2006.

onymous parallelism are out of the question, as they do not fit Paul's normal way of writing.) This means that the question of whether ἄρρητος refers to the esoteric aspect of the heavenly words is ultimately beside the point: one way or another, the idea of an esoteric angelic language almost certainly appears within 2 Cor 12.4, although we cannot tell whether it is found in the modifier preceding ῥήματα or in the one following it. In this connection, it is worth mentioning that Origen cracked the case with an intratextual reading of the New Testament: he used the reference to "unarticulable words" of Rom 8.26 as a hermeneutic clue for understanding the nature of the words "that no one may utter" in 2 Cor 12.4 (*Or.* 2.3), thereby arriving at a sort of heavenly language. But he did not necessarily associate that language with the angels, as he appears to imply that the ascending mystic of 2 Corinthians 12 heard *the Holy Spirit* praying.[70]

C. The Testament of Job

The *Testament of Job* is a pseudepigraphic work imaginatively retailing the end of Job's life. Its importance for our study looms large in the last eight chapters of the work, which describe Job's daughters as singing in angelic tongues. Before discussing these chapters, I must devote a few pages to the question of the author's religious identity.[71]

The range of possible dates for the *Testament of Job* depends a great deal on whether the writing is Jewish or Christian. It is generally agreed that the work was written in Egypt.[72] One school of thought requires that, if the work is Jewish *and* written in Egypt, it must be dated prior to the revolt of 115–117 C.E., as the decimation of the Jewish population in Egypt was (according to this view) too extensive to give rise to literary works of this type. This aligns with the usual dating given by scholars, which extends from the first century B.C.E. through the first century C.E.[73] William

---

[70] See Widdicombe 2000:107.

[71] Charlesworth 1981:135 calls the *Testament of Job* a "midrash in the form of a testament". His use of "midrash" was anticipated by Kohler 1897; M. R. James 1897:lxxxiv). Similarly, Lesses 2007:54. Bickerman 1980:2.15–16 notes that the *Testament of Job* is exceptional among the so-called testaments in that it is truly testamentary – *viz.* it contains the details of the bequeathing of an inheritance, and not just of death-bed instruction. See also Schürer 1973–87:3.552.

[72] See esp. Gruen 2009.

[73] Spittler 1983:833 is representative in dating the *Testament of Job* to the period from 100 B.C.E. to 100 C.E. In a later article, Spittler (2000:1189) simply says that the book "existed in the time of Jesus and Paul". See the review of scholarly opinion in Gunther 1973:36–8. Philonenko 1958 41–53) and J. J. Collins 1974 argue for a date in the first century C.E. J. J. Collins 1974:50 and Jacobs 1970:1 n. 3 both think that the theme of

Gruen III assigns a date slightly after the revolt, however, claiming to find literary fallout from the revolt in the first 27 chapters of the work.[74] On the other hand, if the writing is Christian, there is no compelling reason not to extend this range forward in time, even by as much as three centuries (see below).[75]

The evidence is too equivocal to treat a Jewish origin as virtually certain. As I noted in the introduction to this study, the recent trend of assuming a pseudepigraphon preserved by the church to be Christian unless proven otherwise is methodologically questionable. While this assumption offers a corrective to the long held *opposing* assumption (*viz.* that a Jewish-sounding pseudepigraphon will invariably turn out to be Jewish), it is counterproductive in many cases: given that the church has preserved so many indisputably Jewish writings (*viz. Jubilees, 1 Enoch,* Philo's writings, etc.), why should a Christian origin be the default provenance attributed to any given Jewish-sounding writing preserved by the church?

Scholarship has always been divided on the question of the author's religious identity. William Horbury claimed that the *Testament of Job* "is probably ... closer to the world of *Vetus Testamentum* than to that of *Vigiliae Christianae*."[76] The editors of the "new Schürer," overturning the original Schürer's attribution of this text to a Christian hand, similarly write, "There is nothing indisputably Christian in any of the work, and its Jewish origin should be accepted."[77] Some scholars have suggested that

---

endurance points to a date during a time of persecution. A simple theme of endurance seems too ordinary, however, to be necessarily attributed to a time of persecution. As Frankfurter 1998:436 writes, "We can no longer attribute the consistent references to martyrdom in early Christian apocalyptic literature to historical religious persecution." See Haas 1989. See also Philip Alexander's disqualification of this method of dating texts in his discussion of *3 Enoch* (Alexander 1983:228). See the discussion of these issues in DiTommaso 2007:251–4. Denis 1970:103, dating the text to ca. 40 B.C.E., finds an allusion to the Parthian invasion of Palestine in *T. Job* 17.2–18, but the allusion is weak at best. Kalman 2006 argues that the writing is Jewish and early enough to have influenced a fourth-century C.E. rabbinic discussion.

[74] Gruen 2009. Gruen points to the fifth book of the *Sibylline Oracles* as proof that literary production among Egyptian Jews did not cease in 117 C.E. (2009:174). In response to Kugler and Rohrbaugh 2004's claim that "urgings to perseverance would surely have rung so hollow [after 117 C.E.] as to be unthinkable", Gruen (2009:178) writes that "a recent history of massive destruction of property and loss of life would be the perfect context for urgings of perseverance".

[75] Glatzer 1974:31 assigns the *Testament of Job* a date in the third or second century B.C.E., but provides no support for this early dating.

[76] Horbury 1991. See Begg 1994.

[77] Schürer 1973–87:3.553. Cf. Schürer 1909:3.406–7. Schürer's view was accepted by Beer 1927–31. M. R. James 1897:xcii also supports a Christian origin, "but that he was a Jew by birth is more than a probability". Rahnenführer 1971:71 n. 9 notes that the *Testa-*

chaps. 46–53 (or just 46–52) were added to an earlier writing, so that the question of Christian elements might be asked about these chapters independently of any impression that chaps 1–45 might give.[78] (Christian additions to Jewish pseudepigrapha are common.) Russell Spittler has suggested that the episode involving Job's daughters was tagged on by Montanists, in order to validate that movement's emphasis on ecstatic speech.[79] Not all advocates of a partition theory of the *Testament of Job*, however, assign chaps. 46–53 to a Christian hand: Rebecca Lesses separates the final section from the rest of the work – she even gives it a name (the *Daughters of Job*) – but regards it as a "discarded source" for reconstructing *Jewish* history.[80] James R. Davila notes that the work "contains no indubitably Christian or Jewish signature features," but assigns it to a Christian hand on the strength of parallel themes in Christian texts and on the basis of the above-mentioned policy of assigning pseudepigrapha to the group that preserved them.[81] One factor that might be thought to favor a Jewish origin is the apparent ideology of a holy land in 33.4–7,[82] but Christian groups were also capable of expressing such an ideology, and Patrick Gray's observation that "every verse in *T. Job* 33 – except for v. 1 ... – contains one or more terms found also in James" supports not only the possibility of James' use of the *Testament of Job* but also that of the *Testament of Job*'s use of James.[83]

---

ment of Job is included in the databases of G. W. Lampe's *Patristic Greek Lexicon* and of J. Michl's *Lexikon für Theologie und Kirche*.

[78] E.g., see Nordheim 1980:132.

[79] Spittler 1983:834. Turner (1998a:236) writes that chaps. 48–50 "appear to be part of an addition to the Jewish work, and it is probable they are from a Christian or Gnostic hand" (see Turner 1998b:247 n. 35). Van der Horst 1989:184–5 objects to Spittler's suggestion, however, claiming that such a tactic would not have produced the type of *biblical* warrant for Montanist practice that their detractors would have demanded. But van der Horst's assumption that Montanist authorship of the text would have been motivated by the need for such a warrant is at least questionable. Recent studies have emphasized the literary unity of the *Testament of Job*, but those studies might easily be too dependent on the current trend in scholarship to presume a work's unity – a presumption that is easily overworked. See Schaller 1989; J. J. Collins 1974:48–9; Sullivan 2004:129–30. On the change from first- to third-person narrative at 46.1, see Bauckham 1991.

[80] Lesses 1993:139. Lesses (1993:144) writes that "*Daughters of Job* is clearly a Jewish work," but she supports that statement with a weak line of argument: "There is no mention of Christ or the use of explicitly Christian terminology."

[81] Davila 2005:197–8. Gruen (2009:164 n. 1) is mistaken when he writes, "The idea that the entire work was composed by Christians has recently been proposed in oral presentations of research; however, it has so far not appeared in print." As the present discussion shows, the idea has appeared in print many times.

[82] See Kugel 1996:30.

[83] Gray 2004:410.

There are other reasons, in fact, for regarding the *Testament of Job* as the work of a Christian author. (Whether they are strong enough to over-turn the majority attribution of the work to a Jewish hand is the question before us.) We may begin by noting that the *Decretum Gelasianum* (454 C.E.) lists "the book which is called the Testament of Job" among the 62 books or categories of books that declares "apocryphal," and that of the 61 other items listed, only three ("the book about Gog the giant ...,"[84] "the book which is called the Repentance of Jamne and Mambre," and angel-invoking amulets) are at all open to question concerning their Christian provenance (although the possibility of such is not problematic for any of them). On the face of it, the decree appears to have compiled a list of works thought to have been composed by Christians, but which do not meet the approval of orthodox circles. The *Testament of Job* may have been such a work.[85] There are also some possible internal indications that the *Testament of Job* might be a Christian writing. Thornhill notes a num-ber of places where the *Testament of Job* may be dependent on the New Testament, a possibility which he combines with an observation about some supposedly "late" vocabulary to yield a second-century Christian author.[86] One could, in fact, to build a case for a Christian origin of *T. Job* 46–53 on the basis of possible echoes of NT language. Acts 2.11 describes the content of the Pentecost xenoglossy as "the wonderful deeds of God" (τὰ μεγαλεῖα τοῦ θεοῦ), a phrase which the *Testament of Job* uses to describe the content of the daughters' angelic speech. (See below.) It is also possible that the use of μερισμὸν in *T. Job* 46.1 is an allusion to the use of μερισμοῖς in Heb 2.4: ". . . God added his testimony by signs and wonders and various miracles, and by distributions [μερισμοῖς] of the Holy Spirit, according to his will." The *Testament of Job* uses μερισμὸν to refer to the distribution of Job's inheritance to his sons, but its doing so might be intended to imply that what the daughters receive is also a μερισμὸν of an inheritance, which in turn might be calculated to recall Heb 2.4. (Hebrews is the only NT writing in which the μερισμ- word group appears.) On this model, of course, the theme of angelic languages is itself an echo of 1 Cor 13.1.

While most scholars have assumed a date range falling or touching on Second Temple times, there are some subtle indications that our text might

---

[84] Confusion between "Gog" and "Og" (of Bashan) was widespread in both Christian and Jewish writings. See Bøe 2001:58–61.

[85] Davila (2005:197) says it is "not certain" that the *Decretum Gelasianum*'s reference to a "Testament of Job" has the extant work by that title in mind. See Dobschütz 1912:306.

[86] Thornhill 1984:619. Gray (2004:409) writes that Thornhill's view is "technically possible", but he accords "greater *prima facie* plausibility" to M. R. James's use of the *Testament of Job*.

be a Christian text from a somewhat later period, perhaps even from the time of the Great Church. As far as I know, this position has only just recently begun to make the rounds. Allen Kerkeslager dates the *Testament of Job* to the period 350–420 C.E. (!), and Davila similarly "see[s] no compelling reason to move backwards from the context of late antique Egypt".[87] Both scholars associate the writing with the Coptic Christian context in which it has been preserved. (The oldest extant copy of the *Testament of Job* is an early fifth-century Coptic manuscript.)[88] In favor of a connection with the Great Church's world of ideas, one might consider whether the magical sashes of Job's daughters might not have been intended to remind the reader of a cincture, as worn by priests during the Christian liturgy. That the sash is described in the *Testament* as having angelic associations might actually reinforce this idea, as Christian priestly functions and accoutrements were at that time regularly interpreted in angelic terms.

T. Job 33.1–9 may hold some clues to the religious identity of the author. David M. Hay connects *T. Job* 33.3 with "an early stage of Merkabah mysticism."[89] On the basis of this passage and the purportedly late vocabulary compiled by Berndt Schaller, however, Martin Hengel argues for a late date:

B. Schaller proposes a date in the second century AD on the basis of 'seldom and in part late-Hellenistic or even Byzantine words' and 'some borrowed Latin words'; I ask myself whether one doesn't have to consider the third or fourth century as the Greek-speaking synagogue blossomed for the last time. Even if one denies a Christian origin, which is

---

[87] Davila 2005:198. See Kerkeslager, Setzer, Trebilco, and Goodblatt 2006:63–4 n. 65. (I am thankful to Dr. Kerkeslager for corresponding with me about this matter.) Against a late date, Spittler 1983:847 n. f, Gray 2004:422 n. 45, and Kalman 2006:387 n. 53 all adopt Tertullian's reference to Job being afflicted with worms (*Pat.* 14.2–7) to mark a *terminus ad quem* for the *Testament of Job*, taking the pseudepigraphon to be Tertullian's source not only for a nonscriptural detail but also for its manner of expression (see *T. Job* 20.7–9). While such a line of dependence can by no means be ruled out, it is hardly as secure as Spittler and Gray present it. The worm affliction tradition was more widespread (as Spittler himself shows) and Tertullian's wording is too distant from that of our pseudepigraphon to judge that scenario as probable, esp. when *'Abot de Rabbi Nathan* knows the same tradition as the *Testament of Job* (see Spittler 1983:847 n. f).

[88] See Römer and Thissen 1989. The *Testament of Job* influenced later Coptic iconography in Egypt – see van Loon 1999:158–63. Parmentier (2004:230) *perhaps* tips his hand in favor of a Christian provenance, but speaks directly only to the Christian use of this work: "Through the Septuagint and two apocrypha, the *Testament of Job* and the *Life of Job*, the dominant Christian view of Job also becomes that of the pious sufferer."

[89] Hay 1973:23. Rahnenführer (1971:81) similarly notes, "Die erwähnten ntl. Vorstellungen sowohl betreffs der Heiligen als auch der Throne sind nicht spezifisch christlich, sondern entsprechen vielmehr wie im Hen. und TH jüdischer Eschatologie und Apokalyptik, … gibt es die Vorstellung, daß die Gerechten von Gott den Thron der Herrlichkeit zum Besitz erhalten werden."

argued by some interpreters even today, an indirect or direct Christian influence cannot be ruled out; this is in my opinion probable. A Jewish author could apply christological motifs to Job and his children and thus rob them of their uniqueness. Since the text was transmitted in later times only by Christians, a moderate Christian redaction of the text is possible. Such a Christian influence may appear in the formula ἐκ δεξιῶν τοῦ πατρός.[90]

The point about throne imagery and the point about late vocabulary (dated by Schaller to the time of Justin Martyr) are two separate matters. As Hengel is well aware, there is nothing distinctively Christian about throne imagery.[91] Walter Wink remarks that "some kind of speculative ferment must have existed almost from the publication of Daniel, for what crops up in the Book of Revelation is a full-blown and mature picture of God's throne surrounded by twenty-four thrones, on which were seated twenty-four elders with golden crowns (Rev. 4:4 [twice]; so also 4:2; 11.16; 20:4)."[92] Rahnenführer further notes that Enoch, Seth (Rahnenführer actually replaces Seth with Noah and Shem), Abraham, Isaac, and Jacob are all raised to the right hand "with great joy" in *T. Benj.* 10.6.[93]

The combination of Ps 110.1 with the reference to "Father" (in MS P), however, may suggest a Christian provenance (at least for that manuscript): "My throne is in the upper world, and its splendor and majesty come from the right hand of the Father [*apud* MS P; cf. S ("God") and V ("Savior")]." As is well known, Ps 110.1 is the most widely cited passage in the New Testament.[94] This in itself does not exclude the possibility that a Jewish writer could have employed this verse. Neither does MS P's

---

[90] Hengel 1995:207. Cf. Rahnenführer 1971:80–3; Schaller 1979:352–4.

[91] See esp. the throne imagery in 4Q491c and in 4Q521. See M. Smith 1990; J. J. Collins 1995:136–53; 1997a:143–7; Abegg 1997; Zimmermann 1998:285–310. On the apocalyptic seer's claim to stand in heaven already, see Volz 1934:354. On the throne in 4Q521, see Puech 1991–92:489–90.

[92] Wink 1984:18–19. In discussing the throne imagery of Dan 7.9, Wink (1984:18) remarks, "No surviving documents allude to these thrones again prior to the New Testament." Besides begging the question of the date of the *Testament of Job* (which he does not mention in this context), Wink's view runs aground on account of *T. Levi* 3.8. Recognizing this threat from the *Testament of Levi*, he appeals (1998:18 n. 14) to text history: the "[throne] reading is lacking in one manuscript (Aᵃ), and other manuscripts have been variously interpolated in order to bring an earlier three-heavens view into line with a seven-heavens concept". True enough, but the *terminus a quo* for this development is the end of the second century B.C.E. (See the discussion in A. Y. Collins 1995:62–6.) The passage from 4Q491 (quoted above) also overturns Wink's judgment.

[93] Rahnenführer 1971:84. In light of this comparison between *T. Job* 33.3 and *T. Benj.* 10.8, it is interesting to note Philonenko's belief that the *Testament of Job* was "visibly inspired" by the *Testaments of the Twelve Patriarchs* (Philonenko 1958:43). Philonenko's opinion has not received support, and I fail to see the connection he sees.

[94] Hengel 1995:133 counts 21 references or allusions to Ps 110.1 in the New Testament, "[i]f one includes all of the passages about the exaltation of Christ to the right hand of God".

reference to God as "Father" require a Christian influence by itself: a number of Jewish writings (especially prayer texts) refer to God as "Father."[95] The combination of Psalm 110 with a reference to God as "Father," however, almost certainly requires us to think of P's reading as the product of a Christian writer or redactor.[96] It is to be noted that Job does not claim to be raised to the "right hand of the Father" himself (a position reserved for Christ, according to the earliest *kerygma*), but rather that the "splendor and majesty" of his own throne "come from the right hand of the Father/God" (*T. Job* 33.3).[97]

Although the possibility of a Christian provenance is not as remote as some scholars have assumed, a Jewish provenance is probably more likely for this text. It must be admitted, first of all, that nothing listed above is *decisive* in arguing for a Christian provenance. In fact, nearly everything is compatible with a Jewish origin. The main thing that inclines me toward a Jewish provenance, however, is Gruen's recent argument, tying the *Testament of Job* to events that rocked Egyptian Jewry during and after the revolt of 115–117 C.E.[98] Although Gruen's argument turns only on what is found in chaps. 1–27 of the work, the unity of the text should be presumed, at least in the absence of contrary evidence. In what follows, therefore, I assume that the work is Jewish, although I continue to extend the possibility that this is not the case.

Let us now turn to the intriguing reference to esoteric angelic languages appearing in chaps. 46–53. There we find Job distributing to his seven sons their inheritance, and his three daughters complaining that they are being excluded.[99] Job replies that he has an even better inheritance in store for

---

[95] See Schrenk and Quell 1964–76:978–82; D'Angelo 1999:69–70.

[96] It appears that a distinctively Christian reading of Psalm 110 sometimes activated the use of "Father" and "Son" language for God and Christ (e.g., in Peter's sermon in Acts 2). Kilgallen 2002:84 calls attention to the way Peter, in the Pentecost sermon, changes the language of "God" and "Christ" to "Father" and "Christ". According to Kilgallen, "there is nothing in the speech itself which warrants this change of vocabulary". He fails to see that Peter's appeal to Psalm 110 activates this change.

[97] Engelsen's argument for a relatively early date deserves mention. He argues (1970:53) that R. Yochanan b. Zakkai, who died only ten years after the destruction of the Temple, taught that Job "did all his good deeds only from fear of God," in contrast to Abraham, whose good deeds were motivated by love: "His words may be a protest against the Testament, which makes Job say that he will destroy Satan's temple and image 'from the love of God' (Sotah V)." Bagnall 2009:11–12, 24 tries to problematize the idea of second-century Egyptian Christian texts in general, but his arguments do little more than exploit the margins of error in the dates assigned by earlier scholars.

[98] Gruen 2009.

[99] On inheritance by daughters generally, see Ben-Barak 1980. On inheritance by daughters in rabbinic Judaism, see Ilan 2000; 2006:138–46.

his daughters. He sends one of them to fetch three golden boxes (or "gold-carrying boxes" [see below]) from a vault:

T. Job 46.7–9
And he opened them and brought out three multicolored cords whose appearance was such that no man could describe, since they were not from earth but from heaven, shimmering with fiery sparks like the rays of the sun. And he gave each one a cord, saying, "Place these about your breast, so it may go well with you all the days of your life."[100]

The daughters complain about the apparent uselessness of these cords, but Job assures them that these cords will provide a livelihood. God had given these cords to Job, when he had instructed him, "Arise, gird your loins like a man" (Job 38.3; 40.2). Job then describes these cords in terms of their past usefulness to him:

T. Job 47.6b–9
And immediately from that time [when I began to wear the cords] the worms disappeared from my body and the plagues, too. And then my body got strength through the Lord as if I actually had not suffered a thing. I also forgot the pains in my heart. And the Lord spoke to me in power, showing me things present and things to come.[101]

These cords gave access to heaven to their wearers.[102] Job describes them as amulets "of the Father," and tells his daughters to gird themselves with them "in order that you may be able to see those who are coming for my soul, in order that you may marvel over the creatures of God":

T. Job 48.1–50.2
[W]hen the one called Hemera arose, she wrapped her own string just as her father said. And she took on another heart[103] – no longer minded toward earthly things[104] – but she spoke ecstatically in the angelic dialect [ἀγγελικῇ φωνῇ], sending up a hymn to God in

---

[100] Trans. Spittler 1983:864.

[101] Trans. Spittler 1983:864.

[102] See Lesses 2007. Rahnenführer 1971:90 n. 73 lists (general) studies on the history-of-religions significance of girdles as apotropaic devices. Others have noted a functional similarity between these cords and the robe and the two girdles worn by Aseneth in *Jos. Asen.* 14.16 (Philonenko 1958:52; Standhartinger 1995:209; 1999:142 n. 214). Note also the mantic use of wristbands and veils by the prophetesses in Ezek 13.17–23 (See Isaksson 1965:159–60.)

[103] This change of heart, which happens to all three daughters, recalls the language of Epiphanius' discussion of the Montanists (*Pan.* 48.4.1; also in Eusebius, *Hist. eccl.* 5.16.17). See Vollenweider 1996:170 n. 25. Cf. esp. Wilhelm Schneemelcher's interpretive translation of Epiphanius: "Behold, man is like a lyre and I rush thereon like a plectrum [cf. the musical description of the Delphic oracle in Plutarch, *Moralia* 437d]. ... Behold, the Lord is he who arouses the hearts of men (throws them into ecstasy) and gives to men a new heart" (Schneemelcher 1965:686). See Trevett 1996:83. The conversionist interpretation of the Montanist doctrine in Klawiter 1975:89 stretches the evidence. See also the discussion of the "renewed heart" in Munzinger 2007:105–6.

[104] Cf. *L.A.E.* 33.1 (see M. D. Johnson 1985:287).

accord with the hymnic style of the angels. And as she spoke ecstatically, she allowed "The Spirit" to be inscribed on her garment.[105]

Then Kasia bound hers on and had her heart changed so that she no longer regarded worldly things. And her mouth took on the dialect of the archons [διάλεκτον τῶν ἀρχόντων] and she praised God for the creation of the heights. ...

Then the other one also, named Amaltheia's Horn, bound on her cord. And her mouth spoke ecstatically in the dialect of those on high, since her heart also was changed, keeping aloof from worldly things. For she spoke in the dialect of the cherubim [διαλέκτῳ <τῶν> Χερουβὶμ], glorifying the Master of virtues by exhibiting their splendor.[106]

The "Spirit"-inscription on Hemera's garment presumably effects her ecstasy in some way.[107]

The action of wrapping oneself is perhaps significant. David Halperin has collected a wealth of rabbinic passages that refer to wrapping as a gesture of approach to God (e.g., as preparation for prayer). The one passage that he quotes is especially interesting when compared to the death-bed scene in the *Testament of Job*, and it happens to be a passage that I quoted already in the previous chapter: "It was also taught: the one who enters to visit the invalid does not sit on a bed or on a seat, but must wrap himself and sit in front of him, for the *shekinah* is above the pillow of

---

[105] Several commentators have noted the similarity between εν στολη ("garment") and εν στηλη, opting for the latter wording, although it is unattested in any manuscript, since it is a title attributed to various gnostic and magical writings – e.g., the *Three Steles of Seth* (NHC VII,5) and the *PGM* στήλη τοῦ Ἰέου (Preisendanz 1928–31:no. 5.96). Cf. Schaller 1979:369 n. 3g. Fraser (1972:498) writes, "imaginary stelai containing sacred texts, instructions, and so on, are a common feature of early Hellenistic romantic literature". (See the reference to the "unnecessary discussion" about the word στήλη in Cowley 1923:206–7. He refers esp. to τὴν Ἀκικάρου στήλην [the *Story of Ahiqar?*] in Clement of Alexandria, *Strom.* 1.15.69.) Van der Horst 1989:103 n. 28 writes, "in view of the fact that the words of the second and third daughters are said to have been recorded in a book, it is very likely that here too there is a reference to a piece of writing". (But note that when a stele is thought of as a stone rather than a literary genre, the normal Greek expression is ἐπὶ στήλης.) Philonenko 1968:56 reads εν <επι>στολη and translates "sur son Épître". Cf. Spittler 1983:866 n. h.

[106] Trans. Spittler 1983:865–6.

[107] There are two possible explanations. (I leave aside the explanation of R. A. Kraft 1974:82, first proposed by M. R. James [1897:xcvii], that "The Spirit" is the title of a poem inscribed on Hemera's garment.) In the realm of magic, both Jewish and pagan, the wearing of God's name as a talisman was common. The so-called "seal of Solomon" is a well known example. (See Perdrizet 1903; Scholem 1965:60; Rohrbacher-Sticker 1996:43; Lesses 1998:317–23. See also the discussion of "the ideology of the divine name" in Janowitz 1989:25–8.) Alternatively, we may understand the inscription of "The Spirit" as the key to an enacted metaphor: Hemera's enwrapping of herself in the girdle represents her being enwrapped by/in the "spirit." The metaphor exists already in Jdg 6.34: "The spirit of the LORD clothed Gideon." (The NRSV unfortunately dismisses the metaphor.)

an invalid" (*b. Šabb.* 12b).[108] It should be noted, however, that the *Testament of Job* does not indicate any connection between wrapping and visiting the sick. A more significant parallel, perhaps, can be found in Philo of Alexandria's allegorizing of the Passover girdle (see Exod 12.11) in *QE* I.19. Philo interprets the girdle as a symbol of self-control. While the *Testament of Job* does not say as much, the effect of the girdles for Job's daughters is broadly similar, although it is certainly different enough to be a coincidence.[109]

Not surprisingly, the obvious parallel between this account and the New Testament description of glossolalia has received a lot of attention, and has had a noticeable effect on how the *Testament of Job* is interpreted. One should not pass too quickly over the distinctiveness of the account in the *Testament of Job*. It should be noted, for example, that the designation of the supernaturally endowed language changes with each of the daughters. At first glance, this variation of terms appears to be merely stylistic, like the variation found in the descriptions of the cords (46.6: χορδή; 47.11: φυλακτήριον;[110] 48.1: σπάρτη; 52.1: τεπίζωσις) and of "earthly things" (48.2: μηκέτι φρονεῖν τὰ τῆς γῆς; 49.1: μηκέτι ἐνθυμηθῆναι τὰ κοσμικά; 50.1: ἀφισταμένη ἀπὸ τῶν κοσμικῶν), but the description of the daughters' response to the ascent of Job's soul in a chariot suggests that the variation in terminology might also denote a variation in referents: "And they blessed and glorified God each one in her own distinctive dialect" (52.7). The fact that the daughters spoke successively, and not all together, is another indicator that their dialects may have been distinctive. It is worth noting, in this connection, that the angelic ranks seem to ascend: angel → archon → cherub. Alexander Altmann noted long ago that, in early merkabah mysticism, the class of angels encountered at each level of ascent has its own particular language.[111] Nothing in the narrative suggests that Job's daughters had any sort of rapturous experience – *viz.* that the angeloglossic utterances are connected with an encounter of angelic beings during a heavenly ascent – but the possibility that the daughters are imagined to have seen some sort of vision should not be dismissed.[112] In *T. Job* 52.6–12, apparently only Job and his daughters are able to see the angelic psychopomps with their "gleaming chariots". This ability to see into the angelic realm is apparently limited to those who bear the magical girdles,

---

[108] Halperin 1983:125 n. 88. I quote the text according to my own translation from the preceding chapter.

[109] See also Philo, *Leg.* II.27–8; III.154; Geljon 2002:113–14.

[110] See Schaller 1979:368 n. 11a.

[111] Altmann 1946.

[112] It is worth noting that Gruenwald 1980:17 judges one part of the *Testament of Job* (36.8–38.8) to be anti-apocalyptic in outlook.

so that a connection between speaking in angelic tongues and experiencing angelic visitations may be in evidence.

Van der Horst translates τρία σκευάρια τοῦ χρυσοῦ as "three boxes *with gold*" rather than "three golden boxes."[113] That is, he views the boxes as *containers* for golden objects, implying that the girdles are golden, a detail that may be of some angelological significance: golden girdles are standard angelic wear throughout apocalyptic literature, and beyond.[114] Gold, of course, symbolized divinity throughout the Mediterranean world (and beyond).[115] Golden girdles were also associated with inspired unintelligible speech: Lucian describes Alexander of Abonuteichos as an ecstatic babbler wearing a golden girdle, making such sounds "as may also be heard among Hebrews and Phoenicians."[116]

---

[113] He suggests that for "three golden boxes" we might have expected τρία σκευάρια χρυσᾶ (van der Horst 1989:104–5). Whatever the correct rendering may be, it is worth noting that *m. Meg.* 4.8 identifies one who overlays his phylacteries with gold as a sectarian (*min*). See the discussion of this passage in Segal 1986:149.

[114] Significantly, one of these examples of an angel wearing a golden girdle comes from another apocalyptic episode of humans speaking angelically (*Apoc. Zeph.* 6.12). Cf. *Vis. Paul* 12; Dan 10.5 (in MT and Theodotion); Rev 1.13; 15.6. Cf. also the nondescript belt in Ezek 9.2. On the standard depiction of angels girded with golden belts, cf. Stuckenbruck 1995:228. Cf. also the description of those surrounding the divine throne in the *Ques. Ezra* 27: "There are stations, ..., hollows, fiery ones, girdle wearers, (and) lanterns" (Stone 1983:27 [translator's ellipsis]). Pearson 1976:233 n. 14 notes that "Michael is regularly presented in Coptic literature as girded with a golden girdle". Speyer 1983 lists magicians who wore golden girdles (Kirke, Kalypso, Abaris, Empedocles). Henrichs 1977:139, 141 (esp. nn. 64–5), 156 discusses the maenadic use of girdles, but downplays their possible magical aspect. Aune 1997:94 notes that Mithras is three times depicted as wearing a golden belt around his chest when he slays the bull at Marino. Philonenko (1968:55 [note to 47.3]) writes that the daughters' cords are "en tous points identique" with a sacred Iranian cord called a "kusti", but Schaller 1979:367 n. 7 considers this connection questionable. Besserman 1979:41–51 compares the daughters' cords to the green girdle in *Sir Gawain and the Green Knight*. Girdles also signify nobility. Cf. Aeschylus's (aretalogical) salute to the Persian Queen Atossa: "most exalted of Persia's deep-girdled dames" (quoted in Calvin W. McEwan 1934:19). See Mowinckel 1956:413 n. 2. Golden girdles are also worn by kings (1 Macc 10.89) and priests (Josephus, *A.J.* III.159, 171).

[115] The wearing of gold, of course, often signified the divine. As Pindar writes, "Gold is the child of Zeus, neither moth nor weevil eats it" (frag. 222 [trans. Race 1997:409]). Cf. Callimachus, *Hymn to Apollo* 32–5; Fraser 1972:660–1. Aune 1997:94 writes, "The epiphanies of Zeus in *Iliad* 8.41–46 and of Poseidon in *Iliad* 13.20–27 (both passages nearly identical verbally) became the model for the use of gold in divine epiphanies." For Greek sources associating gold with the divine, see Daumas 1956; Stevenson 1995:261 n. 27; A. S. Brown 1998:392–5. For examples from an earlier period (in the Near East), see Oppenheim 1949.

[116] Van der Horst 1989:112. On Alexander in Lucian, see H. D. Betz 1961:140–7; Benko 1984:108–13. Georgi 1986:71 n. 100 objects to this interpretation: "It is unlikely that only 'an incomprehensible language' is meant here (Gutbrod) or a language of

In other respects, the change wrought in Job's daughter is more closely paralleled in Joshua's resumption of Moses' office in Pseudo-Philo's *Liber Antiquitatum Biblicarum* (based on Deut 34.9):

"[T]ake [Moses'] garments of wisdom [*vestimenta sapientiae*] and clothe yourself, and with his belt of knowledge [*zona scientiae*] gird your loins, and you will be changed and become another man" .. And Joshua took the garments of wisdom and clothed himself and girded his loins with the belt of understanding. And when he clothed himself with it, his mind was afire and his spirit was moved, and he said to the people …[117]

The phrase "another man" seems to come from 1 Sam 10.6–9, where the notion involves ecstatic speech.[118] Pseudo-Philo makes the same connection between spiritual clothing and being changed into "another man" in his account of Kenaz (*L.A.B.* 27.10).[119] Terence E. Fretheim notes the prominence of this clothing imagery in describing the activity of the Spirit in the Bible: it is found in Judg 6.34; 1 Sam 10.6; 1 Chron 12.18; and 2 Chron 24.20, and "perhaps" in Mic 3.8 and Isa 61.1.[120] The description of an inner change toward angelic likeness is also a widespread theme in mystical writings.[121] For example, we read in the *Cologne Mani Codex*, in a passage quoting the so-called *Apocalypse of Sethel*: "when I listened to these things, my heart rejoiced and my mind was changed, and I became like one of the greatest angels" (*CMC* 51.1–6).[122] Although there are many examples of prophets being *seized* by the prophetic spirit, our text is not necessarily one of them.[123]

---

fantasy. The narrator Lucian is, after all, of Syrian origin. When Lucian adds that the words were meaningless, that pertains to the content of the statements, not to the chosen language."

[117] *L.A.B.* 20.2–3 (trans. van der Horst 1989:113).

[118] The constellation of concepts apparently retained its package form for a long time, as shown by a rather precise parallel in a much later writing that invokes the same biblical verse as Pseudo-Philo: according to Maimonides' *Laws of the Principles of the Torah* (12th cent.): "When the spirit rests upon him, his soul conjoins with the rank of angels called *'isham*. He is transformed into a different individual. He understands through an intellect that is not as it had been up to that point. He is elevated above the rank of the rest of the sages, as it says of Saul: *You will prophesy with them and be transformed into a different individual* (1 Samuel 10:6)" (7.1 [quoted in Kreisel 2001:185]).

[119] See Levison 1997:99–101; 2009:161–63, 174–75; Mach 1992:169.

[120] Fretheim 1984:151.

[121] See Grözinger 1980:74–6.

[122] Cameron and Dewey 1979:39. See Fossum 1995:85 n. 65. Fossum notes that the change of heart/mind recorded in the *Cologne Mani Codex* "would seem to be the result of a doctrinal impartation." For a general discussion of the *Apocalypse of Sethel*, see Reeves 1996:119–22; Frankfurter 1997.

[123] See Parke 1988:2.6–20. Price 1997:67 thinks that he sees a possible allusion to Maenadism within the name of Job's third daughter, Amaltheia's Horn (*Amaltheias-Keras*): the goat Amaltheias, according to legend, had suckled the infant Dionysus:

The text describes the daughters' changed hearts appositionally as a disregard for "earthly things". This description closely parallels Ezra's confession of earthly-mindedness in *4 Ezra* 4.23. Ezra's "earthly" concerns, however, are hardly unimportant or ignoble: they concern the plight of Israel. The *Testament of Job*'s intended contrast between earthly and heavenly concerns is probably better illustrated by Luke 10.38–42, in which Jesus reprimands Martha for allowing chores to distract her, while her sister Mary, who had spent her time listening intently to Jesus' teaching, "has chosen the better part, which will not be taken away from her." (Cf. Paul's teaching on the entanglement of marriage, in 1 Cor 7.32–4.) A closer look at what the *Testament of Job* means by "earthly things" is provided in 36.3 (Job is speaking): "My heart is not fixed on earthly concerns, since the earth and those who dwell in it are unstable. But my heart is fixed on heavenly concerns, for there is no upset in heaven."[124]

Characters in this sort of revelatory text are often depicted as writing down their privileged insights or being given a book by a heavenly figure. Our episode continues with Job's brother, Nereus, completing the book after Job's death (*T. Job* 51.1–4):[125]

After the three had stopped singing hymns,
    while the Lord was present as was I, Nereus, the brother of Job, and while the holy angel (ms. P: "the holy spirit") also was present,
    I sat near Job on the couch, And I heard the magnificent things, while each one made explanation (ὑποσημειουμένης) to the other.
    And I wrote out a complete book of most of the contents of hymns that issued from the three daughters of my brother, so that these things would be preserved. For these are the magnificent things of God (τὰ μεγαλεῖα τοῦ θεοῦ).

After a period of ecstatic praise, Job's daughters begin to explain (or interpret?) to one another the content of their angeloglossic praises, as Nereus listens and writes out "a complete book of most of the contents of hymns that issued from the three daughters."[126] According to an alternative

---

"Conceivably the occurrence of the name in the *Testament of Job* may denote a now-untraceable connection, perhaps some syncretism issuing in a kind of Jewish Maenadism." It is more likely, however, that the name "Amaltheias-Keras" had its intended referent in the cornucopia as a symbol of prosperity, and not in the myth from which this association had originated.

[124] See Garrett 1993.

[125] Cf. how the *History of the Rechabites* continues after Zosimos' death with Kruseos as its purported author. Kruseos was a witness to the translation of Zosimos' dead body into heaven, a scene with some similarities to the final scene in the *Testament of Job*. Cf. also how Joshua was widely thought to have written the ending of Deuteronomy.

[126] Charlesworth (1986:423–4) apparently believes that the "Hymns of Kasia" (*T. Job* 49.3) and the "Prayers of Amaltheia's Horn" (*T. Job* 50.3) were real texts. On the "pseudo-pseudepigrapha" mentioned in the *Testament of Job*, see Reymond 2009. I wish to thank Dr. Reymond for sending me a copy of his essay.

translation, preferred by Kraft and van der Horst, the daughters wrote down their own words.[127] The former translation invites comparison with the Pauline charism of the "interpretation of tongues,"[128] while the latter is similar to the seers' experiences in the *Ascension of Isaiah* and *4 Ezra*.[129] The interpretation of the passage turns on the word ὑποσημειουμένης. Although it is not a Pauline term, Gerhard Dautzenberg compares it with the charism of *interpreting* glossolalia.[130] The content of Nereus' writing is described as τὰ μεγαλεῖα τοῦ θεοῦ, a term also used to describe the content of the xenoglossic utterances in Acts 2.11.[131] In both cases, the term τὰ μεγαλεῖα τοῦ θεοῦ is used by listeners within the narrative, rather than by the narrator. The simplest way to account for this parallel, of course, is to suppose the *Testament of Job*'s direct borrowing from Acts, but it is possible that τὰ μεγαλεῖα τοῦ θεοῦ was also a free-floating technical term for the content of glossolalic utterances.[132]

Nothing in my examination of *T. Job* 46–53 should be surprising to more casual readers of these chapters, armed as they invariably will be the idea that glossolalia was sometimes viewed in angeloglossic terms. Clint Tibbs calls *T. Job* 48–52 "[t]he only clear evidence for possible glossolalia

---

[127] Van der Horst 1989:103.

[128] Thiselton 1979 points out that Paul's wording in 1 Corinthians 14 does not require us to think of the "interpreter" as a separate person. Thiselton argues that the phenomenon described is not one of real "interpretation," but cf. Dunn 1975:246–8; Forbes 1995:65–72.

[129] Cf. the interspersed discussion of *readerly* prophetic inspiration in the excursus on "Higher wisdom through revelation" in Hengel 1974:1.210–18.

[130] Dautzenberg (1975:236–7) writes, "*yposemeioomai* ist in Analogie zu *ypokrinomai* vom Deuteausdruck *semeioomai* gebildet. ... Bei Anwendung einer anderen Terminologie (*dialektos yposemeioomai*) als im 1 Kor (*glossa diermeneuo*), wird doch das gleiche Phänomen beschrieben."

[131] Parallel noted by Dautzenberg 1979:col. 241. The translation in R. A. Kraft 1974:83 ("the magnificent compositions of God") fits the context of *T. Job* 51, but obscures the parallelism with Acts 2.11. Conzelmann 1987:15 notes that this phrase "is found in the LXX and also in 1QS 1.21", but the only verbatim parallel is that found in the angeloglossic episode in the *Testament of Job*, which Conzelmann does not cite. The only appearance of the expression in the Septuagint is 2 Macc 3.34. See also Acts 10.46, where Cornelius's household's glossolalic praises are described as μεγαλύνειν τὸν θεόν. Contra Marshall 1977:359 and Menzies 1991:211, the phrase "the magnificent works of God" does not imply that the content of glossolalia is proclamation rather than praise. On Acts 2.11, see Kremer 1973:142–3.

[132] Levison 2009:341 argues that, since Peter recognized the glossolalic speech in Acts 10.46 as an utterance of praise, it must have been done "in comprehensible tongues" (*viz.* human language). The fact that the content of Job's daughters' angeloglossy is given as τὰ μεγαλεῖα τοῦ θεοῦ shows that Peter's recognition of the doxological nature of glossolalia does not imply that it is consists of human languages.

in the Jewish world".[133] This passage is an important witness to the career of angeloglossy, and for its narrative clarity is far less of a puzzle overall than Paul's teasing reference in 1 Cor 13.1. Given the possibility that this passage was written by a Christian, one must seriously consider that it was perhaps based on 1 Cor 13.1. Such a scenario, however, would not imply that its presence within the work is purely unrelated to charismatic activity within the author's community. Charismatic communities, both Jewish and Christian, were probably more prevalent than the literary remains of these two religions might move us to believe.

D. The *Apocalypse of Zephaniah*

The *Apocalypse of Zephaniah* is a fragmentary text reconstructed from three sources: a quotation from Clement of Alexandria (*Strom.* 5.11.77), a short Sahidic fragment, and a longer Akhmimic fragment. These three sources together are generally agreed to amount to only one fourth of the original work.[134] Some scholars doubt that the Akhmimic fragment is part of the *Apocalypse of Zephaniah*, since it does not overlap any positively identified texts and never mentions Zephaniah.[135] O. S. Wintermute finds such reserve to be misplaced, however, noting that three ancient catalog witnesses associate editions of the *Apocalypse of Zephaniah* with the *Apocalypse of Elijah*, and that the latter appears together with the above-mentioned Sahidic and Akhmimic apocalyptic texts. He also reproduces other minor arguments which have been put forth for identifying the Akhmimic fragment as the *Apocalypse of Zephaniah*.[136] K. H. Kuhn takes a median position by printing the two texts in question in sequence in the Sparks edition, but by retaining the title "An anonymous apocalypse" for the larger passage (which includes the passage discussed below).

Lines of literary dependence, running both to and from the *Apocalypse of Zephaniah*, allow us to date the document sometime between 100 B.C.E. and 175 C.E.[137] Its original language was Greek, and the strongest proba-

---

[133] Tibbs 2007:221 n. 23.

[134] See C. Schmidt 1925:319–20.

[135] E.g., J. J. Collins 1992:194–5.

[136] Wintermute 1983:499–500. See K. H. Kuhn 1984:915–18; S. E. Robinson 2000. Texts of the catalog witnesses are collected in Steindorff 1899:3a.22–3. An in-depth review of the manuscripts. of the *Apocalypse of Zephaniah* can be found in Diebner 1978; 1979.

[137] Wintermute 1983:500–1. Himmelfarb 1985:147–58 confirms a relatively early date for the *Apocalypse of Zephaniah* by source-critically locating its descent into Hades within the first extant generation of the Jewish and Christian *descensus* tradition. (See the generational stemma in Himmelfarb 1985:171). See Gunther 1973:41–2. The *Apocalypse*

bility for its place of origin is Egypt.[138] Despite the Coptic dialects of the extant remains, scholars have noted an absence of Christian elements.[139] There have been attempts to draw a line of dependence from the Book of Revelation to the *Apocalypse of Zephaniah*, or vice versa, but the parallels seem rather generic.[140] Wilhelm Lueken characterized the writing as having been "strongly reworked by a Christian" ("stark christlich über-arbeitete").[141]

Apoc. Zeph. 8 follows upon a two-page lacuna in the manuscript, which presumably had recounted the conclusion of the seer's descent into Hades. The extant fragment begins anew near the beginning of the seer's adventure in heaven. It is at this point that the text mentions an esoteric angelic language:

> They helped me and set me on that boat. Thousands of thousands and myriads of myriads of angels gave praise before me. I, myself, put on an angelic garment. I saw all of those angels praying. I, myself, prayed together with them, I knew their language, which they spoke with me. Now, moreover, my sons, this is the trial because it is necessary that the good and the evil be weighed in a balance.[142]

Scholars have paid more attention to the role of the angelic garment – which has been interpreted in terms of its role in other apocalyptic texts – than to the role of the angelic tongues. By reducing the garment motif to its common elements in the *Apocalypse of Zephaniah*, the *Ascension of Isaiah* (8.26; 9.9–13), *2 Enoch* (9.2), and *3 Enoch* (18), Himmelfarb follows R. H. Charles's suggestion that the garments represent "spiritual bodies."[143] It is also possible, however, that Zephaniah's garment duplicates the function of Job's daughters' charismatic sashes in the *Testament of Job*. It may well be that the concept of angeloglossy should be used to shed light on the interpretation of the garment, rather than vice versa. This question bears on

---

of Zephaniah is listed as an apocryphal writing in the 7th-cent. C.E. *Catalogue of the Sixty Canonical Books*. See Schneemelcher 1963b:51–52.

[138] Frankfurter 1998 calls attention to the extensive Egyptian symbolism in the *Apocalypse of Elijah*, a text that was circulated together with the *Apocalypse of Zephaniah*. See Frankfurter 1993. Pearson 1976 thinks it possible that the *Apocalypse of Zephaniah* influenced a later "Coptic Enoch Apocryphon". See also Kugler and Rohrbaugh 2004.

[139] See Stuckenbruck 1995:78–9. Bauckham (1980–1:337 n. 22) thinks that "at least minor Christian editing seems probable". Mach 1992:295–6, on the other hand, thinks that the Christian element in the book is stronger. See also Lacau 1966:170–7.

[140] See Wintermute 1983:504; Briggs 1999:132–3.

[141] Lueken 1898:85.

[142] Trans. Wintermute 1983:514.

[143] Himmelfarb 1985:156. S.v. "Kleider (der Seelen)" in the index to Recheis 1958. "Garments" takes on a very different, but possibly related, meaning in later Jewish mysticism. Cf. Scholem 1965:57–64. Muffs 1992:49–60 discusses a wide range of religious/magical associations with garments. See also Benko 1993:95–108, esp. 101–5.

whether the author of the *Apocalypse of Zephaniah* thought of angelo-glossy, in hymnody and in intercessory prayer, as an accessible phenomenon. Himmelfarb comes close to disclaiming any interpretation in which the author's experience figures largely, but the "absence of techniques for ascent" is not necessarily as complete as she claims.[144]

Perhaps the most important datum about human participation in angeloglossy in the *Apocalypse of Zephaniah* is the use to which it is put: *intercessory prayer* and *hymnody*. The theme of intercession is a constant (and urgent) one throughout apocalyptic literature.[145] This theme has its basis in the Bible,[146] and, in many of the apocalyptic works that formed the continuation of the prophetic tradition, intercession is affirmed as a real duty of the person who has God's ear.[147] For some heroes, the constancy and insistence of their intercession occupies the foreground of their heroic status – cf. esp. Josephus, Philo, Pseudo-Philo, the *Testament of Moses* on Moses,[148] and the *Prayer of Jacob*, the *Prayer of Manasseh,* and *Psalms of Solomon* on Abraham.[149] In addition to texts which depict the heroes of the faith as great intercessors (Esther 13; Daniel 9; Judith 9; Tobit 3; *1 En.* 89.61–65, *T. Jac.* 7.11), there are several[150] in which angels are depicted as interceding for humans (Tob 12.12, 15; *Jub.* 30.20; *1 En.* 15.2; 39.5; 40.6; 47.1–4; 99.3; 104.1; *T. Dan* 6.1–2; *T. Ash.* 6.6; *T. Levi* 3.5–6; 5.5–7;

---

[144] Himmelfarb 1995:132. Himmelfarb's comment is in response to Stone 1990:30–3. See now Stone 2003. On the relation of descriptions of ecstatic phenomena to their authors' experiences, see Block 1988.

[145] See Johansson 1940; Nickelsburg 1972:13 n. 17; Parker 2006.

[146] Idelsohn (1932:5) writes, "As we glance over the Scriptures, we find that almost every outstanding figure in Israel was also an intercessor who would compose prayers on certain occasions." See Johansson 1940; Reventlow 1986:228–64; and P. D. Miller 1994:262–80. According to Balentine 1984, only Abraham, the man of God in 1 Kgs 13.6, Nehemiah, Hezekiah, Moses, Job, Samuel, and Jeremiah are described in the Hebrew Bible as intercessors. Balentine notes that this list is comprised mostly of specifically *northern* figures, and concludes that the tradition of intercession is a product of that geographical area. The list of intercessors in P. D. Miller 1994:263 also includes Elijah, Elisha, Isaiah, Ezekiel, and Amos.

[147] Barton 1986:102 notes that "[t]he heroes of pseudo-prophetic books written in [the postexilic] period are generally skilled in intercession". See the many examples from Jewish and Christian texts in Bauckham 1998:136–42.

[148] Josephus, *A.J.* III.298; Philo, *Mut.* 129; Pseudo-Philo, *L.A.B.* 19.3; *T. Mos.* 11.17. See also *Ques. Ezra* 39–40 (rec. A). Tiede (1972:183) writes, "the most important role that Moses plays for pseudo-Philo is his function as God's spokesman and intercessor for the people". See Tiede 1972:124, 184; 1980:41. See also the rabbinic texts discussed in Mann 1940:515–21.

[149] *Pr. Jac.* 2.270–1; *Pr. Man.* 2.628–35; *Pss. Sol.* 9.9, 18.3. On "the status of Abraham as intermediary," see Siker 1991:24–7.

[150] I.e., more than a "paucity," contra H. B. Kuhn 1948:227.

T. Adam 2.1–12).[151] In some texts, humans are the spiritual heroes, while angels are the ideals to which heroism attains.[152] In the Christian *Vis. Paul* 43–4, an interceding archangel Michael urges humans to pray for themselves.[153] Tigchelaar locates the phenomenon of angelic intercession within an array of angelic activities modeled upon human activities,[154] but angelic intercession stands out among these activities as an idea with its own well-developed career. Both human and angelic intercession are described in priestly terminology, the angelic somewhat more consistently than the human.[155]

Himmelfarb has observed that "it is possible to read the Book of Zephaniah as suggesting topics that an author with an apocalyptic bent might treat as they are treated in the Apocalypse of Zephaniah."[156] It is not difficult to discern a connection between *Apoc. Zeph.* 8 and (biblical) Zeph 3.9 ("Then will I turn to the people a pure language"). But if we are right to hear an echo of Zeph 3.9, then it should be noted that the author of our apocalypse has changed the meaning of the verse from what was originally a reference to the worldwide conquest of the primordial universal language (Hebrew) to the idea that access to the "pure" esoteric language of the angels would be made possible. The latter idea cashes in a couple of pas-

---

[151] On angelic intercession in Jewish literature, see Lueken 1898:7–12; N. B. Johnson 1948:52–3; D. S. Russell 1964:242; Schäfer 1975:28–9, 62–4, 70; Christoffersson 1990:119–20; Davidson 1992:309–13. On angelic intercession in *T. Dan* 6.2, see Dey 1975:89–90.

[152] Enoch refuses to intercede in *2 Enoch*. Sacchi 1990:243 attributes this to the book being written in "an era in which the problem of intercession was felt strongly", but this inference is certainly not straightforward. Sacchi opposes the view of *2 Enoch* to that of *Apoc. Zeph.* 2.9; 6.10; 7.8; and Rom 8.34. We may regard *2 Enoch* as an exception to the general rule, establishing a pattern that would eventually be vindicated by the Islamic tradition, but comprising only a minority stance within Jewish apocalyptic. But cf. *4 Ezra* 7.102–15. Dean-Otting 1984:244–5 opposes the stance of *4 Ezra* 7 to that of the *Testament of Abraham*. Sacchi 1990:244 also notes, "The stance of the *Book of Parables* is interesting ([*1 En.*] 38.6 and 40.6): a very high angel prays, interceding for humans, but it is unclear whether this intercession is useful or not, and in any case the intercession is destined to finish with the judgment." I think that his skepticism is misplaced: if *1 Enoch*, or one of its constituent parts, were against angelic intercession, we probably would hear the objection more clearly.

[153] On Michael as intercessor, see Ego 1989 (esp. the chart of texts on pp. 7–8). Majercik 1989:20 notes that, in the *Chaldean Oracles*, "the souls of the theurgists are said to derive from the angelic order, from which point they incarnate with the purpose of aiding mankind".

[154] Tigchelaar 1996:249–51.

[155] Carlson 1982 surveys the connection between prayer and the sacrificial apparatus.

[156] Himmelfarb 1993:52. Harrisville 1976 suggests that LXX Zeph 3.9 was translated under the influence of a charismatic rendering of Isa 28.11.

sages in Peter Schäfer's *Synopse zur Hekhalot-Literatur* (§§390, 637)[157] in which speaking in a "pure tongue" (לשׁון מח[ו]רה) is demonstrated through a series of *voces mysticae* based solely upon the letters in the Tetragrammaton.

The *Apocalypse of Zephaniah* provides our first example of angeloglossy in a writing whose Jewish provenance is fairly (but not *entirely*) secure. We will later examine another writing in this chapter falling under the same judgment (*Apocalypse of Abraham*), and one whose Jewish provenance is essentially set in stone (*Genesis Rabbah*). A further mix of Jewish and Christian writings in the next chapter will add to the impression that the concept of angeloglossy was current in both religions.

E. The *Ascension of Isaiah*

The *Ascension of Isaiah* is another important text for understanding the idea of an esoteric angelic languages in the pseudepigrapha, although the possible reference to angeloglossy within that text, like that in the *Apocalypse of Abraham* (discussed below), is not as explicit as the references in the *Testament of Job* and *Apocalypse of Zephaniah*. Nevertheless, the reference is secure enough to belong in the present chapter.

The *Ascension of Isaiah* is usually seen as a composite work, although Richard Bauckham has recently argued that it is unified writing.[158] The sharpest division within the work is that separating chaps. 1–5 from 6–11. Chaps. 1–5 can be divided further, however, as 3.13–4.22 (the so-called *Testament of Hezekiah*) appears to be an interpolation. *4 Baruch* seems to know the narrative of chaps. 1–5 with the interpolation already in place, thereby dating this development to the end of the first century C.E., at the latest.[159] The sawing of Isaiah was a well established legend early on,[160] and the material in 1.1–3.12 and 5.1–16 (the so-called *Martyrdom of Isaiah*) was probably composed in the first century C.E., although it may be dependent upon an even earlier narrative. This is the only part of the *Ascension of Isaiah* that does not bear a Christian imprint.

Pier Cesare Bori has argued that the prophetism of the *Ascension of Isaiah* fits best in a pre-Montanist movement, and, on those grounds, places the work in Asia Minor.[161] Others have objected to Bori's thesis, noting

---

[157] Schäfer 1981.

[158] See the discussion in Knibb 1985:147–9; Nordheim 1980:208–19. See Bauckham 1998:363–90.

[159] See Knibb 1985:149.

[160] See Schürer 1973–87:3.338–40.

[161] Bori 1980:385–6.

the presence of gnosticizing Jewish-Christian elements within the work, and supposing these to exclude Montanism.[162] More recent work, however, has shown that Montanism shared a number of exegetical complexes with the more gnosticizing Jewish-Christian stream, which might make differentiating between the two trickier than some realize.[163] Nevertheless, there are no compelling reasons to associate the *Ascension of Isaiah* with the Montanists or their direct forebears in Asia Minor. David Frankfurter also places the *Acension of Isaiah* in Asia Minor, but on the grounds that it "exalts a kind of visionary charismatic leadership much as the Book of Revelation does (3:31; 6–11)".[164] Torleif Elgvin suggests a Syrian provenance, due to "the reference to Tyre and Sidon (5:13), similarities with (the opponents of) Ignatius of Antioch, and the Hebrew roots of the Martyrdom".[165]

Robert Hall, seeking the "community situation" underlying the *Ascension of Isaiah*, notes that chap. 7 begins with what looks like an introduction ("The vision which Isaiah saw ..."),[166] and points out that various details in chap. 6 presuppose the compilation of chaps. 1–5 together with 6–11.[167] Thus Hall attributes chap. 6 to the final redactor (a judgment that he notes is "hardly controversial").[168] He contends that the final author composed the "historical apocalypse" in 3.13–31. This insert is aimed against detractors: "*Asc. Is.* 3:13–20 summarizes the doctrine of the descent and ascent and establishes it as *the* doctrine of the apostles. *Asc. Is.* 3:21–31 attacks those who reject this doctrine of the apostles (3:21) – that is, the vision of the descent and ascent of the Beloved ascribed to Isaiah (3:31)."[169] The author thus represents a "prophetic school":

This description of the prophetic school [in 6.1–17], more detailed and specific than necessary for the story, probably reflects the author's idealized view of his or her own group. If so, the *Ascension of Isaiah* issued from an early Christian prophetic school which periodically gathered from various early Christian communities to form an outpost

---

[162] E.g., Simonetti 1983:204–5.

[163] See Ford 1966; 1970–1; Poirier 1999; Denzey 2001.

[164] Frankfurter 1996:133.

[165] Elgvin 2007:293 n. 56.

[166] Strangely, however, Hall thinks that the final author composed 7.1. I think that the appearance of an *incipit* in the middle of a work more likely betrays an earlier hand.

[167] Hall 1990a.

[168] Hall 1990a:290. Hall (1990a:290–1) writes, "Chapter 6 is isolated from its context. ... Since the early Christian apocalypse bears no essential connection with Isaiah and since this chapter depends on the picture of Isaiah's activity in chaps. 1–5, the final author must have written 6:1–17 to tie the two halves of the work together and to include the Vision within its pseudepigraphical framework." Hannah 1999:84 notes that it is presently the trend to view the *Ascension of Isaiah* as a unity.

[169] Hall 1990a:291. For the *Ascension of Isaiah*'s merkabah-mystical associations, see the discussion of *Ascen. Isa.* 9.1–2 in Norelli 1995:449–51. See also Norelli 1994:234–48; Gruenwald 1980:57–62.

of heaven in which senior prophets imparted the gift of prophecy by laying on of hands and offered instructions to refine the technique and prophetic sensitivity of their juniors. Although the author's school participated with other early Christians in charismatic worship, it distinguished itself from them in experiencing heavenly trips to see God. Probably the Vision of the Descent and Ascent of the Beloved typifies the accounts of such heavenly voyagers and stems from the author's community.[170]

Hall sees evidence of this community situation within retouched passages in chaps. 1–5. Belkira's argument against Isaiah (3.6–12) is particularly telling. Isaiah claims to have seen the Lord and lived to tell it. According to Belkira, Isaiah must be a false prophet, because Moses wrote that no one can see the Lord and live. Hall suggests that Belkira represents the views of those Christians who object to heavenly ascents (a polemic reflected also in John 3.13).[171] (In this connection, it is instructive to read Irenaeus's discussion of prophetic revelation in *Haer.* 4.20.8–10, in which the Isaian passage is brought within the bounds of Moses' words. Irenaeus presumably would have agreed with Belkira.) The author of the *Ascension of Isaiah* has therefore "chosen a pseudonym carefully" – even the school's detractors will have to agree that the real Isaiah saw what he claimed to have seen.[172] As for the author's location and date, Hall suggests the region of Tyre and Sidon (see *Ascen. Isa.* 5.13), and a date in the late first or early second century C.E.

For purposes of this study, it is important to note the work's mystical associations.[173] In attempting to place this writing within the streams of early Christianity, it should be noted that the *Ascension of Isaiah* shares its angelomorphic christology and pneumatology[174] (cf. 3.15; 4.21; 7.23; 8.14 [ms. A]; 9.36, 39, 40; 10.4; 11.4, 33) with Origen (*Princ.* 1.3.4; *Hom. Isa.*

---

[170] Hall 1990a:294. Fekkes (1994:24 n. 4) writes, "An experience of group enthusiasm in a Christian gathering may lie behind the description in *Asc. Isa.* 6."

[171] Hannah (1999:88) thinks, primarily on the basis of 8.11–12, that the *Ascension of Isaiah* presents Isaiah's heavenly journey as possessing "an unrepeatable nature". It is not unlikely, however, that Christian merkabists would have stressed the uniqueness of an OT hero's heavenly journey for *its own day*, even while holding out the possibility of its being repeated. Knight 1996:190 understands *Ascen. Isa.* 3.8–10 as an anti-Mosaic (and therefore anti-Jewish) polemic, since Moses had denied that anyone can see God. Martyn (1997:103 n. 40) writes, "The ancient Israelite traditions that refer to seeing God face to face clearly imply that the experience should bring death. But bold interpreters could have taken advantage of certain ambiguities (e.g. Exod 24:9–11), especially if they claimed their visions as an eschatological blessing. The author of the Fourth Gospel evidently had in mind persons who made a similar claim ... when he said pointedly, 'No one has ever seen God'."

[172] Hall 1990a:295.

[173] See Bauckham 1993:140–2; Rowland 1999a:791–2; Hurtado 2003:595–602.

[174] See Stuckenbruck 1999:78–82; 2004. M. R. Barnes 2008:174–6. On the *Ascension of Isaiah*'s pneumatology, see Norelli 1983. On angelomorphic christology more generally, see Gieschen 1998.

1.2)[175] and the Elkesaites (cf. Hippolytus, *Haer.* 9.13.2–3).[176] This view was probably based upon the identification of Christ and the Holy Spirit as the seraphim of Isaiah 6.[177]

The evidence for angeloglossy is found in chaps. 6–11. These chapters are likely to have been written sometime later, and a date in the second century C.E. is often given.[178] Within this section of the pseudepigraphon, Isaiah is transported to the seventh heaven, and praises God in unison with the angels and the revered saints of the Bible.[179] At the climax of his out-of-body experience, Isaiah is shown the heavenly record of men's deeds:

Ascen. Isa. 9.20–3
And I said to him what I had asked him in the third heaven, ["Show me how everything] which is done in that world is known here." And while I was still speaking to him, behold one of the angels who were standing by, more glorious than that angel who had brought me up from the world, showed me (some) books, and he opened them, and the books had writing in them, but not like the books of this world. And they were given to me, and I read them, and behold the deeds of the children of Jerusalem were written there, their deeds which you know, my son Josab. And I said, "Truly, nothing which is done in this world is hidden in the seventh heaven."[180]

Ioan P. Culianu understands these books filled with writing "not like the books of this world" to be written "in alfabeto celeste."[181] There is little

---

[175] See Stroumsa 1981; Trigg 1991. In 359 or 360 C.E., Serapion, bishop of Thmuis, warned Athanasius of a group of Egyptian Christians who identified the Holy Spirit as a supreme angel. (See Kelly 1977:256–7.) Shenoute (5th cent. C.E.) develops Origen's interpretation of the Isaian seraphim further (see Grillmeier 1996:182–3). For the reaction against Origen's view, see Grillmeier 1975:52–3. Johnston 1970:8 lists a number of sources that equate spirits with angelic beings. See also Ellis 1993:30–6; Bucur 2009:115–19 (on the *Shepherd of Hermas*).

[176] See Luttikhuizen 1985:123, 196–9. (But see also the heavy criticism of Luttikhuizen's views in F. S. Jones 1987.) The merkabah associations of the Elkesaites have been laid bare by J. M. Baumgarten 1986. See Carrell 1997:104–6; Fatehi 2000:133–8. The attempt in J. R. Russell 1994:66 to show that the *Ascension of Isaiah*'s ascent narrative is shaped by Iranian ideas is unconvincing in light of his failure to mention the close similarities with merkabah accounts.

[177] Trigg 1991:39 n. 12 writes, "Kretschmar elegantly demonstrates that an early identification of the Seraphim with the two Cherubim supporting the Ark of the Covenant accounts for the tradition, attested by both written and iconographic evidence, that there were *two* Seraphim, an inference not justified by the actual text of Isa. 6. Origen's identification of the Seraphim with the Son and the Holy Spirit shows that this identification was already taken for granted in his time." See Hannah 1999:90-99.

[178] E.g., see Flemming and Duensing 1965:643.

[179] See Stuckenbruck 1999:74–8.

[180] Adapted from Knibb 1985:171 (emended to the Knibb's second Latin version).

[181] Culianu (1983:105) writes, "Giunto nel settimo cielo, Isaia riceve da un angelo *gloriosior astantibus*, che è indubbiamente l'angelo-scrivano di Dio, la scrittura contenente, in alfabeto celeste – ma non in ebraico, benchéquesto fosse spesso ritenuto lingua

room to doubt that Isaiah is depicted here as interpreting an angelic language.

There are other possible indications of an esoteric angelic language in the *Ascension of Isaiah*, although they are less clear. In 9.27–32, Isaiah joins with the angelic praises, and finds that his praise is tranformed to be "like theirs":

And I saw one standing (there) whose glory surpassed that of all, and his glory was great and wonderful. And when they saw him, all the righteous whom I had seen and the angels came to him. And Adam and Abel and Seth and all the righteous approached first and worshiped him, and they all praised him with one voice, and I also was singing praises with them, and my praise was like theirs. And then all the angels approached, and worshiped, and sang praises. And he was transformed and became like an angel. And then the angel who led me said to me, "Worship this one," and I worshiped and sang praises. And the angel said to me, "This is the LORD of all the praise which you have seen"[182]

In what sense does Isaiah's praise become like that of the angels? It is possible, of course, that the similarity between Isaiah's and the angels' praises consists simply of their repeating the same words in Hebrew (e.g., "קדוש קדוש קדוש" as in the canonical account).[183] It is also possible, however, that the primary obstacle that Isaiah has overcome is a language barrier: there are indications within Isaiah's ascent through the lower heavens that succeeding companies of angels speak different (presumably esoteric) languages. As Isaiah enters the first heaven (7.13–15), he notices that the "voices" of the angels on the left are different from the "voices" of those on the right:[184]

And afterwards [the angel] caused me to ascend (to that which is) above the firmament: which is the (first) heaven. And there I saw a throne in the midst, and on his right and on his left were angels. And (the angels on the left were) not like unto the angels who stood on the right, but those who stood on the right had the greater glory, and they all praised with one voice, and there was a throne in the midst, and those who were on the left gave

---

celeste – il racconto della storia futura del mondo. ... Si noti che Isaia non ha nessuna difficoltà a leggere la scrittura divina, benché sia scritta in alfabeto ignoto."

[182] Trans. Knibb 1985:171.

[183] I cannot see how Forbes (1995:183 n. 2) can write that in the *Ascension of Isaiah* "*at no stage* is it suggested that [Isaiah] takes on or learns the type of praise, or the language of praise, of the angels". Considering that Isaiah is explicitly said to join in with the angels' praise (*Ascen. Isa.* 8.17), and when he is shown a tablet containing a heavenly text, it turns out to be in an unearthly language, the natural inference is that the angels praise God in a heavenly language, and that this is the language that Isaiah employs when he joins the heavenly liturgy.

[184] See Bianchi 1983:162 n. 24. Gruenwald 1980:59 n. 108 points out the similarity of this scheme to that of *Hekhalot Rabbati* 17 (= *Synopse* §§219–24), in which the gatekeepers on the right are more important than those on the left.

praise after them; but their voice was not such as the voice of those on the right, nor their praise like the praise of those.

This passage establishes a pattern for the first five heavens, so that by the time of Isaiah's arrival in the sixth heaven, he has already heard ten different angelic "voices." Since it is universally agreed that the above passage was composed in Greek (the only part of the work to survive in Greek is 2.4–4.4), we may presume that φωνή stood in the original text.[185] The first mention of *voice*, in the phrase "with one voice," almost certainly means "voice" (i.e., "in unison"). This is the sense in which the concept of an angelic φωνή would eventually pass into Byzantine hymnology.[186] In the remaining instances, however, philological and history-of-religions considerations may support the rendering "language." It is first of all worth noting that φωνή is sometimes connected with references to angels within mystical or magical texts. In one textual version of the *Hermetic Corpus*, the ascending mystic, upon entering the ogdoad, hears the supernal powers φωνῇ τινι ἰδίᾳ ὑμνουσῶν τὸν θεόν (1.26).[187] Even if this version is not original (the alternate version writes ἡδεῖα for ἰδίᾳ, i.e. "sweet voice" for "own voice/language"),[188] its existence within a textual tradition still counts as a support for translating φωνή as "language" within an angelological context. Heavenly languages are also presumably in view when the spellbinder, following the recipe in a Hermetic papyrus (*PGM* 13.139–40), utters "I call on you who surround all things, I call in every language and in every dialect..." (ἐπικαλοῦμαί σε, τὸν τὰ πάντα περιέχοντα, πάσῃ φωνῇ καὶ πάσῃ διαλέκτῳ...).[189] To be sure, there are counterexamples – e.g., Angelicus Kropp's collection of Coptic magical texts contains references to an angelic or divine φωνή that can only be construed in terms of

---

[185] For the philological range, see Chantraine 1968–80:1237–38; O. Betz 1964–76. Φωνή as "language" is described by Betz as "a Gk. concept," in listing the use of the word in translating דברים in Gen 11.1 and לשׁון in Deut 28.49 (O. Betz:290). On φωνή as "language" in Philo and Josephus, see Paul 1987:236. The equivocality of the word is perhaps best matched in English by "utterance": substituting this term for "voice" in the *Ascension of Isaiah* accounts for its otherwise baffling ability to change meanings.

[186] See Dubowchik 2002:293 with n. 94.

[187] Dodd 1935:176 compares *Corp. herm.* 1.26 to Ps 102.21; 148.2. Dodd writes, "This idea ... arose naturally in a period when the cults of various countries, each with its own liturgical language, were being assimilated and synthetized."

[188] See Copenhaver 1992:118. This reading is accepted by Rudolph 1987:187. D. B. Martin (1987:458) is apparently unaware of the textual variant, as he refers to Bentley Layton's rendering of 1.26 (*viz.* with "a sweet voice") as "a different translation" which he "cannot explain".

[189] M. Smith 1986:175. See Behm 1964–76:723.

"voice".[190] These examples are not intended simply to show that φωνή can simply "language", a fact that needs little demonstration, but more precisely that φωνή is often used to denote angeloglossy in particular. When Isaiah's praise is described as becoming like that of the angels, therefore, the reader should perhaps imagine this primarily in terms of a miraculous ability to speak in a heavenly language. The appearance of such a scheme in the *Ascension of Isaiah* finds possible support in the *Testament of Job* (see above), a writing that may come from the same circle: *language* differentiation, in the latter work, seems to be a primary marker of *rank* differentiation among the angels. In the *Ascension of Isaiah*, rank differentiation is clearly the reason for the references to each successive heaven's "praise" being unlike that of the preceding heaven (chaps. 7–8), and yet that same differentiation of "praise" is also applied, just like the differentiation of "voice," in comparing the angels on the right with those on the left, in each of the first five heavens.

Although the evidence of the *Ascension of Isaiah* is neither explicit nor incontrovertible, it cannot be left out of any discussion of possible allusions to angeloglossy. The *Ascension of Isaiah* is an important witness to the continuation of angeloglossy as a concept within Christian writings. It also demonstrates the degree to which the Christian use of this concept can follow the way in which it used in Jewish apocalyptic texts.

F. The *Apocalypse of Abraham*

The *Apocalypse of Abraham* appears to date from the period between the destruction of the Temple in 70 C.E. (related in chap. 27 of that work), and the appearance of the Pseudo-Clementine *Recognitiones* (second or third century C.E.), which seems to allude to the *Apocalypse of Abraham* (*Clem. Recogn.* 1.32). Most scholars assign the text a date in the late first century.[191] The work survives today only in Slavonic manuscripts from the

---

[190] See London MS Or. 6794 (Kropp 1930–1:1.29; 2.104), Rossi Gnostic Tractate (Kropp 1930–1:1.73; 2.186), and the comments in Kropp 1930–1:3.42–3; Goodenough 1953–68:2.166.

[191] E.g., A. Y. Collins 1995:70. The *Apocalypse of Abraham* is divided into two major parts: chaps. 1–8 comprise one version of the well known story of the young Abraham's making sport of his father's idol-selling business – the rest of the book (chaps. 9–32) constitutes a mystical ascent text. Recent scholarship cautions against assuming that the extant work is a compilation of two earlier works (see also the early argument for this view in Box 1918:xxi–xxiv [responding to the view of Ginzberg]; see Rubinkiewicz 1979:139–44), yet this verdict must be nuanced, as at least the core of the story of Abraham and his father's idols was not the invention of our author. (See Philonenko-Sayar

fourteenth century and later, but the Slavonic is evidently based upon a Greek version. A few scholars have speculated that the pseudepigraphon was composed in Hebrew, which would perhaps favor a Palestinian provenance.[192]

In *Apoc. Ab.* 15.2–7, Abraham is taken to the seventh heaven, where he encounters humanlike creatures, crying out in a language unknown to him:

And the angel took me with his right hand and set me on the right wing of the pigeon and he himself sat on the left wing of the turtledove, (both of) which were as if neither slaughtered nor divided. And he carried me up to the edge of the fiery flames. And we ascended as if (carried) by many winds to the heaven that is fixed on the expanses. And I saw on the air to whose height we had ascended a strong light which can not be described. And behold, in this light a fiery Gehenna was enkindled, and a great crowd in the likeness of men. They all were changing in aspect and shape, running and changing form and prostrating themselves and crying aloud words [словесъ; Himmelfarb: "in a language"] I did not know.

Rubinkiewicz's translation does not clearly indicate that the angels spoke an esoteric language: the reference to "words" that Abraham "did not know" could simply refer to his inability to hear them clearly. Alexander Kulik, however, has recently reconstructed the Greek behind the present "semantic calque", finding there the term φωνή, denoting a "special angelic language". This reconstruction leads him to translate 15.7 as "They [= the angels] were shouting in the language the words of which I did not know," listing the *Testament of Job* and 1 Corinthians as conceptual parallels.[193] Himmelfarb's translation (presented above in brackets) essentially agrees with the view of Kulik.

---

and Philonenko 1982:416–17.) Certain details of this story appear already in *Jubilees* and in the works of Philo. See Pennington 1984:363–7.

[192] Rubinkiewicz 1983:685–6 comments that the work "provides us with an insight into the literary 'workshop' of the Palestinian writers of the first century A.D.", but he cautions (1983:681–3) that scholarly investigation of this matter is very incomplete. But Turdeanu 1981:194 speaks confidently of having found giveaway clues in his philological study of the manuscripts: "L'origine macédonienne du texte [of the 'Première Version Méridionale Abrégée'] est apparente surtout dans son vocabulaire". He asserts that the *Apocalypse of Abraham* was translated from Greek to Slavonic, in Macedonia, in the twelfth or thirteenth century (Turdeanu 1981:181). Rubinkiewicz 1983:682–3 dates the Slavonic version to "the eleventh or twelfth century A.D. in the south of the Slavic world, probably in Bulgaria". See Rubinkiewicz 1979. Lunt, however, argues (in Rubinkiewicz 1983:686 n. 25) on philological and text-critical grounds that the date of translation must be prior to 1050. Rubinkiewicz's surprising suggestion (1983:683) that the *Apocalypse of Abraham* may have been "translated directly from Hebrew into Slavonic" is perhaps the reason that Charlesworth commissioned a supplementary account of the work's origins from Lunt, although Rubinstein (1953; 1954) appears to hold the same view as Rubinkiewicz. See now Kulik 2003.

[193] Kulik 2000. I would like to thank Dr. Kulik for sending me his dissertation. See now Kulik 2004.

In chap. 17 of the *Apocalypse of Abraham*, Abraham joins in the angelic worship in heaven:

And while [the angel] was still speaking, behold the fire coming toward us round about, and a voice was in the fire like a voice of many waters, like a voice of the sea in its uproar. And the angel knelt down with me and worshiped. And I wanted to fall face down on the earth. And the place of highness on which we were standing now stopped on high, now rolled down low. And he said, "Only worship, Abraham, and recite the song which I taught you." Since there was no ground to which I could fall prostrate, I only bowed down, and I recited the song which he had taught me. And he said, "Recite without ceasing." And I recited, and he himself recited the song.[194]

The text presents Abraham's act of worship simultaneously as a heartfelt adoration, and as an effectual gesture of approach. Abraham is allowed to witness even higher glories, apparently through his obedience to the angel's instructions.[195] Gershom Scholem judges the *Apocalypse of Abraham* to be the point at which the apocalyptic tradition draws closest to the merkabah tradition of the hekhalot texts, partly on the basis of this account of Abraham's hymning in communion with the angels.[196] Scholem points to Abraham's hymning and notes, "this is quite in harmony with the characteristic outlook of these hymns, whether sung by the angels or by Israel, in which the veneration of God the King blends imperceptibly with the conjuring magic of the adept."[197] Himmelfarb interprets Abraham's hymning with the angels as a status symbol.[198] Like Scholem, Himmelfarb also detects a theurgical element: "[T]he Apocalypse of Abraham treats the song sung by the visionary as part of the means of achieving ascent rather than simply as a sign of having achieved angelic status after ascent."[199] She may be correct in what she says about participation in the angelic liturgy as a status indicator, but the point is not made explicit by the text. The text looks beyond the recognition of whatever status Abraham has achieved, and on to the theurgical effect of his hymning.

---

[194] Trans. Rubinkiewicz 1983:696–7.

[195] On prostration in worship, see Sir 50.19–21; *m. Tamid* 7.3. Prostration following the *Amida* is still practiced in some places today – it is not, as Guillaume (1927:157) thought, "a relic ... now only known from the Talmud". See Goldberg 1957:8–29; Haran 1983:133–4 (with nn. 21–2). Baumstark 1958:75 sees Jewish prostration as the liturgical-historical origin of Christian genuflection.

[196] Scholem 1965:23. See Gruenwald 1980:51–7; Halperin 1988:103–14.

[197] Scholem 1954:61.

[198] According to Himmelfarb 1993:61, the *Apocalypse of Abraham* shares this feature with other works: "[T]he Apocalypse of Abraham has in common with the Apocalypse of Zephaniah, the Ascension of Isaiah, and the Similitudes of Enoch an understanding of heavenly ascent in which the visionary's participation in the angelic liturgy marks his achievement of angelic status."

[199] Himmelfarb 1993:64.

Mary Dean-Otting argues that scholars have been too quick to find a connection between the ascents of the pseudepigrapha and those of merkabah mysticism: "A major difference between the Merkabah type of ascent and that of the pseudepigraphical texts has been overlooked: the Merkabah ascent comes about ... as [a] result of theurgic practicies while the ascents depicted in our literature take the one ascending by surprise."[200] However, while this distinction obtains for most of the works that Gruenwald classified as incipient merkabah speculation (i.e. *1 Enoch*, *2 Enoch*, *Ascension of Isaiah*, and Revelation), one should note that the *Apocalypse of Abraham* does not conform neatly to Dean-Otting's dichotomy between "theurgic practices" and "ascent by surprise": Abraham begins his journey as an ascent by surprise, but in the angelic song episode he takes his first steps in the art of theurgy. This is not to describe the work as a hybrid of two traditions, for the motif of "mystagogy by surprise" is not unknown in the major hekhalot texts. Scholem would appear to be justified in regarding the *Apocalypse of Abraham* as an important milestone on the road to full-blown merkabah mysticism.[201]

Soon after Abraham encounters fiery beings whose language he does not understand, he is instructed to sing a hymn taught to him by an angel. We are not told that Abraham himself ever speaks in an angelic language.[202] After all, if Abraham does not understand the words spoken by the angels in the seventh heaven, yet understands his angelic guide perfectly well, there is little reason for the reader to infer that the angelic hymn was taught to him in some language other than his native language. Yet the evidence is fairly clear that Abraham heard angels speak a language he could not understand. As such, the *Apocalypse of Abraham* represents another important witness to the idea of angeloglossy.

---

[200] Dean-Otting 1984:25. Dean-Otting (1984:27) writes, "we could not really refer to the men ascending as shamans for they lack the theurgic practices of those magicians of flight".

[201] This important qualification does not escape Dean-Otting. Indeed, she drives it home with more than due attention, organizing her entire study as a looking-forward to the history-of-traditions event represented by the *Apocalypse of Abraham*. It is at this point, she writes, that we "stand at the cross-section" between the apocalyptic and merkabah traditions (Dean-Otting 1984:255). She notes, "the theurgic song and the vision of the throne-chariot which it brings about are more than vaguely related to the later Merkabah speculation" (Dean-Otting 1984:255), and "[t]he combination of throne and chariot is ... one more aspect of the ApocAbraham which binds it very closely to the Hekaloth literature" (Dean-Otting 1984:261 n. 65). See Poirier 2004b.

[202] As noted in D. B. Martin 1991:560 n. 24; 1995:267 n. 3; Turner 1998b:247 n. 35.

G. The Rabbinic Evidence (*Gen. Rab.* 74.7)

As we have already seen, the dominant view within rabbinic literature is that the angels speak Hebrew. Passages referring to an esoteric angelic language are accordingly few and far between. In the next chapter, we will examine the tradition of R. Yochanan b. Zakkai's legendary "mastery" of angelic "speech" (*b. B. Bat.* 134a ‖ *b. Sukkah* 28a). In this chapter, we will discuss a possible reference to angeloglossy in the fifth- or sixth-century *Genesis Rabbah*. We read in *Gen. Rab.* 74.7:

ויבא אלהים אל לבן הארמי בחלום הלילה מה בין נביאי ישראל לנביאי אומות העולם, ר'
חמא בר חנינה אמר אין הקב״ה נגלה על נביאי האומות אלא בחצי דיבור היך דאת אמי
ויקר אלהים אל בלעם, אמר ר' יששכר דכפר מנדי: אין הלשון הזה ויקר
אלא לשון טומאה היך דאת אמר מקרה ליל אבל נביאי ישראל בדיבור שלם בלשון קדושה
וחיבה בלשון שמלאכי שרת מקלסין בו וקרא זה אל זה ואמר קדוש קדוש קדוש י״י צבאות
מלא כל הארץ כבודו

And God came to Laban the Aramaean in a night dream (Gen 31.24). What is the difference between the prophets of Israel and the prophets of the nations of the world? R. Hama b. Hanina said, "The Holy One, blessed be he, is not revealed to the prophets of the nations except in half speech, as it says, *And God called* (ויקר, rather than ויקרא) *to Balaam* (Num 23.4)." R. Issachar of Kefar Mandi said, "This is the most rewarding interpretation: ויקר means only the language of uncleanness, as it says, *(a man who will not be clean by) what happens* (מקרה) *at night* (Deut 23.11)." But the prophets of Israel are addressed in full speech, in the language of holiness and honor, in the language in which the ministering angels praise: *And this one called* (וקרא) *to that one and said, 'Holy, holy, holy, is the Lord of hosts. The whole earth is full of his glory'* (Isa 6.3).[203]

---

[203] A note on this passage's structure is in order, since Jacob Neusner's translation (1985:3.80–1) is based upon a misunderstanding in that area. Neusner connects the final sentence (beginning with "But the prophets ...") with the words of R. Issachar of Kefar Mandi, rather than with the words of R. Hama b. Hanina. He signifies this supposed connection in three ways: (1) he does not put a closing quotation mark between R. Issachar's reference to Deut 23.11 and the final sentence, but includes it all under one quotation, (2) he altogether omits to translate בדיבור שלם in the final sentence, a phrase that clearly corresponds to בחצי דיבור in the words of R. Hama b. Hanina, (3) he translates בלשון קדושה וחיבה as "in language of holiness, purity, clarity," thereby importing the notion of purity into a passage that contains no such reference, creating a link to R. Issachar's reference to "language of uncleanness." All of these errors are easily explainable by considering the text of *Lev. Rab.* 1.13 : Neusner's translation of *Gen. Rab.* 74.7 seems to be a mere jumbling of a prior translation of *Leviticus Rabbah*. Neusner's rendering is without warrant in the text of *Genesis Rabbah*, and it hides precisely those features that point to the priority of the *Genesis Rabbah* version. The phrase בדיבור שלם clearly shows that the last sentence continues the view of R. Hama b. Hanina. Happily, this is how Grözinger understands the passage (see below), as he replaces R. Issachar's words with an ellipsis.

Unfortunately, the reappearance of this tradition in *Leviticus Rabbah* complicates things, and it is necessary to say a word or two on the relationship between these two versions. *Lev. Rab.* 1.13 reads:

מה בין נביאי ישראל לנביאי אמות העולם? ר' חמא ברבי חנינה ור' יששכר מכפר מנדו.
ר' חמא ברבי חנינה אמר: אין הקב"ה נגלה על נביאי אמות העולם אלא בחצי דבור,
כמו שאתה אומר: "ויקר אלהים אל־בלעם", אבל נביאי ישראל בדבור שלם, שכתוב:
"ויקרא אל־משה". אמר ר' יששכר מכפר מנדו: כך יהא בשכרם. אין לשון זה "ויקר" אלא
לשון טמאה, כמו שאתה אומר: "כי־יהיה בך איש, אשר לא־יהיה טהור, מקרה־לילה". אבל
נביאי ישראל – בלשון קדשה, בלשון טהרה, בלשון ברור; בלשון, שמלאכי השרת מקלסים
בו, כמו שאתה אומר: "וקרא זה אל־זה ואמר".

What is the difference between the prophets of Israel and the prophets of the nations of the world? R. Hama b. R. Hanina and R. Issachar of Kefar Mandu [have commented]. R. Hama b. R. Hanina said, "The Holy One, blessed be he, is not revealed to the prophets of the nations except in half speech, as it says, *And God called* (ויקר, rather than ויקרא) *to Balaam* (Num 23.4)." But the prophets of Israel are addressed in full speech, as it is written: *And the Lord called* (ויקרא) *to Moses* (Lev 1.1). R. Issachar of Kefar Mandu said, "This is the most rewarding interpretation: ויקר means only the language of uncleanness, as it says, *a man who will not be clean by what happens* (מקרה) *at night* (Deut 23.11)." But the prophets of Israel, in the holy language, in the (ritually) pure language, in the (genetically) pure language, in the language that the ministering angels converse in, as it says, *And this one called* (וקרא) *to that one and said* (Isa 6.3).

Leviticus Rabbah was probably compiled later than *Genesis Rabbah*, but that in itself does not decide the question of priority. The priority issue weighs upon the proper interpretation of these two rabbis' words, as the wording of *Leviticus Rabbah* makes it appear that R. Issachar of Kefar Mandu (Mandi) refers to the language of the ministering angels, and by opposing it to the language of uncleanness (*viz.* the languages of the nations), implies that the angels speak Hebrew.[204] This differs considerably from the wording of *Genesis Rabbah*, in which these words expand upon the quite different view of R. Hama b. Hanina. Fortunately, the difference in the wording of this expansion contains redaction-critical direction indicators. There is little question that the Lev 1.1 prooftext used in *Leviticus Rabbah* corresponds perfectly (both morphologically and literarily) with the Num 23.4 prooftext known to both versions, and on that grounds has a good claim to being original. At the same time, however, the compiler of *Leviticus Rabbah*, seeking to record every (worthy?) rabbinic discussion of Lev 1.1 that he knows, may have forged a connection between Lev 1.1 and the exegetical complex associated with R. Hama b. Hanina, thereby dislodging the Isa 6.3 citation from its original connection with the words of that rabbi. While that scenario is not intrinsically preferrable to the claim that *Leviticus Rabbah* gets it right, there are in fact some redaction-critical direction indicators in its favor. For example, it is more likely that the *Le-*

---

[204] See Visotzky 2003:139.

viticus Rabbah version has added a reference to a ritually pure language (לשון טהרה) in answer to R. Issachar's association of the "language of impurity" (לשון טמאה) with the prophets of the nations than that *Genesis Rabbah* has deleted such a reference: there is no discernible reason for *Genesis Rabbah* to delete it, and plenty of reason for *Leviticus Rabbah* to add it. It is furthermore unlikely that the compiler of the tradition in *Genesis Rabbah* would have failed to see the value in *Leviticus Rabbah*'s use of Zeph 3.9's reference to a genetically (or technically) pure language (בלשון ברור) in connection with angeloglossy (cf. the use of this term in the hekhalot texts, where it describes *nomina barbara*). Interestingly, the version that has the most to gain from the fact that Isaiah's angels speak Hebrew stops short of producing the angels' words, while the version that stands to lose from the angels' words includes them.

It would appear, therefore, that *Gen. Rab.* 74.7 preserves an earlier form of the tradition than *Lev. Rab.* 1.13.[205] It should be noted that Balaam represented a more difficult case to resolve than pagan prophets in general, because the Bible explicitly says that the spirit of God came upon him (Num 24.2; also in LXX Num 23.7), so that denying God's part in Balaam's prophetic inspiration was excluded as an option.[206] According to R. Hama b. Hanina, God speaks to foreign prophets in "half speech," while he speaks to the prophets of Israel in "full speech, in the language of holiness and honor, in which the ministering angels praise."[207] The midrash employs Num 23.4 for a prooftext: "And God ויקר to Balaam." R. Hama b. Hanina reads ויקר as a defective rendering of the root קרא, and accordingly infers, from the notion of a defective rendering, that God speaks to foreign prophets (of whom Balaam is prototypical) in a חצי דיבור, while he speaks to the prophets of Israel in a דיבור שלם.[208] The full, triliteral rendering is preserved when God speaks to Moses (Lev 1.1) and when the angels call to one another (Isa 6.3). Furthermore, in the *Genesis Rabbah* account, R.

---

[205] For those who are not convinced of the priority of the *Genesis Rabbah* version, the following discussion will fail to establish only that R. Hama b. Hanina's view of prophetic inspiration lines up with his view of angelic languages, but it should *not* fail to establish what that view of prophetic inspiration is.

[206] See Vermes 1983:144–5.

[207] On rabbinic views of the prophesying of Gentiles, see *Sipre* 357; *Sipre Zuta* 7.89; Lieberman 1946; Levine 1975:210 n. 253. In Jewish writings from the Islamic centuries, the primary contrast is not between the prophets of Israel and the prophets of other nations, but between Moses and *all* other prophets (most notably in that only Moses heard God without an intermediary). While this contrast had always been present in Jewish tradition, its potential for polemic against the claims of Muhammad's prophethood made it a central idea. See Kreisel 2001.

[208] Basing an argument on a word's defective form was typical of R. Hama b. Hanina. See Editorial staff 1971–72. On rabbinic exegesis based on spelling variations, see Barr 1989:8–10.

Hama b. Hanina's description of the higher form of prophetic inspiration
as involving "the language of holiness and honor" is also true to form for
the interpretation I am suggesting – as Deborah Levine Gera notes, Greek
accounts of the language of the gods typically describe this language as
"perfect, true, accurate, euphonious, or majestic."[209] By contrast, the *Leviticus Rabbah* account looks for all the world like a retrofitting, in which an
original description of a divine language as genetically or technically pure
is turned into a description of a ritually pure language.

Karl Erich Grözinger is one of the few scholars who has given serious
attention to the question of angeloglossy in rabbinic texts, although, as we
will see, he probably did not give enough attention to this text.[210] Grözinger detects certain connections between prophetic speech and angelic singing in rabbinic discussions of the differences between Israelite and foreign
prophets. While discussing *Gen. Rab.* 74.7, he handily translates דיבור שלם
as "Vollform" and חצי דיבור as "Halbform".[211] Unfortunately, he does not
attempt to link the notions of *Halbform* and *Vollform* to the concept of divine language. If he had, he might have recognized a possible allusion to
esoteric angeloglossy within this text. Instead, he concentrates solely on
the possibility of the Israelite prophets' participation in the liturgy, comparing this passage with others in which the prophets are associated with
liturgical singing (e.g., *Song Zuta* 1.1; *Midr. Pss.*:45.6). This comparison is
unfortunate, in my opinion, both because *Midrash Psalms* is a very late
text, and because it is not at all clear that *Genesis Rabbah* is discussing the
same thing as *Shir ha-Shirim Zuta* and *Midrash Psalms*. While the latter
two texts seem to leave the prophets' participation in liturgical singing as a
reference to inspired singing, without indicating the involvement of any
sort of angeloglossy, *Genesis Rabbah* may, in fact, contain a specific allusion to an esoteric divine language. This possibility rests on an explanation
of the concepts of *Halbform* and *Vollform*. After rendering בחצי דיבור as
"halbem Wort," Grözinger inserts "Sprechweise" in parentheses, but it is
open to question whether this represents the correct understanding of the
Halbform/Vollform dichotomy that drives the midrashic device.

Another possible reading of *Gen. Rab.* 74.7 emerges from a consideration of the notion of divine language within the wider Mediterranean religious *milieu*. In attempting to explain the similarity of certain "divine"
words (e.g., those found in Homer's divine toponyms or throughout the
myriad texts of *voces mysticae*) to human words, scholars have suggested

---

[209] Gera 2003:54.

[210] Grözinger 1982:99–107.

[211] Grözinger 1982:100 explains: "Wayyiqqar (Nif.1pf.cons. von qrh) wird hier von
der Wurzel qr' abgeleitet und so als Kurzform, als 'Halbform' empfunden, von den
Engeln dagegen heißt es 'qara' ('Vollform')."

that there is an irreducible difference between the language of heaven and all earthly attempts to copy it.[212] Alfred Heubeck argues that this forms the basis of Homer's divine words.[213] The root notion is not that the heavenly language is necessarily inaccessible, but rather that humans lack the linguistic ability to speak it correctly.[214] In reference to *PGM* 13.763–4, Hans Dieter Betz writes,

> The expression τὸ κρυπτὸν ὄνομα καὶ ἄρρητον is to be interpreted to mean that the name 'cannot be pronounced by a human mouth' (ἐν ἀνθρώπου στόματι λαληθῆναι οὐ δύναται). The implication is, first, that the secret names do not represent human but divine language, and that the human mouth is not capable of articulating them, just as human reason cannot comprehend their meaning.[215]

At first, Betz's understanding seems questionable in view of the fact that the pronunciation of this seven-vowel name is actually attempted, as shown by *PGM* 13.206–9 ("Lord, I imitate [you by saying] the 7 vowels; enter and hear me, A EE Ē Ē Ē IIII OOOOO YYYYY Ō Ō Ō Ō Ō Ō Ō ABR ŌCH BRA ŌCH CHRAMMA ŌCH PROARBATH Ō IA Ō OYAE Ē

---

[212] See Gilbert Hamonic's remarks in Detienne and Hamonic 1995:42–3.

[213] Heubeck 1949–50. See also Hirschle 1979:21–5; Gera 2003:52–3.

[214] In this connection, we must consider the portion of Forbes's thoroughgoing revisionist study of glossolalia that deals with Gnostic or pagan *nomina barbara*. Forbes (1995:153–4) writes, "The magical papyri may be rapidly dismissed, as having no demonstrable link with early Christian glossolalia whatsoever. ... It is true that a number of magical papyri are to be dated to the first century A.D. or earlier, and some of these do contain 'nomina barbara'. It is also true that such magic is deeply traditional, and we could safely presume such early documents even if they were not extant. But these invocations and incantations which make up so much of the magical papyri, are not conceived as language, do not need, or receive interpretation, and neither are they seen as in any sense revelatory. ... Neither are they spontaneous: they are incantations to be recited or inscribed precisely as they are written." This passage is a mixture of invalid reasoning and irrelevant facts. How does Forbes know that the *nomina barbara* "are not conceived as language?" And what does the "need" for "interpretation" have to do with the linguistic nature of *nomina barbara*? If the *nomina barbara* neither receive nor express a need for interpretation, would that not be consistent with the use of uninterpreted glossolalia that Paul confronts in 1 Corinthians 12–14? And how does the question of *spontaneity* impinge upon the glossolalic nature of these words? A glossolalic utterance certainly expresses *something* when first spoken (even if it is unknown to the glossolalist), and it presumably would express the same thing when repeated by rote (*viz.* as *nomina barbara* within a magical recipe). In connection with this last question, Forbes 1995:154 n. 11 quotes T. W. Manson: "The complicated mess of alphabetic permutations and combinations, interlarded with battered relics of divine names, which appears in the papyri, is the product of perverted ingenuity rather than religious ecstasy. It is not glossolalia whatever else it may be." Perhaps, but the pertinent question is whether the *nomina barbara* were *intended* to represent a species of glossolalia in a transcriptional form.

[215] H. D. Betz 1995:163. See Delling 1964–76:671–2.

IOY Ō").[216] Betz explains, however, that the attempt is limited to a crude approximation of the true divine name. His explanation is supported by a number of neoplatonic passages, including Nicomachus of Gerasa's *Harmonikon Enchiridion*:

[T]he tones of the seven spheres, each of which by nature produces a particular sound, are the sources of the nomenclature of the vowels. These are described as unspeakable in themselves and in all their combinations by wise men, since the tone in this context performs a role analogous to that of the monad in number, the point in geometry, and the letter in grammar. However, when they are combined with the materiality of the consonants, just as soul is combined with body, and harmony with strings, (the one producing a creature, the other notes and melodies), they have potencies which are efficacious and perfective of divine things.[217]

Iamblichus writes, "those who first learned the names of the Gods, having mingled them with their own proper tongue, delivered them to us, that we might always preserve immoveable the sacred law of tradition, in a language peculiar and adapted to them" (*Myst.* 7.4).[218] This understanding of language had been developed by Plato (esp. in *Cratylus*),[219] and Philo may be counted as the Jewish representative of this linguistic theory *par excellence* (see esp. his famous interpretation of Exod 20.18 ["they *saw* the voice"] in *Migr.* 47–8).[220]

---

[216] M. Smith 1986:175. Forbes 1995:155 challenges the concept that one must pray to the gods in their language: "Men do not know divine languages, but there is no suggestion at all that the gods do not know those of men!" To the contrary: (1) there *are* traditions that limit the divine beings' (e.g., angels') abilities to understand human languages (such as the claim, found in some rabbinic writings, that the angels do not understand Aramaic), and (2) respecting one's ability to understand and observing the correct gestures of approach are two different things: the need to communicate in the language of the gods arises not from their ignorance of human language, but rather from the propriety and greater utility of the divine language. In other words, *voces mysticae* appear to have invoked divine potencies through their "immediate signification". (On the contrast between "immediate" and "mediated signification," see Assmann 1997:102–3.) On the various concepts bound up in the notion of a divine language, see the four models discussed in Detienne and Hamonic 1995, which is the transcript of a discussion between a moderator and specialists in the traditions of Greece, Vedic India, the Cuna tribe, and Caucasus.

[217] Translation from Shaw 1995:184. For a spectacular example of the invocational power of vowel sequences, and their association with planetary angels, see the so-called "Miletus angel inscription" (3rd–5th cent. C.E.), discussed by Deissmann 1927:453–60 and Arnold 1995:83–5. See Dodds 1951:292–5. Planetary angels also figure prominently in *2 Enoch*. On the *voces mysticae* in the neoplatonists, see the bibliography listed in the discussion of 2 Cor 12.1–4 above.

[218] Trans. T. Taylor 1968:293.

[219] See Kretzman 1971; Levin 1997.

[220] Philo's notion that the "Divine Metalanguage" is strictly a language of names also correlates with the Homeric conception. See Niehoff 1995:221. On the "naming" aspect in Philo's theory of language, see further Winston 1991; Weitzman 1999:39. On "nam-

In light of this understanding of human language as a faltering attempt to approximate the language of heaven, it must be said that the terms חצי דיבור and דיבור שלם make a great deal of sense. God speaks to foreign prophets through the imperfect medium of an earthly language, while he speaks to the prophets of Israel through the perfect medium of the heavenly language. According to this understanding, the contrast between *Halbform* and *Vollform* does not represent the difference between ciphers and plain speech, but rather the difference between human and divine language. The implicit equation between the language by which God reveals himself to the prophets and that in which the angels sing suggests that ecstatic speech may be involved, although there are perhaps other ways of imagining the prophets' encounter with the divine language. Of course, it remains *possible* that חצי דיבור and דיבור שלם refer to ciphers and plain speech, but it is difficult, on that view, to understand how God's revelation to the prophets of Israel is in the language "in which the ministering angels praise." Although the notion might excite some modern purveyors of semiotic theory, surely the midrash could not mean to imply that human speech in general is characterized by ciphers, while angelic speech is transparent.

But might not דיבור שלם simply denote Hebrew and חצי דיבור denote other (human) languages? Not really: R. Issachar's gloss ("This is the most rewarding interpretation: ויקר means only the language of uncleanness [לשון טומאה], as it says, *(a man who will not be clean by) what happens* [מקרה] *at night* [Deut 23.11]") would appear to make that option untenable, as he seems to be offering the gentile-languages scheme as *an alternative* to R. Hama b. Hanina's scheme. Notwithstanding the use of "pure tongue" (לשון טה[ו]רה) in hekhalot writings to denote meaningless combinations of the letters of the Tetragrammaton (cf. *Synopse* §§390, 637),[221] we can hardly take R. Issachar's use of לשון טומאה in a corresponding direction, and *Genesis Rabbah* is not employing לשון קדושה וחיבה and לשון טומאה as purely symmetrical opposites.

There are two further supports for my proposed reading of חצי דיבור and דיבור שלם in *Gen. Rab.* 74.7, which, taken together, permit this pur-

---

ing" in Plato, see Sawyer 1999:112. On the use of names in merkabah mysticism, see Elior 1993:10–12. See also Hahn 1969:9–10.

[221] In Schäfer 1981. Lesses (2007:70) states concerning *Synopse* §637, "The adjuration of the Sar ha-Panim in the Hekhalot texts mentions a special 'language' that the angels understand: the 'language of purity' (*lashon taharah*), or as it is also referred to, 'the language of YHWH' (*lashon YHWH*). In this adjuration, a progressively more powerful series of *voces mysticae* is used to adjure and call upon the Sar ha-Panim to do the will of the adjurer, finally ending with his name itself, which lacks only one letter from the divine name of four letters 'by which He formed and established all and sealed with it all the work of His hands.'"

ported example of esoteric angeloglossy to be placed in the present chapter (*viz.* as representative of "relatively certain cases" of angeloglossy). The first is found in a fascinating passage in a much later midrash, the thirteenth-century Yemenite *Midrash ha-Gadol*. The tradition recorded in *Midrash ha-Gadol* adds an interesting twist to the biblical account of God appointing Aaron as Moses' spokesperson: God tells Moses, "You shall speak in the holy tongue like an angel, and Aaron your brother will speak in the Hebrew language, as it says, *See, I have made you a god* (אלהים) *unto Pharaoh, and Aaron your brother will be your prophet*" (Exod 7.1).[222] Aaron's designation as "prophet" is taken to imply that he interprets words spoken in the angelic language, which, we are told, is *not* Hebrew. The envisioned scheme of the full oracular event, *viz.* that of a "prophet" rendering another functionary's unintelligible utterance in an understandable language, is not unlike that of an earlier (pre-Amandry) understanding of how the Delphic oracle worked.[223] This midrash says nothing about the perfection of the heavenly language or the imperfection of a given earthly language, but in other respects it appears to invoke the same theory of prophetic inspiration that I suggest lies behind *Gen. Rab.* 74.7. Moreover, based on its content, exegetical base, and interpretive method, there is even a possibility that the tradition in *Midrash ha-Gadol* stems from R. Hama b. Hanina himself – in fact, earlier rabbinic texts even represent him deducing a different point from the same verse in Exodus (cf. *Exod. Rab.* 8.2)[224] – although it is impossible to press such possibilities across so great a stretch of time. *Midrash ha-Gadol* contains much older material, much of which may have been preserved in a written form prior to its incorporation into a Yemenite midrash, but it is impossible to date that material on internal grounds alone. For those who are reticent about citing undatable parallels from such late compilations, the passage from *Midrash ha-Gadol* is still

---

[222] Text from Hoffmann 1913:35:

אתה דבר בלשון קדש כמלאך ואהרן אחיך ידבר בלשון עברי שנ' ראה נתתיך אלהים
לפ' ואהרן אחיך יהיה נביאך

Judah Halevi's reference to the giving of the Decalogue through "pure speech" (*Kuzari* 1.87) is too late and enigmatic to be of much help in this context.

[223] If pagan oracles really worked this way (contrary to what most current scholarship thinks), then it would be worth noting that Aaron's designation as a "prophet" could bear a more technical sense of the word.

[224] Cf. also *Exod. Rab.* 21.8. By my count, roughly 40% of R. Hama b. Hanina's prooftexts preserved in the Babylonian Talmud come from Exodus, and the point of most of this 40% appears to be haggadic rather than halakhic (see *b. B. Bat.* 102a, 123b, *b. B. Meṣiʿa* 86b, *b. Ned.* 38a, *b. Šabb.* 10b, 88a, *b. Sotah* 11a, 12a, 12b, 13b, 14a), which suggests that he was known for lecturing on the Exodus narrative. (He is said to have presided over Rabbi Judah's academy shortly after his death [*b. Ketub.* 103a], and perhaps continually lectured on Exodus in that capacity.)

not without value: it at least tells us that such an understanding of the inner workings of prophetic inspiration is, from a strictly conceptual standpoint, eminently possible within rabbinic circles.

The second further support for my reading is found in the presence of this same theory of prophetic inspiration within early Sufism, a movement that spans much of the chronological gap between *Genesis Rabbah* and *Midrash ha-Gadol*. According to David Christie-Murray,

> In earlier times, the Sufi of Islam continued a tradition of God's unintelligible speech. This had originated from the prophet Mohammed's telling that he had heard sounds and confused speech which he understood only after they had ceased, and that it was a great effort for him to pass to the state of logical and intelligible language. The later writers described such speech, and it is possible that their descriptions relate to a practice comparable to tongues, although they specify hearing and translating a speech beyond comprehension, not uttering one.[225]

It is not surprising that Jewish and Islamic thinkers should light upon the same conceptions in their respective theories of prophetic inspiration, and when borrowing from one to the other seems inevitable, it is not easy in many given case to tell which way the borrowing went.[226] Of course, if *Genesis Rabbah* is to be dated to the fifth or sixth century,[227] then the theory of inspiration it attributes to R. Issachar of Kefar Mandi could not be a borrowing from Sufism, all the less so if the idea should be traced back to R. Hama b. Hanina. But the kinship in conceptions can perhaps be explained through a more widespread understanding of how prophetic inspiration worked.

R. Hama b. Hanina's theory of prophetic inspiration appears to represent a rare instance of a Palestinian rabbi espousing an esoteric-language view of angeloglossy. One does not have to assume that R. Hama b. Hanina believes in the angelic mediation of prophecy to infer a connection with angels – he makes the connection himself in appositionally referring to the "full speech" of Israel's prophetic inspiration as "the language of holiness

---

[225] Christie-Murray 1978:10. Unfortunately, Christie-Murray does not give references for these claims. The 14th-century Shams al-Dīn Aḥmad-e Aflākī-ye ʿĀrefī refers to the "language of states" or "of being" (*zabān-e ḥāl*) in at least four of his nine descriptions of famous Islamic holy men (O'Kane 2002:53, 121, 272–3, 362, 478, 557 [§§2.24; 3.89, 90, 329, 511; 4.98; 7.12]). The "language of states" is opposed to the "language of words" in §2.24, but the episode of an ox speaking to Mowlānā in the "language of states" which "the people of ecstatic states (*ahl-e ḥāl*) understand" (§3.90) suggests that it may be an audible phenomenon. This speaking in the "language of states" appears to be one type of "uttering higher meanings" (= prophesying?; cf. §3.89), for which Mowlānā demanded silence from croaking frogs. The phenomenon of "the glorious Koran" damning someone through "the language of its being" (§3.511), however, is difficult to understand on these terms.

[226] See Wolfson 1979.

[227] See Strack and Stemberger 1992:303–5.

and honor" and "the language in which the ministering angels praise". It is thus impossible to take R. Yochanan's view of angelic languages, which I discussed in the preceding chapter, as representative of *every* rabbi (although it is probably fairly representative of the movement as a whole). R. Hama b. Hanina was slightly earlier than R. Yochanan (with some probable overlap), and may represent a body of eclectic, unsystematized beliefs that R. Yochanan's generation successfully effaced,[228] although in this case it survived long enough to make it into a fifth-century midrash.

H. Ephrem Syrus, *Hymn* 11

It is not my intention to treat merely literary echoes of 1 Cor 13.1 as examples of a belief in angeloglossy, but the dividing line between literary echo and a more reflective reemployment of that idea is sometimes difficult to draw. In this connection, we must consider a stanza from a poem by Ephrem Syrus (c. 306–373), "the most important personage in the history of early Syrian Christianity" (Petersen).[229] While the reception history of 1 Cor 13.1 is fairly full, there is reason to think that Ephrem Syrus's reference to angelic languages in his eleventh *Hymn upon the Faith* is more than just a clever refurbishing of Paul's words. We read in stanza 8 of that hymn (according to the newer versification),

Lo! [the] ear [of the deceived] is not able to hear the mighty crash, neither can it hear the still silence; how then shall he hear the voice of the Son or the silence of the Father, when the silence too is vocal? The heavens declare the glory of God. Lo! a silence, the whole whereof muttereth among all languages to all languages! This firmament, lo! it declareth day by day the glory of its Maker. Man is too little to be able to hear all languages, and if he sufficed to hear the tongue of Angels that are spirits, so might he life himself up to hear the silence which speaketh between the Father and the Son. Our tongue is estranged to the voice of beasts; the tongue of Angels is estranged to every [other] tongue. That silence wherewith the Father speaketh with His Well-beloved, is strange unto the Angels.[230]

This passage reads almost like a compromise between the view attributing a single primordial language to God and angels alike, and the view attributing a purely mental means of communication to the heavenly beings. Put in these terms, Ephrem seems to dovetail one view with the other, tak-

---

[228] We should like to know more about the relationship between R. Yochanan's circle and the academy in Sepphoris, where R. Hama b. Hanina purportedly presided.

[229] Petersen 1994:114.

[230] Morris 1897:149–50. P. S. Russell's translation (2000:34) highlights the parallelism of the last two sentences: "The speech of animals is foreign to our tongue. | The speech of angels is foreign to every tongue. | The silence by which the Father speaks to His Beloved is foreign to the angels."

ing his view of divine communication from one, and his view of angelic communication from the other. Yet his scheme differs from other schemes in another important way: Hebrew does not figure anywhere in it.

It might be supposed that the words "Man is too little to be able to hear all languages, and if he sufficed to hear the tongue of Angels that are spirits,..." is an echo of 1 Cor 13.1, but if it is, it has had a different design cast upon it. For one thing, 1 Corinthians 13 refers to *speaking* in angelic languages, while Ephrem's hymn refers merely to *hearing* angelic languages. What is most interesting is that Ephrem presents angelic languages as an intermediary tier between human language and divine communicative silence, and that the difference between our linguisticality and that of the angels is compared with the difference between us and the beasts. This comparison may also imply a corresponding intellectual gap, but that is hardly clear: Ephrem is addressing language, and the angels do not speak the same language(s) as humans.

Paul S. Russell has published a fascinating article on this passage. His approach has the advantage of appealing to a broad and deep interest in divine silence within Ephrem's writings, including a number of applications of the divine silence to the propriety of human silence as an element of piety. Russell writes, "We must not allow ourselves to see Ephraem as an Eastern obscurantist. He *never* argues against the use of speech in theology, only against the *inappropriate* use of speech."[231] This involves recognizing that human speech is capable of praising God, but only to an extent, beyond which true worship consists of silence, as in the high priest's yearly approach to the Holy of Holies (*Hymn* 8.7). According to Russell, "the farther down the ontological scale of existence *any* language is directed, the more fully that language will inherently be able to address the task for which it is intended."[232]

Unfortunately, Russell takes the significance of the divine silence in *Hymn* 11.8 in a direction not supported by Ephrem's own explanation. According to Russell, Ephrem here as well interprets the divine silence as expressing the limitation of our sublunary perspective, and its orientation to a world completely unlike that of the highest heaven. While it is true that the idea that God speaks in silence was widespread, and is especially noticeable in apocalyptic writings of the time, in which the silence of the highest heaven (or innermost sanctuary) is contrasted with the loud praises of the heavenly host throughout the other heavens (or sanctuaries). Of course, such an idea is widespread within sources of the period, but it is not clear that it represents the reason for divine silence in our text. According to Ephrem's own explanation, divine silence, as *communication*, has nothing

---

[231] P. S. Russell 2000:29.
[232] P. S. Russell 2000:31.

to do with the bursting of a given world's grammar of understanding, but rather with a lack of need for God to use nouns and verbs, either in what he "speaks" to his creation, or in what he "hears" from that creation. Russell seems to be confusing two different ideas, that of the ascending mystic's apophatic impasse, and that of God's absolute non-objectifiability (which was interpreted [strangely] within neoplatonic circles as a lack of God's need to use objective references in communication). The latter was famously held much later by Thomas Aquinas and Dante (for whom this mode of communication was angelic), but it could also be found in our period in Augustine (for whom this mode was strictly divine).[233] *Hymn* 11.8 seems to differentiate between the levels of creation according to the rarefaction of their respective languages (in which the use of a subject/object grammar is the coarseness from which "rarefaction" escapes).[234] Thus I cannot follow Russell when he states that "the silence of creatures can be genuinely communicative."[235] He assumes that "silence ... is not obviously differentiated in one instance from another," but it seems clear that we are dealing with two different things: silence as an apophatic lack of an adequate linguistic resource (what Ninian Smart refers to as "going off the top of the word-scale"),[236] and silence as *symbolic* (rather than constitutive) of God's superlinguistic way of communicating. While I agree that "Ephrem's ... mind is [generally] clearly fixed on what he is trying to say more than on how to say it beautifully ... and that he has a completely coherent theological understanding that rests on a foundation that has been carefully considered and constructed,"[237] Ephrem's intellectual rigor is not enough to insure that every block he uses fits perfectly within its context.

An *Encomium* falsely attributed to Gregory of Nyssa, and which served as the source for Simeon Metaphrastes's *Life of Ephrem*, makes an appar-

---

[233] On angelic communicative silence in Aquinas and Dante, see Gera 2003:50. See Aquinas, *Summa Theologiæ*, question 107. See also William of Ockham's words in Freddoso and Kelley 1991:34–8, in which appeal is made to Augustine. See Kobusch 1987:95, 97. Aquinas had his detractors on this subject – see McDannell and Lang 1988:93.

[234] P. S. Russell (2000:35) writes, "The 'speech' of animals and angels mentioned in the quotation from *Hymn* 11 ... should be thought of as foreign languages we humans cannot understand that have varied suitability for discussing elevated topics but are still inherently limited by their nature as languages." While animals and angels do speak in "foreign languages", and Ephrem may explain that fact through the topics they discuss, the point of *Hymn* 11.8 is simply that animals and angels do not speak the same language as God.

[235] P. S. Russell 2000:36.

[236] Smart 1972:29. Cf. Otto 192:203: "[God's] personal character is that side of His nature which is turned manward ... only to be expressed by the suspension of speech and the inspiration of sacred song." But cf. Raphael 1997:162–5.

[237] P. S. Russell 2000:23.

ent reference to his communicating with the angels through silence as a desert hermit:

[Ephrem] despised all worldly things ... fled the world and the things of the world, and, as Scripture says, "he wandered far and dwelt I the desert," heedful of only himself and God and there received a lavish increase in virtue for he knew precisely that the eremitical life would free the one who desired it from the turmoil of the world and would provide silent converse with the angels.[238]

Gregory of Nyssa himself held to a notion of angelic speech as silent communication, but the translators of the above passage insist that its attribution to Gregory is bogus, and others have noted a lack of any demonstrable influence of the Cappadocians on Ephrem.[239] More interesting, perhaps, is the fact that the above *Encomium* attributes to Ephrem's hermit life a mode of conversation belonging to the angels, suggesting that Ephrem achieved the monastic ideal of the *vita angelica*.

Ephrem Syrus is thus an important and independent witness to the idea that angels speak nonhuman languages. While his intensely anti-Jewish theology may have predisposed him against Hebrew-speaking angels, it is significant that he also does not know of Aramaic-speaking angels. While the view he adumbrates could be dependent solely upon 1 Cor 13.1, his use of Paul's concept of angelic languages is anything but empty.

I. The *Book of the Resurrection*
(attributed to Bartholomew the Apostle)

According to Wilhelm Schneemelcher's conjecture, the *Book of the Resurrection of Jesus Christ*, narrated in the voice of the Apostle Bartholomew, goes "back to a special Bartholomew-tradition of the 3rd or 4th centuries."[240] (The antiquity of other Bartholomew works can be established with relative certainty: the *Decretum Gelasianum* [454 C.E.] lists the *Gospel of Bartholomew* among the apocrypha, and Jerome had already alluded to the same work.) Schneemelcher is properly cautious in how he says this: he notes how much of the extant Coptic work is likely to be a later development, and how unsure we must be of its original shape.[241] The original language of this pseudepigraphon is agreed, on all hands, to have been Greek. The Coptic version may have originated two to four centuries

---

[238] (Pseudo-)Gregory of Nyssa, *De Vita S. Patris Ephraem Syri* 832d (trans. Mathews and Amar 1994:14).

[239] See esp. Rompay 1996:628.

[240] Schneemelcher 1963a:508.

[241] See the attempt to assemble the pieces of the Bartholomaic-tradition puzzle in Haase 1915.

later than the conjectured date for the Greek text. Although older works often describe the *Book of the Resurrection* as Gnostic, this judgment appears to have been based on a few minor features (e.g., injunctions to secrecy, the use of white garments) that are more indicative of the work's general tenor than of its relation to Gnosticism. M. R. James has summarized the more intentional aspects of the work's character well: "This writing may be better described as a rhapsody than a narrative. ... The interest of the author is centred in the hymns, blessings, salutations, and prayers, ... which occupy a large part of the original text."[242]

The full Coptic text was first published, along with a translation, by E. A. Wallis Budge, in 1913, although W. E. Crum's translation had been made available earlier (without the Coptic text) as a part of Robert de Rustafjaell's *The Light of Egypt from Recently Discovered Predynastic and Early Christian Records* (1909).[243] Matthias Westerhoff published a new bi-recensional edition (with translation and commentary) in 1999.[244] Wallis Budge's text was taken from a manuscript in the British Museum (London MS Or. 6804), which give a nearly complete copy of the text (missing five leaves at the beginning). This manuscript had been acquired by Rustafjaell from an antiquities dealer in Egypt, and the exact origin of the writing cannot be determined, although it is purported to have been held by the library of the White Monastery near Achmim. In a letter from Crum to Rustafjaell (quoted by the latter), it is noted that the monastery would have acquired some of its holdings from other churches, making it even riskier to attribute the text to scribes from that area. According to Wallis Budge, the manuscript dates "probably" from the tenth or eleventh century, but James, following the verdict of Crum, states that it "is assigned to the twelfth century."[245] The colophon pins it to the church in "Illarte," but that place name is a mystery. Portions of the *Book of the Resurrection*, extant in various fragments kept in Paris and Berlin, had been published earlier.[246] Westerhoff dates the original text to the eighth or ninth century.[247] Given

---

[242] M. R. James 1924:186.

[243] Crum 1909; Wallis Budge 1913:1–48 (Coptic text of MS 6804), 179–215 (translation of MS 6804 and other fragments). Wallis Budge apparently had published a facsimile edition earlier, almost immediately on the British Museum's reception of the manuscript (as mentioned by Rustafjaell). M. R. James (1924:181–6) published a translation of select passages, which is not at all helpful for the discussion at hand.

[244] Westerhoff 1999. See Schenke 2001.

[245] Wallis Budge 1913:vi; M. R. James 1924:186.

[246] The London, Paris, and Berlin texts represent three separate recensions. See the overviews in Wallis Budge 1913:xv–xvii; M. R. James 1924:181–2; Schneemelcher 1963a.

[247] Westerhoff 1999:226–7.

such a late date, some readers might wish to classify this text as part of the post-history of the developments discussed in this book.

In the notes to his translation of the *Testament of Job*, Spittler notes, more than once, similarities within certain isolated ingredients between the *Testament of Job* and the *Book of the Resurrection*. Some of these similarities are particularly interesting: Spittler has provided a series of shared ideas, all involving the same hymn from Elihu in the *Testament of Job*.[248] He wisely avoids trying to account for these similarities through direct literary dependence: "both hymns must arise from the same literary stock, the roots of which reach through Job 18 LXX as far back as the 'mocking dirges' in Isa 14 and Ezek 28."[249] For our purposes, another shared feature of these two texts is more significant, that of "virgins" singing in the language of the cherubim. But even in this, a comparison reveals a great difference: the "virgins" in the *Book of the Resurrection* are representative of an angelic order. (See below.) Other surface similarities can also be noted, but nothing strong enough to suggest direct literary dependence. At most, there is a sharing of a general *milieu*.

At several places in the *Book of the Resurrection*, we read of the angels singing in their own language. From the end of the fifth folio, to the second half of the sixth, we read of an exchange between Mary and Philogenes the gardener ("Philoges" in the Paris fragments), concerning what transpired after Jesus' body was placed in the tomb. Philogenes is speaking:

Now in the middle of the night I rose up, and I went to the door of the tomb of my Lord, and I found all the armies of the angelic host drawn up there. ... And there was a great chariot standing there, and it was formed of fire [which sent forth bright flames]. And there were also there twelve [Virgins, who stood upon the fiery chariot], and they were singing hymns in the language of the Cherubim, who all made answer unto them, "Amen. Hallelujah!"[250]

---

[248] The list of parallels in Spittler 1983:862 n. d is as follows: *T. Job* 43.5: "Elihu ... will have no memorial among the living" || *Book of the Resurrection*: "Judas' inheritance has been taken away from among the living"; *T. Job* 43.5: "his quenched lamp lost its luster" || *Book of the Resurrection*: "the light departed and left him, and darkness came upon him"; *T. Job* 43.7: "His kingdom is gone, his throne is rotted, and the honor of his tent lies in Hades" || *Book of the Resurrection*: "his crown has been snatched away ... the worm has inherited his substance ... his house hath been left a desert"; *T. Job* 43.8: "He loved the beauty of the snake and the scales of the dragon. Its venom and poison shall be his food" || *Book of the Resurrection*: "His mouth was filled with thirty snakes so that they might devour him." (Spittler uses the translation of the *Book of the Resurrection* in Wallis Budge 1913. The translation of the *Testament of Job* is Spittler's own.) See also Westerhoff 1999:83 n. 9, 85 n. 1, 293.

[249] Spittler 1983:862 n. d.

[250] Trans. Wallis Budge 1913:188–9.

The purported reference to twelve "virgins" singing hymns in the language of the Cherubim falls at the bottom of folio 6a and at the top of folio 6b, making reading the text of MS 6804 difficult. Crum's translation therefore contains more ellipses at this point. Wallis Budge, however, restores the text (as above) with help from fragments belonging to the Bibliothèque Nationale in Paris.[251] The plausibility of restoring the word "Virgins" is also supported by a later passage in MS 6804: folio 11b clearly refers to "the Powers and the Virgins" singing to Eve "in the celestial language" (see below). There are also other points of difference between Crum and Wallis Budge: the former questioningly suggests that the unidentified group sang in the language "of the Seraphim," rather than "of the Cherubim," but the latter again has the benefit of the Paris fragments for his restoration.[252] "Virgins" apparently denotes an angelic order: the fourth rank of heavenly beings seen by Philogenes (in addition to cherubim, seraphim, and powers) consists of 30,000 "Virgins" (folio 6a). This is an interesting variation on the creation of angelic orders in the image of church offices, perhaps following upon the example of the twenty-four elders in Revelation 5 (who may or may not be angelic).

When Philogenes finished relating his vision, Christ appeared in their midst, and spoke to Mary in the heavenly language:

> And the Saviour appeared in their presence mounted upon the chariot of the Father of the Universe, and He cried out in the language of His Godhead, saying, 'MARI KHAR MARIATH,' whereof the interpretation is, 'Mary, the mother of the Son of God.' Then Mary, who knew the interpretation of the words, said, HRAMBOUNE KATHIATHARI MIÔTH,' whereof the interpretation is, 'The Son of the Almighty, and the Master, and my Son.'[253]

We cannot know for sure whether "the language of the cherubim" and "the language of his Godhead" are the same: in other texts, we have seen examples of different angelic orders apparently speaking different languages. The hints that the angelic language(s) mentioned in this text may correspond to glossolalia appear to be stronger than in most other texts (see below, in connection with Jesus' ascension): it would be interesting (but difficult) to learn whether the belief in such a correspondence had the effect of homogenizing the celestial languages, or whether the glossolalist was imagined to speak a number of celestial languages.

On folio 11b (within the "third hymn of the angels"), following a description of Adam's glorious appearance, we read that "Eve herself was adorned with the adornments of the Holy Spirit, and the Powers and the

---

[251] See Wallis Budge 1913:219–21.

[252] Crum 1909:116. On the angelic orders in the *Book of the Resurrection*, see Westerhoff 1999:262–4.

[253] Trans. Wallis Budge 1913:189.

Virgins sang hymns to her in the celestial language, calling her 'Zôê', the mother of all the living."[254] Here the retention of the Greek word for "life" may simply be a matter of the Coptic translator's understanding, so that "Zôê" need not be taken as a pronouncement of angeloglossic speech (although it is not impossible that "Zôê" had been part of a stream of *nomina barbara*). The reference to "adornments of the Holy Spirit" is reminiscent of the *Testament of Job*'s reference to "the Spirit" being inscribed on Hemera's garment (see above), but there is a crucial difference: in the *Testament of Job*, the one wearing a "Spirit garment" sings in a celestial language, while the one wearing "Holy Spirit adornments" in the *Book of the Resurrection* has hymns *sung to her* in the celestial language.[255]

On folio 14b, we read of Jesus speaking in an unknown tongue immediately before his ascension:

When the Saviour took us up on the Mount [of Olive], the Saviour spake unto us [in a language] which we did not understand, but straightway He revealed it unto us. [He said unto us . . . .] ATHARATH THAURATH. And [straightway] the Seven Firmaments [were opened] . . . . our bodies . . . . . . saw, and we looked and we' saw our Saviour. His body was going up into the heavens, and His feet were firmly fixed upon the mountain with us.[256]

The central significance of this passage perhaps lies in its connection with the power to bestow the Holy Spirit: at the top of folio 15a, after a break of five lines, we read,

[He who is ordained by any authority save] that of thy hand and thy throne [shall be repulsed and shall not prosper]. Thy [breath shall be filled] with My breath, and with the breath of [My Son], and with the breath of the Holy spirit, so that every man whom thou shalt baptize . . . . shall receive a portion of the Holy Spirit, in [the Name of] the Father, and the Son, and the Holy Spirit.' Then the Cherubim, [and the Seraphim], and the Archangels, and [all] the angels answered [and said, 'Amen. Hallelujah.']>[257]

The giving of the Holy Spirit through breathing recalls the Johannine narrative (see John 20.22), while the delay in bestowing the Holy Spirit

---

[254] Trans. Wallis Budge 1913:197.

[255] Immediately before Eve is introduced, we are told that "the Name[s] of the Father, and the Son, and the Holy Spirit were written" upon Adam's body "in seven [symbolic signs?]" (trans. Wallis Budge 1913:197). On angeloglossic singing in the *Book of the Resurrection*, see Westerhoff 1999:246–8.

[256] Trans. Wallis Budge 1913:202. In the Paris fragments, only one word in the heavenly language is written: "Anetharath." See Wallis Budge 1913:228.

[257] Trans. Wallis Budge 1913:202. I have removed a single bracket from the translation, as Wallis Budge places a left bracket before "Then the Cherubim" (with no corresponding right bracket anywhere). "Cherubim" is a certain reading in the Coptic text. (See Wallis Budge 1913:29.)

until after the ascension recalls the Lukan narrative.[258] At any rate, Jesus' last words are spoken in a strange language, which at once strikes a common note from within the text (the theme of a celestial language), and a common note from the ascension/Pentecost narrative in the New Testament (the disciples' speaking in "other tongues"). By incorporating the celestial language at this point in the narrative, the author of the *Book of the Resurrection* strongly hints that glossolalia is nothing other than angeloglossy. The promise that "every man whom thou shalt baptize ... shall receive a portion of the Holy Spirit" may suggest the continued existence of glossolalia within the circles that first used this text.

Even considering the earliest possible date for its composition, the *Book of the Resurrection* represents the latest classical Christian work whose reference to angeloglossy can be considered "certain" or "likely". (See the chart below.) It is nevertheless an important witness, not least because it represents a monastic *milieu* more clearly than the other works.

J. Conclusion

The works discussed above all contain relatively certain references to the idea of an esoteric angelic language. The phenomenon is found in both Christian and Jewish texts (certainly Christian: 1–2 Corinthians, *Book of the Resurrection*, Ephrem's *Hymn* 11, and the *Ascension of Isaiah*; probably Jewish: *Testament of Job*, *Apocalypse of Zephaniah*, and *Apocalypse of Abraham*; certainly Jewish: *Genesis Rabbah*), and it appears in both pseudepigraphic and non-pseudepigraphic works. The references in some of the works are more sustained and spectacular than in others. I regard the references to angeloglossy in 1 Cor 13.1, the *Book of the Resurrection*, Ephrem's *Hymn* 11, the *Testament of Job*, and the *Apocalypse of Zephaniah* as certain, but I regard those in 2 Cor 12.1–7, the *Ascension of Isaiah*, the *Apocalypse of Abraham*, and *Genesis Rabbah* as merely likely, but *more* likely than the references discussed in the next chapter. It should be noted that these texts differ from one another in a number of ways in their basic presentation of angeloglossy. Some of these texts envision humans participating in angelic speech (1 Cor 13.1 [hypothetically only?], *Ascension of Isaiah*, *Testament of Job*, and *Apocalypse of Zephaniah*), while others confine the phenomenon to angels (2 Cor 12.1–7, Ephrem's *Hymn* 11, and *Genesis Rabbah*), and still others are unclear as to whether the phenomenon extends to humans (*Book of the Resurrection* and *Apocalypse of Abraham*).

---

[258] On the echoes of the canonical gospel tradition in the *Book of the Resurrection*, see Haase 1915:103.

In the next chapter, I discuss a number of additional works that may refer to angeloglossy. But whereas the works discussed above are judged to be either "certain" or "likely" references to angeloglossy, the references discussed in the next chapter are all listed as merely (but eminently) "possible". Although we cannot speak about these works with as much confidence as the works we have already discussed, we cannot leave them out altogether.

Chapter 5

The Esoteric Heavenly Language Continued:
Less Certain Cases

The cases that we examined in the preceding chapter represent fairly certain references to the esoteric nature of angelic languages. There remain a few less certain references. These include the Qumran *Songs of the Sabbath Sacrifice*, R. Yochanan b. Zakkai's legendary mastery of the "conversation" of angels, demons, and palm trees (*b. B. Bat.* 134a ‖ *b. Sukkah* 28a), the fourth-century Nanas inscription (from Kotiaeion, Asia Minor), and the Christian liturgical jubilus. This chapter will examine these four cases.

A. The Qumran *Songs of the Sabbath Sacrifice*

Before discussing possible references to an esoteric angelic language in the *Songs of the Sabbath Sacrifice*, we should devote a little space to the question of whether the Qumran community participated in glossolalic speech. The majority of Qumran scholars probably do not take such a suggestion seriously, but the fact that more than a handful of scholars have cautiously suggested such a scenario calls for a brief discussion. The main support for a glossolalic Qumran community is found in the attention that the scrolls give to Isa 28.11–13, a text that the early church interpreted as a reference to glossolalia. This has also been supported by reference to the intensity of the Qumranic expressions of piety, an intensity that some believe suggests the type of religious enthusiasm that often typifies glossolalic communities.[1] Roy Harrisville, attempting to reconstruct the readings of Isa 28.11–

---

[1] The Qumran texts are filled with just the sort of imminent angelology and towering boundary markers that elsewhere typify glossolalic conventicles. Cf. Sheres and Blau 1995:84: "But the angels' speech [in the *Songs of the Sabbath Sacrifice*] is not recorded. Why do we not hear what they are saying? One commentator has suggested that the big difference between the 'tongues of men and of angels' rendered their idiom unintelligible. Perhaps also, at such auspicious moments the sectarians themselves spoke in tongues (an ecstatic incomprehensible language), a chanting that would drown out what was going on. The sectarians' taste for the esoteric is evident elsewhere in their use of magical incantations written backwards and in circles." Dale Allison (see below) is the "one commentator" to whom Sheres and Blau refer.

13 available to the Apostle Paul, writes of the sect's "preoccupation" with that passage.[2] Although it is for him a side issue, Harrisville tentatively suggests that Qumran might have "furnished an atmosphere congenial to the emergence of the technical terms" related to glossolalia.[3]

Harrisville's suggestion that glossolalia stands behind the Qumranic use of Isa 28.11–13 has not been well received within scholarship, especially because the form of this passage found in 1QH 2.18 and 4.16 is much closer to the septuagintal wording (directed against false prophets) than it is to the proto-Aquilanic wording that provided the prooftextual support for Paul's discussion.[4] William Schniedewind has recently suggested a more efficient interpretation of Isa 28.10–14 within Qumran ideology. He writes that the term קו (Isaiah:28.10) held a special significance for the Qumranites, as it signified *true revelation* (cf. esp. Ps 19.2–5), in contradistinction to the teachings of nonsectarians, within the Qumranic theology of the Word: "Apparently, Qumranites interpreted Isa 28.10 in two parts, with *Qav* being the divine word and *Tzav*, false precepts. The use of this particular code terminology ... underscores the importance of Isaiah 28 to the Qumran linguistic ideology."[5] The scope of Schniedewind's reconstruction of the Qumranic "relexicalization" of קו (esp. in 1QH) is impressive, and his argument can perhaps be strengthened by noting extra-Qumranic evidence for a (sometimes) nationalistic valuation of Hebrew, such as the prohibition of gentile languages in the eighteen items transmitted in a baraita attributed to R. Shimon b. Yohai.[6] Whether or not one accepts all of Schniedewind's reconstruction of the Qumranic meaning of קו, or his anth-

---

[2] Harrisville 1976:42. See O. Betz 1968. For a review of Isa 28.11 in Qumranic, Targumic, and New Testament texts, see Maly 1967:229–36. In connection with approaches that look for terminological parity between Paul's discussion of glossolalia and the discussion of praise in the *Hodayot*, mention should be made of the comparison between Pauline prayer "with the spirit" (1 Cor 14.14–15) and divine preordination of the hymnist's praise in 1QH 11.5–7 in Flusser 1965:251. Flusser stops short of suggesting that the Qumranites spoke glossolalically. Forbes (1995:46) writes that Harrisville's "if" (in his statement "if something akin to glossolalia was practised in Jewish circles") is "a very large one indeed". Unaware of Allison 1988 (see below), he writes, "I know of no suggestion that glossolalia was practised at Qumran, nor any evidence that might suggest it" (Forbes 1995:46).

[3] Harrisville 1976:45. S. E. Johnson 1957:131 denies that there was glossolalia at Qumran.

[4] See Theissen 1983:290 n. 58.

[5] Schniedewind 2000:249–50. צו is used as a technical term for a false preacher in CD – see Watson 2004:109–10.

[6] *y. Šabb.* 1.3c. Tomson (1990:174 n. 134) writes, in connection with this baraita, that a "prohibition of 'non-Jewish' languages is difficult to imagine in actual life (Aramaic, like Greek, being spoken by many Jews including Sages) but reflects general resentment". Perhaps so, but such a prohibition presumably could have been actualized at a commune like Qumran.

ropological interpretation of the Qumranites' Hebrew ideology, the most readily acceptable aspects of his discussion of Isa 28.10–14 appear to exhaust the significance of that passage for Qumran. Despite the glossolalic associations that this passage has for early Christianity, we will have to look elsewhere for evidence of Qumran angeloglossy/glossolalia.

Dale C. Allison, asking why the *Songs of the Sabbath Sacrifice* never discloses the specific content of the angels' praise, lists the view that the angels spoke in esoteric language as one possibility among several.[7] According to Allison, certain features of the Qumran description of the angelic realm may imply the existence of an esoteric angelic language:

> Admittedly, *4QShirot 'Olat Ha-Shabbat* nowhere unambiguously or explicitly states that the praise of angels is made in an otherworldly tongue. Yet the several references to "wondrous words" or "songs" *might* be so understood; and *4Q403*, frag. 1, col. i, 36 mentions "the tongue of all [godlike beings] who chant with knowledge." These words could very well advert to the special language of those in heaven. For this reason one cannot exclude the possibility that the angelic blessings and chants find no place in the Sabbath songs because their idiom would be unintelligible.[8]

These words from Allison will concern us below, but I quote them here because he builds on them in order to add another possible scenario, one he calls a "bit more speculative": "the Qumran sectarians may have spoken 'in tongues,' that is, in inspired, incomprehensible ecstatic utterance."[9] Allison mentions this last scenario simply in order to have all the options on the table. Philip Alexander responds in the expected manner: "there is no hard evidence that the Qumranites subscribed to the idea that the angels spoke a special angelic language. They could just as easily have held that Hebrew, the 'holy tongue', is the language of heaven."[10]

In the end, Allison argues that the common association of silence with the most holy precincts explains the silence of the angels.[11] It is worth noting that the scenario that he counts as most likely is actually the *least* likely of those that he names, as it is hard to imagine that the angels worshipped in silence if the text continually refers to the "psalm of praise in/by [?] the tongue of the *n*th chief prince," to the regular recitation of "seven wonderful words," and to the fact that each chief angel's praise is repeated seven times louder by the succeeding angel. It is not surprising

---

[7] Allison 1988. See Schwemer 1991:97–9. Newsom 1999:11 suggests that the *Songs of the Sabbath Sacrifice* may contain an implicit "polemical rejection ... of the speculations of those who set the Qedushah at the center of their recitation of angelic song".

[8] Allison 1988:190–1.

[9] Allison 1988:191–2.

[10] Alexander 2006:113. In Allison's defense, it should be pointed out that he is fully aware of where "hard evidence" is lacking.

[11] On silence as worship, see Kaufmann 1927:2.476–7; Potin 1971:1.187; Wilcox 1991:241–4; Knohl 1995:148–52; 1996; Wick 1998.

that others posing the same question as Allison should think in terms of an esoteric angelic language. Although she does not mention angeloglossy in particular, Esther G. Chazon is not far off from this interpretation when she writes that the "qualitative distinction ... drawn [in 4Q400 2.1–8] between angelic praise and human praise ... may provide a clue to the *Shirot*'s puzzling omission of the angels' words in general, and of the *trishagion* (Isa 6:3) and the blessing of God's glory (Ezek 3:12) in particular. ... Human inadequacy rather than angelic silence appears to be the reason for the omission of the angels' precise words."[12] But here we must beware of asking a question ill-suited to the text, and we should first ask whether the silence of the angels is even hermeneutically significant. In this regard, Carol Newsom plausibly suggests that the omission of the angels' words results from the angels themselves (rather than God) being the true focus of the text.[13]

In addition to the occasional argument that the Qumranites themselves spoke in tongues, one also encounters the argument that they made sport of other groups who spoke in tongues. Thus Martin Hengel suggests that the Qumranites directed their reference to Isa 28.10 against glossolalic activity

---

[12] Chazon 2000:99–101.

[13] Newsom 1985:16. Elior 1993:27 refers to a similar shift from emphasis upon God within Hekhalot literature: "The Hekhalot traditions reflect a transition from a religious conception focused on God to a worldview centered on the Merkabah." It should be noted, however, that there is no paucity of angelic words in the Hekhalot texts. Fletcher-Louis (1998:372) suggests, in support of his contention that the "angels" within the text are really the angelified Qumran community, that the omission of the angels' words "is readily explicable if those words were well known to the Qumran sectarians. We know from a passage in Josephus (*A.J.* XX.216–18) that the temple singers could recite by heart the psalms for the daily liturgy. ... The *Songs* are a conductor's or a lead chorister's score. His call for angelic worship is met by the response of the community members themselves." The most immediate problems with this interpretation are found in carrying it to what is subsequently said about the chief princes' praise: this involves separating their "seven wonderful words" from the merkabah-mystical tradition of hearing heavenly *voces mysticae* that are illegal to repeat, and it is difficult to imagine how the sevenfold volumizing of each angels' praise by a succeeding angel is actually accomplished if the "angels" are really humans. There are also more general problems with Fletcher-Louis's overall interpretation of the *Songs of the Sabbath Sacrifice*: to note only one of the more strained claims, he writes that the notion of angels purifying themselves in 4Q400 1.1.15 could not possibly refer to suprahuman angels: "I do not know of any instances of angels being sanctified, much less angels sanctifying themselves" (Fletcher-Louis 1998:377). Although the classic merkabah texts are centuries later than the texts that Fletcher-Louis discusses, it should be pointed out that they prominently portray the angels purifying themselves (e.g., *Synopse* §§54; 180–1; 196; *Sefer ha-Razim*, level 4, lines 6–7 [see Margalioth 1966:96; Morgan 1983:67; Rebiger and Schäfer 2009:70*–71*], *Visions of Ezekiel* 65–6 [Gruenwald 1972:126; see Halperin 1988:267]), which would seem to unsettle Fletcher-Louis's case to some degree. See Elior 1993:47.

among the *Pharisees*, and offers, as a parallel to this, Hippolytus' reference to the Naasenes' use of Isa 28.10.[14] Hengel's view echoes that of
Isaiah Sonne, except that the latter thinks that the Gnostic sect mentioned
by Hippolytus is itself the target of the Qumranic polemic.[15] It is interesting to note that this view turns on the same piece of Qumranic biblical exegesis as that of Harrisville and company, but that the argument is different. Whereas Harrisville considers an implicit continuity between the use
of Isaiah 28 at Qumran and in Paul's letters, Hengel and Sonne refer to an
element not found in Paul, *viz.* the apparently nonsensical phrases in Isa
28.10. This biblical passage apparently had a fascinating career, but I am
unable to find any continuity between its use at Qumran and in Paul, while
the similarity between Qumran and the Naasenes is likely to be coinciden-
tal, especially since the reinterpretation in both cases amounts to a simple
pesher-like adjustment of the object of critique.

---

[14] Hengel (1996:20) writes, "[I]n CD 4.18ff. there is a sharp polemic against the
'builders of the wall' who 'follow after' a false prophet bearing the 'cover-name' of *Zaw*,
taken from Is 28.10,13 ... who falsifies the law as a deceiving 'preacher'. ... There are
good reasons for the supposition of A. S. van der Woude and R. Meyer that these opponents were the Pharisees." Hengel was preceded in some of his judgments by Teicher
1953:10–11. Teicher's formulation of the matter is full of uncontrolled speculation and
bizarre reasoning: he even infers from the lack of any mention of glossolalia and prophecy in 1QS that these two charisms were not pre-Pauline phenomena within the church.
(Two years earlier, Teicher [1951:93–94] had argued that the Qumran scrolls represented
the library of Ebionites, and had been placed in hiding seeking to foil Diocletian's book
burning.) On Hippolytus' reference to the Naasenes' use of Isa 28.10, cf. Layton
1987:424 n. m: "St. Hippolytus, writing in Rome A.D. ca. 222–35, reports in *Against
Heresies* 5.8.4, that a gnostic-like sect named the Naasenes spoke of Adamas, the prototypical human being (cf. [*Apocryphon of John*] 8:28f) as 'Kaulakau'; of earthly Adam as
'Saulasau'; and of the river that flows from earth back to the spiritual realm as 'Zeēsar.'
These three esoteric names ultimately correspond to Hebrew phrases occurring in Is
28:10: 'Therefore the word of the Lord will be to them precept upon precept (*tsau la-
tsau*), precept upon precept, line upon line (*kau la-lau*) [*sic*], line upon line, here a little
(*zᵃ'ir šam*), there a little'."

[15] Sonne 1950–1:302–3 writes, "A reference to the same passage from Isaiah with the
same polemical import is to be found, I surmise, in the *Damascus Document*, ed. Schechter, p. 4, line 19: אחרי צו הצו הוא המטיף המטיף אשר הכלו. The editor in his translation (p.
xxxvi: ... who walked after the commandng one. – The commanding one etc.) separating
צו from הצו missed the allusion to Isa. 28.10, 13: צו לצו קו לקו. These words, according
to Jerome in his commentary, were used by certain heretics as *glossalalia* [*sic*] to impress
the populace. Those heretics may be identified with the Gnostic sect worshipping Jesus
under the name *caulacau* which is but the Hebrew קו לקו (see Philastrius, *De Haeresi-
bus*, 33, and Alb. Fabricius' notes). The passage in the *Damascus Document* seems to be
directed against the *caulacau* sect. The correct translation should read: ... 'who followed
the prophet of (צו לצו) צו לצו,' i.e. *caulacau*." It is instructive to note that the Isaiah
Targum redirects Isa 28.1–13 (along with 5.1–7 and 22.20–5) against first-century
priests. See Chilton 1983:20–3.

In light of the above, the notion that there was glossolalia at Qumran should probably be dismissed. It does not necessarily follow, however, that the Qumran scrolls are not open to the idea that the angels spoke an esoteric language. This, in fact, is the view of a few scholars discussing the *Songs of the Sabbath Sacrifice*.

On the basis of the breadth of the Qumran library, we should perhaps not be surprised that texts witnessing to the notion of human-angelic communion should be found there. What we find in the way of Qumranic witnesses to this idea, however, is much more impressive than what we find in a representative cross section of other Second Temple Jewish writings. Communion with angels was evidently a very important idea at Qumran.[16] The *Damascus Document* (CD), *Community Rule* (1QS), the *Hodayot* (1QH), the *War Scroll* (1QM) and the *Songs of the Sabbath Sacrifice* (4Q400–7; 11Q17; MasShirShabb) are all replete with the notion of righteous humans communing with the angels.[17] As Jacob Licht notes, the motif is used to support the sectarianism of Qumran: "The companionship of the angels is claimed *through* membership of the sect."[18]

The writing that concerns us most is a thirteen-week liturgy called the *Songs of the Sabbath Sacrifice*. It is extant in hands dating from the late-Hasmonean period (i.e., from 75 B.C.E.) to the end of the Qumran era (ca. 68 C.E.). Carol Newsom, the original editor, argues that it was used only for the first quarter of the liturgical year, and her view has been accepted by many scholars,[19] but David K. Falk suggests that it was repeated

---

[16] Although I accept the dominant view that the Qumranites were Essenes, I refer to them here only as Qumranites. The question of their Essene identity does not affect my discussion.

[17] Nitzan 1994a:166–8 offers a helpful division of the basic schemes of human-angelic communion: a scheme typically corresponds to the (1) the *cosmological approach*: human and angelic praise of God is included within the praises of all creation, (2) the *celestial approach*: the heavenly liturgy proceeds at a level totally off-limits to human participation, or (3) the *communionist approach*: humans and angels praise God together in liturgical communion (also in Nitzan 1994b:273–6). After a careful consideration of the relevant texts, Nitzan concludes that the *Songs of the Sabbath Sacrifice* reflects a *mystical* understanding of the communion of humans and angels. Nitzan's threefold division is further developed by Chazon 2003, who gives examples of each from the Qumran scrolls. See also Chazon 2000. Caquot 1988:424 writes on the "inherent gulf" between humans and angels: "Mais cette communion espérée ou anticipée de façon mystique n'est pas une assimilation. Il reste une distance entre les êtres célestes qui servent Dieu dans ses palais et les créatures de chair et de sang que Dieu a élues pour le servir sur terre." See also Tantlevskij 1997; Regev 2007:359–61, 368–73.

[18] Licht 1956:101. See B. P. Kittel 1980:79–80; Schäfer 1975:36–40. Reif (1993:51) writes, "the members of [the Qumran] sect looked upon their liturgies as reflections of the angelological variety".

[19] Newsom 1985:5, 9. Against Newsom, see Maier 1992:544; J. J. Collins 1997a:136–37. Newsom's study brought to light a number of important manuscripts whose contents

throughout the year, which could explain why no separate liturgy survives for the other thirty-nine weeks of the year.[20] Angels are depicted throughout the *Songs of the Sabbath Sacrifice* offering their sacrifices of praise to God, and their activities are described in cultic terms.[21] The participation of angels in the Qumran cult perhaps suggests a heavenly *imprimatur* upon the worship apparatus at Qumran, or upon the Qumran community itself.[22]

Who wrote the *Songs of the Sabbath Sacrifice*? The Qumran find consists of texts composed both at Qumran and elsewhere, so one cannot simply assume that a given text found there reflects the religious genius of the Qumran community.[23] The provenance of the *Songs of the Sabbath Sacrifice* is currently a matter of intense debate. Newsom, who once argued in favor of the Qumran authorship of this text, now doubts that position, as do Esther G. Chazon and James Davila.[24] The fact that a copy of this text was found at Masada suggests to some scholars that it may have circulated in various Palestinian circles.[25] Adam S. van der Woude thinks it not un-

---

had been previously revealed to the scholarly public only fragmentarily in Strugnell 1960, and, much later, in van der Woude 1982.

[20] Falk 1999:859–60.

[21] On spiritual offerings at Qumran, and the biblical roots of this idea, see Klinzing 1971:93–106. See the comparison between Qumran's angelic priests and the Mandaean *'Utria* in Cinal 1988. The identification of angels as priestly also appears in Christian sources: see Héring 1962:106.

[22] Newsom 1985:71–2; Davidson 1992:237. Ego 1989:62 interprets *y. Yoma* 7.2 along the same lines: "Dieses Korrespondenzverhältnis fungiert einerseits im Hinblick auf eine Legitimation des irdischen Gottesdienstes, und begründet andererseits eine Kultusgemeinschaft von Engeln und Priestern." So also Schwemer 1991:92: "Die Grundanschauung, daß sich himmlischer und irdischer Kult entsprechen und der irdische Kult seine Legitimation durch den himmlischen erhält, galt auch in Jerusalem." This use of the communion-with-angels doctrine as a legitimation of Qumran practices and piety could function both positively and negatively. Positively, it lends assurance that God approves of, and therefore will vindicate the Qumranites on account of the worship that they offer. Negatively, it insinuates that the worship at Jerusalem is a waste of time and material.

[23] Criteria for determining Qumran authorship are discussed in Lichtenberger 1980:13–19; Lange 2003.

[24] See Newsom 1990; Chazon 1998–9:260; Davila 1998:479. Golb 1995:130–50 counts the discovery of the *Songs of the Sabbath Sacrifice* at Masada as a support for his view that the Qumran caves were the repository of a Jerusalem library. Newsom (2000:887) now writes that the evidence for Qumran authorship is "ambiguous," but that "on balance a pre-Qumran origin seems most likely," and that "one should probably seek its origin in the priestly scribal circles that produced works such as *Jubilees* or Aramaic Levi".

[25] Schiffman (1994:355–60) writes, "We now believe that the reason these sites share literary remains is simply because the texts were widespread in Judaea at the time. Hence, it may be that this angelic liturgy and the mystical approach it follows were not limited to the Qumran sectarians in the last years of the Second Temple but had spread much farther among the Jewish community of Palestine. If so, we can now understand

likely, however, that a Qumranite brought the scroll to Masada after Qumran had been destroyed, and Kocku von Stuckrad thinks that there are "strong reasons" for viewing the *Songs of the Sabbath Sacrifice* as part of a "much older" pre-Qumranic priestly liturgy.[26] In judging supposed differences between this text and others written at Qumran, however, it would be wrong to expect the level of thoroughgoing consistency that is sometimes expected. Thus, while the seven princes of the liturgies of weeks six and eight are archangels, it probably matters little that that view is at variance with the four-archangel scheme of 1QM 9.14–16.[27] I am persuaded by Crispin H. T. Fletcher-Louis's study of the *Urim* and *Thummim* in that particular text, and its similarity in that regard with texts of undisputed Qumranic origin (e.g., the *Hodayot*), that the *Songs of the Sabbath Sacrifice* is either narrowly Qumranic or, at most, broadly Essene.[28]

The texts discussed in this chapter were selected because they all give at least partial evidence of angels speaking in heavenly languages. The case for placing the *Songs of the Sabbath Sacrifice* in this category is one that needs to be made, rather than read off the page (of the scroll). There is an important question of translation in the *Songs of the Sabbath Sacrifice* that has strangely been ignored, even within word-by-word commentaries on the text. A formulaic phrase recurs in one part of the songs that *may* refer to a differentiation in language among the seven angelic princes, although most scholars have translated the phrase in a way that obscures this possibility. If the text intends to say that each of the seven angels speaks a different language, then presumably the text does not envision Hebrew as the language of the angels (or, at most, that it is one angelic language among several). This would comprise a point of contrast between the *Songs of the*

---

why ideas such as those reflected in this text appeared in rabbinic literature and in the *Merkavah* mysticism of the third through eighth centuries C.E."

[26] Van der Woude 1998–9:5; Stuckrad 2000:12 n. 24. As Wise, Abegg, and Cook (1995:365) write, "There is no mention of *Yahad*" in the *Songs of the Sabbath Sacrifice*. See also Sevenster 1968:174–5; Cross 1995:50–1. On the relationship between Masada and the Qumran writings, see Tov 2000.

[27] On the seven princes in the *Songs of the Sabbath Sacrifice*, see Newsom 1985:34. For other examples of the seven-archangel scheme, see Ezekiel 9; Tob 12.15; *T. Levi* 8.2; *1 En.* 20. Cf. the four-archangel scheme of *1 En.* 9; 40.1–10. See Lueken 1898:35–8; Dupont-Sommer 1973:329–33; Schäfer 1975:20–3; Szabó 1980:145–7; van Henten 1995:cols. 150–3; Bucur 2009:39 n. 145. On the number of archangels in Christian texts, see Kropp 1930–1:3.70–83; Grant 1969:286–9.

[28] Fletcher-Louis 2002:222–51. J. J. Collins 2000:13 argues that the "whole atmosphere of the work ... and especially its putative function" fit better with Qumran than with any other context. Alexander (2006:97) similarly writes, "[Newsom's] original judgement was probably correct", pointing to the mention of the *maskil* (*viz.* the head of the Qumran community) in the writing's opening.

Sabbath Sacrifice and the Hebrew-speaking heaven(s) that one normally expects, given the exalted status of Hebrew at Qumran.

The words in question appear in several places in the *Songs of the Sabbath Sacrifice* (4Q401 29.1; 4Q403 1.1.2; 1.1.3; 1.1.4–5; 1.1.6; 1.2.36; 4Q406 3.3; MasShirShabb 2.12; 2.14; 2.16) as prayer headings. 4Q403 1.1.2 is typical:

תהלת שבח בלשון הרבי[עי] לגבור ... על כול[אלוהים] בשבע גבורות פלאה

These words have been rendered variously by different translators:

Psalm of praise by the tongue of the fou[rth] to the Warrior who is above all [heavenly beings] with its seven wondrous powers ... (Newsom)[29]

Psalm of exaltation by the tongue of the fourth to the Warrior who is above all heavenly beings with its seven wondrous powers ... (Elior)[30]

Psalm of praise by the tongue of the four[th] to the Mighty One over all [divinities] with its seven wondrous mighty acts ... (Davila)[31]

Psalm of praise, on the tongue of the fou[rth], to the Powerful One who is above all [the gods] with its seven wonderful powers ... (García Martínez/Tigchelaar)[32]

Psalm of praise (uttered) by the tongue of the four[th] to the Mighty One above all the [gods], seven wonderful mighty deeds ... (Vermes)[33]

A psalm of praise will be spoken in the language of the four[th] to the Warrior who is over all the godlike beings, incorporating his language's seven wondrous warrior utterances ... (Wise/Abegg/Cook)[34]

Newsom, Elior, Davila, García Martínez/Tigchelaar, and Vermes all understand בלשון הרביעי differently from Wise/Abegg/Cook. But Wise, Abegg, and Cook are not alone: Christopher Rowland writes, "The mention of the different heavenly languages (4Q403 1 i 1–29) suggests a peculiar language for different parts of heaven that may be akin to the glossolalia mentioned in the New Testament and alluded to in works like the Testament of Job 48."[35] We must briefly consider the virtues of each translation.

---

[29] Newsom 1985:193.

[30] Elior 1999:140.

[31] Davila 2000:118.

[32] García Martínez and Tigchelaar 1997–8:815. The translation in García Martínez 1996:421 differs in two respects: it removes the brackets from "fou[rth]," and writes "his" for "its."

[33] Vermes 1997:323.

[34] Wise, Abegg, and Cook 1996:369. Cf. the introductory remarks in Wise, Abegg, and Cook 1996:365: "The apostle Paul wrote of 'the tongues of men and of angels' (1 Cor. 13:1), and, indeed, our author supplies the angels with different languages, each endowed with its own particular character, each singularly specialized to praise God."

[35] Rowland 1996:406.

Unfortunately, none of the translators gives an explanation for the choices reflected above. Even the formal commentaries (Newsom [two], Davila) are silent about their reasoning.[36] The rendering that does *not* imply a diversity of angelic languages is clearly the more widely accepted. I do not intend to show that the other view is preferable: I only mean to show that it is more probable than the *opinio communis* seems to allow. Although the notion of seven different angelic languages may conflict with the presumably official status of the *Jubilees* scheme at Qumran (*viz.* that Hebrew is the heavenly language), the appearance of this notion within the *Songs of the Sabbath Sacrifice* may have been a trifle in the eyes of the Qumranites who appreciated the text for its more obvious features. The fact that this reading conflicts with Qumran ideology, therefore, should not be taken as contradictory evidence for this reading, although it may perhaps be admitted as evidence against Qumran authorship.

In support of reading -ב (in בלשון) as "in" (*apud* Wise/Abegg/Cook), mention should be made of Altmann's discussion of early merkabah mysticism, where he points out that the ascending mystic often encounters different orders of angels speaking different languages.[37] In light of the patent merkabah associations of the *Songs of the Sabbath Sacrifice*, therefore, we should not be surprised to find different languages spoken among the seven angelic princes. But the fit is not perfect: language differentiation usually signifies a difference of angelic order, and there is no indication in the *Songs of the Sabbath Sacrifice* that the seven angelic princes belong to different ranks or orders.

In support of reading -ב as "with" (or "by" or "on"), one must consider the formulaic references to each angel's לשון in the continuation of a given week's liturgy:

[... ולשון הראישון תגבר שבעת בלשון משנה לו ולשון משניו תגבר]
שבע משלישי ל[ו ולש]ון השל[ישי ת]גבר שבע[ה מרביעי לו
ולשון הרביעי תגבר
שבעה בלשון החמישי לו ולשון החמישי תגבר שבעה בלשון]
הששי לו ולשו[ן] הששי תגבר שבעה ב[ל]ש[ון השביעי לו
ובלשון השביעי תגבר ...

[... The tongue of the first will be strengthened seven times with the tongue of the second to him. The tongue of the second to him will be strengthened] seven times with (that) of the third compared to [him. The tong]ue of the thi[rd will] be strengthened seve[n times with (that) of the fourth compared to him. The tongue of the fourth will be strengthened seven times with the tongue of the fifth compared to him. The tongue of the fifth will be

---

[36] Newsom 1985:*passim*; 1998; Davila 2000:83–167. (Newsom 1998 borrows extensively [verbatim] from Newsom 1985.) Commenting on the same phrase within the copy of the *Songs of the Sabbath Sacrifice* found at Masada, Newsom 1998:251 writes "הרביע׳ בלשון is elliptical for 'by the tongue of the fourth chief prince'."

[37] Altmann 1946.

strengthened seven times with the tongue of] the sixth compared to him. The tongu[e of the sixth will be strengthened seven times with the] to[ngue of the seventh compared to him. The tongue of the seventh will be strengthened ...[38]

James Davila explains: "Although the grammar is somewhat obscure, this passage appears to state that the praise of each successive secondary prince resounds seven times louder than that of his predecessor."[39] The idea of *strengthening* also implies that the praise of these seven angelic princes is uttered in unison. In connection with seven heavenly beings praising in unison, the content of which praise is too wonderful to report ("seven wonderful words"), we might compare *2 En.* 19.6: "And in the midst of them are 7 phoenixes and 7 cherubim and 7 six-winged beings, having but one voice and singing in unison. And their song is not to be reported."[40]

I can garner nothing further for one side or the other of this issue, which is why the possibility of finding angeloglossy in the *Songs of the Sabbath Sacrifice* belongs here, and not in the preceding chapter. That does not mean, however, that nothing of interest surrounding this question can be said. Indeed, the fact that the angeloglossic scenario has more going for it than scholars working with this text typically think is reason enough to take another look at this text. As things now stand, the question of angeloglossy in the Qumran scrolls is still open.

B. The Rabbinic Evidence Continued
(*b. B. Bat.* 134a || *b. Sukkah* 28a)

Despite the rabbis' clear preference for a hebraeophone angeloglossy (see chap. 3), the concept of humans speaking in, or listening to, esoteric angel-

---

[38] Text and translation: García Martínez and Tigchelaar 1997–8:820–23.

[39] Davila 2000:134 continues, "The idea is similar to the description of the praise offered by the many myriad chariots in the seven heavenly palaces in *Ma'aseh Merkavah* §§554–55." Although his rendering of what this passage "appears to state" is probably correct, the example that Davila gives from *Ma'aseh Merkabah* is not very instructive: *Synopse* §554 lists ascending figures for the angelic beings inhabiting the successive heavens, while §555 lists what the beings in each heaven speak in praise to God. By implication of the fact that each successive heaven has more beings offering praise, the sound of praise presumably increases as one ascends. This implication cannot be attached to our text from Qumran, however, in which there is no account of an increasing number of angelic beings. The similarity between the two passages, therefore, obtains only in the final effect. It is important to note that *Ma'aseh Merkabah* (*Synopse* §§554–5) does not explicitly testify to the notion of individual angels praising louder than others. Alexander 2006:33 understands the sevenfoldness as follows: "As each prince comes in the praises are swelled sevenfold. In other words, the celestial praises to God are sung like a sevenfold canon, or, perhaps, a fugue."

[40] Trans. Andersen 1983.134.

ic languages can perhaps also be found in rabbinic writings. Although an esoteric-language angeloglossy is scarce in the Babylonian Talmud, two parallel references to the "conversation of angels" (מלאכי שיחת) are well known.[41] The tradition preserved in these passages gives a spectacular list of R. Yochanan b. Zakkai's accomplishments:

b. B. Bat. 134a (cf. *b. Sukkah* 28a)

אמרו עליו על רבן יוחנן בן זכאי שלא הניח מקרא ומשנה תלמוד הלכות ואגדות דקדוקי
תורה ודקדוקי סופרים וקלין וחמורין וגזרות שוות ותקופות וגמטריאות ומשלות כובסים
ומשלות שועלים שיחת שדים ושיחת דקלים ושיחת מלאכי השרת ודבר גדול ודבר קטן
דבר גדול מעשה מרכבה דבר קטן הויות דאביי ורבא

They said of R. Yochanan b. Zakkai that he did not neglect Scripture and mishnah, gemara, halakhot, aggadot, the minutiae of Torah and the minutiae of the scribes, the arguments *a minore ad maius*, the arguments by catchword association, astronomy and mathematics, fuller's parables and fox parables, the discourse of demons and the discourse of palm trees and the discourse of the ministering angels, and the great matter and the small matter. "Great matter" refers to *ma'aseh merkabah* – "small matter" refers to the arguments of Abaye and Rava.

A number of scholars have already discussed this tradition block, but no one, to my mind, has satisfactorily explained its meaning or origin. Daniel Boyarin points to the fact that "the discourse ... of the ministering angels" is listed toward the end of Yochanan b. Zakkai's abilities as an indication of its relative unimportance compared with "the various branches of Torah-knowledge proper".[42] Be that as it may (and what else should one expect from the Talmud?), this passage is intensely interesting, both for its own sake and for our larger investigation.

The date of this tradition is difficult to pin down. Most of the abilities listed in this aretalogy cannot be attributed to the historical Yochanan b. Zakkai, and Christopher Rowland has put forth a strong argument against the founding rabbi's involvement in the mystical tradition altogether.[43] We

---

[41] An almost exact parallel to these references appears in the (post-talmudic) minor midrash *Ma'ayan ha-Hochmah* (see Eisenstein 1915:308). The passage in question has a kabbalistic tinge, and refers to two of the above-mentioned discourse circles: "Become wise in the ascent, and in the uppermost step, to understand the discourse of demons [שיחת שדים] and the discourse of angels who minister [שיחת מלאכים המשרתים] before the dignitaries". Rowland 1999b:224 claims that "there is a clear reference to charismatic or ecstatic speech" in *m. 'Abot* 2.8, but the reference, if real, is anything but "clear." Rowland is presumably referring to the phrase "Eleazar b. Arak is an ever-flowing spring" (Danby 1933:448).

[42] Boyarin 1993:111–12.

[43] Rowland 1999b:222–6. According to Rowland, it was Eliezer b. Hyrcanus and Eleazar b. Arak who represented the mystical-ascent trajectory within early rabbinism. For the contrary view, see Neusner 1970:134–41; Séd 1973; Gruenwald 1980:83–5; 1988:141–2. More generally, see the bibliography in DeConick 2001:51 n. 72. Alon 1980:89–90 appears to accept *b. Sukkah* 28a's account of Yochanan b. Zakkai's abilities

are not concerned here with the historical Yochanan b. Zakkai, however, but with the tradition told about him. One possible indication of an early date for this tradition is the likelihood that a knowledge of the demons' language may be a part of an early conception of the means of warding off demons. According to Eli Yassif, "Knowing the habits of the demons, the times when one must be wary of them and the like are limited, 'technical' means of grappling with them," a means not necessary for the true Torah scholar, whose "safety in this demon-infested world" is "guarantee[d]".[44] But this is a perilous distinction to press as a chronological indicator, especially given the attention paid to "technical means" within the later *hekhalot* tradition, and the fact that in our text understanding the demons' language is paired with understanding the angels' language – a fact probably indicating that technical control is out of the picture. Our task is to determine what religious-historical developments lay behind Yochanan b. Zakkai's supposed mastery of "the discourse of demons and the discourse of palm trees and the discourse of the ministering angels."[45]

The most peculiar item within Yochanan b. Zakkai's linguistic abilities, *viz.* the "discourse of palm trees," may provide us with a handle by which we can determine the signifying context for the "the discourse of demons ... and the discourse of the ministering angels." If we can find a probable context for understanding the reference to palm trees, then that same context may provide the correct understanding for the references to angels and demons. This presumption depends upon our viewing these three groups as related, and our solution will accordingly have to be graded on the basis of this presumption.

It should first be noted that there are many instances in ancient writings of trees talking. In his treatise "On the Improvement of Understanding", "trees speaking" is the first of several "fictitious ideas" that Spinoza claimed to be the product of human ignorance of nature.[46] N. Wyatt recently discussed a number of examples of "oracular trees" from Ugaritic and

---

as historical, although he fails to make specific mention of the alleged linguistic abilities. Halperin 1983 has argued against *any* of the tannaim being involved in ecstatic mysticism. Halperin's view is argued further by Swartz 1996:9–13. In Goodenough's view (1953–68:5.109), the rabbinic suit against merkabah mysticism was real but not totally effective: "The rabbis as a group did not like [merkabah mysticism] and did all possible to repress it in the interests of halachic Judaism, although many individual rabbis succumbed to its lures." See Hoffman 1981.

[44] Yassif 2006:732–3.

[45] Mention was made above to the reference to angelic languages in the minor *Ma'ayan ha-Hochmah*. The "discourse of demons" is also attributed to Hillel in *Massekhet Soferim* 16.7. As the Babylonian Talmud comprises the late limit for classical Judaism, our investigation will not consider the presence of similar traditions in the Zohar, or in other later compilations.

[46] Spinoza 1951:2.3–41, esp. 21–2.

biblical passages.[47] Dale C. Allison Jr. provides a convenient list of talking trees in his commentary on the *Testament of Abraham*:

Ovid, *Metam.* 8.771–773 (a nymph inside or identical with a tree prophesies punishment to its slayer); Pliny the Elder, *Nat.* 17.243 (included in the "Notes" of a certain "Gaius Epicius" are "Cases of trees that talked"); Apollonius of Rhodes, *Argon.* 4.603–605 (lamenting women are turned into or encased inside trees); *Gos. Pet.* 10:42 (Jesus' cross speaks); Philostratus, *Vit. Apoll.* 6.10 (a tree salutes Apollonius "in accents articulate and like those of a woman"); Ps.-Callisthenes, *Hist. Alex. Magn.* Rec. α 3.29 (trees foretell Alexander's death; ...); *CMC* 6.1–8.12; 9.1–10.15; 98.9–99.9 (date-palms protest being cut and having their fruit eaten). In Exodus 3, God speaks to Moses from a סנה or "bush," and *b. Šabb.* 67a classifies this as a "tree" (אילן). *Y. Ḥag.* 77a and *b. Ḥag.* 14b report that trees sang when R. Johanan b. Zakkai expounded the *Merkabah*, and the latter has them quoting parts of Ps 148:7, 8, 14.[48]

In one obvious way, of course, these examples do not shed much light on Yochanan b. Zakkai's ability, as his was either an ability to hear what normally cannot be heard or an ability to understand an esoteric tongue. As the trees in Allison's list all apparently spoke out loud and in the vernacular, our talmudic passages appear to refer to something else. Wyatt's examples are better on this score, as he refers to oracular trees that spoke by the sound of wind rustling through the branches, as in 2 Sam 5.23–4. Wyatt's list also contains a specific example of a palm tree: the palm under which Deborah sat and judged Israel was perhaps an oracular tree.

Ithamar Gruenwald and Burton Visotzky have both argued that the talmudic references to the "discourse of palm trees" can be clarified by the accounts in the *Cologne Mani Codex* mentioned by Allison, as the trees in that text are specified as *palm* trees. This codex depicts a palm tree vocally objecting to the harvesting of its dates.[49] Two passages in the codex employ this motif:

CMC 6.12–8.7
We went away to a certain [date-palm tree], and he climbed up ...
    . . [The palm tree spoke:] "If you keep the [pain] away from us (trees), you will [not perish] with the murderer."
    Then that Baptist, gripped by fear of me [Mani], came down from it in confusion, and fell at my feet and said: "I did not know that this secret mystery is with you. Whence was the [agony of the date-palm tree] revealed to you?" ...
    (Mani is now speaking) "... [When the date-palm tree said] this to you, why did you become [greatly] frightened and change your complexion? How much more will [that one], with whom all the [plants] speak, be disturbed?"

---

[47] Wyatt 2007:497–507.

[48] Allison 2003b:108. To this list should be added the passage that Allison seeks to illuminate: *T. Ab.* 3.3–4. One should also add the Greek idea of a spirit dwelling within a tree – see Parke 1967:22–7. See the discussion in J. A. Robinson 1892:59–64.

[49] Gruenwald 1988:253–77, esp. 275–7 (originally published as Gruenwald 1983); Visotzky 1994. On speaking trees in rabbinic literature, see Marmorstein 1914:132–3.

CMC 98.8–99.9

Again he (Mani) points out that a date-palm tree spoke with Aianos, the Baptist from Koche, and commanded him to say to <its> lord: "Don't cut (me) down because my fruit is stolen, but grant me this [year]. And in [the] course of this year I shall give you [fruit] proportionate to [what] has been stolen, [and in all] the [other years hereafter]." But [it] also commanded (him) to say to that man who was stealing its fruit: "Do not come at this season to steal my fruit away. If you come, I shall hurl you down from my height and you will die."[50]

One obvious advantage of this comparison is that both the Babylonian Talmud and the *Cologne Mani Codex* refer to *palm* trees, rather than generic trees. Although there are other speaking trees in rabbinic and pseudepigraphic writings, there are no other references to speaking *palm* trees. Another advantage, as Visotzky points out, is that the *Cologne Mani Codex* is a product of the same geographical area as the Babylonian Talmud.[51] Although the *Cologne Mani Codex* is extant only in Greek, most scholars agree that its original language was Syriac. This means that both the Talmud and the Mani tradition relate *Semitic* accounts of speaking palm trees. There are, however, two disadvantages to Gruenwald's and Visotzky's interpetation, and they seem to outweigh the advantages: (1) as Albert Henrichs's seminal article makes clear, Mani's talking palm tree belongs to a wider mythical motif of trees that spoke *when threatened*, and not to the idea that trees carried on conversations with each other,[52] and (2) this interpretation seeks to interpet the "conversation of palm trees" in isolation from the other two discourse circles that the Talmud attributes to Yochanan b. Zakkai (*viz.* angels and demons). An interpretation of the "discourse of palm trees" that can simultaneously account for the "discourse of angels" and the "discourse of demons" has parsimony on its side. We should also question the relevance of Visotzky's claim that the Talmud, the *Cologne Mani Codex*, and the Qumranic *Genesis Apocryphon* all connect the speech of palm trees with the careers of "towering religious figures": although this connection does exist in every case, it is probably more the result of pseudepigraphy's attraction to figures of exalted spiritual stature

---

[50] *CMC* 98.8–99.9, trans. Cameron and Dewey 1979:79 (quoted in Visotzky 1994:208). Text and photographs can be found in Koenen and Römer 1985:194–97.

[51] On this, see also Gruenwald 1988:253–77; Visotzky 1983. Visotzky dates the redaction of the Talmudic passage to the "late fifth century," but it could be either earlier or later. Oberhänsli-Widmer (1998:53) thinks that most of the items in this "Bildungskatalog" come from the tannaitic period, and that only the references to the 4th-century figures Abaye and Raba are later: the references to Abaye and Raba belong to an attempt to explain the "great" and "small" matters. Oberhänsli-Widmer bases this judgment on the references to types of parables, and on the assumption that these come from the tannaitic period.

[52] Henrichs 1979. See Dillon 1997:119. Cf. Carlo Severi's discussion of the Cuna belief in tree languages, in Detienne and Hamonic 1995.

than of any necessary connection between talking trees and founders of new religions.[53]

Gruenwald and Visotzky both give such a limited range of solutions for שיחת דקלים, which may be due to the fact that שיחה primarily means "conversation" rather than "language." As such, they may not have searched for parallels involving esoteric tree languages. But שיחה can also refer to a particular group's distinctive language: e.g., according to Marcus Jastrow's *Dictionary of the Targumim, the Talmud Babli and Yerushalmi, and the Midrashic Literature*, שיחת כנענים means "the language of the Canaanites."[54] Accordingly, one cannot dismiss the possibility that שיחת דקלים means "language of palm trees" – a possibility that admits solutions other than those explored by Gruenwald and Visotzky.

The Talmud records that Yochanan b. Zakkai mastered "the great matter and the small matter." The "great matter," we are told, is merkabah speculation. Although this explanation has the appearance of a secondary accretion, the mystical tinge of the abilities listed suggests that the interpretation fits. One obvious way in which the merkabah tradition can illuminate the image of a speaking palm tree lies in the frequent mention that merkabah texts make of trees praising God, a detail derived from the Bible. In typical fashion, the merkabah texts narrativize the biblical description of these trees into a sampling of the things one might encounter during the ascent to the highest heaven: some of the texts mention trees that break forth into songs of praise for their creator, recalling Ps 96.12, 148.14, Isa 5.12, 44.23.[55] In both the Bible and the cultural and intellectual milieu of merka-

---

[53] Allison 2003a, however, appreciates Visotzky's observation.

[54] Jastrow 1989:977.

[55] E.g., *y. Ḥag.* 2.1 reads, "And a fire descended from heaven and surrounded them. And the Ministering Angels were leaping about them like guests at a wedding rejoicing before the bridegroom. One angel spoke from out of the fire and said: The Account of the Chariot is precisely as you described it, Eleazar ben 'Arakh! Immediately all the trees opened their mouths and began to sing 'Then shall all the trees of the wood sing for joy!' [Ps 96.12]". The account in *b. Ḥag.* 14b differs somewhat: "Immediately, Rabbi Eleazar ben 'Arakh began the Account of the Chariot and he expounded, 'and a flame descended from heaven and encompassed all the trees in the field. All broke out in song.' Which song did they utter? 'Praise the Lord from the earth, ye sea-monsters, and all deeps...fruitful trees and all cedars Hallelujah.' (Ps 148:7, 9, 14). An angel answered from the flame and said: 'This indeed is the Account of the Chariot!'." This paragraph (in either form) is not in the parallel portions to this teaching in the Tosefta or in the *Mekilta de Rabbi Simeon b. Yohai*. Cf. *Hekhalot Rabbati* 25.1 (= *Synopse* §253). On the singing of trees in merkabah texts, see Gruenwald 1980:83–5. The *Testament of Abraham* also records that Abraham heard a cypress tree recite the thrice-holy "in human voice" (3.1–3; see Allison 2003a). J. A. Robinson 1891:38 suggests that a similar scene obtains in the *Martyrdom of Perpetua and Felicitas*: reading *canebant* ("singing") for *cadebant* ("falling") in 11.6, Robinson posits that the *folia* are described as *canebant sine cessatione*, and that this belongs together with the subsequent detail that Saturus and his friends

bah mysticism, this image would have found support in a general belief that all creation worships its creator.[56] Merely citing the theme of trees praising God, however, still leaves too much in the dark, because it does not explain why *palm* trees are specified (שיחת דקלים) when relating Yochanan b. Zakkai's abilities.

A better context for understanding "the conversation of palm trees" is found in a different component of the merkabah tradition, the well known narrative conceit of animating the heavenly Temple's ornaments and accouterments. Just as merkabah texts envision the four creatures of Ezekiel 1 and 10 comprising the very throne of God (as opposed to merely carrying it), so also they imagine other elements of the Temple architecture and furnishings to be alive.[57] The notion of the heavenly Temple itself praising God is found throughout merkabah literature. The idea is prominent within the Qumran *Songs of the Sabbath Sacrifice*:

4Q403 1.1.39b–41a

39 ... זמרו לאלוהי עז
40 במנת רוח רוש ל[מזמו]ר בשמחת אלוהים וגיל בכול קדושים לזמרות פלא בשמחת עול[מים]
41 באלה יהללו כול יסודי קודש קודשים עמודי משא לזבול רום רומים וכול פנות מבניתו ...

39 ... Chant to the powerful God
40 with the chosen spiritual portion, so that it is [a melo]dy with the joy of the gods, and celebration with all the holy ones, for a wonderful song in eter[nal] happiness.
41 With them praise all the fou[ndations of the hol]y of holies, the supporting columns of the most exalted dwelling, and all the corners of his building. ...[58]

"heard the sound of voices in unison chanting 'Holy, holy, holy!' *sine cessatione*". See also J. A. Robinson 1892:59–64. Robinson's reconstruction is accepted by Robeck 1992:76–7, a number of scholars listed in Robeck 1992:255 n. 27, and Butler 2006. Robinson's emendation is challenged, however, by Bremmer 2003:61–2, and by Heffernan 2007:358. Bowersock (1995:34) writes that Saturus' vision "is likely ... to be an authentic document both from the simplicity of its narration and the social context within which the action of the dream takes place". See also Barnes 1971:263. On the liturgical context of this scene, see Spinks 1991:51.

[56] See the passages collected in Downing 1964:24, and the discussion there (Ps 19.1–4; 30.9b; 50.6; 89.5; 97.6–7). Studies on Psalm 19 are numerous – see esp. Barr 1993:85–9. On Psalms 19 and 104, see Maier 1979:348–52. On Psalm 148, see Fretheim 1987. Westermann's description (1982:165) of creation's praise in the Psalms is remarkably reminiscent of the theurgical theory that we examined above: "All creatures can be called to praise because it is a much wider concept. It brings to expression that joy of existence which can be attributed to all creatures – one does not need human language for it (Ps. 19:3: 'There is no speech, nor are there words; their voice is not heard'). This joy of existence alludes to their meaning for existence: turned towards the creator." For the praise of creation in rabbinic texts, see Grözinger 1982:292–301.

[57] See Grözinger 1982:286–9.

[58] Text and translation: García Martínez and Tigchelaar 1997–8:818–19.

4Q403 1.2.13b–16

13 ... וכול מחשבי הדביר יחושו בתהלי פלא בדבי]ר ... [

14 פלא דביר לדביר בקול המוני קודש וכול מחשביהם [...]

15 והללו יחד מרכבות דבירו וברכו פלא כרוביהם ואופניה]ם ... [

16 ראשי תבנית אלוהים והללוהו בדביר פודשו *vacat* [...]

13 ... And all the decorations of the inner shrine hurry with wonderful psalms in the inner sh[rine ...]

14 wonder, inner shrine to inner shrine, with the sound of holy multitudes. And all their decorations [...]

15 And the chariots of his inner shrine praise together, and his cherubim and the[ir] ofanim bless wonderfully [...]

16 the chiefs of the construction of the gods. And they praise him in his holy inner shrine. *Blank* [...].[59]

Allison notes a similarity between the *Songs of the Sabbath Sacrifice*'s depiction of parts of a building as offering praise to God and certain passages in the book of Revelation.[60] Joseph Baumgarten mentions this use of the Temple's trappings for constructing a list of the heavenly choir's different sections: in 4Q405,

[t]he figures embroidered in the vestibules of the royal chambers were capable of joining in hymns of praise: RWQMWTM YRNNW. Newsom has identified *1 Kings* 6, 29 and *Ezekiel* 41, 15–26 as the biblical sources for the image of angelic figures carved on the walls and doors of the Temple. However, in biblical Hebrew the verb RQM is used for embroidering cloth and garments. In *1QM* the word RWQMH is extended to ornamental designs carved on shields or spears. Yet the idea that such designs were capable of singing hymns seems quite strange.

---

[59] Text and translation: García Martínez and Tigchelaar 1997–8:820–21.

[60] Allison 1985–7. Note that the Vulgate removes the scandal of a speaking altar in Rev 16.7, by substituting for it a speaking angel. Clifford 1972:73–4 posits a similar understanding of an ancient Near Eastern text, which reads "The speech of wood and the whisper (?) of stone, the converse (?) of heaven with the earth, the deeps with the stars, speech which men do not know, and the multitude of the earth do not understand. Come and I will seek it." Clifford posits that "the speech of wood and the whisper of stone" may "be related to the cedar and precious stone that went into Baal's temple". Some scholars, taking their cue from 4Q405 and later merkabah texts, identify the throne in Revelation 4–5 *as comprised of* the four living creatures (e.g., Hall 1990b), but Briggs 1999:47 n. 5, 174–5 n. 113 correctly notes that the throne and the living creatures are differentiated in Rev 5.11, and that the living creatures are described as falling down to worship the Lamb in Rev 5.8, making it difficult to imagine them as comprising the throne. On the hymning altar in 4Q405, see Moyise 1995:89–91. Segert 1988: 223 sees similarities between the poetic structures of the *Songs of the Sabbath Sacrifice* and certain passages in Revelation. Fujita (1986:163) writes, "The [*Songs of the Sabbath Sacrifice*] text ... is not intended to be a commentary on Ezekiel's chapters. ... The structural portions of the temple were mentioned not for the sake of offering a detailed blueprint but in order to summon the architectural parts to join the chorus in praise of God!" On the general comparison of Revelation with Qumran, see Aune 1998.

In his study of *Merkabah* mysticism Scholem referred to the song of the kine who drew the ark of the covenant. According to the Talmud the song depicted the ark as "girdled in golden embroidery" HMHWŠQT BRQMY ZHB. Scholem compared this with the hymn in *Hekhalot Rabbati* where God is described as HMHWDR BRQMY ŠYR, "he who is glorified with embroideries of song." He also speculated on a possible Greek source, *hymnos* as 'woven speech', for this unusual phrase. We now recognise that the root RQM was already used at Qumran for the embroideries of angelic figures which uttered songs of adoration.[61]

Alexander's commentary on *Songs of the Sabbath Sacrifice* gives more attention than any other treatment to these elements. Pointing out that the references to the parts of the Temple praising God "is probably more than a fanciful, poetic figure of speech", he suggests that תבנית אלהים should be rendered "a structure of ¹Elohim" (*viz.* a structure *made up* of *elohim*) rather than (as per Newsom) "divine structure".[62] The idea of the (true) animation of cult objects bears some similarity to ideas once widespread in Egyptian religion.[63]

Since carved palm trees have always been a part of the Temple's decorations (see 1 Kgs 6.29, 32, 35; cf. Josephus, *A.J.* VIII.77–8, 84–5), and are frequently and prominently mentioned in Ezekiel's account of the heavenly Temple (40.16, 26, 31, 34, 37; 41.16–20, 23–6) and in Ps 92.13–16, the idea of animating the Temple's furnishings and decorations would appear to be pregnant with meaning for the image of the discourse of palm trees.[64]

---

[61] J. M. Baumgarten 1988:202–3. See Newsom 1998:359. For the motif of the throne praising God, see also *Hekhalot Rabbati* 3.2 (= *Synopse* §99); 24.1 (= *Synopse* §251); Kuyt 1995:148–9. See the discussion of the gradual transformation of the אופנים into animate beings in Elior 1999:154–6. On the mystical "song of the kine," see Scholem 1965:24–7; Yahalom 1987:113–14.

[62] Alexander 2006:31. See Alexander 2006:30–2, 34, 36–7, 39–40, 54.

[63] The animation of thrones was particularly common in Egyptian thought, and was perhaps a formative idea behind Isis worship. See Frankfort 1948:43–4.

[64] Metzger 1993 has shown that palm trees have always been a part of the Temple's iconography. See Goodenough 1953–68:4.132, 7.125; Bloch-Smith 1994:22–24. On palm trees in the iconography of Ezekiel's eschatological Temple (chaps. 40–8), see Busink 1980:754, 765–6; Metzger 1993; Rudnig 2000:130–3, 247–50. On the relation of Ezekiel 40–8 to Ezekiel's other three visions, see Rudnig 2000:55–8. Rahmani 1994:48–50 suggests that the predominance of palm trees over other trees in ossuary iconography has to do with the relative ease of its depiction. Such an explanation, if plausible, could help explain the use of the palm tree in Temple iconography. On palm tree iconography in the ruins of the Temple Mount and in the synagogues excavated at Capernaum, Chorazin, Delos, Eshtemoa (?), and Gamla, see Goodenough 1953–68:1.184–6, 196, 235, 246. On palm tree iconography at Gamla, see Binder 1997:168–9. On palm tree iconography at Delos, see Binder 1997:306. Palm trees even appear in the iconography of the Islamic Dome of the Rock (built on the Temple Mount in the 7th century C.E.), although one cannot be confident of a conscious attempt to revisit Temple iconography. See Rosen-Ayalon 1989:21–4, 61. The original exterior mosaics of the Dome of the Rock were covered with ceramic tiles during the restoration work of Suleiman the Magnificent, but a

Presumably, the notion of animated palm trees offering praise to God would have followed upon any effort to animate the Temple, all the more so for the prominence that the sources give to the palm tree decorations. It would not be strange, therefore, for a merkabah mystic to refer to speaking or singing palm trees in the course of a relating an ascent to the heavenly Temple.

This study is interested in the idea of singing palm trees, not for its own sake, but rather for the light it sheds on Yochanan b. Zakkai's involvement with the שׂיחה of the ministering angels. The foregoing scenario invokes an interpretive context explicitly mentioned elsewhere within the Talmud's listing of Yochanan b. Zakkai's abilities: merkabah mysticism. If we suppose that Yochanan b. Zakkai's abilities in the "conversation" or "tongues" of angels, demons, and palm trees are all part of the same package (as the Talmud seems to present them), then a context that best renders the designation of these three discourse circles comprehensible should be regarded as a more likely context for understanding the reference to the language of angels. The merkabah tradition provides such a context. That שׂיחה of angels plays a role in the merkabah tradition goes without saying: angels figure everywhere in these texts, and they are usually not silent. That the שׂיחה of demons also plays a role in this tradition is less obvious, yet it unmistakably does play a role within the wider set of heavenly ascent traditions.[65] (It is also possible, given the Babylonian Talmud's bent toward re-

---

report of the original iconography has been left by Felix Fabri (a visitor to Jerusalem in 1483), who, viewing the Dome of the Rock from afar, claims to have seen "... trees, palm trees, olive trees and angels." Rosen-Ayalon surmises that the "angels" that Fabri saw were really winged crowns, like those that can still be seen on the interior mosaics (1989:21–2), but also that these crowns may be "a schematized interpretation of an angelic figure proper" (1989:21–2). Even on the Dome of the Rock, therefore, the palm tree motif may have been depicted in an angelological context. On the place of palm trees in ancient Jewish iconography in general, see Fine 1989. Palm tree iconography is also found in holy scenes related to other Near Eastern gods – e.g., see Baudissin 1876–8:2.211–16; Porter 1993. See Taglicht 1917:414. A few earlier NT scholars denied that palm trees grew in Jerusalem, which of course is wrong (see J. A. T. Robinson 1985:231 n. 53).

[65] According to the opening line of the *Testament of Adam* (2nd–5th cent. C.E.), "The first hour of the night is the praise of the demons; and at that hour they do not injure or harm any human being" (S. E. Robinson 1983:993). Despite the fact that the *Testament of Adam* invokes the dominant Jewish and Christian understanding of demons as creatures bent on destruction and devilment – and this in fact is the understanding bound up in the term שׁדים – the image of demons worshipping God recalls the morally neutral *daimons* of Neoplatonic speculation. The latter do little more than occupy one of the lesser stations in the celestial order, and are often described performing the same acts of worship as the angels. See Detienne 1963:25–9, 38–42; A. Scott 1991:59–61. Philo equates angels and demons in *Somn.* I.141, *Gig.* VI.16, and *QG* IV.188 (A. Scott 1991:70–1). An invo-

ferring to demons as often as angels, that "שׂיחה of demons" is a late addition.)[66] And, as we have shown, the notion of the שׂיחה of palm trees also makes sense, as palm trees are a constant feature of the Jewish Temple's iconography, and the merkabah tradition liked to bring this iconography to life.

The investigation thus far leads us to suspect a particular context for understanding Yochanan b. Zakkai's mastery of the שׂיחה of angels, that of the mystical ascent, but I have done little to negotiate the meaning of שׂיחה, other than to note that it possesses a wider range of meaning than Gruenwald and Visotzky admit. The meaning of שׂיחה is a matter of crucial importance for our study. Are Gruenwald and Visotzky correct in understanding שׂיחה as "conversation", or does it rather mean "language"?[67] Perhaps we can extrapolate from the general nature of R. Yochanan b. Zakkai's superhuman abilities: "They said of R. Yochanan b. Zakkai that he did not neglect Scripture and mishnah, gemara, halakhot, aggadot, the minutiae of Torah and the minutiae of the scribes, the arguments *a minore ad maius*, the arguments by catchword association, astronomy and mathematics, fuller's parables and fox parables, the discourse of demons and the discourse of palm trees and the discourse of the ministering angels, and the great matter and the small matter." All of the items in the list that can be clearly identified appear to represent bodies of knowledge rather than supernatural abilities.[68] Thus Yochanan b. Zakkai's knowledge of "the discourse of demons and the discourse of palm trees and the discourse of the ministering angels" would appear to be knowledge of the *content* of these discourses, content which is probably ineffable and almost certainly mysterious. This makes it unlikely (yet still possible) that Yochanan b. Zakkai's mastery of the שׂיחה of angels refers to some species of glossolalia.

The evidence for the continuation of angeloglossy among Jews beyond the classical age of pseudepigrapha is scarce and ambiguous, although, as we saw in the preceding chapter, it is not altogether lacking. Yochanan b.

---

cation to Harpokrates describes him as "praised among all gods, angels and daimons" (*PGM* 4.1000 [trans. Grese and O'Neil 1986:58]).

[66] See Ginzberg 1955:22.

[67] Gruenwald 1980:142 n. 3 notes the possibility that merkabah mystics spoke glossolalically: commenting on the phrase "Do not investigate the words of your lips" in *Hekhalot Zutreti* ("in all likelihood the oldest *Hekhalot* text proper that we possess"), he writes, "The phrase … can be interpreted as meaning that one should not venture explaining words uttered as *glossolalia*. However, the more simple meaning, namely, that there are matters relating to the secret lore which should not be discussed in public, cannot be ruled out."

[68] Elsewhere in rabbinic tradition, Yochanan b. Zakkai is credited with what *might* be viewed as an extraordinary ability for exorcism (*Pesiq. Rab Kah.* 4.5), yet it might be his exceptional *knowledge* of exorcistic recipes that underlies this ability.

Zakkai's mastery of the discourse of angels is a *possible* reference to angeloglossy, but is not as clear as we would like it to be, and the use of שׁיחה instead of לשׁון makes it unlikely. It probably refers to the privilege of listening in on what the angels say.[69]

Two more possible interpretations of "the conversation of palm trees" are discussed in an appendix at the end of this book.

C. The Nanas Inscription

The Nanas inscription is a fourth-century Montanist[70] epitaph found a few miles southeast of Kotiaeion, in the Tembris valley (Asia Minor). The inscription remembers the prophetess buried there for continual "prayer and intercession" (Εὐχῆς καὶ λιτανίης)[71] and "hymns and adulation" (ὕμνοις καὶ κολακίης). It reads as follows:

```
    ΠΡΟΦΗΤΙϹΑ
    ΝΑΝΑϹΕΡΜΟΓΕΝΟΥ
    ΕΥΧΗϹΚΑΙΛΙΤΑΝΙΗϹ[ΤΟΝ]
    ΠΡΟϹΕΨΝΗΤΟΝΑΝΑΚΤΑ
 5  ΥΜΝΟΙϹΚΑΙΚΟΛΑΚΙΗϹ
    ΤΟΝΑΘΑΝΑΤΟΝΕΔΥϹΩΠΙ
    ΕΥΧΟΜΕΝΗΠΑΝΗΜΕΡΟΝ
    ΠΑΝΝΥΧΙΟΝΘΕΟΥΦΟΒΟΝ
    ΕΙΧΕΝΑΠΑΡΧΙϹ
10  ΑΝΓΕΛΙΚΗΝΕΠΙϹΚΟΠΗΝ
    ΚΑΙΦΩΝΗΝΕΙΧΕΜΕΓΙϹΤΟΝ
    ΝΑΝΑϹΗΥΛΛΟΓΗΜΕΝΗ
    ΗϹΚΗΜΗΤΗΡ[ΙΟΝ    ]
    ΜΑΕΙΤΟΛΠΗ[    ]ϹΥ[72]
15  ΝΕΥΝΟΝΠΟΛΥΦΙΛΤΑΤΟΝΑΝ
```

---

[69] It is worth noting, in this context, that the 15th/16th-century Christian magician Heinrich Cornelius Agrippa von Nettesheim separated the language of the angels from the *divine* language, and held that, although the latter might be accessible to the true magus, it is not accessible to the angels. See Lehrich 2003:200. Across so great a span of time, of course, the value of noting this scheme can only lie in its instantiating a possibility that we might otherwise overlook.

[70] Tabbernee 1997:575 lists the inscription as "definitely Montanist", yet registers room for doubt by heading his main discussion "Nanas, a Montanist(?) prophetess" (1997:419). The Montanist identification has been challenged by Lane Fox 1987:747 n. 11, Trevett 1999 (reversing an earlier judgment in Trevett 1996:171), and Eisen 2000:63–85), but see Poirier 2004a. Tabbernee now (2007:375) writes that "it seems that the Montanist nature of the Nanas inscription is assured".

[71] On the perception of women as especially effective intercessors, see Torjeson 1998.

[72] The conjectural siglum below the H in line 14 follows Tabbernee's drawing of the inscription, but departs from his edition of the text.

ΔΡΑΝΗΛΘΕ ΜΕΤΑ[   ]
ΕΠΙΧΘΟΝΙΠΟΥ[ΛΥΒΟΤΕΙΡΗ]
ΝΟΥCΕΡΓΟΝ[   ]
ΑΝΤΕΠΟΙΗCΕ[   ]
20 ΠΟΘΕΟΝΤΕC[ΕΤΙΜ]ΗC
ΑΝΤΟΜΕΓΙCΤΟΝ[   ]
ΕΙCΥΠΟΜΝΗΜΑ

Two of the lines in this inscription touch upon the topic of this study: if ἐπισκοπὴν is understood to refer to "visitations",[73] then, according to ll. 10–11, Nanas is credited either with "angelic visitations and speech ... in greatest measure" (as read by Tabbernee, Trevett) or, reading μέγιστον as the equivalent of μεγίστων, "visitations from angels and voices ... from the exalted ones" (as read by Merkelbach, Haspels).[74] On the terms of the first reading, one can readily appreciate the possibility that this inscription refers to angeloglossy. Taking ἀγγελικὴν to modify both ἐπισκοπὴν and φωνήν, and translating φωνήν as "languages", one might infer that Nanas spoke in angelic tongues "in greatest measure" (μέγιστον).[75] This, however, is not the only way to understand the Tabbernee/Trevett rendering of this inscription: the intent could be that Nanas *heard* "angelic speech", that is, that she was adept at delivering prophecies mediated by angels.[76] Alternatively, the reference could very well be to Nanas holding open conversations with angels (*a la* the OT saints of old, the desert fathers, Symeon the Fool, and, nearer our own time, Emanuel Swedenborg and John Chapman [a.k.a. "Johnny Appleseed"], etc.), presumably when they "visited" her (cf.

---

[73] I must say "if" because Hirschmann 2004:165–7 has made the interesting suggestion that ἐπισκοπὴν refers to the episcopal office, and that ll. 10–11 credit Nanas with being both a bishop and a prophetess powerful in her charism. Hirschmann's suggestion is an appealing one, but one might have expected, if she were a bishop, that such an office would have been mentioned more prominently toward the beginning of the inscription – unless, of course, Montanism construed the bishop's office as much less powerful than the rest of the Church did at this time in history.

[74] Text from Tabbernee 1997:420–1 (cf. the edited text there as well as fig. 77, and see there for epigraphical details). See also Eisen 2000:63–4; Merkelbach and Stauber 2001:349–50 (no. 16/41/15).

[75] Strobel (1980:99–100), who follows Emilie Haspels's parsing of the text (see below), understands φωνήν *by itself* as a reference to glossolalia ("(die Gabe der) Zunge"), with no connection to the mention of angels.

[76] Φωνή can signify angelic voices (e.g., London MS Or. 6794 [Kropp 1930–1:1.29; 2.104], Rossi Gnostic Tractate [Kropp 1930–1:1.73; 2.186], and the comments in Kropp 1930–1:3.42–3; Goodenough 1953–68:2.166), but it can also signify angelic languages (e.g., *PGM* 13.139–40 – cf. the reading φωνῇ τινι ἰδίᾳ ὑμνουσῶν τὸν θεόν for *Corp. herm.* 1.26: it is difficult to judge whether the reading ἰδίᾳ is more original than the alternative reading ἡδεῖα, but the latter was perhaps influenced by the "sweet" singing of the muses in Hesiod, *Theog.* 7–14, 39–43, 68–70 [see Most 2006:2–9]). On angelic mediation of prophecy, see Levison 1995; Tibbs 2007:125–6.

ἐπισκοπὴν).[77] By itself, therefore, the term ἀγγελικὴν ... φωνὴν could refer to any of a variety of activities.

Merkelbach and Haspels parse ll. 10–11 differently. Merkelbach translates these lines as "Wartung durch die Engel hatte sie und Stimme der Höchsten" and Haspels attributes to Nanas "the gift of hearing voices."[78] This rendering is superior to that of Tabbernee and Trevett, given the fact that this pairing of "angelic visitations" with "voices of exalted ones" closely parallels an apparently formulaic expression by which Origen refers to the primordial humanity: "And the divine word according to Moses introduces the first humans as hearing divine voices and oracles, and often beholding the angels of God coming to visit them" (Καὶ ὁ θεῖος δὲ κατὰ Μωυσέα λόγος εἰσήγαγε τοὺς πρώτους ἀκούοντας θειοτέρας φωνῆς καὶ χρησμῶν καὶ ὁρῶντας ἔσθ᾿ ὅτε ἀγγέλων θεοῦ ἐπιδημίας γεγενημένας πρὸς αὐτούς; Cels. 4.80 [author's translation]; cf. 8.34). Thus we see that the protological glory is represented in Origen by the same experiences attributed to Nanas. There is reason to believe that Origen is calling upon a stock image of the protological glory, which suggests that the formula he employs was more widespread than appears at first.[79] This could shed light on the Nanas inscription: the ἀγγελικὴν ἐπισκοπὴν καὶ φωνὴν ... μέγιστον ascribed to Nanas may have served to identify her with a bygone era. That is, Nanas' prophetic experiences appear to be described in terms of Edenic access to God and the angels.[80]

---

[77] For a list of angels conversing with humans in the Old Testament, see McKane 1965:60 n. 1. Cf. Sozomen, Hist. eccl. 3.14.9 (on Pachomius); Symeon the Holy Fool 154 (see Krueger 1996). In the latter, an artisan witnesses Symeon "at the baths conversing with two angels". Ca. 400 C.E. Postumianus wrote of a hermit on Mt. Sinai, who, when asked why he separated so from humankind, answered that "One who is frequented by humans cannot possibly be frequented by angels [qui ab hominibus frequentaretur, non posse ab angelis frequentari]" (recorded in Sulpicius Severus, Dialogus 1.17.13–16; see Skrobucha 1966:20). On Swedenborg and (the Swedenborgian) Chapman, see L. E. Schmidt 2005:45, 92–3. (Swedenborg appealed to the fact that "the ancients frequently did so" as a warrant for his conversing with angels – see Pelikan 1989:169; Katz 2004:169–70.) Cf. also the Acts of Paul, in which Paul speaks glossolalically with an angel face to face. In b. Ned. 20a–b, R. Yochanan b. Dabai says that the "ministering angels" explained why some children are born with disabilities, but Amemar (in the same sugya) takes that title as a reference to the Rabbis. See Boyarin 1993:109–13.

[78] Merkelbach and Stauber 2001:349; Haspels 1971:216.

[79] Origen uses these divine privileges in an argument that they do not precisely serve: they symbolize God's assistance before "progress had been made toward understanding ... and the discovery of the arts," and as a means of subduing threatening beasts. He shows no real interest in these privileges per se.

[80] Conversation with angels was a universal emblem of blessed estate. E.g., this privilege is dealt to Abraham, Isaac, and Jacobs in the respective Testaments ascribed to their names – see Gunther 1973:195–6.

The idea of conversing with angels is already known from a probably Montanist context: Tertullian's well known reference to a woman in his congregation who "converses with angels, and sometimes even with the Lord; she both sees and hears mysterious communications" (*conversatur cum angelis, aliquando etiam cum domino, et uidet et audit sacramenta* [*An.* 9]). Although it is abundantly clear that glossolalia was widespread among the Montanists,[81] Martin Parmentier's claim that Tertullian's account refers to glossolalia is dubious at best: his judgment seems to draw from an *a priori* identification of all references to angelic speech, even "*conversatur cum angelis*", as glossolalic.[82] It is more likely that the references to "angels" and "the Lord" simply denote different sources of prophetic inspiration.

---

[81] See Lombard 1915:299–300; Schepelern 1929:153; Currie 1965:286–9; Kydd 1984:34–6; Trevett 1996:89–91, Poirier 2004a, Tabbernee 2007:92–100. Forbes's denial of this view is based on a bizarre line of argument: he (1995:160) writes, "the evidence of Eusebius, who knows of collections of Montanist oracles, and actually cites the contents of some of them, makes it luminously clear that these oracles were delivered in plain Greek". The supposition that a community was not glossolalic if it also exhibited the gift of *vernacular* prophecy is curious, to say the least, especially in the light of Paul's discussion of the spiritual gifts in 1 Corinthians 12–14, in which Paul both describes and prescribes this precise mixture of charismatic workings. (Froehlich [1973:97] commits himself to the same problematic either/or: the "very existence [of intelligible Montanist oracles] contradicts the repeated charge that the Montanist prophets uttered inarticulate speech".) Tabbernee 2007:95–6 notes other evidence that Montanist oracles stood in need of interpretation, suggesting that at least some of these oracles were glossolalic: "Sotas of Anchialus['] attempt at casting out Priscilla's 'demon' was frustrated because the ὑποκριταί did not give their permission (Aelius P. Julius, *ap.* Eusebius, *Hist. eccl.* 5.19.3). Although frequently overlooked because of the modern sense of the word ὑποκριτής as 'hypocrite,' in the ancient world a ὑποκριτής was primarily an 'interpreter.' It appears that the New Prophets were assisted by persons who, according to Apollonius (*ap.* Eusebius, *Hist. eccl.* 5.18.12), cooperated with the 'spirit' 'inspiring' them. In Maximilla's case, the attempt by Zoticus of Cumane and Julian of Apamea "to converse with the spirit [of Maximilla] as it spoke" was frustrated because Themiso (the main interpreter?) and his companions "would not allow the false and people-deceiving spirit to be put to the text by them" (Anonymous, *ap.* Eusebius, *Hist. eccl.* 5.16.17; cf. Apollonius, *ap.* Eusebius, *Hist. eccl.* 5.18.13). The most likely way Themiso and the others could have prevented Zoticus and Julian from conversing with the 'spirit' was by refusing to 'interpret' the unintelligible aspects of the prophetess' utterances."

[82] Parmentier 1994:289 supposes that this passage illustrates a connection "zwischen den Gaben der Prophetie und der Zungen". His ability to read glossolalia into the text so easily – a reading that is not impossible but which requires more of an explanation than he offers – is probably owed to his consistent use of the term "Engelsprache" to denote the simple alternative to a xenoglossic understanding of glossolalia. Yet there is much to be said for the view that the New Testament supports such a scenario. See the previous chapter.

To the degree that the Origenist parallel does not mislead us in understanding the Nanas inscription, Merkelbach's rendering of ἀγγελικὴν
ἐπισκοπὴν καὶ φωνὴν ... μέγιστον as "Wartung durch die Engel hatte sie
und Stimme der Höchsten" is preferable. Although it would not be impossible to combine this rendering with the notion of an esoteric angelic language, it is scarcely possible to find that notion within this rendering itself.
This understanding of the wording finds further support in another passage
from Tertullian, in which he cites the Montanist leader Prisca's (Priscilla's) claims that Montanists "see visions; and, turning their face down-
ward, they even hear manifest voices, as salutary as they are withal secret"
("visiones vident, et ponentes faciem deorsum etiam voces audiunt mani-
festas tam salutares quam et occultas" [*Exh. cast.* 10]). The Nanas inscription, therefore, is a possible but perhaps not probable support for the notion of angeloglossy.

D. The Liturgical Jubilus

Christian liturgists have always associated the *alleluia* with angelic
praise.[83] By the Middle Ages – scholars have not determined exactly how
early the development took place – the *alleluia* had been expanded by a
sequence of nonsensical syllables called the "jubilus" (*jubilatio*), which
was often said to represent the sounds of angelic praise.[84] In assessing the
existence of angeloglossy in the early church, we must deal with the possibility that an early form of the jubilus existed in the early Christian liturgy.
The scenario of an early *liturgical* jubilus is problematic, but it is assumed
by a number of scholars, and must be discussed.

Although the positive evidence for the liturgical jubilus dates from the
Middle Ages, the medieval musical theorists seeking a theological or traditional justification for this development looked to Augustine. Two passages from Augustine's commentary on the Psalms were seminal for the medieval *alleluia*:

Enarrat. Ps. 32.2
What is it to sing in jubilation? To be unable to understand, to express in words, what is
sung in the heart. For they who sing, either in the harvest, in the vineyard, or in some

---

[83] Werner ([1945–6:325–6) writes, "[T]he Hallelujah is considered a song of human
beings and angels. It is from this aspect that the Hallelujah assumed both in Hellenistic
Judaism and in the Early Church a distinctly mystic-esoteric character, greatly enhanced
through its ecstatic musical rendition. This conception is reflected in countless statements, explanations, poems, prayers, throughout Judaism and Christianity. The Targum
of Psalm 148, discussing the Hallelujah, is full of angelological associations." See esp.
Hammerstein 1962:39–44.

[84] *S.v.* 'Jubilus', in Eggebrëcht 1967:427. See Hiley 1993:130–7.

other arduous occupation, after beginning to manifest their gladness in the words of songs, are filled with such joy that they cannot express it in words, and turn from the syllables of words and proceed to the sound of jubilation. The jubilus is something which signifies that the heart labors with what it cannot utter. And whom does jubilation befit but the ineffable God?[85]

Enarrat. Ps. 99.3–5
One who jubilates does not speak words, but it is rather a sort of sound of joy without words, since it is the voice of a soul poured out in joy and expressing, as best it can, the feeling, though not grasping the sense. ... When, then, do we jubilate? When we praise what cannot be said. ... Let us notice the whole creation, ... in all of it there is something, I do not know what invisible, which is called spirit or soul, ... which understands God, which pertains to the mind properly speaking, which distinguishes between just and unjust, just as the eye does between white and black.[86]

Several other ancient authors discuss this phenomenon – e.g., Cassiodorus refers to the jubilus as singing "non articulatis sermonibus, sed confusa voce" (*Expos. in ps.* 46.1). References can also be found in Marcus Terentius Varro (pre-Christian), Lucius Apuleius, Calpurnius Siculus, Hilary of Poitiers, and Sidonius Apollinaris.[87] Medieval composers employ these au-

---

[85] Translated in McKinnon 1987:155. "Quid est in iubilatione canere? Intellegere, uerbis explicare non posse quod canitur corde. Etenim illi qui cantant, siue in messe, siue in uinea, siue in aliquo opere feruenti, cum coeperint in uerbis canticorum exsultare laetitia, ueluti impleti tanta laetitia, ut eam uerbis explicare non possint, auertunt se a syllabis uerborum, et eunt in sonum iubilationis. Iubilum sonus quidam est significans cor parturire quod dicere non potest. Et quem decet ista iubilatio, nisi ineffabilem Deum?" (Augustine 1956a:254).

[86] Translation partially based on McKinnon 1987:158. "Qui iubilat, non uerba dicit, sed sonus quidam est laetitiae sine uerbis; uox est enim animi diffusi laetitiae, quantum potest, exprimentis affectum, non sensum comprehendentis. ... Quando ergo nos iubilamus? Quando laudamus quod dici non potest. Adtendimus enim uniuersam creaturam, ... inque his omnibus nescio quid inuisibile, quod spiritus uel alma dicitur, ... quod intellegat Deum, quod ad mentem proprie pertineat, quod sicut oculus album et nigrum, ita aequitatem iniquitatemque discernat" (Augustine 1956b:1394).

[87] All of these authors are discussed in Wiora 1962. (Wiora views the jubilus as a product of pagan influences.) Parmentier (1994) also points to the 5th-century Syriac father John of Apamea as an eyewitnesse of this phenomenon, but the text to which he makes reference speaks only of a purely silent mode of prayer, typical of Eastern Christian spirituality. (On the text from John of Apamea, see Brock 1979. On John of Apamea's angelology, see Strothmann 1972:74–7, 86–8.) Werner 1959:169–70 argues for the Jewish roots of the jubilus. Elsewhere, Werner (1966:30 n. 2) notes that the "rabbis" took a rather dim view of "songs without words", but he may have had the rather late figure of Solomon b. Adret (14th cent.) in mind (cf. Werner 1959:304). Avenary 1978:36 apparently thinks that the thesis of the jubilus's Jewish origin conflicts with the thesis of its glossolalic origin: in arguing that the jubilus was borne out of glossolalic praise (which he defines as "a psycho-physical behavior resulting from the religious ecstasy or trance of the believers who are lost in transcendent visions", he does not give a reasoned explanation for his assumption that this excludes the relevance of Jewish models. His attempt to distance the jubilus from Judaism causes him to write some surprising things about

thors (esp. Augustine) as supports for the liturgical jubilus, and modern scholars have construed them as early witnesses to this feature of the liturgy. As James McKinnon points out, however, when the patristic writers mention singing in "jubilus," they do not appear to have had the *alleluia* in mind. Rather, they refer to a general (secular) practice of singing nonsensical syllables, and relate that practice to the wordless jubilation of the heart in praise to God.[88] McKinnon writes,

> Music historians continue to assume that authors like Augustine, Jerome and Hilary were referring to the alleluia in their vivid descriptions of the *jubilus*. They identify the melismatic style of the alleluia of the Mass as known from medieval sources with the most striking characteristic of the *jubilus*, its lack of text. This is a completely arbitrary identification, however, not hinted at by the patristic authors themselves. On the contrary they describe the *jubilus* as a secular genre, not an ecclesiastical chant; it is a kind of wordless song with which workers, especially farmers, accompanied their labors (Wiora, 1962). They introduce it into the psalm commentaries when the word *jubilare* – not *alleluia* – appears in a psalm, and then in the accustomed manner of allegorical exegesis they attempt to discover in its wordlessness some facet of spiritual truth.[89]

In noting that the connection between the *alleluia* and the jubilus is not explicit in patristic writings, McKinnon makes a good point – a necessary revision, in fact, of a widespread scholarly assumption.[90] (The absence of a connection is especially clear in Hilary of Poitiers, an author often cited in support of an early liturgical jubilus.) It should be noted, however, that the question of arbitrariness attaches not to whether the identification was *ever* made, but to *how early* it had been made. In pursuing that question (if only

---

Judaism, e.g., that the idea of liturgical union with the angels "is not germane to Jewish imagination" (Avenary 1978:39; Avenary excepts Qumran). Avenary attempts to meet the evidence for a Jewish origin head-on: he (1978:34–5) interprets "*Laudes, hoc est Alleluia canere, canticum est Hebraeorum*" (Isidore of Seville, 7th cent.) to mean "Singing the lauds, i.e. 'alleluia', is an utterance of joy with the Hebrews," rather than as "Lauds, i.e. singing 'alleluia,' is a Hebrew song". Avenary finds the use of extended melisma to be rather exceptional within Judaism, but see Gerson-Kiwi 1961:43–9; 1967:526–8. In the present discussion, I deal only with the jubilus in a Christian setting, for which the evidence of an angeloglossic understanding is unambiguous.

[88] Ensley (1977) holds the two together (*viz.* workaday melodies and liturgical *sequentia*) in a conscious and theologically resonant way throughout his popular-level book. He helpfully differentiates between "musical", "congregational", and "mystical" jubilation.

[89] McKinnon 1987:10. Wiora's note about the farmer's *jubilus* is reminiscent of a passage in which Jerome describes the singing of field hands near Bethlehem, in which "the farm hand grasping the plough handle sings Alleluia, the sweating reaper cheers himself with psalms, and the vine dresser sings something of David as he prunes the vine with his curved knife" (*Epist.* 46 [translated in McKinnon 1987:140]). On the *alleluia*'s melismatic embellishment (mostly later than Augustine), see Fassler 1993:30–43.

[90] But some writers had recognized the distinction all along – e.g. thirty years before McKinnon, Chambers 1956:5 wrote of jubilation being "[t]ransferred to Catholic worship and prayer".

summarily), it will be necessary to differentiate between the workaday jubilus (of Augustine *et al*) and the liturgical jubilus (of medieval and later figures).

Four hundred years after Augustine, Amalarius of Metz's discussion of the jubilus would have a defined liturgical moment in mind, and would seek the phenomenon's significance in the mental state it creates, rather than in the sound it produces: "This *jubilatio*, which singers call a *sequentia*, brings such a state to our mind that the utterance of words is not necessary, but by thought alone will show mind what it has within itself" (*De eccl. offic.* 3.16).[91] It should be said that Amalarius was regularly given to mystical explanations of the church's liturgy.

Most scholars discussing the origins of the liturgical jubilus simply had assumed that Augustine, Hilary, etc. knew and wrote about a melismatic expansion of the *alleluia*. It is with this assumption in mind that several have suggested that the jubilus represents the liturgical routinization of glossolalic praise – that is, that the singing of the *alleluia* originally represented a moment of (semi-spontaneous?) glossolalia.[92] Eric Werner writes,

> In Church and Synagogue, extended melismatic chant was regarded as an ecstatic praise of God, 'sonus quidam est laetitiae sine verbis' as St Augustine puts it. Such a conception places this type of singing in close proximity to the glossolaly of the Paulinian age (I Cor. 12:30; 14:5; Acts 10:46; 19:6). Augustine in another remark about *Jubilus*, seems to connect it with the early Christian practice of 'talking in tongues'. Jerome, too, attempts an explanation of melismatic chant along the very same lines. I venture to put forward my own conviction that the whole concept of the pure, wordless, melismatic jubilation should be considered the last, jealously guarded remnant of an organized musical form of glossolaly, if we permit ourselves a slight contradiction in terms.[93]

Werner further suggests that the church's *alleluia* grew in an "atmosphere of esoteric exaltation," and that its separation "[f]rom its original contexts, its use as spontaneous acclamation, together with its 'pneumatic' colour,

---

[91] *Haec iubilatio, quam cantores sequentiam vocant, illum statum ad mentem nostram ducit, quando non erit necessaria locutio verborum, sed sola cogitatione mens menti monstrabit quod retinet in se* (Hanssens 1948 – 50:2.304).

[92] E.g., Werner 1959:155, 168–9; Avenary 1978; Parmentier 1994. See also Hammerstein 1962:39–44. Richstaetter (1936:334) had made a comparison between glossolalia and the jubilus some seventy years ago. Congar 1983b:184 n. 1 approves of the comparison, but does not commit himself to a genetic relationship between the two. Whether or not the theory of a glossolalic origin is correct, the routinization of the jubilus certainly would have ruined that connection. As Werner 1959:201 notes, "When, in the course of centuries, the melismatic element became so predominant in the Alleluias that the melodies of the *Jubili* (the wordless parts) could no longer be kept in memory by the singers, these melismata were provided with new, non-scriptural texts, made to fit these tunes in syllabic order–the so-called sequences."

[93] Werner 1959:168–9. See also Werner 1945–46:325–7.

led to a certain disembodiment, to a spiritualization of the Hallelujah, which finally resulted in the omission of the word Hallelujah itself, so that only certain vowels of it were sung – AEOUIA."[94] Although this latter development was not dominant within the practice of jubilus, its pronounced resemblance to *voces mysticae* provides further evidence that the melismatic tropes of the jubilus were not merely a stylistic coloratura, but rather something of a presumed esoteric nature. The title *jubilatio* would eventually be given (synonymously with *sequentia, neuma,* and *melodia*) to an assortment of melismatic compositions accompanying the final syllable in the "alleluia" preceding the *versus alleluiaticus.*

Hanoch Avenary posits that the "new song" in Rev 14.3 that "no one could learn ... but the redeemed of the earth" represents singing in an esoteric angelic language, and calls attention to similar ideas in 2 Cor 12.2–4, *2 En.* 17 (A), and *Apoc. Ab.* 15.6.[95] Glossolalia enabled the apocalyptic visionaries to join the heavenly hosts in their singing of *sanctus* and *alleluia.* As for the extended melismas of the Eastern branch of the church, Avenary reproduces transcriptions that recall the *voces mysticae.*[96] He suggests that these nonsensical syllables represent the formalization of glossolalia. Combining this formalized glossolalia with the "self-identification of the church singers with the angelic choir in heaven,"[97] we are brought face to face with the concept of angeloglossy. Martin Parmentier also argues that the jubilus represents the attenuation of glossolalia to a purely liturgical role, and a consequent loss in the church's awareness of glossolalia.[98] He contends that the earliest jubilus was indeed glossolalic, but that the wide-

---

[94] Werner 1959:303.

[95] Cf. also *Pss. Sol.* 15.3. See the discussion of "new song" within the New Testament in Dorda 1999; Tomes 2007:248–50. Fenske 1999 argues that the "new song" in Rev 14.3 is to be equated with the "song of Moses" in Rev 15.3, which in turn is to be identified with Deuteronomy 32.

[96] *Viz.* "Alle-ye-ye / e-ye-e-ye e-ye / (etc. etc.) / ye ye lo-go / lo-go-lo güo-go uo güo ... / and so on" (18th cent. Coptic, *apud* G. A. Villoteau); "ye, ye, ma, ma, etc." (Syrian, *apud* J. Jeannin); "ya, ye, yo, amma, meme, momo, etc." (Jacobite, *apud* J. Jeannin); "eia, enga" (Chaldean, *apud* J. Jeannin); "e - ye - ye - elu; oyemu, oya-yema" (Syrians and Jacobites at Epiphany, *apud* J. Parisot); "A - a - u - u - u - a - a - kha - u - a / a - u - a - anga - a - na - a, u - a - au - a / le - u - e - e / e - khe - khe, (etc., till the end) lu - - a - nga - a - nga - a ..." (Byzantine, *apud* E. Wellesz); "a - ne - na" (Russian [until ca. 1660], *apud* O. von Riesemann). See Riesemann 1961:142–3.

[97] Avenary 1978:41.

[98] Parmentier 1994: See Parmentier 1999:71–3. Parmentier 1999:72 n. 52 cites Paul Hinnebusch as an early (1976) proponent of the equation of jubilus with glossolalia. Ensley 1977:112–13 writes, "The Fathers ... did not see their experience as 'tongues' or relate it to the New Testament experience of tongues. They were either confused by the tongues passages in the New Testament or took those passages to mean speaking in languages that one had never learned."

spread mistake of associating glossolalia with xenoglossy caused the church fathers not to recognize glossolalia when they witnessed it.

Regardless of whether Augustine had a specifically Christian parallel to what he described as *jubilatio*, it is difficult to read his words without thinking of the spirit's "wordless groaning" in Rom 8.26.[99] Furthermore, since the *alleluia* was thought to represent angelic praise, the theory of a glossolalic origin to the jubilus would appear to represent an understanding of glossolalia as an esoteric angelic language. (Although Paul knows of a hymnic role for glossolalia [1 Cor 14.15], the jubilus is more reminiscent of the angeloglossic episodes in the pseudepigrapha than of anything found in the New Testament.) On the grounds of a liturgical construal of Augustine's words (dismissed by McKinnon), the chronological component of this theory coincides roughly with the gradual disappearance of glossolalia in the first few centuries of the church, leading to the suggestion that the jubilus represents the mode of continuance of the glossolalic form.[100] There is clear evidence that glossolalia was still around throughout the second and most of the third centuries, and the fact that some patristic writers mistakenly equate glossolalia with xenoglossy does not controvert their claims to be witnesses of it. (How could they tell the difference, and what else were they to think after reading Acts 2?)[101]

---

[99] Boenig (1995:81) writes, "Given ... the new convert Augustine's tendency to burst into tears at the singing of hymns in church, we are not too far from the mark in assuming that there is something autobiographical about these [Augustinian] passages." To the contrary, I find that, although Augustine appears to write as an eyewitness, he does not seem to write from first-hand experience.

[100] One still encounters the view that glossolalia died out in the first century, only to be carried on by the Montanists and other groups discounted by later orthodoxy. E.g., see Currie 1965.

[101] The chief witnesses to the survival of glossolalia are in no sense obscure. Irenaeus refers to "many" in the church who "through the Spirit" speak different kinds of languages (*Haer.* 5.6.1). See Lawson 1948:97–9; Burgess 1984:61; Kydd 1984:45; Hinson 1986:184–5. Schöllgen 1999:100 notes, "keine der antimontanistischen Quellen des 2. und frühen 3. Jahrhunderts die Legitimität von Prophetie und Prophetentum generell in Frage stellt". Novatian may also have been a witness to glossolalia in the third century, although his remarks (in *De Trinitate* 29.167) are perhaps only based upon an exegesis of Paul. Tertullian seems to affirm the continuing existence of the charisms in *Marc.* 5.8.4–12. Clement of Alexandria's listing of the Pauline charisms as evidence of the *true* gnostic would have lost some of its force if these charisms (including glossolalia) were not extant in the congregations that he knew. (See Burgess 1984:72). In the fourth century, Eusebius (*Comm. Isa.* 41 [*ad* Isa 6.2]) and Hilary of Poitiers (*De Trinitate* 2.33–4; 8.30) also comment on glossolalia in a way that may imply its continued existence within the church. Justin Martyr writes that the "prophetical gifts" remained in the church until his day, without, however, specifically mentioning glossolalia (*Dial.* 82). Some patristic writers, including Hippolytus (*Antichr.* 2) and Augustine (*De baptismo libri septem* 3.16.21) denied the continued existence of prophecy and/or glossolalia. John Chrysostom

Is there a connection between the liturgical jubilus and a belief in esoteric angelic languages? Almost certainly. Is there also a connection between the liturgical jubilus and an angeloglossic understanding of glossolalia? That is less certain. Did the liturgical jubilus develop from glossolalia? That is still less certain. The angelic associations of the *alleluia* are patent, and the question of whether the jubilus really developed from (once spontaneous) glossolalia is unnecessary for our including the jubilus in this discussion. Even if the latter scenario was invented wholecloth by liturgists, the original significance of the liturgical jubilus was probably still wrapped up in the notion of an esoteric angelic tongue.

E. Conclusion

This chapter has examined four additional possible references to angeloglossy, including a possible *trace* of angeloglossy, two of which are certainly Christian (the Nanas inscription and liturgical jubilus), and the other two certainly Jewish (*Songs of the Sabbath Sacrifice* and the Babylonian Talmud). The reference to (or trace of) angeloglossy in these four is in every case distinctly possible, but it is neither as certain or likely as in the cases presented in the preceding chapter. Human participation in angeloglossy is found in the talmudic passages (*b. Baba Batra / b. Sukkah*), and it *might* be found in the Nanas inscription, but it does not appear in the *Songs of the Sabbath Sacrifice*. The liturgical jubilus is a special case: if the angeloglossic background sometimes posited for the jubilus is at all creditable, then it points to a time when human participation in angeloglossy was understood to be normal.

(*Hom. 1 Cor.* 29) stated that they were "rare" in his day. See Rancillac 1970:124, 142; Ritter 1972; Shogren 1999:120–1. The reasons for the decline of the charismatic gifts in the catholic church are debated. Ash 1976 argues that the rise of episcopal power was construed as a theoretical challenge to the authority of charismatic utterances. See also H. Kraft 1977; Congar 1983a:65–6; Trocmé 1997; Schöllgen 1999. More generally, see Campenhausen 1969:178–212. Kydd (1984:57) thinks that no evidence exists for the continuation of the charismata after 260 C.E., but it seems hazardous to claim that there was a definitive end. See McDonnell and Montague 1991. The only real drawback of McDonnell and Montague's otherwise excellent discussion is that they uncritically dismiss the Montanists as an aberration. See also Ruthven 1993:26–30.

It is not certain whether the unintelligible utterances described by Celsus (Origen, *Cels.* 7.9), and whose continued existence Origen denies (7.11), should be understood as glossolalia: as Celsus describes the utterances, they appear to *follow*, rather than precede, a prophetic message. This makes them look more like (Gnostic?) *nomina barbara* than Pauline glossolalia. See Engelsen 1970:41–3; Kydd 1984:36–40; Hauck 1989:83–4; Cook 2000:77–9.

Chapter 6

Conclusion

The concept of angelic languages appears in a number of Jewish and Christian writings from the second century B.C.E. until the Italian Renaissance. In some of these writings the angels speak Hebrew, and in others they speak an unearthly esoteric language. This study has attempted to collect and comment on all such references from the classical period, beginning with the writing of *Jubilees* (mid-second century B.C.E.) and ending with the main redaction of the Babylonian Talmud (seventh century C.E. or earlier). While it has discussed these references as an end in itself, it has also attempted to answer a number of questions that arise from these references: How did the view that angels speak an esoteric language develop and spread in the first place, especially in the apparent absence of such a view in the Hebrew Bible? Why did the view that angels speak an unearthly esoteric language make so little impact upon rabbinic Judaism before the fifth century C.E., despite the existence of this view in indisputably Jewish apocalyptic writings? Why did the idea of Hebrew-speaking angels make so little impact on developing Christianity? And most especially: What did Paul mean when he referred to "the tongues of men and of angels" (1 Cor 13.1)?

Although the concept of angelic languages is recurrent in a number of Jewish and Christian writings beginning in the second century B.C.E., until now it had somehow escaped treatment in a book-length study all its own. The need for such a discussion was made even greater by the fact that the scant scholarly references to the concept of angelic languages have hardly ever looked at the two views of angelic language in mutual perspective. This study has tried to fill that gap by providing both a survey of the writings in which this concept appears and an account of the currency enjoyed by the two views of angelic languages. To this end, this study examined possible references or allusions to angelic languages (both Hebrew and esoteric languages) in an assortment of Jewish and Christian writings, as well as in a celebrated inscription from Asia Minor and in the ideas assigned with the liturgical jubilus. Hopefully, the survey in this study has accomplished two things: (1) it has provided a sort of religious profile (as it were) for the two views, in the form of a list of writings adhering to each view, and (2) it has allowed a clearer view of the concept of angelic languages, and of how that concept might be joined to other concepts. The clearest references to angeloglossy tend to be from Christian sources. This can be accounted for in a couple of ways: (1) within Christianity, the Hebrew language was stripped of almost all its religious value, and (2) the continuation (and democratization) of the prophetic spirit was a more central and consistent part of Christian than of Jewish theology.

In chapter two, we saw that the view that angels speak Hebrew is more widespread within Jewish sources for our period than the view that angels speak an esoteric language all their own. One should not assume, however, that the former view was predominant within all forms of Jewish expression. The religion of ancient Judaism varied at different times and in different localities, social groupings, and schools of thought. In the person of R. Hama b. Hanina, for example, we see that the view that angels speak an esoteric language was not unknown within rabbinic circles of the late tannaitic/early amoraic period. Nevertheless, the idea that angels speak Hebrew appears to have dominated most forms of Palestinian Judaism, and the reason for this may have as much to do with social history as with the history of ideas.

Scholars have been exploring the relationship between the rabbis and the rest of Jewish society, including those groups who have been written into the self-histories of the rabbinic movement. In this connection, I have used R. Yochanan's attempt to corral popular piety by removing the theoretical supports of extra-synagogal prayer as a window onto the power relations between the rabbinic movement in the vicinity of third-century Tiberias and its circle of influence. This use of R. Yochanan is partly emblematic of how power relations might operate in other areas of rabbinic social history, partly an attempt to understand an important source of rabbinic thought (given the R. Yochanan's influence on later generations), and partly a yielding to the way made available by our limited evidence.

In chapter three, I argued that the hebraeophone view of angelic speech was promulgated by groups who were ideologically invested in the use of Hebrew. In arguing that Hebrew was *not* the predominant spoken language among Palestinian Jews during the Second Temple and early rabbinic periods, I showed that the attaching of religious value to speaking, reading, or praying in Hebrew might be an expression of a need rather than a description of a dominant practice. I then sought to establish the existence of groups that pursued the use of Hebrew within religious contexts (and perhaps within nonreligious contexts as well). These groups are mostly to be identified with the rabbinic movement, although the rabbis were not all of one mind on these matters. It would be difficult to provide any sort of timeline of these developments, although it will appear that the last generation of tannaim and first generation of amoraim were principal players in the spread of these linguistic ideologies. The build-up toward this trend as well as the rabbinic movement's eventual wider acceptance of Aramaic are difficult to treat in detail.

How should one account for the particular shape of R. Yochanan's dictum that the angels, implicitly understood to speak Hebrew, do not understand Aramaic (*b. Soṭah* 33a; *b. Šabb.* 12b)? The rise of the idea that the angels speak Hebrew is not in itself terribly problematic – after all, angels speak Hebrew throughout the Bible, even when they are overheard in their praise of God (Isa 6.3; Ezek 3.12) – but when the idea that the angels speak Hebrew is coupled with the idea that they do not speak Aramaic, we are met with a double proposition that apparently represented a matter of some rhetorical urgency. The suggestion is ready to hand that R. Yochanan sought to censure the use of Aramaic, at least within a certain context. But why would he do so? I suggested a couple of reasons: (1) R. Yochanan sought to proscribe the practice of extra-synagogal prayer (of which petitionary prayer is the most representative), thereby placing all liturgical activity under the control of whatever group was running the synagogue, and (2) he sought to exalt Hebrew in general as a way of empowering the *literati* (*viz.* the rabbis). While I think that one or the other reason is likely to be the correct explanation for R. Yochanan's insistence, I know of no way to get beyond their pairing as mutual possibilities to the question of which is the *real* (or more dominant) reason. This is a limitation of social history (which does much of its work through models that are sometimes mutually compatible), but the results of that approach remain useful even when they are equivocal.

The scenario obtaining in R. Yochanan's dictum can be contrasted with that of R. Hama b. Hanina. In chapter four, I suggested that the theory of prophetic inspiration adduced in *Gen. Rab.* 74.7 presupposes that angels speak an esoteric language, and that it is in this "holy" language that the angels bear prophetic messages to the prophets of Israel (but not to the prophets of other nations). The concept has a conceptual parallel in the (later) Yemenite *Midrash ha-Gadol*.[1] Whether this view actually goes back to R. Hama b. Hanina is a matter of importance for whether the variation of views should be understood in chronological terms: he was a contemporary of R. Yochanan, and the two purportedly belonged to the same circle. To the degree that R. Hama b. Hanina appears to be a proponent of an "esoteric language" view of angelic speech, we must be prepared to envision both views as competing on common ground. To be sure, there is nothing unlikely about this: by no stretch of the imagination can we suppose that the question of angelic languages was divisive. (We should also remember that R. Yochanan's dictum may have become more widely oper-

---

[1] See Hoffmann 1913:35.

ational in later generations than it was in his own.) In truth, most rabbis probably could not have cared less about what language the angels speak. But as we have seen, in the case of R. Yochanan, it was also a question with rhetorical potential for the rabbis' linguistic policy, and it is in the direction of that rhetorical usefulness that we gain a possible glimpse into the sociological and ideological aspects of the third-century amoraim.

The bulk of this study, however, did not pursue sociological questions, but aimed simply to undertake the first sustained survey of early Jewish and Christian texts evincing the notion of angelic language(s). Casual readers of the New Testament will have been familiar with 1 Cor 13.1, while seasoned academics will have also known about the *Testament of Job* (and possibly a few other references). Very few, I think, will have been aware of most of the references to angelic language(s) surveyed here. Thus simply listing the witnesses is perhaps a more worthwhile contribution to the study of ancient Judaism and early Christianity than the attempt to comment intelligently on those witnesses. Be that as it may, I hope the survey offered above will advance the field on a number of levels.

Appendix 1

Two Additional Solutions for "the Speech of Palm Trees"
(*b. B. Bat.* 134a ‖ *b. Sukkah* 28a)

The best way to understand R. Yochanan b. Zakkai's mastery of angelic "speech", in my view, is the one that I outlined in chapter four. Nevertheless, two other eminently possible solutions to the problem of the "speech of palm trees" deserve to be mentioned. The first solution derives from a straightforward exegesis of two magical texts from the Cairo Geniza. The second is a construct involving the hermetic/neoplatonic art of theurgy.

A. The *Palmgeister* in T.-S. K 1.56 and 1.147

An interesting passage appears in a couple of Cairo Geniza texts, which Peter Schäfer and Shaul Shaked date, on palaeographic grounds, to the eleventh century:[1]

T.-S. K 1.56, folio 1a, ll. 13b–20a

13 [...] בשם אל אתיה אסיה
14 ??? ??? הוה אהה שתפקון ותרחקון ותתבטלון מן
15 ??? ??? ומן מאתים וארבעום ושמנה אברים שיש בו
16 ??? ??? עמיה ודיתיב עמה ודשכיב עמיה
17 ??? ??? ??? ??? ??? ? ין ופתכברין בישין ובני אוגרי
18 ??? ??? ??? ??? ??? ?בני דקלי בשם יה יה יה וה צבאות
19 ??? ??? א?ו יה שלא תבואו אליו לא ביום ולא בלילה
20 ??? ?נים בעולם [...]

13 [...] With the names ʾL ʾTYH ʾSYH,
14 ??? ??? HWH ʾHH, that you come forth, and distance yourself, and desist from
15 ??? ??? and from the two hundred forty eight limbs that he has,
16 [and each, that dwells in him and stays][2] in him and sits with him and lies with him,
17 ??? ??? and evil idols and incubi,
18 [ŠB Ṭ-spirits, astral spirits] and palm tree [spirits] with the names YH YH YH WḤṢBʾWT
19 ??? ??? Y?W YH, that you not come upon him, either by day or by night,
20 or in any case. [...]

---

[1] See Schäfer and Shaked 1994:31, 222.
[2] Reconstruction according to Schäfer and Shaked 1994:34.

T.-S. K 1.147, folio 1a, ll. 30–6

[...]

30 בנדפה וכל דדאיר עימה ודקאים עימה

31 ודיתיב עימה ודשכיב עימה

32 ונפי?ין בושין וומילין

33 בישין ומזיקין בישין

34 ושטנין בישין ורוחין בישין ופהכברין בישין ובני איגרי ובני הצבט

35 ובני מזלי ובני דיקלי שלא תבואו אליה עוד ולא תבלבלו את דעתה

36 לא ביום ולא בלילה בשום פנים בעולם ולא

37 תתראו אליה עוד ולא בדמות אדם ולא בדמות

38 בהמה וחיה ועוף [...]

[...]
30 with her body and each, that dwells with her and stays with her
31 and sits with her and lies with her,
32 and evil *ne[f]ilim*,
33 and evil words and evil demons (of destruction)
34 and evil satans and evil spirits and evil idols and incubi and ḤṢB Ṭ-spirits,
35 and astral spirits and palm tree spirits, that you no more come to her, and that you no more confuse her mind,
36 either by day or by night, or in any case,
37 and that you appear to her no more, not in human form, and not in the form
38 of a beast, wild animal, or bird. [...]

In these two roughly parallel texts, "palm tree spirits" (בני דיקלי; *Palmgeister*) appear alongside shades, incubi, and other demons of affliction. I can offer no explanation for why a *Palmgeist* belongs in such company,[3] or what type of affliction it might specialize in, but these texts demonstrate that a connection between palm trees and demons existed, at least by the eleventh century. Supposing that a transcultural mythologem might be at work, it is worth noting that Carl Jung refers to a Nigerian soldier who claims to have heard the voice of an *oji* tree calling to him.[4] The significance of Jung's account for the present study is deepened somewhat with Jung's ascribing the voice to a spirit or "tree demon". If Jung is right, then we have here, in the form of this Nigerian soldier's belief, a connection between a *tree demon* and a human's privileged ability to hear the *voice of a tree*. The problem with this comparison, however, is that Jung's Nigerian seems to regard the tree demon as a beneficent power (or at least as an ally), while the *Palmgeister* in T.-S. K 1.56 and 1.147 are clearly maleficent.

To arrive at the triad "angels, demons, and palm trees" (requisite for understanding R. Yochanan b. Zakkai's abilities), we need only to imagine

---

[3] Schäfer and Shaked (1994:233) cite Joshua Trachtenberg in connection with the medieval Jewish and German traditions that associate demons with trees, but, on this explanation, it is not clear why these Cairo Geniza texts refer to *Palmgeister* rather than *Baumgeister*. See Trachtenberg 1939:34, 276 n. 25.

[4] Jung 1967:247–9.

a context in which angels are considered together with these demonic powers. This presents no problem, as the expression "angels, demons, and palm
trees" simply signifies that the extent of Yochanan b. Zakkai's linguistic
abilities extends to both good and evil invisible powers. Of course, the
greatest problem facing this solution is the fact that these two texts belong
to the eleventh century. Virtually all of the demonic species apart from the
Palmgeist were known in late antiquity (for incubi, see Tob 6.15 [short re-
cension]; *Gos. Phil.* 65.1–26 [late 2nd to early 3rd century C.E.]),[5] but we
do not know whether the *Palmgeist* was also known in late antiquity.
Without a clearer link back to an earlier demonology the argument is not
very strong.

B. Palm Trees as Neoplatonic Heliotropes

It is also possible to explain Yochanan b. Zakkai's mastery of the language
of palm trees through neoplatonic theurgy, a means of mystical ascent that
became popular with figures like Iamblichus and Proclus.[6] These theurgical techniques were influential in certain Jewish circles, and are a regular
feature of Hekhalot texts.[7] The details of theurgy that concern us here are
those associated with Proclus (412–485 C.E.). His *On the Hieratic Art* is an
extract from a lost work, presumably the *Commentary on the Chaldean
Oracles*.[8] In it, Proclus describes the sound heliotropes (*viz.* plants that turn

---

[5] See Ego 2003:312–13; Quispel 1975:164–5. The short-recensional Tobit reading
was found at Qumran – see 4QTob[a] ar 6.15.

[6] Cumont (1911:188) is still worth quoting: "Neo-Platonism, which concerned itself to
a large extent with demonology, leaned more and more towards theurgy, and was finally
completely absorbed by it."

[7] See the discussion of "theurgy in the Hekhalot texts" in Alexander 1973–87:361–3.
Leo Baeck attempted to show that the Jewish magical work *Sefer Yezira* was influenced
by Proclus' system (Baeck 1926; 1934), but Scholem (1974:26) argued, on stylistic
grounds, that the work precedes Proclus. In later works, Scholem (1987:29 n. 46) tempers
his dismissiveness of Baeck's thesis, and admits that "on some points of detail Baeck's
intepretations appear plausible and valuable". Ultimately, the only damage Scholem in-
flicts on Baeck's thesis is in the latter's insistence that *Proclus* (and not some other neoplatonist) is responsible for the influence. See Merlan 1965. According to Merlan,
"Ersetzen wir das Wort 'Proclus' durch 'Proclus und seine Gesinnungsgenossen im
Neuplatonismus,' so scheint die These Baecks im wesentlichen richtig zu sein" (Merlan
1965:181). The name "Proclus", of course, is ultimately not necessary for the thesis aired
in this section of my discussion.

[8] Greek text from Bidez 1924–32:6.139–51. The translation in T. Taylor 1968:343–7
is based on the Latin paraphrase of Marsilio Ficino, *De sacrificio et magia*, which is re-
produced in Copenhaver 1988:106–9. The English translation in Copenhaver 1988 is
based upon the Greek text of Bidez, which had been discovered subsequently to Taylor's
translation. (Copenhaver presents the text in English, Greek, and Latin.)

toward the sun)[9] make as they turn toward the sun – a sound imperceptible to (most) humans – as a hymn that these plants sing to their "king":

On the Hieratic Art 7–14
Why do heliotropes move together with the sun, selenotropes with the moon, moving around to the extent of their ability with the luminaries of the cosmos? All things pray according to their own order and sing hymns, either intellectually or rationally or naturally or sensibly (ἢ νοερῶς ἢ λογικῶς ἢ φυσικῶς ἢ αἰσθητῶς), to heads of entire chains. And since the heliotrope is also moved toward that to which it readily opens, if anyone hears it striking the air as it moves about, he perceives in the sound that it offers to the king the kind of hymn that a plant can sing.[10]

A few paragraphs later, Proclus compares the opening and closing of the lotus's petals, in time with the sun's circuit, with the opening and closing of the human mouth in hymning. Although the palm tree is neither a heliotrope nor a lotus,[11] Proclus includes it within his list of plants that have a

---

[9] See Sheppard 1982:220. The Proclean heliotrope may belong to a broader range of plants than modern botany considers heliotropic – e.g., neoplatonists apparently regarded the mallow as a heliotrope (see Clark 47 [note]) while Thessalus (a Hermetist) writes, "there are many kinds of 'heliotropes,' and of all these most efficacious is the one called chicory" (Thessalus, *Power of Herbs* 2.1, trans. Scarborough 1991:155 [an almost verbatim discussion appears in Scarborough 1988:30–1]; see the discussion in Delatte 1961:62–3). For other classical references to the heliotrope, see the "explanatory note" to Proclus, *On the Hieratic Art* 8, in Copenhaver 1988:105. In the ancient world, the heliotrope had widely celebrated magical properties, some of which are listed within the Pseudo-Solomonic *Epistle to Rehoboam* (7.4): see Ness 1999:151. Ness's dating of the *Letter of Rehoboam* to "the first century CE or the early second century" (Ness 1999:149) echoes the judgment of S. Carroll 1989. See also Festugière 1950–4:1.339–40. An early dating of the *Letter of Rehoboam* is purportedly helped by the first-century C.E. date that Scarborough 1988:144–8 assigns to Thessalus' *Power of Herbs*, on the basis of the "inclusion of exotic Eastern substances". Magical recipes are not immune from literary forces, however, and the inclusion of "exotic Eastern substances" possesses an enduring literary value: e.g., Stannard (1988:348) writes, of medieval writing, that "[r]eference to Near Eastern species growing in a literary garden was a common technique to indicate an exotic provenance".

[10] This is Copenhaver's translation (see below), which renders the Greek but apparently versifies according to the Latin. On this Proclean passage, see Hirschle 1979:14–15; Copenhaver 1988; Fauth 1995:143–4; Shaw 1995:48–9. On heliolatry in Proclus in general, see the introduction in Bidez 1924–32:6.139–47, esp. 144–8; Saffrey 1984; Fauth 1995:121–64; Shaw 1995:216–28. See also the discussion of the "simile of light" in Gersh 1973:90–4.

[11] In ancient iconography, the palm and the lotus represent opposing stylized renderings of leafy plants. See Danthine 1937:46–8. Magical recipes often involve herbs, but seldom trees. There is a possible use of the palm tree within the Greek magical papyri, but the reference is problematic. One of the recipes found there calls for νεῦρα φοίνικος, which can perhaps be translated as "fibers of the palm." Van den Broek (1972:56–7) prefers to translate the phrase as "sinews of the phoenix," citing Dioscurides' claim that magicians use this phrase to signify the *habrotonon* plant, and that "[i]t is highly unlikely

special association with the sun, in view of the manner in which its fronds radiate in imitation of the sun's rays:

On the Hieratic Art 65–9
In brief, then, such things as the plants mentioned above follow the orbits of the luminary; others imitate the appearance of its rays (e.g., the palm) or the empyrean substance (e.g., the laurel) or something else. So it seems that properties sown together in the sun are distributed among the angels, demons, souls, animals, plants, and stones that share them.

Proclus does not ascribe any sort of motion to the palm tree, such as comprised the "physical singing" of the heliotrope and lotus. It is possible, however, that Proclus, or at least some of his readers, had such a concept in mind: a gaonic responsum based on *b. Sukk.* 28a (now known as *Otzar ha-Gaonim* 67) would later describe the speech of palm trees precisely in terms of the movement of their fronds on a perfectly windless day:

אמרו כי יום שאין בו נשיבת הרוח וכשאתה פורם סדין אינה מתנענעת והיודע עומד בין שני דקלים שהם קרובים זה לזה ורואה איך ינועו [חריותיהם] זה לזה

It is said that on a day when no wind is blowing and if you spread a sheet it will not flap; then the one who knows stands between two date palms which are close to one another and observes how the fronds sway.[12]

This equation of a plant's speech with its movement recalls what Proclus wrote concerning the heliotrope and lotus. The connection between motion and creation's perpetual hymning is also found in Iamblichus, best known for his theurgical theorizing: "Sound and melodies are consecrated appropriately to each of the gods, and a kinship with them has been assigned appropriately according to the proper ranks and powers of each, and (according to) the motions in the universe itself and the harmonious sounds whirring as a result of these motions" (*Myst.* 118.6–119.4).[13] The extension of the hymn-singing ability to moving objects other than the mouth was an idea known to Jews: the notion that *bodies* can hymn through the movement of their parts is familiar from merkabah speculations based upon the

---

that they would have given this plant a magic name that was borrowed from another plant," *viz.* the palm. If van den Broek is right, then the herbal magical interpretation is left with no explanation for the choice of a palm tree – or of *any* tree, for that matter. See Deutsch 1999–2000:217. The fact that both Mandaean and Manichaean sources find religious symbolism in the palm tree may suggest the antiquity of this symbolism.

[12] Translation adapted from Visotzky 1994:206–7. Text from Lewin 1934:31. Gruenwald 1983 was the first to connect this gaonic responsum with the *Cologne Mani Codex*. This passage represents the most common attempt to explain "the discourse of palm trees." E.g., see Oberhänsli-Widmer 1998:54 n. 72. The Soncino translation of *b. B. Bat.* 134a (quoted in Forbes 1995:186 n. 12) seems to presuppose such an interpretation: it translates שיחת דקלים as "the whispering of the palms".

[13] Trans. Pearson 1992:265–6.

description of the heavenly creatures in Ezek 3.12–13 (cf. 10.5), in which the cherubim hymn God through the motion of their wings.[14] The (crudely correct) notion that sound is produced by moving objects vibrating the air apparently extends even to the understanding of how the tongue produces a voice. In the *Apostolic Constitutions*, we read that God created "living air for breathing in and out and rendering sound by the tongue striking the air."[15]

The supposition that Yochanan b. Zakkai (according to his doxographers) might have participated in neoplatonic theurgy is perhaps enhanced by the persistence of solar imagery within certain streams of late antique Judaism.[16] The Essene morning ritual (Josephus, *B.J.* II.128)[17] and the pronounced presence of Helios in third- and fourth-century C.E. synagogues[18] are two obvious examples of how heliolatry influenced Jewish religious expressions. The most telling evidence for a possible neoplatonic use of Helios within Jewish circles is found within the *Sefer ha-Razim*, a manual

---

[14] See *b. Ḥag.* 13b; *Gen. Rab.* 65.21; *Hekhalot Rabbati* 11.4 (= *Synopse* §189); Newsom 1987:27–8; 1998:353; Halperin 1988:52–3, 59, 388–9, 398; Weinfeld 1995:137. Cf. Maimonides's doubts on this matter (derived from Aristotle) in *Guide of the Perplexed* 2.8 (Pines 1963:267), and the discussion of his inconsistencies in Kreisel 2001:291. In the later Islamic speculations of al-Suhrawardī, the sound of Gabriel's wings would become the command that produces all things (see Schimmel 1988). It is also possible that Proclus' notion of the palm's theurgical "sympathy" comprises the true essence of this "physical singing." Certainly, modern mystical appreciations of Proclus do not see such an inference as involving any sort of leap at all – cf. esp. the detailed use of these Proclean passages as a heuristic for understanding the *sympathy* of Sufism in Corbin 1969:105–12. The problem with resorting to these modern reappropriations, of course, is that their eclecticism compromises their usefulness for the history of religions in late antiquity. The assumption that Proclus predicated the "praying" ability of all things upon their ability to move is not totally secure, but, in the light of *Otzar ha-Gaonim* 67, it is perhaps better founded than Corbin's attempt to equate prayer to the sun with an apparently motion-independent "heliopathy."

[15] Trans. Fiensy 1985:101. The characterization of sound as vibrating air remained prominent up until the Italian Renaissance, and afterwards: see Boyle 1977:20 (on Quintilian, Varro, Erasmus).

[16] On the importance of Helios for neoplatonism, see Porphyry, *Letter to Anebo* 2.9 (reconstructed text in Parthey 1857:xxix–xlv; ET in T. Taylor 1968:1–16); Iamblichus, *Myst.* 7.2, 4; and esp. Julian's *Hymn to Helios* (in W. Wright 1913:1.353–435). See Rosán 1949:126, 188, 212–14.

[17] See Mendels 1979:218–19; M. Smith 1982; 1984 (with a response: Milgrom 1985); J. M. Baumgarten 1983; and Philonenko 1985. See also Ulfgard 1998:53–4. The Qumranic morning ritual echoed that of pagans throughout the Mediterranean world. See Halsberghe 1972:35–6 n. 10.

[18] Among the many treatments of the zodiac in synagogue mosaics, the following emphasize the presence of Helios: Goodenough 1953–68:8.214–15; Dothan 1968; Maier 1979:382–5. See also Hoffman 1981:22–3; Stuckrad 2000.

of magic that includes spells invoking Helios,[19] along with the prayer to Helios in the so-called "Eighth Book of Moses" (*PGM* 13.254–63), and in the elements of Helios devotion embedded in the so-called "Prayer of Jacob" found in the pseudepigraphic *Ladder of Jacob*.[20] This belief that the sun was in some way identified with the highest God, perhaps as the face of God or some similar manifestation of divine glory,[21] may be a holdover from heretical expressions of Yahwism during the days of the prophets (see 2 Kgs 23.5, 11; Ps 18.5; 19.6; Jer 44.15–20; Ezek 8.16).[22] The renewed interest that pagans took in the sun god would also have been an influence in this direction. The role of this god within Roman imperial policy is especially important for understanding the religious milieu of the early rabbinic (tannaitic and amoraic) period.[23]

The principal shortcoming of the neoplatonist interpretation of "the conversation of palm trees" is that it is unable to account for the teaming of "palm trees" with "angels" and "demons". This alone perhaps makes the Temple iconography scenario more tenable.

---

[19] See Maier 1979:375–80; Ness 1999:155–8; Lesses 1996:49–51. Cf. the numerous appearances of Helios in the Greek magical papyri, discussed in Fauth 1995:34–120. Cf. also the divine figure σεμες ειλαμ, mentioned in numerous magical texts, and whose name is taken by most scholars to be a transliteration of עולם שמש ("Eternal Sun") – but cf. the alternative view in Sperber 1994:81–91.

[20] On the "Eighth Book of Moses," see Dieterich 1891:137. On *Sefer ha-Razim* and the "Eighth Book of Moses," see Lesses 1998:292–6. On the *Prayer of Jacob*, see Leicht 1999:153–9. More generally, see Goodman 2007:205–17.

[21] See Plutarch, *Moralia* 781f–782a (=*To an Uneducated Ruler* 5), and the discussion thereof in Chesnut 1986:151–3.

[22] See Hollis 1933; Saggs 1960; Morgenstern 1963; Sarna 1967; Stähli 1985; R. P. Carroll 1986:733–8; M. S. Smith 1990:115–24; G. Taylor 1993; Boyd-Taylor 1998. On the possible connection between sun worship and Sukkoth, see the works listed in Rubenstein 1995:138–9 n. 133. Maier (1979:354) writes, "Von der Kulttheologie her bleibt die Sonne weiterhin das nächstliegende Vergleichsobjekt für die 'Herrlichkeit' Gottes (Sir 42,16) und dient somit als Theophanie-Symbol (vgl. Sir 50,7)."

[23] Ness 1999 notes the attention that emperors had given to this god: Vespasian's soldiers greeted the rising sun "after the Syrian custom" (first century C.E.), Aurelian named *Sol Invictus* the official protector of the Empire (third century C.E.), Constantine worshipped *Sol Invictus* (fourth century C.E.), and Julian, writing as a popularizing Neoplatonist, composed a *Hymn to Helios* (fourth century C.E.). On Julian's hymn, see Fauth 1995:121–64.

Appendix 2

A Partial Response to Christopher Forbes on the Nature of
New Testament Glossolalia

In 1995, Christopher Forbes published *Prophecy and Inspired Speech in Early Christianity and its Hellenistic Environment*. The main thesis of the book is that Christian glossolalia is a unique phenomenon, not comparable to the varieties of ecstatic speech or notions of divine language found in hellenistic sources. As a setup for this larger thesis, or possibly as a supporting argument for it, Forbes also argues that glossolalia, as known from the New Testament, is a supernatural speaking in *human languages* – that is, he finds the description of the miracle in Acts 2 to be normative for *all* the accounts and discussions of glossolalia throughout the New Testament. The purpose of the following is to examine Forbes's argument for the human linguistic nature of glossolalia, especially as it relates to his explicit suggestion that NT glossolalia is (usually) *not* angeloglossy.

As the scheme Forbes promotes is pitted against several alternative schemes with varying degrees of overlap, he sometimes appears to have difficulty keeping his arguments aligned with what it is they purport to show. Thus Forbes enlists, as arguments for glossolalia's being composed of specifically *human* languages, a number of arguments that work equally well for an angeloglossic understanding of glossolalia. He lists five possible views of glossolalia:

(a) Paul, like Luke, thought of glossolalia as the miraculous ability to speak unlearned human languages. (b) Paul thought of glossolalia as the miraculous ability to speak heavenly or angelic languages. (c) Paul thought of glossolalia as some combination of (a) and (b). (d) Paul thought of glossolalia as a kind of sub- or pre-linguistic form of speech, or possibly as a kind of coded utterance, analogous but not identical to speech. ... (e) Paul thought of glossolalia as (or glossolalia actually was) an idiosyncratic form of language, a kind of dialect for prayer, in which archaic or foreign terms dominated.[1]

Here we see that Forbes differentiates the human-language view (designated "(a)") from the angeloglossic view ("(b)"). Yet most of the arguments that he puts forward in support of (a) work equally well with (b):

[1] Forbes 1995:57–8. Cf. the list of 12 views of glossolalia in Cartledge 2002:63. See also the various understandings explored in Cartledge 2006.

The following contentions are advanced in favour of (a): the parallel with Luke suggests *a priori* that a miraculous gift of language is intended, as does the closely related terminology. The Greek γλῶσσα, like the English "tongue", can mean little else in this context, and the related gift, "interpretation" (1 Corinthians 12.30, 14.5, 13, etc.), is most naturally understood in its primary sense of (inspired) "translation". Paul's explicit statement, "If I speak in the tongues of men and angels" (13.1) is clearly central here. Likewise important is his argument that "If I do not grasp the meaning of what someone is saying, I am a foreigner (βάρβαρος) to the speaker, and he is a foreigner to me" (14.11). It is further urged that the plain meaning of Paul's quotation from Isaiah 28.11–12, in ch. 14.20ff., has to do with foreign languages.[2]

Certainly, the meaning of γλῶσσα, the significance of 1 Cor 13.1, and Paul's point about being a foreigner to one whom one does not understand all stand equally in support of an angeloglossic understanding of glossolalia. Forbes in fact admits that "several of these passages" (he does not refer directly to his "arguments") can support an angeloglossic understanding. In fact, only the first and the last of the arguments he lists would (if cogent) favor a human-language view of glossolalia over an angeloglossic view. He also writes that the reference to "the tongues of men" in 1 Cor 13.1 would be "something of a puzzle" on the terms of the angeloglossic view. The arguments he gives against the angeloglossic view are therefore primarily three: (1) angeloglossy is not in view in Acts 2, (2) the original, contextual meaning of Isa 28.11–12 (which Paul quotes) has to do with foreign rather than angelic languages, and (3) the reference to "the tongues of men" in 1 Cor 13.1 is left unexplained. I will discuss each of these in turn.

Given the way in which scholarship usually cordons off the Acts 2 description of xenoglossy as a special case – not at all normative for the NT understanding of glossolalia – the reader of Forbes's book may find his questioning of this state of affairs somewhat bold. (That in itself is not bad, and can even be a good thing.) Indeed, readers who know the field might be surprised that Forbes assumes that Luke's description of the speech miracle in Acts 2 applies equally to the speech miracles in Acts 10 and 19! We might well ask, therefore, whether Forbes gives proper consideration to the reasons scholars usually judge Acts 2 to be a special case. As far as I

---

[2] Forbes 1995:58. Forbes is not the only one to argue that glossolalia comprises a supernatural speaking of human languages that one has not learned. Although this view is rare, Gundry (1996) argued it forty years ago, and Turner (1998a:227–9; 1998b:236) has argued it more recently than Forbes. Luke Timothy Johnson unfortunately confuses the question of what the early Christians understood glossolalia to be with what it really was. He does this twice in L. T. Johnson 1992:596–7, once in dispensing with the "angelic language" theory and once again in dispensing with the "unknown human languages" theory. Thus he speaks disparaging of the angeloglossic understanding of glossolalia as "patently folkloric rather than scientific" (L. T. Johnson 1992:597) and reasons as if Paul's understanding, whatever it might be, would have to be "scientifically" sound.

can see, he does not address the issue: his effort to join Acts 2 and the other NT accounts and descriptions of glossolalia into a single model seems to focus entirely on rehabilitating Acts 2 as an account substantially unaltered by Luke. That is, Forbes argues against the (almost standard) view that Luke took what was originally an account of a (non-xenoglossic) glossolalic miracle and turned it into an account of xenoglossy. He writes that "many [have] argue[d] that Luke's interpretation of (at least) the Pentecostal glossolalia of ch. 2 as unlearned foreign languages is secondary and unhistorical, and determined by his theological interests", and therefrom tells us why this understanding of Acts 2 is inadequate.[3] The problem with this, of course, is that dismissing the fruits of redaction criticism still leaves us with a Pentecost account that looks like a one-time event fraught with special theological significance for the birth of the Church. The prophetic significance of God gathering the nations together in Jerusalem is too transparent within the symbolism of Acts 2 not to be tied to what happens, and, as a fulfillment of prophecy that could only happen in Jerusalem, the aspects of the miracle that contribute to that scenario scarcely commend themselves as constituent elements of glossolalia. There is also a strong traditions-historical presumption against Forbes's reading of Acts 2, as scholars regularly note that Acts 2 recalls Jewish traditions surrounding the Sinai event found in a variety of sources. That the people heard a divine word in a "familiar language" appears, in fact, to be indebted to this history of traditions, as Philo wrote, in his commentary on the Decalogue, that the flame that the people saw on Sinai "became articulated speech in the *language familiar* to the audience" (*Dec.* 46).[4] These two objections represent two serious strikes against the historicity of Luke's presentation of the Pentecost miracle as xenoglossy. But even if there were no question of the historicity of Luke's account, there would still be a serious doubt as to whether the xenoglossic form of the disciples' utterances was normative for Christian glossolalia in general, including the other accounts of glossolalia within Acts. Forbes does not seem to recognize this.

Forbes also contends that, since the original, contextual meaning of Isa 28.11–12 is about foreign languages, it stands to reason that anyone using this verse as a prooftext for glossolalia would assume that that charism had something to do with speaking foreign languages. The chief problem with this is that first-century Christian authors often did not respect the original, contextual meaning of Scripture in the way Forbes imagines.[5] The really

---

[3] Forbes 1995:48.

[4] See Park 2008:212–13.

[5] One recent school of thought, associated esp. with the works of Richard B. Hays, understands many of Paul's citations of Scripture to be "metaleptic" or intertextual in nature, implicitly invoking the wider context of an original quotation from Scripture.

strange thing about this is that Forbes comes close to saying precisely that: he writes that "the most plausible reconstruction" is that "Paul cites Isaiah 28.11 with very little regard for the nuances of the context".[6] Forbes seems to put Paul on a tightrope: Paul wanted to preserve the original signific-ance of the passage, but he has little use for the "nuances" that comprise or shape that significance. A better solution, I suggest, would be to say that Paul used the verse just as recklessly as he appears to have used it, or, bet-ter yet, that Paul's use of the verse answers to a prior Corinthian use of that verse – a solution suggested by a number of details, including the textual form of the quotation.[7]

Forbes furthermore thinks that the reference to "the tongues of men" in 1 Cor 13.1 is troubling for the thesis that glossolalia is primarily angelog-lossic. In response, I would steer the reader to my comments in the rele-vant section of Chapter 4 (above).[8] There (at the end of that section) I put forward an alternative understanding of "the tongues of men and of angels" that I believe supports an angeloglossic understanding of glossolalia while doing full justice to the reference to "the tongues of men".[9]

After giving these three objections to an angeloglossic understanding of glossolalia, Forbes's most consistent strategy for keeping the readers' doubts about angeloglossy alive is to call attention to the fact that that

---

(See esp. Hays 1989.) But even if this might sometimes be the case – I am not convinced that it usually is – it cannot be assumed to be so in a given instance, and would scarcely obtain when Paul cites a verse out of deference to his opponents' battery of texts. The attempt in Watson 2004:128–9, 193 to bridge the chasm between the original meaning of Paul's quotations and what Paul thought they meant is hardly convincing, as it relies on the mistaken notion that a "dialogical" hermeneutic can stand in for "the 'literal sense' of the text".

[6] Forbes 1995:180.

[7] Elsewhere I have argued that the form of Isa 28.11–12 found in 1 Cor 14.21 actually comes from a testimonium that the Corinthians used as a prooftextual support for their understanding of glossolalia, and that 14.22 is a continuation of the Corinthian view: Poirier 2004c.

[8] See pp. 49–51 above. Cf. also D. B. Martin's response (1995:267 n. 3) to Forbes's reading of 1 Cor 13.1: "Contrary to Forbes's exegesis, Paul's statement about 'tongues of men' in 1 Cor. 13:1 is in opposition to 'tongues of angels.' The latter refers to glossola-lia, the former to normal speech. The construction is the rhetorical commonplace 'from the lesser to the greater'."

[9] As a final comment on the angeloglossy view, Forbes 1995:58–9 examines E. Earle Ellis's argument that angeloglossic glossolalia was tied to the role of angels in conveying prophecies. Here it only needs to be said that, although Ellis's argument for angelic spi-rits of prophecy is convincing, his argument that this explains the need for glossolalia seems to be uniquely his. As such, Forbes's objections to Ellis's view hardly count as arguments against the angeloglossy view in general. See Ellis 1993:23–44.

view hangs on just two words in 1 Cor 13.1.[10] I doubt that this can carry much weight: two words in Paul are still two words. They can be marginalized in terms of their importance for Paul, but they cannot be swept under the rug.

In addition to Forbes's arguments for questioning an angeloglossic understanding of glossolalia, we should briefly consider an argument that Max Turner puts forth (in response to James D. G. Dunn): "If Paul thought all tongues were angelic he is unlikely to have maintained they belong only to our pre-resurrection 'childhood' (1 Cor. 13.11) and will pass away."[11] This argument, I think, scarcely can withstand even the briefest consideration of the context of 1 Cor 13.11. Certainly, Paul's reference to "the tongues of men and of angels" (1 Cor 13.1) should be taken to set the semantic range of the reference to the "tongues" that will be obsolesced at the *parousia* (13.8). If one objects to Paul's thinking that "the tongues of angels" will cease at the *parousia*, then one must also judge the composition of 1 Corinthians 13 to be somewhat dishonest. There are, in fact, ways of accounting for what Paul says that do not problematize the angeloglossic understanding of glossolalia. For example, it may be that the cessation of tongues, knowledge, prophecy, etc. relates to a neoplatonic-style reabsorption of creation into the pleroma. Or it may be that the cessation of, say, knowledge really refers to the end of *spiritually derived* knowledge – some day "we will know even as we are known", which will make the gift of knowledge obsolete. In that day, our participation in heavenly language will not have to be effected by a charism. And so, an angeloglossic understanding of glossolalia is not incompatible with the idea that tongues will one day cease.

---

[10] E.g., Forbes 1995:62 n. 40, 155–6. Elsewhere, Forbes (1995:58–9) writes, "It would seem to me that the widely held view that Paul must *primarily* mean heavenly languages is implausible, being as it is based heavily on the phrase 'and angels' in 1 Corinthians 13.1, which does look like a rhetorical flourish. 'Or even those of angels' may well be the sense Paul intended."

[11] Turner 1998a:228. But Turner continues, "Given this, however, we need not reject that Paul thought some types of 'tongue' (cf. *genē glōssōn*; 12:10) were angelic (as, e.g., in *Test. Job* 48–50; *Apoc. Zeph.* 8, ...)."

Bibliography

A. Primary Literature

Adriaen, M. (ed.), 1958. Cassiodorus, *Expositio psalmorum*, CCSL 97–98, Turnholt: Brepols.

Alexander, Philip S. (trans.), 1983. '3 (Hebrew Apocalypse of) Enoch', 223–316, In *Old Testament Pseudepigrapha*, Vol. 1: *Apocalyptic Literature and Testaments*, Edited by James H. Charlesworth, Garden City, NY: Doubleday.

Andersen, F. I. (trans.), 1983. '2 (Slavonic Apocalypse of) Enoch', 91–221, In *Old Testament Pseudepigrapha*, Vol. 1: *Apocalyptic Literature and Testaments*, Edited by James H. Charlesworth, Garden City, NY: Doubleday.

Archambault, Georges (ed. and trans.), 1909. *Dialogue avec Tryphon*, 2 vols., Textes et Documents Pour l'Étude Historique du Christianisme, Paris, A. Picard.

Augustine, 1956a. *Sancti Aurelii Augustini, Enarrationes in psalmos I – L*, *Aurelii Augustini Opera*, Part 10, Vol. 1, CCSL 38, Turnhout: Brepols.

Augustine, 1956b. *Sancti Aurelii Augustini, Enarrationes in psalmos LI – C*, *Aurelii Augustini Opera*, Part 10, Vol. 2, CCSL 39, Turnhout: Brepols.

Babbitt, Frank Cole (ed. and trans.), 1999. Plutarch, *Moralia*, Vol. 5, Loeb Classical Library 306, Cambridge: Harvard University Press.

Bidez, Joseph (ed.), 1924–32. *Catalogue des manuscrits alchimiques Grecs*, 8 vols., Brussels: Maurice Lamertin.

Blackman, Philip (ed. and trans.), 1983. *Mishnayoth*, 7 vols., 2nd ed., Gateshead: Judaica.

Borret, Marcel (ed. and trans.), 1967–76. Origen, *Contre Celse*, 5 vols., Sources Chrétiennes 132, 136, 147, 150, 227, Paris: Cerf.

Box, G. H., 1918. *The Apocalypse of Abraham*, London: SPCK.

Brock, Sebastian (ed.), 1967. *Testamentum Iobi*, Pseudepigrapha Veteris Testamenti Graece 2 (Part 1), Leiden: Brill.

–, 1979. 'John the Solitary, *On Prayer*', *JTS* 30: 84–101.

Burchard, Christoph, 1985. 'Joseph and Aseneth', 177–247, In *Old Testament Pseudepigrapha*, Vol. 2: *Expansions of the "Old Testament" and Legends, Wisdom and Philosophical Literature, Prayers, Psalms and Odes, Fragments of Lost Judeo-Hellenistic Works*, Edited by James H. Charlesworth, Garden City, NY: Doubleday.

Cameron, Ron, and Arthur J. Dewey (trans.), 1979. *The Cologne Mani Codex (P. Colon. inv. nr. 4780): "Concerning the Origin of his Body"*, SBLTT 15, Missoula, MT: Scholars Press.

Caster, Marcel (trans.), 1951. Clément d'Alexandrie, *Les stromates*, Book 1, Sources Chrétiennes 30, Paris: Cerf.

Charles, R. H., 1913. *The Apocrypha and Pseudepigrapha of the Old Testament*, 2 Vols., Oxford: Clarendon.

Charlesworth, J. H. (trans.), 1985. 'Prayer of Jacob', 715–23, In *Old Testament Pseudepigrapha*, Vol. 2: *Expansions of the "Old Testament" and Legends, Wisdom and Philosophical Literature, Prayers, Psalms and Odes, Fragments of Lost Judeo-Hellenistic Works*, Edited by James H. Charlesworth, Garden City, NY: Doubleday.

– (trans.), 1985. 'Prayer of Manasseh', 625–37, In *Old Testament Pseudepigrapha*, Vol. 2: *Expansions of the "Old Testament" and Legends, Wisdom and Philosophical Literature, Prayers, Psalms and Odes, Fragments of Lost Judeo-Hellenistic Works*, Edited by James H. Charlesworth, Garden City, NY: Doubleday.

Clark, Gillian (trans.), 1989. *Iamblichus: On the Pythagorean Life*, Translated Texts for Historians 8, Liverpool: Liverpool University Press.

Clarke, Emma C., John M. Dillon, and Jackson P. Hershbell (trans.), 2003. *Iamblichus: De mysteriis*, Writings from the Greco-Roman World 4, Atlanta: Society of Biblical Literature.

Cohen, Abraham (ed.), 1984. *Minor Tractates*, London: Soncino.

Colson, F. H., G. H. Whitaker, and Ralph Marcus (trans.), 1958–62. Philo, 12 vols., Loeb Classical Library, Cambridge: Harvard University Press.

Copenhaver, Brian (trans.), 1992. *Hermetica: The Greek* Corpus Hermeticum *and the Latin* Asclepius *in a New English Translation, with Notes and Introduction*, Cambridge: Cambridge University Press.

Crum, W. E. (trans.), 1909. 'Translation' (of the Coptic *Book of the Resurrection*), 110–36, In *The Light of Egypt from Recently Discovered Predynastic and Early Christian Records*, Edited by Robert de Rustafjaell, London: Kegan Paul, Trench, Trübner & Co.

Danby, Herbert, 1933. *The Mishnah*, Oxford: Oxford University Press.

des Places, Edouard (ed.), and Marguerite Forrat (trans.), 1986. Eusebius, *Contre Hiéroclès*, Sources chrétiennes 333, Paris: Cerf.

Diels, Hermann (ed.), 1917. Philodemos, *Über die Götter, Drittes Buch: Griechischer Text*, Abhandlungen der königlich preussischen Akademie der Wissenschaften: Philosophisch-Historische Klasse 4, Berlin: Königliche Akademie der Wissenschaften.

Doutreleau, Louis (ed. and trans.), 1976. Origen, *Homélies sur la Genèse*, Sources chrétiennes 7, Paris: Cerf.

Eisenstein, J. D. (ed.), 1915. *Ozar Midrashim: A Library of Two Hundred Minor Midrashim*, Vol. 2, New York: J. D. Eisenstein.

Epstein, Isidore (ed.), 1935–78. *The Babylonian Talmud*, 35 vols., London: Soncino.

Evans, Ernest (ed. and trans.), 1972. Tertullian, *Adversus Marcionem*, Books 4–5, Oxford Early Christian Texts, Oxford: Clarendon.

Festugière, R. P., 1950–54. *La révélation d'Hermès Trismégiste*, 4 vols., Paris: J. Gabalda.

Finkelstein, Louis, and H. S. Horovitz (ed.), 1969. *Sifre 'al Sefer Devarim*, New York: Jewish Theological Seminary of America.

Flemming, J., and H. Duensing (trans.), 1965. 'The Ascension of Isaiah', 642–63, In Edgar Hennecke, *New Testament Apocrypha*, (ed. by Wilhelm Schneemelcher) Vol. 2: *Writings Relating to the Apostles; Apocalypses and Related Subjects*, Philadelphia: Westminster.

Fowler, Harold North (ed. and trans.), 1969. Plutarch, *Moralia*, Vol. 10, Loeb Classical Library 321, London: William Heinemann.

Freddoso, Alfred J., and Francis E. Kelley (trans.), 1991. William of Ockham, *Quodlibetal Questions*, New Haven: Yale University Press.

Fredouille, Jean-Claude (ed. and trans.), 1984. Tertullien, *De la patience*, Sources Chrétiennes 310, Paris: Cerf.

Friedrich, Hans-Veit (ed. and trans.), 1990. Tertullian, *De exhortatione castitatis = Ermahnung zur Keuschheit*, Beiträge zur Altertumskunde 2, Stuttgart: B. G. Teubner.

García Martínez, Florentino (trans.), 1996. *The Dead Sea Scrolls Translated: The Qumran Texts in English*, 2nd ed., Leiden: E. J. Brill.

García Martínez, Florentino, and Eibert J. C. Tigchelaar (trans.), 1997–8. *The Dead Sea Scrolls Study Edition*, 2 Vols., Leiden: E. J. Brill.

Grese, W. C., and E. N. O'Neil (trans.), 1986. '*PGM* IV.930–1114', 156–60, In *The Greek Magical Papyri in Translation, Including the Demotic Spells*, Edited by Hans Dieter Betz, Vol. 1: *Texts*, 2nd ed., Chicago: University of Chicago Press.

Gruenwald, Ithamar, 1972 (ed.). 'Visions of Ezekiel,' 101–39, In *Temirion: Texts and Studies in Kabbala and Hasidism*, Vol. 1, Edited by Israel Weinstock, Jerusalem: Mossad Harav Kook.

Ha-Levi, Judah, 1997–2002. *Ha-Kuzari*, 3 vols., Jerusalem: Nezer-David.

Halm, Carolus (ed.), 1983. Sulpicius Severus, *Libri qui supersunt*, New York: Hildesheim.

Hansen, Günther Christian (ed. and trans.), 2004. Sozomen, *Historia ecclesiastica = Kirchengeschichte*, 4 vols., Fontes Christiani 73, Turnhout: Brepols.

Hanssens, Jean Michel (ed.), 1948–50. Amalarius of Metz, *Opera liturgica omnia*, Studi e testi 138–40, Vatican City: Biblioteca apostolica vaticana.

Harrington, Daniel J. (ed.), and Jacques Cazeaux (trans.), 1976. Pseudo-Philo, *Les antiquités bibliques*, Vol. 1, Sources Chrétiennes 229, Paris: Cerf.

Hieronymus, 1970. *S. Hieronymi presbyteri opera*, Part 1, *Opera exegetica*, Vol. 6, *Commentarii in prophetas minores*, CCSL 76A, Turnhout: Brepols.

Hoffmann, David Zvi (ed.), 1913. *Midrasch ha-Gadol zum Buche Exodus*, Vol. 1, Schriften des Vereins Mekize Nirdamim 3/19, Berlin: Itzkowski.

Migne, J.-P., 1857. Origen, *Opera omnia*, Patrologiæ Cursus Completus, Series Graeca 11–17, Paris: Garnier Fratres.

Migne, J.-P., 1879. Hugonis de S. Victore, *Opera omnia*, Patrologiæ Cursus Completus, Series Latina Prior 177, Rev. ed., Paris: Garnier Fratres.

James, Montague Rhodes (trans.), 1924. *The Apocryphal New Testament*, Oxford: Clarendon.

Johnson, M. D. (trans.), 1985. 'Life of Adam and Eve', 249–95, In *Old Testament Pseudepigrapha*, Vol. 2: *Expansions of the "Old Testament" and Legends, Wisdom and Philosophical Literature, Prayers, Psalms and Odes, Fragments of Lost Judeo-Hellenistic Works*, Edited by James H. Charlesworth, Garden City, NY: Doubleday.

Knibb, M. A. (trans.), 1985. 'Martyrdom and Ascension of Isaiah', 143–76, In *Old Testament Pseudepigrapha*, Vol. 2: *Expansions of the "Old Testament" and Legends, Wisdom and Philosophical Literature, Prayers, Psalms and Odes, Fragments of Lost Judeo-Hellenistic Works*, Edited by James H. Charlesworth, Garden City, NY: Doubleday.

Kraft, Robert A. (ed.), 1974. *The Testament of Job, According to the SV Text*, SBLTT 5, Pseudepigrapha Series 4, Missoula: Scholars Press.

Kropp, Angelicus M., 1930–1. *Ausgewählte koptische Zaubertexte*, 3 vols., Bruxelles: La Fondation Égyptologique Reine Élisabeth.

Krueger, Derek, 1996. *Symeon the Holy Fool: Leontius' Life and the Late Antique City*, Transformation of the Classical Heritage 25, Berkeley: University of California Press.

Kuhn, K. H. (trans.), 1984. 'The Apocalypse of Zephaniah and an Anonymous Apocalypse', 915–25, In *The Apocryphal Old Testament*, Edited by H. F. D. Sparks, Oxford: Clarendon.

Lake, Kirsopp (ed. and trans.), 1980. Eusebius, *The Ecclesiastical History*, Vol. 1, Loeb Classical Library 153, Cambridge: Harvard University Press.

– (ed. and trans.), 1985–92. *The Apostolic Fathers*, 2 vols.; Loeb Classical Library 24–25, Cambridge: Harvard University Press.

Layton, Bentley (trans.), 1987. *The Gnostic Scriptures*, Garden City: Doubleday.

Lewin, Benjamin Manasseh (ed.), 1934. *Otzar ha-Gaonim: Thesaurus of the Ganoic Responsa and Commentaries, Following the Order of the Talmudic Tractates*, Vol. 6, Book 2: *Tractate Sukkah*, Jerusalem: Central Press.

Liebermann, Saul (ed.), 1974. *Midrash Devarim Rabbah*, Jerusalem: Wahrmann.

Loi, Vincenzo (ed. and trans.), 1975. Novatian, *La Trinità*, Corona Patrum, Torino: Società Editrice Internazionale.

Luz, Ulrich, 2004. 'Paul as Mystic', 131–43, In *The Holy Spirit and Christian Origins: Essays in Honor of James D. G. Dunn*, Edited by Graham N. Stanton, Bruce W. Longenecker, and Stephen C. Barton, Grand Rapids: Eerdmans.

Luzzatto, Maria Jagoda, and Antonius la Penna (eds.), Babrius, *Mythiambi Aesopei*, Bibliotheca Scriptorum Graecorum et Romanorum Teubneriana, Leipzig: Teubner.

Macho, Alejandro Díez (ed.), R. Le Déaut, Martin McNamara, and Michael Maher (trans.), 1968. *Neophyti 1: Targum Palestinense ms. de la Biblioteca Vaticana*, Vol. 1: *Génesis*, Textos y estudiios / Seminario Filológico 'Cardenal Cisneros' del Instituto Arias Montano 7, Madrid: Consejo Superior de Investigaciones Científicas.

Maher, Michael (trans.), 1992. *Targum Pseudo-Jonathan, Genesis*, The Aramaic Bible 1B, Collegeville, MN: Liturgical.

Mair, G. R. (trans.), 1977. Callimachus, *Hymns and Epigrams*, Lycophron, Aratus, Loeb Classical Library 129, Cambridge: Harvard University Press.

Marcus, Ralph (trans.), 1953–61. Philo, *Supplement*, 2 vols., Loeb Classical Library, Cambridge: Harvard University Press.

Margalioth, Mordecai (ed.), 1966. *Sepher Ha-Razim: A Newly Recovered Book of Magic from the Talmudic Period*, Jerusalem: American Academy for Jewish Research.

Mathews, Edward G. Jr., and Joseph P. Amar (trans.), 1994. *St. Ephrem the Syrian: Selected Prose Works*, (ed. Kathleen McVey) The Fathers of the Church, Washington, DC: Catholic University of America.

Merkelbach, Reinhold, and Josef Stauber, 2001. *Steinepigramme aus dem griechischen Osten*, Vol. 3: *Der "Ferne Osten" und das Landesinnere bis zum Tauros*, Munich/Leipzig: K. G. Saur.

Metzger, Bruce M., and Roland E. Murphy (eds.), 1994. *The New Oxford Annotated Bible*, New York: Oxford University Press.

Mohrmann, Christine (intro.), G. J. M. Bartelink (ed.), and Marino Barchiesi (trans.), 1974. Palladius, *La storia lausiaca*, Scrittori Greci e Latini, Vite dei santi 2, Milano: Fondazione Lorenzo Valla.

Morales, Edgardo M. (ed.), and Pierre Leclerc (trans.), 2007. Jerome, *Trois vies de moines (Paul, Malchus, Hilarion)*, Sources Chrétiennes 508, Paris: Cerf.

Morgan, Michael A. (trans.), 1983. *Sepher Ha-Razim: The Book of the Mysteries*, SBLTT 25, Pseudepigrapha Series 11, Chico, CA: Scholars Press.

Morris, J. B. (trans.), 1897. *Select Works of S. Ephrem the Syrian: Translated Out of the Original Syriac*, Oxford: John Henry Parker.

Most, Glenn W. (ed. and trans.), 2006. Hesiod, *Theogony, Works and Days, Testimonia*, Loeb Classical Library 57, Cambridge: Harvard University Press.

Neusner, Jacob (trans.), 1985. *Genesis Rabbah: The Judaic Commentary to the Book of Genesis: A New American Translation*, 3 vols., BJS 106, Atlanta: Scholars Press.

Newsom, Carol A., 1985. *Songs of the Sabbath Sacrifice: A Critical Edition*, Atlanta: Scholars Press.

–, 1998. 'Shirot ʿOlat HaShabbat', 173–402, In *Qumran Cave 4, VI: Poetical and Liturgical Texts, Part 1*, Edited by Esther Eshel, Hanan Eshel, Carol Newsom, Bilhah Nitzan, Eileen Schuller, and Ada Yardeni, DJD 11, Oxford: Clarendon.

Norelli, Enrico (ed.), 1987. Hippolytus, *L'Anticristo = De antichristo*, Biblioteca Patristica 10, Firenze: Nardini.

Nestle, Eberhard, Barbara Aland, Kurt Aland, Johannes Karavidopoulos, Carlo M. Martini, and Bruce M. Metzger (eds.), 1996. *Novum Testamentum Graece*, Stuttgart: Deutsche Bibelgesellschaft.

O'Brien, T. C. (ed. and trans.), 1964. Thomas Aquinas, *Summa theologiæ*, Vol. 14, New York: Blackfriars.

O'Kane, John (trans.), 2002. Shams al-Dīn Aḥmad-e Aflākī-ye ʿĀrefī, *The Feats of the Knowers of God*, Islamic History and Civilization: Studies and Texts 43, Leiden: E. J. Brill.

Parthey, Gustavus (ed.), 1857. *Jamblichi: de mysteriis liber*, Berlin: Prostat in Libraria Friderici Nicolai.

Pennington, A. (trans.), 1984. 'The Apocalypse of Abraham', 363–91, In *The Apocryphal Old Testament*, Edited by H. F. D. Sparks, Oxford: Clarendon.

Petschenig, M. (ed.), 1908–10. Sancti Aureli Augustini, *Scripta contra donatistas*, Corpus Scriptorum Ecclesiasticorum Latinorum 51–53, Vienna: F. Tempsky.

Philonenko, Marc, 1968. 'Le Testament de Job: Introduction, Traduction et Notes', *Semitica* 18: 1–75.

Pines, Shlomo (trans.), 1963. Moses Maimonides, *The Guide of the Perplexed*, 2 vols., Chicago: University of Chicago Press.

Preisendanz, Karl (trans.), 1928–31. *Papyri graecae magicae: Die griechischen Zauberpapyri*, 2 vols., Leipzig: B. G. Teubner.

Priest, J. (trans.), 1983. 'Testament of Moses', 919–34, In *Old Testament Pseudepigrapha*, Vol. 1: *Apocalyptic Literature and Testaments*, Edited by James H. Charlesworth, Garden City, NY: Doubleday.

Race, William H. (ed. and trans.), 1997. Pindar, *Nemean Odes, Isthmian Odes, Fragments*, Loeb Classical Library 485; Cambridge: Harvard University Press.

Rahmani, L. Y., 1994. *A Catalogue of Jewish Ossuaries in the Collections of the State of Israel*, Jerusalem: Israeli Antiquities Authority.

Rebiger, Bill, and Peter Schäfer (eds.), 2009. *Sefer ha-Razim I und II = Das Buch der Geheimnisse I und II*, Vol. 1: *Edition*, TSAJ 125, Tübingen: Mohr Siebeck.

Ricciotti, Giuseppe, 1932. *L'Apocalisse di Paolo Siriaca*, Brescia: Morcelliana.

Robinson, J. Armitage, 1891. *The Passion of S. Perpetua*, Texts and Studies 1/2, Cambridge: Cambridge University Press.

–, 1892. *The Testament of Abraham*, Texts and Studies 2/2, Cambridge: Cambridge University Press.

Robinson, Stephen Edward (trans.), 1983. 'Testament of Adam', 989–95, In *Old Testament Pseudepigrapha*, Vol. 1: *Apocalyptic Literature and Testaments*, Edited by James H. Charlesworth, Garden City, NY: Doubleday.

Rosati, Gianpiero (intro.), Giovanna Faranda Villa (trans.), and Rossella Corti (annot.), 1994. Ovid, *Le metamorfosi*, Vol. 1, Rizzoli editore 946, Milano: R.C.S. Libri & Grandi Opere.

Rousseau, Adelin, Louis Doutreleau, and Charles Mercier (eds. and trans.), 1965–82. Irenaeus of Lyons, *Contre les hérésies*, Sources Chrétiennes 100, 152–53, 210–11, 23–64, 293–94, Paris: Cerf.

Rubinkiewicz, Ryszard (trans.), 1983. 'Apocalypse of Abraham', 681–706, In *Old Testament Pseudepigrapha*, Vol. 1: *Apocalyptic Literature and Testaments*, Edited by James H. Charlesworth, Garden City, NY: Doubleday.

Sanford, Eva Matthews (trans.), 1965. Augustine, *De civitate dei*, Loeb Classical Library 5, Cambridge: Harvard University Press.

Schäfer, Peter, 1981. *Synopse zur Hekhalot-Literatur*, TSAJ 2, Tübingen: Mohr Siebeck.

Schäfer, Peter, and Shaul Shaked, 1994. *Magische Texte aus der Kairoer Geniza*, Vol. 1, Tübingen: Mohr Siebeck.

Schechter, Salomon (ed.) 1887, *Aboth de Rabbi Nathan*, Vienna: Ch. D. Lippe.

Septuaginta, 1979. Edited by Alfred Rahlfs, Stuttgart: Deutsche Bibelgesellschaft.

Shinan, Avigdor (ed.), 1984. *Midrash Shemot Rabbah*, Jerusalem: Dvir.

Smith, Morton (trans.), 1986. '*PGM* XIII.1–343', 172–82, In *The Greek Magical Papyri in Translation, Including the Demotic Spells*, Hans Dieter Betz, Vol. 1: *Texts*, 2nd ed., Chicago: University of Chicago Press.

Smulders, P. (ed.), 1979. Sancti Hilarii Pictaviensis Episcopi, *De trinitate*, Preface, Books 1-7, Corpus Christianorum Series Latina 62, Turnhout: Brepols.

Spittler, Russell P. (trans.), 1983. 'Testament of Job', 829–68, in *Old Testament Pseudepigrapha*, Vol. 1: *Apocalyptic Literature and Testaments*, Edited by James H. Charlesworth, Garden City, NY: Doubleday.

Sprenger, Hans Norbert (ed.), 1977. Theodore of Mopsuestia, *Commentarius in XII prophetas*, Göttinger Orientforschungen 5/1, Wiesbaden: Otto Harrassowitz.

Stec, David M. (trans.), 1980. *The Targum of Psalms*, The Aramaic Bible 16, Collegeville, MN: Liturgical.

Steindorff, Georg, 1899. *Die Apokalypse des Elias, eine unbekannte Apokalypse und Bruchstücke der Sophonias-Apokalypse*, TU 2, Leipzig: J. C. Hinrichs.

Stone, Michael E. (trans.), 1983. 'Questions of Ezra', 591–99, In *Old Testament Pseudepigrapha*, Vol. 1: *Apocalyptic Literature and Testaments*, Edited by James H. Charlesworth, Garden City, NY: Doubleday.

Stone, Michael, and Esther Eshel, 1995. '4QExposition on the Patriarchs', 215–30, In *Qumran Cave 4*, Vol. 14: *Parabiblical Texts, Part 2*, Edited by Magen Broshi *et al*, DJD 19, Oxford: Clarendon.

Tabbernee, William, 1997. *Montanist Inscriptions and Testimonia: Epigraphic Sources Illustrating the History of Montanism*, NAPS Patristic Monograph Series 16, Macon: Mercer University Press.

Talmud Yerushalmi, 1968–69. 7 vols, Jerusalem: Mekhon Ḥatam Sofer.

Taylor, Thomas (trans.), 1968. Iamblichus, *On the Mysteries of the Egyptians, Chaldeans, and Assyrians*, 3rd ed., London: Stuart and Watkins.

Thackeray, H. St. J., Ralph Marcus, Allen Wikgren, and Louis Feldman (trans.), *Josephus*, 10 vols., Loeb Classical Library, Cambridge: Harvard University Press, 1958–65.

Theodor, J. and Ch. Albeck (eds.), 1912–29. *Bereschit Rabba: mit kritischem Apparat und Kommentar*, 3 vols., Veröffentlichungen der Akademie für die Wissenschaft des Judentums, Berlin: Schwetschke.

Thornhill, R. (trans.), 1984. 'The Testament of Job', 617–48, In *The Apocryphal Old Testament*, Edtied by H. F. D. Sparks, Oxford: Clarendon.

VanderKam, J., and J. T. Milik, 1995. '4QpseudoJubilees^a', 141–56, In *Qumran Cave 4*, Vol. 8: *Parabiblical Texts, Part 1*, Edited by Harold Attridge *et al*, DJD 13, Oxford: Clarendon.

Vermes, Geza, 1997. *The Complete Dead Sea Scrolls in English*, New York: Allen Lane.

Wallis Budge, E. A., 1913. *Coptic Apocrypha in the Dialect of Upper Egypt*, Oxford: Horace Hart.

Waszink, J. H. (ed.), 1947. Tertullian, *De anima*, Amsterdam: J. M. Meulenhoff.

West, Martin L., 1966. Hesiod, *Theogony*, Oxford: Oxford University Press.

Westerhoff, Matthias, 1999. *Auferstehung und Jenseits im koptischen 'Buch der Auferstehung Jesu Christi, unseres Herrn'*, Orientalia Biblica et Christiana 11, Wiesbaden: Harrassowitz.

Williams, Frank (trans.), 1994. *The Panarion of Epiphanius of Salamis: Books II & III (Sects 47–80, De Fide)*, NHMS 36, Leiden: E. J. Brill.

Wintermute, O. S. (trans.), 1983. 'Apocalypse of Zephaniah', 497–515, In *Old Testament Pseudepigrapha*, Vol. 1: *Apocalyptic Literature and Testaments*, Edited by James H. Charlesworth, Garden City, NY: Doubleday.

– (trans.), 1985. 'Jubilees', 35–142, In *Old Testament Pseudepigrapha*, Vol. 2: *Expansions of the "Old Testament" and Legends, Wisdom and Philosophical Literature, Prayers, Psalms and Odes, Fragments of Lost Judeo-Hellenistic Works*, Edited by James H. Charlesworth, Garden City, NY: Doubleday.

Wise, Michael, Martin Abegg Jr., and Edward Cook, 1996. *The Dead Sea Scrolls: A New Translation*, San Francisco: Harper.

Worrell, William H., 1929–30. 'A Coptic Wizard's Hoard', *American Journal of Semitic Languages and Literatures* 46: 239–62.

Wright, R. B. (trans.), 1985. 'Psalms of Solomon', 639–70, In *Old Testament Pseudepigrapha*, Vol. 2: *Expansions of the "Old Testament" and Legends, Wisdom and Philosophical Literature, Prayers, Psalms and Odes, Fragments of Lost Judeo-Hellenistic Works*, Edited by James H. Charlesworth, Garden City, NY: Doubleday.

Wright, Wilmer Cave, 1913. *The Works of Julian the Apostate*, 3 vols., London: Heinemann.

Young, Robert (trans.), 1953. *Young's Literal Translation of the Holy Bible*, Rev. ed., Grand Rapids: Baker.

Ziegler, Joseph (ed.), 1975. Eusebius, *Der Jesajakommentar*, Die griechischen christlichen Schriftsteller der ersten Jahrhunderte, Eusebius, Vol. 9, Berlin: Akademie-Verlag.

B. Secondary Literature

Abegg, Martin G. Jr., 1997. 'Who Ascended to Heaven? 4Q491, 4Q427, and the Teacher of Righteousness', 61–73, In *Eschatology, Messianism, and the Dead Sea Scrolls*, Edited by Craig A. Evans and Peter W. Flint, Studies in the Dead Sea Scrolls and Related Literature, Grand Rapids: Eerdmans.

Adler, William, 1996. 'Introduction', 1–31, In *The Jewish Apocalyptic Heritage in Early Christianity*, Edited by James C. VanderKam and William Adler, CRINT 3/4, Van Gorcum: Assen.

Albeck, Chanoch, 1969. *Introduction to the Talmud, Babli and Yerushalmi*, Tel Aviv: Davir (Hebrew).

Alexander, Patrick H. et al., 1999. *The SBL Handbook of Style: for Ancient Near Eastern, Biblical, and Early Christian Studies*, Peabody: Hendrickson.

Alexander, Philip S., 1973–87. 'Incantations and Books of Magic', 3.342–79, In Emil Schürer, *The History of the Jewish People in the Age of Jesus Christ (175 B.C. –A.D.*

135), 3 Vols., (rev. and ed. by G. Vermes, F. Millar, M. Black, and M. Goodman) Edinburgh: T. & T. Clark.

–, 2006. *The Mystical Texts: Songs of the Sabbath Sacrifice and Related Manuscripts*, Companion to the Qumran Scrolls; Library of Second Temple Studies 61, London: T & T Clark International.

–, 2009. 'What Happened to the Jewish Priesthood after 70?', In *A Wandering Galilean: Essays in Honour of Seán Freyne*, Edited by Zuleika Rodgers with Margaret Daly-Denton and Anne Fitzpatrick McKinley, JSJSup 132, Leiden: Brill.

Allison, Dale C. Jr., 1985–87. '4Q403 Fragm. 1, Col. i, 38–46 and the Revelation to John', *RevQ* 12: 409–14.

–, 1988. 'The Silence of Angels: Reflections on the Songs of the Sabbath Sacrifice', *RevQ* 13: 189–97.

–, 2003a. 'Abraham's Oracular Tree (*T. Abr.* 3:1–4)', *JJS* 54: 51–61.

–, 2003b. *Testament of Abraham*, Commentaries on Early Jewish Literature, Berlin: Walter de Gruyter.

Alon, Gedaliah, 1980. *The Jews in Their Land in the Talmudic Age (70–640 C.E.)*, Vol. 1, Jerusalem: Magnes.

Alston, William P., 1956. 'Ineffability', *Philosophical Review* 65: 506–22.

Altmann, Alexander, 1946. 'The Singing of the Qedushah in the Early Hekhalot Literature', *Melilah* 2: 1–24 (Hebrew).

Arnold, Clinton E., 1995. *The Colossian Syncretism: The Interface Between Christianity and Folk Belief at Colossae*, WUNT 2.77, Tübingen: Mohr Siebeck.

Ash, James L., 1976. 'The Decline of Ecstatic Prophecy in the Early Church', *TS* 37: 227–52.

Assmann, Jan, 1995. 'Unio Liturgica: Die kultische Einstimmung in götterweltlichen Lobpreis als Grundmotiv 'esoterischer' Überlieferung im alten Ägypten', 37–60, In *Secrecy and Concealment: Studies in the History of Mediterranean and Near Eastern Religions*, Edited by Hans G. Kippenberg and Guy G. Stroumsa, SHR 65, Leiden: E. J. Brill.

–, 1997. *Moses the Egyptian: The Memory of Egypt in Western Monotheism*, Cambridge: Harvard University Press.

Aune, David E., 1997. *Revelation 1–5*, WBC 52A, Dallas: Word.

–, 1998. 'Qumran and the Book of Revelation', 2.622–48, In *The Dead Sea Scrolls After Fifty Years: A Comprehensive Assessment*, Edited by Peter W. Flint and James C. VanderKam, 2 Vols.; Leiden: E. J. Brill.

–, 2006. *Apocalypticism, Prophecy, and Magic in Early Christianity: Collected Essays*, Tübingen: Mohr Siebeck.

Avenary, Hanoch, 1978. 'Reflections on the Origins of the Alleluia-Jubilus', *Orbis Musicae* 6: 34–42.

Avery-Peck, Alan J., 1992. 'Oral Tradition: Early Judaism', 5.34–37, In *The Anchor Bible Dictionary*, Edited by David Noel Freedman, 6 Vols.; New York: Doubleday.

Baeck, Leo, 1926. 'Zum Sepher Jezira', *MGWJ* 70: 371–76.

–, 1934. 'Die zehn Sephirot im Sepher Jezira', *MGWJ* 78: 448–55.

Bagnall, Roger S., 2009. *Early Christian Books in Egypt*, Princeton: Princeton University Press.

Baldry, H. C., 1965. *The Unity of Mankind in Greek Thought*, Cambridge: Cambridge University Press.

Balentine, Samuel E., 1984. 'The Prophet as Intercessor: A Reassessment', *JBL* 103: 161–73.

Bar-Ilan, Meir, 2004. 'Prayers of Jews to Angels and Other Mediators in the First Centuries CE', 79–95, In *Saints and Role Models in Judaism and Christianity*, Edited by Marcel Poorthuis and Joshua Schwartz, J&CP 7; Leiden: E. J. Brill.

Barnes, Michel René, 2008. 'The Beginning and End of Early Christian Pneumatology', *Augustinian Studies* 39: 169–86.

Barnes, Timothy David, 1971. *Tertullian: A Historical and Literary Study*, Oxford: Clarendon.

Barr, James, 1966. *Old and New in Interpretation: A Study of the Two Testaments*, London: SCM.

–, 1980. *The Scope and Authority of the Bible*, Explorations in Theology 7, London: SCM.

–, 1983. *Holy Scripture: Canon, Authority, Criticism*, Philadelphia: Westminster.

–, 1989. *The Variable Spellings of the Hebrew Bible*, Oxford: Oxford University Press.

–, 1993. *Biblical Faith and Natural Theology: The Gifford Lectures for 1991 Delivered in the University of Edinburgh*, Oxford: Clarendon.

–, 1999. *The Concept of Biblical Theology: An Old Testament Perspective*, Minneapolis: Fortress.

Barth, Markus, 1974. *Ephesians 1–3*, AB 34, Garden City: Doubleday.

Barth, Markus, and Helmut Blanke, 1994. *Colossians: A New Translation with Introduction and Commentary*, AB 34B, New York: Doubleday.

Barton, John, 1986. *Oracles of God: Perceptions of Ancient Prophecy in Israel after the Exile*, London: Darton, Longman, & Todd.

Bauckham, Richard, 1980–81. 'The Worship of Jesus in Apocalyptic Christianity', *NTS* 27: 322–41.

–, 1991. Review of *Studies on the Testament of Job*, Edited by Michael A. Knibb and Pieter W. van der Horst, in *JTS* 42: 182–84.

–, 1993. *The Climax of Prophecy: Studies on the Book of Revelation*, Edinburgh: T. & T. Clark.

–, 1998. *The Fate of the Dead: Studies on the Jewish and Christian Apocalypses*, NovTSup 93, Leiden: E. J. Brill.

Baudissin, Wolf Wilhelm Grafen, 1876–78. *Studien zur semitischen Religionsgeschichte*, 2 Vols, Leipzig: F. W. Grunow.

Baumgarten, A. I., 2001. 'Literacy and the Polemics Surrounding Biblical Interpretation in the Second Temple Period', 27–41, In *Studies in Ancient Midrash*, Edited by James L. Kugel, Cambridge: Harvard University Press.

Baumgarten, Joseph M., 1983. 'The "Sons of Dawn" in *CDC* 13:14–15 and the Ban on Commerce among the Essenes,' *IEJ* 33: 81–85.

–, 1986. 'The Book of Elchesai and Merkavah Mysticism', *JSJ* 17: 212–23.

–, 1988. 'The Qumran Sabbath Shirot and Rabbinic Merkabah Traditions', *RevQ* 13: 199–213.

Baumstark, Anton, 1958. *Comparative Liturgy*, London: A. R. Mowbray.

Becker, Adam H., and Annette Yoshiko Reed (eds.), 2003. *The Ways that Never Parted: Jews and Christians in Late Antiquity and the Early Middle Ages*, TSAJ 95, Tübingen: Mohr Siebeck.

Beer, G., 1927–31. 'Hiobtestament', 2.1930–31, In *Die Religion in Geschichte und Gegenwart: Handwörterbuch für Theologie und Religionswissenschaft*, Edited by Hermann Gunkel and Leopold Zscharnack, Tübingen: Mohr Siebeck.

Begg, Christopher, 1994. 'Comparing Characters: The Book of Job and the *Testament of Job*', 435–45, In *The Book of Job*, Edited by W. A. M. Beuken, BETL 114, Leuven: Leuven University Press.

Behm, Johannes, 1964–76. 'γλῶσσα', 1.719–26, In *Theological Dictionary of the New Testament*, Edited by Gerhard Kittel and Gerhard Friedrich, 10 Vols., Grand Rapids: Eerdmans.

Ben-Barak, Zafrira, 1980. 'Inheritance by Daughters in the Ancient Near East', *JSS* 25: 22–33.

Benko, Stephen, 1984. *Pagan Rome and the Early Christians*, Bloomington: Indiana University Press.

–, 1993. *The Virgin Goddess: Studies in the Pagan and Christian Roots of Mariology*, Studies in the History of Religions 59, Leiden: E. J. Brill.

Besserman, Lawrence L., 1979. *The Legend of Job in the Middle Ages*, Cambridge: Harvard University Press.

Betz, Hans Dieter, 1961. *Lukian von Samosata und das Neue Testament: Religionsgeschichtliche und paränetische Parallelen, ein Beitrag zum Corpus Hellenisticum Novi Testamenti*, Berlin: Akademie-Verlag.

–, 1995. 'Secrecy in the Greek Magical Papyri', 153–75, In *Secrecy and Concealment: Studies in the History of Mediterranean and Near Eastern Religions*, Edited by Hans G. Kippenberg and Guy G. Stroumsa, SHR 65, Leiden: E. J. Brill.

Betz, Otto, 1964–76. 'φωνή', 9.278–301, In *Theological Dictionary of the New Testament*, Edited by Gerhard Kittel and Gerhard Friedrich, 10 Vols., Grand Rapids: Eerdmans.

–, 1968. 'Zungenreden und süßer Wein: Zur eschatologischen Exegese von Jesaja 28 in Qumran und im Neuen Testament', 20–36, In *Bibel und Qumran: Beiträge zur Erforschung der Beziehungen zwischen Bibel- und Qumranwissenschaft*, Edited by Siegfried Wagner, Berlin: Evangelische Haupt-Bibelgesellschaft.

Bianchi, Ugo, 1983. 'L'*Ascensione di Isaia*: tematiche soteriologiche di *descensus/ascensus*', 155–83, In *Isaia, Il Diletto e la Chiesa: Visione ed esegesi profetica cristiano-primitiva nell'*Ascensione di Isaia: *Atti del Convegno di Roma, 9–10 aprile 1981*, Edited by Mauro Pesce, Testi e ricerche di Scienze religiose 20, Brescia: Paideia.

Bickerman, Elias, 1980. *Studies in Jewish and Christian History*, 3 Vols., AGJU 9, Leiden: E. J. Brill.

Binder, Donald D., 1997. *Into the Temple Courts: The Place of the Synagogues in the Second Temple Period*, SBLDS 169, Atlanta: Scholars Press.

Bloch-Smith, Elizabeth, 1994. '"Who Is the King of Glory?": Solomon's Temple and Its Symbolism', 18–31, In *Scripture and Other Artifacts: Essays on the Bible and Archaeology in Honor of Philip J. King*, Edited by Michael D. Coogan, J. Cheryl Exum, and Lawrence E. Stager, Louisville: Westminster/John Knox.

Block, Daniel I., 1988. 'Text and Emotion: A Study in the "Corruptions" in Ezekiel's Inaugural Vision (Ezekiel 1:4–28)', *CBQ* 50: 418–42.

Boccaccini, Gabriele, 1994. 'Targum Neofiti as a Proto-Rabbinic Document: A Systemic Analysis', 254–63, In *The Aramaic Bible: Targums in their Historical Context*, Edited by D. R. G. Beattie and M. J. McNamara, JSOTSup 166, Sheffield: Sheffield Academic Press.

–, 1998. *Beyond the Essene Hypothesis: The Parting of the Ways between Qumran and Enochic Judaism*, Grand Rapids: Eerdmans.

Boenig, Robert, 1995. 'St Augustine's *Jubilus* and Richard Rolle's *Canor*', 75–86, In *Vox Mystica: Essays on Medieval Mysticism in Honor of Professor Valerie M. Lagorio*, Edited by Anne Clark Bartlett, Cambridge: D. S. Brewer.

Bøe, Sverre, 2001. *Gog and Magog: Ezekiel 38–39 as Pre-text for Revelation 19,17–21 and 20,7–10*, WUNT 2.135; Tübingen: Mohr Siebeck.

Boers, Hendrikus, 2006. *Christ in the Letters of Paul: In Place of a Christology*, BZNW 140, Berlin: Walter de Gruyter.

Böhlig, Alexander, 1967. 'Die himmlische Welt nach dem Ägypterevangelium von Nag Hammadi', *Le Muséon* 80: 5–26.

Bömer, Franz, 1969. *P. Ovidius Naso, Metamorphosen: Kommentar. Buch I–III*, Heidelberg: Carl Winter – Universitätsverlag.

Bori, Pier Cesare, 1980. 'L'estasi del profeta: "Ascensio Isaiae" 6 e l'antico profetismo cristiano', *Cristianesimo nella storia* 1: 367–89.

Boring, M. Eugene, 1991. *The Continuing Voice of Jesus: Christian Prophecy and the Gospel Tradition*, Louisville: Westminster/John Knox.

Borst, Arno, 1957–63. *Der Turmbau von Babel: Geschichte der Meinungen über Ursprung und Vielfalt der Sprachen und Völker*, 6 Vols., Stuttgart: Anton Hiersemann.

Bousset, Wilhelm, 1970. *Kyrios Christos: A History of the Belief in Christ from the Beginnings of Christianity to Irenaeus*, Nashville: Abingdon.

Bowersock, G. W., 1995. *Martyrdom and Rome*, Cambridge: Cambridge University Press.

Bowker, John, 1969. *The Targums and Rabbinic Literature: An Introduction to Jewish Interpretations of Scripture*, Cambridge: Cambridge University Press.

Boyarin, Daniel, 1993. *Carnal Israel: Reading Sex in Talmudic Culture*, Berkeley: University of California Press.

–, 1999. *Dying for God: Martyrdom and the Making of Christianity and Judaism*, Figurae, Stanford: Stanford University Press.

Boyd-Taylor, Cameron, 1998. 'A Place in the Sun: The Interpretative Significance of LXX-Psalm 18:5c', *BIOSCS* 31: 71–105.

Boyle, Marjorie O'Rourke, 1977. *Erasmus on Language and Method in Theology*, Toronto: University of Toronto Press.

Braaten, Carl E., 1990. *Justification: The Article by Which the Church Stands or Falls*, Minneapolis: Fortress.

Branham, Joan R., 1995. 'Vicarious Sacrality: Temple Space in Ancient Synagogues', 319–45, In *Ancient Synagogues: Historical Analysis and Archaeological Discovery*, Edited by Dan Urman and Paul V. M. Flesher, 2 Vols., StPB 47, Leiden: E. J. Brill.

Bremmer, Jan N., 2003. 'The Vision of Saturus in the *Passio Perpetuae*', 55–73, In *Jerusalem, Alexandria, Rome: Studies in Ancient Cultural Interaction in Honour of A. Hilhorst*, Edited by Florentino García Martínez and Gerard P. Luttikhuizen, JSJSup 82, Leiden: E. J. Brill.

Breuer, Yochanan, 2006. 'Aramaic in Late Antiquity', 457–91, In *The Cambridge History of Judaism*, Vol. 4, *The Late Roman-Rabbinic Period*, (ed. by Steven T. Katz) Cambridge: Cambridge University Press.

Briggs, Robert A., 1999. *Jewish Temple Imagery in the Book of Revelation*, Studies in Biblical Literature 10, New York: Peter Lang.

Brin, Gershon, 1993. 'Regarding the Connection between the *Temple Scroll* and the Book of *Jubilees*', *JBL* 112: 108–109.

Brown, A. S., 1998. 'From the Golden Age to the Isles of the Blest', *Mnemosyne* 51: 385–410.

Brown, Dennis, 1992. *Vir Trilinguis: A Study in the Biblical Exegesis of Saint Jerome*, Kampen: Kok Pharos.

Brown, John Pairman, 2001. *Israel and Hellas*, Vol. 3, *The Legacy of Iranian Imperialism and the Individual*, BZAW 299, Berlin: Walter de Gruyter.

Bucur, Bogdan Gabriel, 2009. *Angelomorphic Pneumatology: Clement of Alexandria and Other Early Christian Witnesses*, VCSup 95, Leiden: E. J. Brill.

Bunn, John T., 1986. 'Glossolalia in Historical Perspective', 165–78, In *Speaking in Tongues: A Guide to Research on Glossolalia*, Edited by Watson E. Mills, Grand Rapids: Eerdmans.

Burgess, Stanley M., 1984. *The Spirit and the Church: Antiquity*, Peabody, MA: Hendrickson.

Busink, Th. A., 1980. *Der Tempel von Jerusalem – Von Salomo bis Herodes: Eine archäologisch-historische Studie unter Berücksichtigung des westsemitischen Tempelbaus*, Vol. 2: *Von Ezechiel bis Middot*, SFSMD 3; Leiden: E. J. Brill.

Butler, Rex D., 2006. *The New Prophecy and "New Vision": Evidence of Montanism in the Passion of Perpetua and Felicitas*, Washington DC: Catholic University of America Press.

Campenhausen, Hans von, 1969. *Ecclesiastical Authority and Spiritual Power in the Church of the First Three Centuries*, London: Adam & Charles Black.

–, 1972. *The Formation of the Christian Bible*, Philadelphia: Fortress.

Caquot, André, 1988. 'Le Service des Anges', *RevQ* 13: 421–29.

Carabine, Deirdre, 1995. *The Unknown God: Negative Theology in the Platonic Tradition: Plato to Eriugena*, Louvain Theological & Pastoral Monographs 19, Louvain: Peeters.

Caragounis, Chrys C., 1977. *The Ephesian Mysterion: Meaning and Content*, ConBNT 8, Lund: Gleerup.

Carlson, David C., 1982. 'Vengeance and Angelic Mediation in *Testament of Moses* 9 and 10', *JBL* 101: 85–95.

Carrell, Peter R., 1997. *Jesus and the Angels: Angelology and the Christology of the Apocalypse of John*, SNTSMS 95, Cambridge: Cambridge University Press.

Carroll, Robert P., 1986. *Jeremiah: A Commentary*, OTL, Philadelphia: Westminster.

Carroll, Scott, 1989. 'A Preliminary Analysis of the *Epistle to Rehoboam*', *JSP* 4: 91–103.

Cartledge, Mark J., 2002. *Charismatic Glossolalia: An Empirical-Theological Study*, Ashgate New Critical Thinking in Theology & Biblical Studies, Aldershot: Ashgate.

— (ed.), 2006. *Speaking in Tongues: Multi-Disciplinary Perspectives*, Studies in Charismatic and Pentecostal Issues, Carlisle: Paternoster.

Chambers, G. B., 1956. *Folksong – Plainsong: A Study in Musical Origins*, London: Merlin.

Chantraine, Pierre, 1968–80. *Dictionnaire étymologique de la langue grecque: Histoire des Mots*, 4 Vols., Paris: Klincksieck.

Charlesworth, James H., 1981. *The Pseudepigrapha and Modern Research with a Supplement*, SBLSCS 7S, Chico, CA: Scholars Press.

–, 1986. 'Jewish Hymns, Odes, and Prayers (ca. 167 B.C.E.–135 C.E.)', 411–36, In *Early Judaism and Its Modern Interpreters*, Edited by Robert A. Kraft and George W. E. Nickelsburg, Philadelphia: Fortress.

Chase, Steven, 2000. Review of David Keck, *Angels and Angelology in the Middle Ages*, In *JR* 80: 138–39.

Chazon, Esther G., 1998–9. 'Hymns and Prayers in the Dead Sea Scrolls', 244–70, In *The Dead Sea Scrolls After Fifty Years: A Comprehensive Assessment*, Edited by Peter W. Flint and James C. VanderKam, 2 Vols., Leiden: E. J. Brill.

–, 2000. 'Liturgical Communion with the Angels at Qumran', 95–105, In *Sapiential, Liturgical and Poetical texts from Qumran: Proceedings of the Third Meeting of the International Organization for Qumran Studies, Oslo 1998, Published in Memory of Maurice Baillet*, Edited by Daniel K. Falk, Florentino García Martínez, and Eileen M. Schuller, STDJ 35, Leiden: E. J. Brill.

–, 2003. 'Human and Angelic Prayer in Light of the Dead Sea Scrolls', 35–47, In *Liturgical Perspectives: Prayer and Poetry in Light of the Dead Sea Scrolls. Proceedings of the Fifth International Symposium of the Orion Center for the Study of the Dead Sea Scrolls and Associated Literature, 19–23 January, 2000*, Edited by Esther G. Chazon, STDJ 48, Leiden: E. J. Brill.

Chesnut, Glenn F., 1986. *The First Christian Histories: Eusebius, Socrates, Sozomen, Theodoret, and Evagrius*, 2nd ed., Macon: Mercer University Press.

Chilton, Bruce, 1983. *Glory of Israel: The Theology and Provenience of the Isaiah Targum*, JSOTSup 23, Sheffield: JSOT.

Chomsky, W., 1951–52. 'What was the Jewish Vernacular During the Second Commonwealth?', *JQR* 42: 193–212.

Christie-Murray, David, 1978. *Voices from the Gods: Speaking with Tongues*, London: Routledge & Kegan Paul.

Christoffersson, Olle, 1990. *The Earnest Expectation of the Creature: The Flood-Tradition as Matrix of Romans 8:18–27*, ConBNT 23, Stockholm: Almqvist & Wiksell.

Cinal, Stanisław, 1998. 'Les anges-prêtres dans les *Šîrôt 'Ôlat haš-Šabbat* de Qumrân (4Q400–407) et les *'Utria* dans le *Dīwān Nahrawāṭā* des Mandéens', 123–36, In *Mogilany 1995: Papers on the Dead Sea Scrolls Offered in Memory of Aleksy Klawek*, Edited by Zdzisław J. Kapera, Krakow: Enigma, 1998).

Clifford, Richard J., 1972. *The Cosmic Mountain in Canaan and the Old Testament*, HSM 4, Cambridge: Harvard University Press.

Cohen, Shaye J. D., 1992. 'Judaism to the Mishnah: 135–220 C.E.', 195–223, In *Christianity and Rabbinic Judaism: A Parallel History of Their Origins and Early Development*, Edited by Hershel Shanks, Washington DC: Biblical Archaeology Society.

–, 1999a. 'The Rabbi in Second-Century Jewish Society', 922–90, In *The Cambridge History of Judaism*, Vol. 3: *The Early Roman Period*, Edited by William Horbury, W. D. Davies, and John Sturdy, Cambridge: Cambridge University Press.

–, 1999b. 'The Temple and the Synagogue', 298–325, In *The Cambridge History of Judaism*, Vol. 3: *The Early Roman Period*, Edited by William Horbury, W. D. Davies, and John Sturdy, Cambridge: Cambridge University Press.

–, 1999c. 'Were Pharisees and Rabbis the Leaders of Communal Prayer and Torah Study in Antiquity?: The Evidence of the New Testament, Josephus, and the Early Church Fathers', 89–105, In *Evolution of the Synagogue: Problems and Progress*, Edited by Howard Clark Kee and Lynn H. Cohick, Harrisburg: Trinity Press International.

Collins, Adela Yarbro, 1995. 'The Seven Heavens in Jewish and Christian Apocalypses', 59–93, In *Death, Ecstasy, and Other Worldly Journeys*, Edited by John J. Collins and Michael Fishbane, Albany: State University of New York Press, 1995.

Collins, John J., 1974. 'Structure and Meaning in the Testament of Job', in *SBLSP* 13: 1.35–52.

–, 1992. *The Apocalyptic Imagination*, New York: Crossroad.

–, 1995. *The Scepter and the Star: The Messiahs of the Dead Sea Scrolls and Other Ancient Literature*, ABRL, New York: Doubleday.

–, 1997a. *Apocalypticism in the Dead Sea Scrolls*, London: Routledge.

–, 1997b. *Seers, Sibyls and Sages in Hellenistic-Roman Judaism*, JSJSup 54, Leiden: E. J. Brill.

–, 2000. 'Powers in Heaven: God, Gods, and Angels in the Dead Sea Scrolls', 9–28, In *Religion in the Dead Sea Scrolls*, Edited by John J. Collins and Robert A. Kugler, Studies in the Dead Sea Scrolls and Related Literature, Grand Rapids: Eerdmans.

Congar, Yves M. J., 1983a. *I Believe in the Holy Spirit*, Vol. 1: *The Holy Spirit in the 'Economy': Revelation and Experience of the Spirit*, New York: Seabury.

–, 1983b. *I Believe in the Holy Spirit*, Vol. 2: *'He is Lord and Giver of Life'*, New York: Seabury.

Constable, Giles, 1995. *Three Studies in Medieval Religious and Social Thought*, Cambridge: Cambridge University Press.

Conzelmann, Hans, 1975. *1 Corinthians: A Commentary on the First Epistle to the Corinthians*, Hermeneia, Philadelphia: Fortress.

–, 1987. *Acts of the Apostles*, Hermeneia, Philadelphia: Fortress.

Cook, John Granger, 2000. *The Interpretation of the New Testament in Greco-Roman Paganism*, Studien und Texte zu Antike und Christentum 3, Tübingen: Mohr Siebeck.

Copenhaver, Brian, 1988. 'Hermes Trismegistus, Proclus, and the Question of a Philosophy of Magic in the Renaissance', 79–110, In *Hermeticism and the Renaissance: Intellectual History and the Occult in Early Modern Europe*, Edited by Ingrid Merkel and Allen G. Debus, Washington: The Folger Shakespeare Library.

Corbin, Henry, 1969. *Creative Imagination in the Sūfism of Ibn 'Arabī*, London: Routledge and Kegan Paul, 1969.

Corley, Jeremy, 2004. 'The Pauline Authorship of 1 Corinthians 13', *CBQ* 66: 256–74.

Cornford, F. M., 1957. *From Religion to Philosophy: A Study in the Origins of Western Speculation*, New York: Harper & Bros..

Coseriu, Eugenio, 1988. *Einführung in die allgemeine Sprachwissenschaft*, Tübingen: Francke.

Cothenet, E., 1971–2. 'Prophétisme dans le Nouveau Testament', cols. 1222–1337. In *Supplément au Dictionnaire de la Bible*, Fasc. 46–47, Paris: Letouzey & Ané.

Cowley, A., 1923. *Aramaic Papyri of the Fifth Century B.C.*, Oxford: Clarendon.

Cross, Frank Moore, 1995. *The Ancient Library of Qumran*, 3rd ed., Minneapolis: Fortress.

Culianu, Ioan P., 1983. 'La *Visione di Isaia* e la tematica della *Himmelsreise*', 95–116, In *Isaia, il diletto e la chiesa: visione ed esegesi profetica cristiano-primitiva nell'*Ascensione di Isaia*: atti del convegno di Roma, 9–10 aprile 1981*, Edited by Mauro Pesce, Testi e ricerche di Scienze religiose 20; Brescia: Paideia.

Cumont, Franz, 1911. *Oriental Religions in Roman Paganism*, Chicago: Open Court.

Currie, Stuart D., 1965. 'Speaking in Tongues: Early Evidence Outside the New Testament Bearing on Γλώσσαις Λαλεῖν', *Int* 19: 274–94.

Dahl, Nils A., 1936. 'Apostelen Paulus' Høisang om Kjaerligheten, Fortolkning av 1 Kor. 13 med Behandling av de Litteraere og Teologiske Problemer', *NTT* 37: 5–135.

Dalman, Gustaf, 1929. *Jesus–Jeshua: Studies in the Gospels*, London: SPCK.

D'Angelo, Mary Rose, 1999. 'Intimating Deity in the Gospel of John: Theological Language and "Father" in "Prayers of Jesus"', *Semeia* 85: 59–82.

Danthine, Hélène, 1937. *Le palmier-dattier et les arbres sacrés dans l'iconographie de l'Asie occidentale ancienne*, Paris: P. Geuthner.

Daumas, F., 1956. 'La valeur de l'or dans la pensée égyptienne', *RHR* 149: 1–17.

Dautzenberg, Gerhard, 1975. *Urchristliche Prophetie: Ihre Erforschung, ihre Voraussetzungen im Judentum und ihre Struktur im ersten Korintherbrief*, BWANT 104; Stuttgart: Kohlhammer.

–, 1979. 'Glossolalie', Cols. 225–46, In *Reallexikon für Antike und Christentum: Sachwörterbuch zur Auseinandersetzung des Christentums mit der antiken Welt*, Vol. 11, No. 82, Edited by Theodor Klauser, Carsten Colpe, Ernst Dassmann, Albrecht Dihle, Bernhard Kötting, Wolfgang Speyer, Jan Hendrik Waszink, Stuttgart: Anton Hiersemann.

Davenport, Gene L., 1971. *The Eschatology of the Book of Jubilees*, StPB 20, Leiden: E. J. Brill.

Davidson, Maxwell J., 1992. *Angels at Qumran: A Comparative Study of 1 Enoch 1–36, 72–108 and Sectarian Writings from Qumran*, JSPSup 11, Sheffield: JSOT.

Davies, Philip R., 1998. *Scribes and Schools: The Canonization of the Hebrew Scriptures*, Library of Ancient Israel, Louisville: Westminster/John Knox.

Davila, James R., 1998. 'Heavenly Ascents in the Dead Sea Scrolls', 461–85, In *The Dead Sea Scrolls After Fifty Years: A Comprehensive Assessment*, Edited by Peter W. Flint and James C. VanderKam, 2 vols., Leiden: E. J. Brill.

–, 2000. *Liturgical Works*, Eerdmans Commentaries on the Dead Sea Scrolls 6, Grand Rapids: Eerdmans.

–, 2005. *The Provenance of the Pseudepigrapha: Jewish, Christian, or Other?*, JSJSup 105, Leiden: E. J. Brill.

Dean-Otting, Mary, 1984. *Heavenly Journeys: A Study of the Motif in Hellenistic Jewish Literature*, Judentum und Umwelt 8, Frankfurt am Main: Peter Lang.

DeConick, April D., 2001. *Voices of the Mystics: Early Christian Discourse in the Gospels of John and Thomas and Other Ancient Christian Literature*, JSNTSup 157, Sheffield: Sheffield Academic Press.

Deissmann, Adolf, 1927. *Light from the Ancient East: The New Testament Illustrated by Recently Discovered Texts of the Graeco-Roman World*, Rev. ed., New York: Doran.

de Lacey, D. R., 1987. 'Jesus as Mediator', *JSNT* 29: 101–21.

Delatte, Armand, 1961. *Herbarius: recherches sur le cérémonial usité chez les anciens pour la cueillette des simples et des plantes magiques*, 3rd ed., Mémoires du Académie Royale de Belgique 54/4, Brussels: Palais des Académies.

Delling, Gerhard, 1964–76. 'στοιχεῖον', 7.670–87, In *Theological Dictionary of the New Testament*, Edited by Gerhard Kittel and Gerhard Friedrich, 10 Vols., Grand Rapids: Eerdmans.

Denis, Albert-Marie, 1970. *Introduction aux pseudépigraphes grecs d'Ancien Testament*, SVTP 1, Leiden: E. J. Brill.

Denzey, Nicola, 2001. 'What Did the Montanists Read?', *HTR* 94: 427–48.

Detienne, Marcel, 1963. *La notion de daïmôn dans le pythagorisme ancien*, Bibliothèque de la Faculté de Philosophie et Lettres de l'Université de Liège 165, Paris: Société d'Édition 'Les Belles Lettres'.

Detienne, Marcel, and Gilbert Hamonic, 1995. *La déesse parole: quatre figures de la langue des dieux*, Paris: Flammarion.

Deutsch, Nathaniel, 1999–2000. 'The Date Palm and the Wellspring: Mandaeism and Jewish Mysticism', *Aram* 11–12: 209–23.

Dey, Lala Kalyan Kumar, 1975. *The Intermediary World and Patterns of Perfection in Philo and Hebrews*, SBLDS 25, Missoula, MT: Scholars Press.

Dibelius, Martin, 1909. *Die Geisterwelt im Glauben des Paulus*, Göttingen: Vandenhoeck & Ruprecht.

Diebner, Bernd Jörg, 1978. 'Literarkritische Probleme der Zephanja-Apokalypse', 152–53, In *Nag Hammadi and Gnosis*, Edited by R. McL. Wilson, NHS 14; Leiden: E. J. Brill.

–, 1979. 'Bemerkungen zum Text des sahidischen und des achmimischen Fragments der sog. Zephanja-Apokalypse', *Dielheimer Blätter zum Alten Testament* 14 (Oct 1979): 54–60.

Dierauer, Urs, 1977. *Tier und Mensch im Denken der Antike: Studien zur Tierpsychologie, Anthropologie und Ethik*, Studien zur antiken Philosophie 6, Amsterdam: Grüner.

Dieterich, Albrecht, 1891. *Abraxas: Studien zur Religionsgeschichte des spätern Altertums: Festschrift Hermann Usener zur Feier seiner 25jährigen Lehrtätigkeit an der Bonner Universität*, Leipzig: B. G. Teubner.

Dillon, Matthew P. J., 1997. 'The Ecology of the Greek Sanctuary', *ZPE* 118: 113–27.

DiTommaso, Lorenzo, 2007. 'Apocalypses and Apocalypticism in Antiquity (Part I)', *Currents in Biblical Research* 5: 235–86.

Dobschütz, Ernst von, 1912. *Das Decretum Gelasianum de Libris Recipiendis et Non Recipiendis*, TU 38/4, Leipzig: J. C. Hinrichs.

Dodd, C. H., 1935. *The Bible and the Greeks*, London: Hodder & Stoughton.

Dodds, E. R., 1951. *The Greeks and the Irrational*, Sather Classical Lectures 25, Berkeley: University of California Press.

Dohmen, Christoph, and Manfred Oeming, 1992. *Biblischer Kanon: Warum und wozu?: Eine Kanontheologie*, Quaetiones Disputatae 137, Freiburg: Herder.

Dorda, Esteban Calderón, 1999. 'Estudio sobre el léxico musical neotestamentario', *Filología Neotestamentaria* 12: 17–24.

Dornseiff, Franz, 1925. *Das Alphabet in Mystik und Magie*, 2nd ed., ΣΤΟΙΧΕΙΑ 7, Leipzig: Teubner.

Dothan, Moshe, 1968. 'The Representation of Helios in the Mosaic of Hammath-Tiberias', 99–104, In *Atti del convegno internazionale sul tema: tardo antico e alto medioevo: la forma artistica nel passaggio dall'antichità al medioevo (Roma 4–7 aprile 1967)*, Quaderno 105, Rome: Accademia Nazionale dei Lincei.

–, 1983. *Hammath Tiberias: Early Synagogues and the Hellenistic and Roman Remains*, Jerusalem: Israel Exploration Society.

Downing, F. Gerald, 1964. *Has Christianity a Revelation?*, Philadelphia: Westminster.

Dubowchik, Rosemary, 2002. 'Singing with the Angels: Foundation Documents as Evidence for Musical Life in Monasteries of the Byzantine Empire', *Dumbarton Oaks Papers* 56: 277–96.

Dunn, James D. G., 1975. *Jesus and the Spirit*, Philadelphia: Westminster.

–, 1995. 'The Colossian Philosophy: A Confident Jewish Apologia', *Bib* 76: 153–81.

–, 1996. 'Deutero-Pauline Letters', 130–44, In *Early Christian Thought in Its Jewish Context*, Edited by John Barclay and John Sweet, Cambridge: Cambridge University Press.

Dupont-Sommer, A., 1973. *The Essene Writings from Qumran*, Gloucester, MA: Peter Smith.

Eco, Umberto, 1995. *The Search for the Perfect Language*, The Making of Europe, Oxford: Blackwell.

Editorial staff, 1971–72. 'Ḥama bar Ḥanina', 7.1219, In *Encyclopaedia Judaica*, Edited by Cecil Roth, 16 vols., New York: Macmillan.

Edwards, James R., 2009. *The Hebrew Gospel and the Development of the Synoptic Tradition*, Grand Rapids: Eerdmans.

Eggebrecht, Hans Heinrich (ed.), 1967. *Riemann Musik Lexikon*, Vol. 3: *Sachteil*, 12th ed., Mainz: B. Schott's Söhne.

Ego, Beate, 1989. *Im Himmel wie auf Erden: Studien zum Verhältnis von himmlischer und irdischer Welt im rabbinischen Judentum*, WUNT 2.34; Tübingen: Mohr Siebeck.

–, 2003. '"Denn er liebt sie" (Tob 6,15 Ms. 319) Zur Rolle des Dämons Asmodius in der Tobit-Erzählung', 309–17, In *Die Dämonen: Die Dämonologie der israelitsich-jüdischen und frühchristlichen Literatur im Kontext ihrer Umwelt*, Edited by Armin Lange, Hermann Lichtenberger, and K. F. Diethard Römheld, Tübingen: Mohr Siebeck.

Eisen, Ute E., 2000. *Women Officeholders in Early Christianity: Epigraphical and Literary Studies*, Collegeville, MN: Liturgical.

Eissfeldt, Otto, 1966. *The Old Testament: An Introduction*, Oxford: Blackwell.

Elgvin, Torleif, 2007. 'Jewish Christian Editing of the Old Testament Pseudepigrapha', 278–304, In *Jewish Believers in Jesus: The Early Centuries*, Edited by Oskar Skarsaune and Reidar Hvalvik, Peabody, MA: Hendrickson.

Elior, Rachel, 1993. 'Mysticism, Magic, and Angelology: The Perception of Angels in Hekhalot Literature', *JSQ* 1: 3–53.

–, 1999. 'The *Merkavah* Tradition and the Emergence of Jewish Mysticism: From Temple to *Merkavah*, from *Hekhal* to *Hekhalot*, from Priestly Opposition to Gazing upon the *Merkavah*', 101–58, In *Sino-Judaica: Jews and Chinese in Historical Dialogue: An International Colloquium, Nanjing, 11–19 October 1996*, Edited by Aharon Oppenheimer, Tel Aviv: Tel Aviv University, 1999.

Ellis, E. Earle, 1989. *Pauline Theology: Ministry and Society*, Grand Rapids: Eerdmans.

–, 1993. *Prophecy and Hermeneutic in Early Christianity*, Grand Rapids: Eerdmans.

Engelsen, Nils Ivar Johan, 1970. 'Glossolalia and Other Forms of Inspired Speech According to I Corinthians 12–14', Ph.D., Yale University.

Ensley, Eddie, 1977. *Sounds of Wonder: A Popular History of Speaking in Tongues in the Catholic Tradition*, New York: Paulist.

Enslin, Morton Scott, 1938. *Christian Beginnings*, New York: Harper & Brothers.

Eshel, Esther, and Michael Stone, 1992. 'An Exposition on the Patriarchs (4Q464) and Two Other Documents (4Q464^a and 4Q464^b)', *Le Muséon* 105: 243–64.

–, 1992–93. 'The Holy Tongue in the Last Days in the Light of a Fragment from Qumran', *Tarbiz* 62: 169–77 (Hebrew).

Falk, Daniel K., 1999. 'Prayer in the Qumran Texts', 852–76, In *The Cambridge History of Judaism*, Vol. 3: *The Early Roman Period*, Edited by William Horbury, W. D. Davies, and John Sturdy, Cambridge: Cambridge University Press.

Fassler, Margot, 1993. *Gothic Song: Victorine Sequences and Augustinian Reform in Twelfth-Century Paris*, Cambridge Studies in Medieval and Renaissance Music, Cambridge: Cambridge University Press.

Fatehi, Mehrdad, 2000. *The Spirit's Relation to the Risen Lord in Paul: An Examination of Its Christological Implications*, WUNT 2.128, Tübingen: Mohr Siebeck.

Fauth, Wolfgang, 1995. *Helios Megistos: Zur synkretistischen Theologie der Spätantike*, Religions in the Graeco-Roman World 125, Leiden: E. J. Brill.

Fee, Gordon D., 1987. *The First Epistle to the Corinthians*, NICNT, Grand Rapids: Eerdmans.

–, 1990. *God's Empowering Presence: The Holy Spirit in the Letters of Paul*, Peabody: Hendrickson.

–, 2007. *Pauline Christology: An Exegetical-Theological Study*, Peabody: Hendrickson.

Fekkes, Jan III, 1994. *Isaiah and Prophetic Traditions in the Book of Revelation: Visionary Antecedents and their Development*, JSNTSup 93, Sheffield: Sheffield Academic Press.

Fenske, Wolfgang, 1999. '"Das Lied des Moses, des Knechtes Gottes, und das Lied des Lammes" (Apokalypse des Johannes 15,3f.): Der Text und seine Bedeutung für die Johannes-Apokalypse', *ZNW* 90: 250–64.

Fiensy, David A., 1985. *Prayers Alleged to Be Jewish: An Examination of the Constitutiones Apostolorum*, BJS 65, Chico, CA: Scholars Press.

Fine, Steven, 1989. 'On the Development of a Symbol: The Date Palm in Roman Palestine and the Jews', *JSP* 4: 105–18.

–, 1996. 'From Meeting House to Sacred Realm: Holiness and the Ancient Synagogue', 21–46, In *Sacred Realm: The Emergence of the Synagogue in the Ancient World*, Edited by Steven Fine, Oxford: Oxford University Press.

–, 1997. *This Holy Place: On the Sanctity of the Synagogue During the Greco-Roman Period*, Christianity and Judaism in Antiquity 11, University of Notre Dame Press.

–, 2005. 'Between Liturgy and Social History: Priestly Power in Late Antique Palestinian Synagogues?,' *JJS* 56: 1–9.

Fishman, Joshua A., 1985. 'The Sociology of Jewish Languages from a General Sociolinguistic Point of View', 3–21, In *Readings in the Sociology of Jewish Languages*, Edited by Joshua A. Fishman, Contributions to the Sociology of Jewish Languages 1, Leiden: E. J. Brill.

Fitzmyer, Joseph A., 1957–58. 'A Feature of Qumran Angelology and the Angels of 1 Cor 11:10', *NTS* 4: 48–58.

–, 1971. *The Genesis Apocryphon of Qumran Cave I: A Commentary*, 2nd ed., Rome: Pontifical Biblical Institute Press.

Fletcher-Louis, Crispin H. T., 1998. 'Heavenly Ascent or Incarnational Presence?: A Revisionist Reading of the Songs of the Sabbath Sacrifice', *SBLSP* 37: 367–99.

–, 2002. *All the Glory of Adam: Liturgical Anthropology in the Dead Sea Scrolls*, STDJ 42, Leiden: E. J. Brill.

Flusser, David, 1965. 'The Dead Sea Sect and Pre-Pauline Christianity', 215–66, In *Scripta Hierosolymitana*, Vol. 4: *Aspects of the Dead Sea Scrolls*, Edited by Chaim Rabin and Yigael Yadin, 2nd ed., Jerusalem: Magnes.

Forbes, Christopher, 1995. *Prophecy and Inspired Speech in Early Christianity and Its Hellenistic Environment*, WUNT 2.75, Tübingen: Mohr Siebeck.

Ford, J. Massyngberde, 1966. 'Was Montanism a Jewish Christian Heresy?', *JEH* 17: 145–58.

–, 1970–71. 'A Note on Proto-Montanism in the Pastoral Epistles', *NTS* 17: 338–46.

Fossum, Jarl E., 1995. *The Image of the Invisible God: Essays on the Influence of Jewish Mysticism on Early Christology*, NTOA 30, Freiburg: Universitätsverlag/Göttingen: Vandenhoeck & Ruprecht.

Fraade, Steven D., 1991. *From Tradition to Commentary: Torah and Its Interpretation in the Midrash* Sifre *to Deuteronomy*, Albany: State University of New York Press.

–, 1999. 'Shifting from Priestly to Non-priestly Legal Authority: A Comparison of the Damascus Document and the Midrash Sifra', *DSD* 6: 109–25.

–, 2002. 'Priests, Kings, and Patriarchs: Yerushalmi Sanhedrin in its Exegetical and Cultural Settings', 315–33, In *The Talmud Yerushalmi and Graeco-Roman Culture III*, Edited by Peter Schäfer, TSAJ 93, Tübingen: Mohr Siebeck.

Francis, Fred O., 1962. 'Humility and Angelic Worship in Col 2:18', *ST* 16: 109–34.

–, 1967. 'Visionary Discipline and Scriptural Tradition at Colossae', *LTQ* 2: 71–81.

Frankfort, Henri, 1948. *Kingship and the Gods: A Study of Ancient Near Eastern Religion as the Integration of Society and Nature*, Chicago: University of Chicago Press.

Frankfurter, David, 1993. *Elijah in Upper Egypt: The Apocalypse of Elijah and Early Egyptian Christianity*, Minneapolis: Fortress.

–, 1996. 'The Legacy of Jewish Apocalypses in Early Christianity: Regional Trajectories', 129–200, In *The Jewish Apocalyptic Heritage in Early Christianity*, Edited by James C. VanderKam and William Adler, CRINT 3.4, Minneapolis: Fortress.

–, 1997. 'Apocalypses Real and Alleged in the Mani Codex', *Numen* 44: 60–73.

–, 1998. 'Early Christian Apocalypticism: Literature and Social World', 415–53, In *The Encyclopedia of Apocalypticism*, Vol. 1: *The Origins of Apocalypticism in Judaism and Christianity*, Edited by John J. Collins, New York: Continuum.

Franklin, Eric, 1994. *Luke: Interpreter of Paul, Critic of Matthew*, JSNTSup 92, Sheffield: Sheffield Academic Press.

Fraser, P. M., 1972. *Ptolemaic Alexandria*, Vol. 1: *Text*, Oxford: Oxford University Press.

Freehof, Solomon B., 1923. 'Devotional Literature in the Vernacular', *CCAR Yearbook* 33: 375–424.

Fretheim, Terence E., 1984. *The Suffering of God: An Old Testament Perspective*, OBT, Philadelphia: Fortress.

–, 1987. 'Nature's Praise of God in the Psalms', *ExAud* 3: 16–30.

Frey, Jörg, 1998. 'Zum Weltbild im Jubiläenbuch', 261–92, In *Studies in the Book of Jubilees*, Edited by Matthias Albani, Jörg Frey, and Armin Lange, TSAJ 65; Tübingen: Mohr Siebeck.

Froehlich, Karlfried, 1973. 'Montanism and Gnosis', 91–111, In *The Heritage of the Early Church: Essays in Honor of the Very Reverend Georges Vasilievich Florovsky*, Edited by David Neimann and Margaret Schatkin, OrChrAn 195, Rome: Pont. Institutum Studiorum Orientalium.

Fujita, Neil S., 1986. *A Crack in the Jar: What Ancient Jewish Documents Tell Us About the New Testament*, New York: Paulist.

Garrett, Susan R., 1993. 'The "Weaker Sex" in the *Testament of Job*', *JBL* 112: 55–70.

Geljon, Albert C., 2002. *Philonic Exegesis in Gregory of Nyssa's* De Vita Moysis, BJS 333, Studia Philonica Monographs 5, Providence: Brown Judaic Studies.

Georgi, Dieter, 1986. *The Opponents of Paul in Second Corinthians*, Philadelphia: Fortress.

Gera, Deborah Levine, 2003. *Ancient Greek Ideas on Speech, Language, and Civilization*, Oxford: Oxford University Press.

Gersh, S. E., 1973. *ΚΙΝΗΣΙΣ ΑΚΙΝΗΤΟΣ: A Study of Spiritual Motion in the Philosophy of Proclus*, Philosophia Antiqua 26, Leiden: E. J. Brill.

Gerson-Kiwi, Edith, 1961. 'Halleluia and Jubilus in Hebrew-Oriental Chant', 43–49, In *Festschrift Heinrich Besseler zum sechzigsten Geburtstag*, Edited by Eberhardt Klemm, Leipzig: Musik Leipzig.

–, 1967. 'Der Sinn des Sinnlosen in der Interpolation sakraler Gesänge', 520–28, In *Festschrift für Walter Wiora zum 30. Dezember 1966*, Edited by Ludwig Finscher and Christoph-Hellmut Mahling, Basel: Bärenreiter Kassel.

Gieschen, Charles A.. 1998. *Angelomorphic Christology: Antecedents and Early Evidence*, AGJU 42, Leiden: E. J. Brill.

Ginzberg, Louis, 1955. *On Jewish Law and Lore*, Philadelphia: Jewish Publication Society of America.

Glatzer, Nachum N., 1974. 'Jüdische Ijob-Deutungen in den ersten christlichen Jahrhunderten', *Freiburger Rundbrief* 26: 31–34.

Gmirkin, Russell, 2000. 'The War Scroll, the Hasidim, and the Maccabean Conflict', 486–96, In *The Dead Sea Scrolls–Fifty Years After Their Discovery: Proceedings of the Jerusalem Congress, July 20–25, 1997*, Edited by Lawrence H. Schiffman, Emanuel Tov, and James C. VanderKam, Jerusalem: Israel Exploration Society.

Golb, Norman, 1995. *Who Wrote the Dead Sea Scrolls? The Search for the Secret of Qumran*, New York: Scribner.

Goldberg, P. Selvin, 1957. *Karaite Liturgy and Its Relation to Synagogue Worship*, Manchester: Manchester University Press.

Golitzin, Alexander, 2001. '"Earthly Angels and Heavenly Men": The Old Testament Pseudepigrapha, Niketas Stethatos, and the Tradition of "Interiorized Apocalyptic" in

Eastern Christian Ascetical and Mystical Literature', *Dumbarton Oaks Papers* 55: 125–53.

Goodblatt, David, 1980. 'Towards the Rehabilitation of Talmudic History', 33–38, In *History of Judaism: The Next Ten Years*, Edited by Baruch M. Bokser, BJS 21, Chico, CA: Scholars Press.

–, 1994. *The Monarchic Principle: Studies in Jewish Self-Government in Antiquity*, TSAJ 38, Tübingen: Mohr Siebeck.

Goodenough, Erwin Ramsdell, 1953–68. *Jewish Symbols in the Greco-Roman Period*, Bollingen 37, 13 vols., New York: Pantheon.

Goodman, Martin, 2007. *Judaism in the Roman World: Collected Essays*, AGJU 66, Leiden: E. J. Brill.

Goodwin, Deborah L., 2006. *"Take Hold of the Robe of a Jew": Herbert of Bosham's Christian Hebraism*, Studies in the History of Christian Traditions 126, Leiden: E. J. Brill.

Goody, Jack, 1986. *The Logic of Writing and the Organization of Society*, Studies in Literacy, Family, Culture and the State, Cambridge: Cambridge University Press.

Grant, Robert M., 1969. 'Chains of Being in Early Christianity', 279–89, In *Myths and Symbols: Studies in Honor of Mircea Eliade*, Edited by J. M. Kitagawa and C. Long, Chicago: University of Chicago Press.

Gray, Patrick, 2004. 'Points and Lines: Thematic Parallelism in the Letter of James and the *Testament of Job*', *NTS* 50: 406–24.

Green, William Scott, 1978. 'What's in a Name? – The Problematic of Rabbinic "Biography"', 77–96, In *Approaches to Ancient Judaism:Theory and Practice*, Edited by William Scott Green, BJS 1, Missoula, MT: Scholars Press.

Grillmeier, Aloys, 1975. *Christ in Christian Tradition*, Vol. 1: *From the Apostolic Age to Chalcedon (451)*, Rev. ed., Atlanta: John Knox.

–, 1996. *Christ in Christian Tradition*, Vol. 2: *From the Council of Chalcedon (451) to Gregory the Great (590–604)*, Pt. 4: *The Church of Alexandria with Nubia and Ethiopia after 451*, London: Mowbray.

Grözinger, Karl-Erich, 1980. 'Singen und ekstatische Sprache in der frühen jüdischen Mystik', *JSJ* 11: 66–77.

–, 1982. *Musik und Gesang in der Theologie der frühen jüdischen Literatur: Talmud Midrasch Mystik*, TSAJ 3, Tübingen: Mohr Siebeck.

–, 1998. 'Sprache und Identität – Das Hebräische und die Juden', 75–90, In *Sprache und Identität im Judentum*, Edited by Karl E. Grözinger, Jüdische Kultur 4, Wiesbaden: Harrassowitz.

Gruen, William "Chip", III, 2009. 'Seeking a Context for the *Testament of Job*', *JSP* 18: 163–79.

Gruenwald, Ithamar, 1980. *Apocalyptic and Merkavah Mysticism*, AGJU 14, Leiden: E. J. Brill.

–, 1983. 'Manichaeism and Judaism in Light of the Cologne Mani Codex', *ZPE* 50: 29–45.

–, 1988. *From Apocalypticism to Gnosticism: Studies in Apocalypticism, Merkavah Mysticism and Gnosticism*, BEATAJ 14, Frankfurt am Main: Peter Lang.

Guillaume, Alfred, 1927. 'The Influence of Judaism on Islam', 129–71, In *The Legacy of Israel*, Edited by Edwyn R. Bevan and Charles Singer, Oxford: Oxford University Press.

Gundry, R. H., 1996. '"Ecstatic Utterance" (N.E.B.)?', *JTS* 17: 299–307.

Güntert, Hermann, 1921. *Von der Sprache der Götter und Geister: Bedeutungsgeschicht-liche Untersuchungen zur homerischen und eddischen Göttersprache*, Halle: Max Niemeyer.

Gunther, John J., 1973. *St. Paul's Opponents and Their Background: A Study of Apocalyptic and Jewish Sectarian Teachings*, NovTSup 35, Leiden: E. J. Brill.

Gutierrez, Pedro, 1968. *La paternité spirituelle selon Saint Paul*, Paris: LeCoffre.

Haas, Cees, 1989. 'Job's Perseverance in the Testament of Job', 117–54, In *Studies on the Testament of Job*, Edited by Michael A. Knibb and Pieter W. van der Horst, SNTSMS 66, Cambridge: Cambridge University Press.

Haase, Felix, 1915. 'Zur Rekonstruktion des Bartholomäusevangeliums', *ZNW* 16: 93–112.

Hahn, E. Adelaide, 1969. *Naming-Constructions in Some Indo-European Languages*, Philological Monographs of the American Philological Association 27, Cleveland: Case Western Reserve University.

Hailperin, Herman, 1963. *Rashi and the Christian Scholars*, Pittsburgh: University of Pittsburgh Press.

Halbertal, Moshe, 1997. *People of the Book: Canon, Meaning, and Authority*, Cam-bridge: Harvard University Press.

Halivni, David Weiss, 1981. 'The Reception Accorded to Rabbi Judah's Mishnah', 204–12, In *Jewish and Christian Self-Definition*, Vol. 2: *Aspects of Judaism in the Greco-Roman Period*, Edited by E. P. Sanders, A. I. Baumgarten, and Alan Mendelsen, Phil-adelphia: Fortress.

Hall, Robert G., 1990a. 'The *Ascension of Isaiah:* Community Situation, Date, and Place in Early Christianity', *JBL* 109: 289–306.

–, 1990b. 'Living Creatures in the Midst of the Throne: Another Look at Revelation 4.6', *NTS* 36: 609–13.

Halperin, David J., 1983. *The Merkabah in Rabbinic Literature*, New Haven: American Oriental Society.

–, 1988. *The Faces of the Chariot: Early Jewish Responses to Ezekiel's Vision*, TSAJ 16, Tübingen: Mohr Siebeck.

Halsberghe, Gaston H., 1972. *The Cult of Sol Invictus*, EPRO 23, Leiden: E. J. Brill.

Hammerstein, Reinhold, 1962. *Die Musik der Engel: Untersuchungen zur Musikan-schauung des Mittelalters*, Bern: Francke.

Hannah, Darrell D., 1999. 'Isaiah's Vision in the Ascension of Isaiah and the Early Church', *JTS* 50: 80–101.

Haran, Menahem, 1983. 'Priesthood, Temple, Divine Service: Some Observations on Institutions and Practices of Worship', *HAR* 7: 121–35.

Harnack, Adolf, 1904–5. *The Expansion of Christianity in the First Three Centuries*, 2 Vols., Theological Translation Library 19, New York: G. P. Putnam's Sons.

Harrisville, Roy A., 1976. 'Speaking in Tongues: A Lexicographical Study', *CBQ* 38: 35–48.

Haspels, Emilie, 1971. *The Highlands of Phrygia: Sites and Monuments*, Vol. 1: *The Text*, Princeton: Princeton University Press.

Hauck, Robert J., 1989. *The More Divine Proof: Prophecy and Inspiration in Celsus and Origen*, AAR Academy Series 69, Atlanta: Scholars Press.

Hay, David M., 1973. *Glory at the Right Hand: Psalm 110 in Early Christianity*, SBLMS 18, Nashville: Abingdon.

Hays, Richard B., 1989. *Echoes of Scripture in the Letters of Paul*, New Haven: Yale University Press.

Heffernan, Thomas J., 2007. Review of Rex D. Butler, *The New Prophecy and "New Vision": Evidence of Montanism in the Passion of Perpetua and Felicitas*, in *VC* 61: 357–9.

Heiligenthal, Roman, 1992. *Zwischen Henoch und Paulus: Studien zum theologie-geschichtlichen Ort des Judasbriefes*, Texte und Arbeiten zum neutestamentlichen Zeitalter 6, Tübingen: Francke.

Hengel, Martin, 1974. *Judaism and Hellenism: Studies in their Encounter in Palestine during the Early Hellenistic Period*, 2 vols., Philadelphia: Fortress.

–, 1994. 'The Scriptures and their Interpretation in Second Temple Judaism', 158–75, In *The Aramaic Bible: Targums in their Historical Context*, Edited by D. R. G. Beattie and M. J. McNamara, JSOTSup 166; Sheffield: Sheffield Academic Press.

–, 1995. *Studies in Early Christology*, Edinburgh: T. & T. Clark.

–, 1996. *The Charismatic Leader and His Followers*, Rev. ed., Edinburgh: T. & T. Clark.

Henrichs, Albert, 1977. 'Greek Maenadism from Olympias to Messalina', *HSCP* 82: 121–60.

–, 1979. '"Thou Shalt not Kill a Tree": Greek, Manichaean and Indian Tales', *BASP* 16: 85–108.

–, 2003. 'Writing Religion: Inscribed Texts, Ritual Authority, and the Religious Discourse of the Polis', 38–58, In *Written Texts and the Rise of Literate Culture in Ancient Greece*, Edited by Harvey Yunis, Cambridge: Cambridge University Press.

Héring, Jean, 1962. *The First Epistle of Saint Paul to the Corinthians*, London: Epworth.

Herr, Moshe, 1979. 'Continuum in the Chain of Torah Transmission', *Zion* 44: 43–56 (Hebrew).

Heubeck, Alfred, 1949–50. 'Die homerische Göttersprache', *Würzburger Jahrbücher für die Altertumswissenschaft* 4: 197–218.

Hezser, Catherine, 2001. *Jewish Literacy in Roman Palestine*, TSAJ 81, Tübingen: Mohr Siebeck.

Hiley, David, 1993. *Western Plainchant: A Handbook*, Oxford: Clarendon.

Hilhorst, Ton, 2007. 'The Prestige of Hebrew in the Christian World of Late Antiquity and Middle Ages', 777–802, In *Flores Florentino: Dead Sea Scrolls and Other Early Jewish Studies in Honour of Florentino García Martínez*, Edited by Anthony Hilhorst, Émile Puech, and Eibert Tigchelaar, JSJSup 122, Leiden: E. J. Brill.

Himmelfarb, Martha, 1985. *Tours of Hell: An Apocalyptic Form in Jewish and Christian Literature*, Philadelphia: Fortress.

–, 1993. *Ascent to Heaven in Jewish and Christian Apocalypses*, New York: Oxford University Press.

–, 1995. 'The Practice of Ascent in the Ancient Mediterranean World', 123–37, In *Death, Ecstasy, and Other Worldly Journeys*, Edited by John J. Collins and Michael Fishbane, Albany: State University of New York Press.

–, 1997. '"A Kingdom of Priests": The Democratization of the Priesthood in the Literature of Second Temple Judaism', *Journal of Jewish Thought and Philosophy* 6: 89–104.

Hinson, E. Glenn, 1986. 'The Significance of Glossolalia in the History of Christianity', 181–203, In *Speaking in Tongues: A Guide to Research on Glossolalia*, Edited by Watson E. Mills, Grand Rapids: Eerdmans.

Hirschle, Maurus, 1979. *Sprachphilosophie und Namenmagie im Neuplatonismus: Mit einem Exkurs zu 'Demokrit' B 142*, Beiträge zur klassischen Philologie 96, Meisenheim am Glan: Anton Hain.

Hirschmann, Vera, 2004. '"Nach Art der Engel" – Die phrygische Prophetin Nanas', *Epigraphica Anatolica* 37: 160–68.

Hoffman, Lawrence A., 1981. 'Censoring In and Censoring Out: A Function of Liturgical Language', 19–37, In *Ancient Synagogues: The State of Research*, Edited by Joseph Gutmann, BJS 22; Chico, CA: Scholars Press.

Hogeterp, Albert L. A., 2009. *Expectations of the End: A Comparative Traditio-Historical Study of Eschatological, Apocalyptic and Messianic Ideas in the Dead Sea Scrolls and the New Testament*, STDJ 83, Leiden: Brill.

Holladay, Carl R., 1990. '1 Corinthians 13: Paul as Apostolic Paradigm', 80–98, In *Greeks, Romans, and Christians: Essays in Honor of Abraham J. Malherbe*, Edited by David L. Balch, Everett Ferguson, and Wayne Meeks, Minneapolis: Fortress.

Hollis, F. J., 1933. 'The Sun-Cult and the Temple in Jerusalem', 87–110, In *Myth and Ritual: Essays on the Myth and Ritual of the Hebrews in Relation to the Cultural Pattern of the Ancient East*, Edited by S. H. Hooke, Oxford: Oxford University Press.

Horbury, William, 1991. Review of *Studies on the Testament of Job* (ed. by Michael A. Knibb and Pieter W. van der Horst), in *VT* 41: 381.

Horn, Friedrich Wilhelm, 1992. *Das Angeld des Geistes: Studien zur paulinischen Pneumatologie*, FRLANT 154, Göttingen: Vandenhoeck & Ruprecht.

Hornblower, Simon, and Antony Spawforth (eds.), 1996. *Oxford Classical Dictionary*, 3d ed., Oxford: Oxford University Press.

Hovenden, Gerald, 2002. *Speaking in Tongues: The New Testament Evidence in Context*, JPTSup 22, Sheffield: Sheffield Academic Press.

Howard, W. F., 1929. 'First and Second Corinthians', 1169–1206, In *The Abingdon Bible Commentary*, Edited by Frederick Carl Eiselen, Edwin Lewis, and David G. Downey, New York: Abingdon-Cokesbury.

Hruby, Kurt, 1971. *Die Synagoge: Geschichtliche Entwicklung einer Institution*, Schriften zur Judentumskunde 3, Zürich: Theologischer Verlag.

Hultgård, Anders, 1977. *L'eschatologie des Testaments des Douze Patriarches*, Vol. 1: *Interpretation des textes*, Stockholm: Almqvist & Wiksell International.

Hurd, John Coolidge Jr., 1983. *The Origin of 1 Corinthians*, Macon: Mercer University Press.

Hurtado, Larry W., 2000. 'Religious Experience and Religious Innovation in the New Testament', *JR* 80: 183–205.

–, 2003. *Lord Jesus Christ: Devotion to Jesus in Earliest Christianity*, Grand Rapids: Eerdman.

Idelsohn, A. Z., 1932. *Jewish Liturgy and Its Development*, New York: Henry Holt.

Ilan, Tal, 2000. 'The Daughters of Zelophehad and Women's Inheritance: The Biblical Injunction and its Outcome', 176–86, In *A Feminist Companion to The Bible: Exodus to Deuteronomy*, Edited by Athalya Brenner, Sheffield: Sheffield University Press.

–, 2006. *Silencing the Queen: The Literary Histories of Shelamzion and Other Jewish Women*, TSAJ 115, Tübingen: Mohr Siebeck.

Isaksson, Abel, 1965. *Marriage and Ministry in the New Temple*, ASNU 24, Lund: C. W. K. Gleerup.

Jacobs, Irving, 1970. 'Literary Motifs in The Testament of Job', *JJS* 21: 1–10.

Jaffee, Martin S., 2001. *Torah in the Mouth: Writing and Oral Tradition in Palestinian Judaism, 200 BCE – 400 CE*, New York: Oxford University Press.

James, Montague Rhodes, 1897. *Apocrypha anecdota II*, Texts and Studies 5, Cambridge: Cambridge University Press.

James, William, 1982. *The Varieties of Religious Experience: A Study in Human Nature*, Penguin American Library, Hammondsworth: Penguin.

Janowitz, Naomi, 1989. *The Poetics of Ascent: Theories of Language in a Rabbinic Ascent Text*, Albany: State University of New York Press.

–, 1991. 'Theories of Divine Names in Origen and Pseudo-Dionysius', *HR* 30: 359–72.

Jastrow, Marcus, 1989. *A Dictionary of the Targumim, the Talmud Babli and Yerushalmi, and the Midrashic Literature*, New York: Judaica.

Johansson, Nils, 1940. *Parakletoi: Vorstellungen von Fürsprechern für die Menschen vor Gott in der alttestamentlichen Religion, im Spätjudentum und Urchristentum*, Lund: Gleerup.

–, 1964. '1 Cor 13 and 1 Cor 14', *NTS* 10: 383–92.

Johnson, Luke Timothy, 1992. 'Tongues, Gift of', 6.596–600, In *The Anchor Bible Dictionary*, Edited by David Noel Freedman, 6 vols., New York: Doubleday.

Johnson, Norman B., 1948. *Prayer in the Apocrypha and Pseudepigrapha: A Study of the Jewish Concept of God*, JBLMS 2, Philadelphia: Society of Biblical Literature and Exegesis.

Johnson, Sherman E., 1957. 'The Dead Sea Manual of Discipline and the Jerusalem Church of Acts', 129–42, In *The Scrolls and the New Testament*, Edited by Krister Stendahl, New York: Harper & Brothers.

Johnston, George, 1970. *The Spirit-Paraclete in the Gospel of John*, SNTSMS 12, Cambridge: Cambridge University Press.

Jones, F. Stanley, 1987. Review of Gerard P. Luttikhuizen, *The Revelation of Elchasai: Investigations into the Evidence for a Mesopotamian Jewish Apocalypse of the Second Century and its Reception by Judeo-Christian Propagandists*, In *JAC* 30: 200–209.

Jones, Gareth Lloyd, 1999. 'Robert Wakefield (d. 1537): The Father of English Hebraists?', 234–48, In *Hebrew Study from Ezra to Ben-Yehuda*, Edited by William Horbury, Edinburgh: T & T Clark.

Jones, Maurice, 1918. 'St. Paul and the Angels', *The Expositor* 15: 356–70, 412–25.

Jung, C. G., 1967. *Alchemical Studies*, The Collected Works of C. G. Jung 13, Princeton: Princeton University Press.

Kaestli, Jean-Daniel, 1995. 'Les écrits apocryphes chrétiens: pour une approche qui valorise leur diversité et leurs attaches bibliques', 27–42, In *Le mystère apocryphe: introduction à une littérature méconnue*, Edited by J.-D. Kaestli and D. Marguerat, Essaia Bibliques 26, Geneva: Labor et Fides.

Kalman, Jason, 2006. 'Job Denied the Resurrection of Jesus? A Rabbinic Critique of the Church Father's Use of Exegetical Traditions Found in the Septuagint and the *Testament of Job*', 371–97, In *The Changing Face of Judaism, Christianity and Other Greco-Roman Religions in Antiquity*, Edited by Ian H. Henderson and Gerbern S. Oegema, Studien zu den jüdischen Schriften aus hellenistisch-römischer Zeit 2, Gütersloh: Gütersloher Verlagshaus.

Kalmin, Richard, 1994. *Sages, Stories, Authors, and Editors in Rabbinic Babylonia*, BJS 300, Atlanta: Scholars Press.

–, 2006. *Jewish Babylonia between Persia and Roman Palestine*, Oxford: Oxford University Press.

Kasher, Rimmon, 1996. 'Angelology and the Supernal Worlds in the Aramaic Targums to the Prophets', *JSJ* 27: 168–91.

Katz, David S., 2004. *God's Last Words: Reading the English Bible from the Reformation to Fundamentalism*, New Haven: Yale University Press.

Kaufmann, Yehezkel, 1927. *Generations of Israelite Faith* (Hebrew), Tel Aviv: Dvir.

Kedar, Benjamin, 1990. 'The Latin Translations', 299–336, In *Mikra: Text, Translation, Reading and Interpretation of the Hebrew Bible in Ancient Judaism and Early Christianity*, Edited by Martin Jan Mulder, CRINT 2/1, Maastricht: Van Gorcum.

Keener, Craig S., 1997. *The Spirit in the Gospels and Acts: Divine Purity and Power*, Peabody: Hendrickson.

Keith, Chris, 2009. *The* Pericope Adulterae, *the Gospel of John, and the Literacy of Jesus*, New Testament Tools, Studies and Documents 38, Leiden: Brill.

Kelly, J. N. D., 1977. *Early Christian Doctrines*, 5th ed., London: Adam & Charles Black.

Kerkeslager, Allen, Claudia Setzer, Paul Trebilco, and David Goodblatt, 2006. 'The Diaspora from 66 to c. 235 CE', 53–92, In *The Cambridge History of Judaism*, Vol. 4: *The Late Roman-Rabbinic Period*, (ed. by Steven T. Katz) Cambridge: Cambridge University Press.

Kiley, Mark, 1986. *Colossians as Pseudepigraphy*, The Biblical Seminar, Sheffield: JSOT Press.

Kilgallen, John J., 2002. '"With many other words" (Acts 2,40): Theological Assumptions in Peter's Pentecost Speech', *Bib* 83: 71–87.

Kimelman, Reuven, 1981. 'The Conflict Between R. Yohanan and Resh Laqish on the Supremacy of the Patriarchate', 1–20, In *Proceedings of the Seventh World Congress of Jewish Studies*, Vol. 3, Jerusalem: Perry Foundation for Biblical Research.

–, 1983. 'The Conflict between the Priestly Oligarchy and the Sages in the Talmudic Period', *Zion* 48: 135–48 (Hebrew).

–, 1999. 'Identifying Jews and Christians in Roman Syrio-Palestine', 301–33, In *Galilee Through the Centuries: Confluence of Cultures*, Edited by Eric M. Meyers, Duke Judaic Studies 1, Winona Lake, IN: Eisenbrauns.

–, 2006. 'Rabbinic Prayer in Late Antiquity', 573–611, In *The Cambridge History of Judaism*, Vol. 4: *The Late Roman-Rabbinic Period*, (ed. by Steven T. Katz) Cambridge: Cambridge University Press.

Kittel, Bonnie Pedrotti, 1980. *The Hymns of Qumran: Translation and Commentary*, SBLDS 50, Chico, CA: Scholars Press.

Kittel, Gerhard, 1964–76. 'ἄγγελος', 1.74–87, In *Theological Dictionary of the New Testament*, Edited by Gerhard Kittel and Gerhard Friedrich, 10 Vols., Grand Rapids: Eerdmans.

Klauck, Hans-Josef, 1999. 'Von Kassandra bis zur Gnosis: Im Umfeld der frühchristlichen Glossolalie', *TQ* 179: 289–312.

–, 2000. 'Mit Engelszungen? Vom Charisma der verständlichen Rede in 1 Kor 14', *ZTK* 97: 276–99.

Klawiter, Frederick Charles, 1975. 'The New Prophecy in Early Christianity: The Origin, Nature, and Development of Montanism, A.D. 165–220', Ph.D., University of Chicago.

Klinzing, Georg, 1971. *Die Umdeutung des Kultus in der Qumrangemeinde und im Neuen Testament*, SUNT 7, Göttingen: Vandenhoeck & Ruprecht.

Knight, Jonathan, 1996. *Disciples of the Beloved One: The Christology, Social Setting and Theological Context of the Ascension of Isaiah*, JSPSup 18, Sheffield: Sheffield Academic Press.

Knohl, Israel, 1995. *The Sanctuary of Silence: The Priestly Torah and the Holiness School*, Minneapolis: Fortress.

–, 1996. 'Between Voice and Silence: The Relationship between Prayer and Temple Cult', *JBL* 115: 17–30.

Kobusch, Theo, 1987. *Sein und Sprache: Historische Grundlegung einer Ontologie der Sprache*, Studien zur Problemgeschichte der antiken und mittelalterlichen Philosophie 11, Leiden: E. J. Brill.

Koenen, Ludwig, and Cornelia Römer (eds.), 1985. *Der Kölner Mani-Kodex: Abbildungen und Dipolomatischer Text*, Papyrologische Texte und Abhandlungen 35, Bonn: Rudolf Habelt.

Kofsky, Aryeh, 2002. *Eusebius of Caesarea Against Paganism*, Boston: E. J. Brill.

Kohler, Kaufmann, 1897. 'The Testament of Job, an Essene Midrash on the Book of Job', 264–338, In *Semitic Studies in Memory of Rev. Dr. Alexander Kohut*, Edited by Georg Alexander Kohut, Berlin: S. Calvary & Co..

Kraemer, David C., 1989. 'On the Reliability of Attributions in the Babylonian Talmud', *HUCA* 60: 175–90.

–, 2006. 'The Mishnah', 299–315, In *The Cambridge History of Judaism*, Vol. 4: *The Late Roman-Rabbinic Period*, (ed. by Steven T. Katz) Cambridge: Cambridge University Press.

Kraft, Heinrich, 1977. 'Vom Ende der urchristlichen Prophetie', 162–85, In *Prophetic Vocation in the New Testament and Today*, Edited by J. Panagopoulos, NovTSup 45, Leiden: E. J. Brill.

Kraft, Robert A., 1994. 'The Pseudepigrapha in Christianity', 55–86, In *Tracing the Threads: Studies in the Vitality of Jewish Pseudepigrapha*, Edited by John C. Reeves, SBLEJL 06, Atlanta: Scholars Press.

–, 2001. 'Setting the Stage and Framing Some Central Questions', *JSJ* 32: 371–95.

–, 2009. *Exploring the Scripturesque: Jewish Texts and their Christian Contexts*, JSJSup, Leiden: Brill.

Krämer, Helmut, 1959. 'Zur Wortbedeutung "Mysteria"', *Wort und Dienst* 6: 121–25.

Kreisel, Howard, 2001. *Prophecy: The History of an Idea in Medieval Jewish Philosophy*, Amsterdam Studies in Jewish Thought 8, Dordrecht: Kluwer.

Kremer, Jacob, 1973. *Pfingstbericht und Pfingstgeschehen: Eine exegetische Untersuchung zu Apg 2, 1–13*, Stuttgarter Bibelstudien 63/64, Stuttgart: KBW Verlag.

Kretzman, N., 1971. 'Plato on the Correctness of Names', *American Philological Quarterly* 8: 126–38.

Kugel, James, 1996. 'The Holiness of Israel and the Land in Second Temple Times', 21–32, In *Texts, Temples, and Traditions: A Tribute to Menahem Haran*, Edited by Michael V. Fox, Victor Avigdor Hurowitz, Avi Hurvitz, Michael L. Klein, Baruch J. Schwartz, and Nili Shupak, Winona Lake, IN: Eisenbrauns.

Kugler, Robert A., and Richard L. Rohrbaugh, 2004. 'On Women and Honor in the *Testament of Job*', *JSP* 14: 43–62.

Kuhn, Harold B., 1948. 'The Angelology of the Non-Canonical Jewish Apocalypses', *JBL* 67: 217–32.

Kulik, Alexander, 2000. 'Apocalypse of Abraham: Towards the Lost Original', Ph.D., Hebrew University.

–, 2003. 'The Gods of Nahor: A Note on the Pantheon of the *Apocalypse of Abraham*', *JJS* 54:228–32.

–, 2004. *Retroverting Slavonic Pseudepigrapha: Toward the Original of the* Apocalypse of Abraham, SBLEJL 3, Atlanta: Society of Biblical Literature.

Kuyt, Annelies, 1995. *The 'Descent' of the Chariot: Towards a Description of the Terminology, Place, Function and Nature of the Yeridah in Hekhalot Literature*, TSAJ 45, Tübingen: Mohr Siebeck.

Kydd, Ronald A. N., 1984. *Charismatic Gifts in the Early Church*, Peabody, MA: Hendrickson.

Lacau, Pierre, 1966. 'Remarques sur le manuscrit akhmimique des apocalypses de Sophonie et d'Élie', *Journal Asiatique* 254: 169–95.

Lane Fox, Robin, 1987. *Pagans and Christians*, New York: Albert A. Knopf.

Lang, Bernhard, 1988–2002. 'Buchreligion', 2.143–65, In *Handbuch religionswissenschaftlicher Grundbegriffe*, Edited by Hubert Cancik, Burkhard Gladigow, and Matthias Laubscher, 5 vols., Stuttgart: Kohlhammer.

Lange, Armin, 2003. 'Kriterien essenischer Texte', 59–69, In *Qumran kontrovers: Beiträge zu den Textfunden vom Toten Meer*, Edited by Jörg Frey and Hartmut Stegemann, Bonifatius: Paderborn.

Laplanche, François, 1986. 'La Bible chez les réformés', 459–80, In *Le siècle des lumières et la Bible*, Edited by Yvon Belaval and Dominique Bourel, Bible de tous les temps 7, Paris: Beauchesne.

Lapin, Hayim, 2006. 'The Origins and Development of the Rabbinic Movement in the Land of Israel', 206–29. In *The Cambridge History of Judaism*, Vol. 4: *The Late Roman-Rabbinic Period*, (ed. by Steven T. Katz) Cambridge: Cambridge University Press.

Lawson, John, 1948. *The Biblical Theology of Saint Irenaeus*, London: Epworth.

Leaney, A. R. C., 1976. 'Greek Manuscripts from the Judaean Desert', 283–300, In *Studies in New Testament Language and Text: Essays in Honour of George D. Kilpatrick on the Occasion of his Sixty-fifth Birthday*, Edited by J. K. Elliott, NovTSup 44; Leiden: E. J. Brill.

Lehrich, Christopher I., 2003. *The Language of Demons and Angels: Cornelius Agrippa's Occult Philosophy*, Brill's Studies in Intellectual History, Leiden: E. J. Brill.

Leicht, Reimund, 1999. '*Qedushah* and Prayer to Helios: A New Hebrew Version of an Apocryphal Prayer of Jacob', *JSQ* 6: 140–76.

Lesses, Rebecca, 1993. 'The Daughters of Job', 139–49, In *Searching the Scriptures*, Edited by Elisabeth Schüssler Fiorenza, Vol. 2: *A Feminist Commentary*, New York: Continuum.

–, 1996. 'Speaking with Angels: Jewish and Greco-Egyptian Revelatory Adjurations', *HTR* 89: 41–60.

–, 1998. *Ritual Practices to Gain Power: Angels, Incantations, and Revelation in Early Jewish Mysticism*, HTS 44, Harrisburg, PA: Trinity.

–, 2007. 'Amulets and Angels: Visionary Experience in the Testament of Job and the Hekhalot Literature', 49–74, In *Heavenly Tablets: Interpretation, Identity and Tradition in Ancient Judaism*, Edited by Lynn LiDonnici and Andrea Lieber, JSJSup 119, Leiden: Brill.

Levin, Susan B., 1997. 'Greek Conceptions of Naming: Three Forms of Appropriateness in Plato and the Literary Tradition', *Classical Philology* 92: 46–57.

Levine, Lee I., 1975. *Caesarea Under Roman Rule*, SJLA 7, Leiden: E. J. Brill.

–, 1979. 'The Jewish Patriarch (Nasi) in Third Century Palestine', 649–88, In *Aufstieg und Niedergang der römischen Welt: Religion (Judentum: Allgemeines, Palästinisches Judentum)* II.19.2, Edited by Wolfgang Haase, Berlin: Walter de Gruyter, 1979.

–, 1989. *The Rabbinic Class of Roman Palestine in Late Antiquity*, Jerusalem: Yad Izhak Ben-Zvi.

Levison, John R., 1995. 'The Prophetic Spirit as an Angel According to Philo', *HTR* 88: 189–207.

–, 1997. *The Spirit in First Century Judaism*, AGJU 29, Leiden: E. J. Brill.

–, 2009. *Filled with the Spirit*, Grand Rapids: Eerdmans.

Lewis, Bernard, 1984. *The Jews of Islam*, Princeton: Princeton University Press.

Licht, Jacob, 1956. "The Doctrine of the Thanksgiving Scroll', *IEJ* 6: 1–13, 89–101.

Lichtenberger, Hermann, 1980. *Studien zum Menschenbild in Texten der Qumrangemeinde*, SUNT 15, Göttingen: Vandenhoeck & Ruprecht.

Lieberman, Saul, 1945–46. 'Palestine in the Third and Fourth Centuries', *JQR* 36: 329–70.

–, 1946. 'Two Lexicographical Notes', *JBL* 65: 67–72.

Lieu, Judith, 1994. '"The Parting of the Ways": Theological Construct or Historical Reality?', *JSNT* 56: 101–19.

Lightstone, Jack N., 1984. *The Commerce of the Sacred: Mediation of the Divine among Jews in the Graeco-Roman Diaspora*, BJS 59, Chico: Scholars Press.

–, 2002. *Mishnah and the Social Formation of the Early Rabbinic Guild: A Socio-Rhetorical Approach*, Studies in Christianity and Judaism 11, Waterloo: Wilfrid Laurier University Press.

Lignée, Hubert, 1988. 'La place du livre des Jubilés et du Rouleau du Temple dans l'histoire du mouvement essénien: ces deux ouvrages ont-ils été écrits par le maître de justice?', *RevQ* 13: 331–45.

Lim, Timothy H., 2000. 'The Qumran Scrolls, Multilingualism, and Biblical Interpretation', 57–73, In *Religion in the Dead Sea Scrolls*, Edited by John J. Collins and Robert A. Kugler, Studies in the Dead Sea Scrolls and Related Literature, Grand Rapids: Eerdmans.

Lincoln, Andrew T., 1981. *Paradise Now and Not Yet: Studies in the Role of the Heavenly Dimension in Paul's Thought with Special Reference to his Eschatology*, SNTSMS 43, Cambridge: Cambridge University Press.

Lombard, Emile, 1915. 'Le montanisme et l'inspiration: A propos du livre de M. de Labriolle', *RTP* 3: 278–322.

Lueken, Wilhelm, 1898. *Michael: Eine Darstellung und Vergleichung der jüdischen und der morgenländisch-christlichen Tradition vom Erzengel Michael*, Göttingen: Vandenhoeck & Ruprecht.

Lührmann, Dieter, 1965. *Das Offenbarungsverständnis bei Paulus und in paulinischen Gemeinden*, WMANT 16, Neukirchen-Vluyn: Neukirchener.

Luttikhuizen, Gerard P., 1985. *The Revelation of Elchasai: Investigations into the Evidence for a Mesopotamian Jewish Apocalypse of the Second Century and its Reception by Judeo-Christian Propagandists*, TSAJ 8, Tübingen: Mohr Siebeck.

Mach, Michael, 1992. *Entwicklungsstadien des jüdischen Engelglaubens in vorrabbinischer Zeit*, TSAJ 34, Tübingen: Mohr Siebeck.

Maier, Johann, 1979. 'Die Sonne im religiösen Denken des antiken Judentums', 346–412, In *Aufstieg und Niedergang der römischen Welt: Religion (Judentum: Allgemeines, Palästinisches Judentum)* II.19.1, Edited by Wolfgang Haase, Berlin: Walter de Gruyter, 1979.

–, 1992. 'Shîrê 'Ôlat hash-Shabbat: Some Observations on their Calendric Implications and on their Style", 543–60, In *The Madrid Qumran Congress: Proceedings of the International Congress on the Dead Sea Scrolls, Madrid 18–21 March, 1991*, Edited by Julio Trebolle Barrera and Luis Vegas Montaner, 2 vols., STDJ 11, Leiden: E. J. Brill.

–, 1993. 'Self-Definition, Prestige, and Status of Priests Towards the End of the Second Temple Period', *BTB* 23: 139–50.

Majercik, Ruth, 1989. *The Chaldean Oracles: Text, Translation, and Commentary*, Studies in Greek and Roman Religion 5, Leiden: E. J. Brill.

Malkiel, David, 2003. 'Between Worldliness and Traditionalism: Eighteenth-Century Jews Debate Intercessory Prayer', *Jewish Studies, an Internet Journal* 2: 169–98.

Maly, Karl, 1967. *Mündige Gemeinde: Untersuchungen zur pastoralen Führung des Apostels Paulus im 1. Korintherbrief*, Stuttgarter Biblische Monographien 2, Stuttgart: Katholisches Bibelwerk.

Mann, Jacob, 1940. *The Bible as Read and Preached in the Old Synagogue*, Vol. 1: *The Palestinian Triennial Cycle: Genesis and Exodus*, Cincinnati: Jacob Mann.

Markschies, Christoph, 1994. 'Hieronymus und die "Hebraica Veritas" – ein Beitrag zur Archäologie des protestantischen Schriftverständnisses?', 131–81, In *Die Septuaginta zwischen Judentum und Christentum*, Edited by Martin Hengel and Anna Maria Schwemer, WUNT 1.72, Tübingen: Mohr Siebeck.

Marmorstein, A., 1914. 'Legendenmotive in der rabbinischen Literatur', *Archiv für Religionswissenschaft* 17: 132–38.

Marshall, I. Howard, 1977. 'The Significance of Pentecost', *SJT* 30: 347–69.

Martin, Dale B., 1991. 'Tongues of Angels and Other Status Indicators', *JAAR* 59: 547–89.

–, 1995. *The Corinthian Body*, New Haven: Yale University Press.

Martin, Matthew J., 2004. 'Origen's Theory of Language and the First Two Columns of the Hexapla', *HTR* 97: 99–106.

Martin, Ralph P., 1992. 'Gifts, Spiritual', 2.1015–18, In *The Anchor Bible Dictionary*, Edited by David Noel Freedman, 6 vols., New York: Doubleday.

Martyn, J. Louis, 1997. *Theological Issues in the Letters of Paul*, Nashville: Abingdon.

May, L. Carlyle, 1956. 'A Survey of Glossolalia and Related Phenomena in Non-Christian Religions', *American Anthropologist* 58: 75–96.

McDannell, Colleen, and Bernhard Lang, 1988. *Heaven: A History*, New Haven: Yale University Press.

McDonnell, Kilian, and George T. Montague, 1991. *Christian Initiation and Baptism in the Holy Spirit: Evidence from the First Eight Centuries*, Collegeville, MN: Liturgical.

McEwan, Calvin W., 1934. *The Oriental Origin of Hellenistic Kingship*, Chicago: University of Chicago Press.

McKane, William, 1965. *Prophets and Wise Men*, SBT 44, Naperville, IL: Alec R. Allenson.

McKinnon, James, 1987. *Music in Early Christian Literature*, Cambridge: Cambridge University Press.

Mendels, Doron, 1979. 'Hellenistic Utopia and the Essenes', *HTR* 72: 207–22.

Menzies, Robert P., 1991. *The Development of Early Christian Pneumatology with Special Reference to Luke-Acts*, JSNTSup 54, Sheffield: Sheffield Academic Press.

Merlan, Philip, 1965. 'Zur Zahlenlehre im Platonismus (Neuplatonismus) und im *Sefer Yezira*', *Journal of the History of Philosophy* 3: 167–81.

Metzger, Martin, 1993. 'Keruben und Palmetten als Dekoration im Jerusalemer Heiligtum und Jahwe, "der Nahrung gibt allem Fleisch"', 503–29, In *Zion: Ort der Begegnung: Festschrift für Laurentius Klein zur Vollendung des 65. Lebensjahres*, Edited by Ferdinand Hahn, Frank-Lothar Hossfeld, Hans Jorissen, and Angelika Neuwirth, BBB 90, Bodenheim: Athenäum Hain Hanstein.

Milbank, John, 1990. *Theology and Social Theory: Beyond Secular Reason*, Oxford: Blackwell.

Milgrom, Jacob, 1985. 'Challenge to Sun-Worship Interpretation of Temple Scroll's Gilded Staircase', *BAR* 11/1: 70–3.

Miller, Patricia Cox, 1986. 'In Praise of Nonsense', 481–505, In *Classical Mediterranean Spirituality: Egyptian, Greek, Roman*, Edited by A. H. Armstrong, World Spirituality 15, New York: Crossroad.

Miller, Patrick D., 1994. *They Cried to the Lord: The Form and Theology of Biblical Prayer*, Minneapolis: Fortress.

Miller, Stuart S., 1984. *Studies in the History and Traditions of Sepphoris*, SJLA 37, Leiden: E. J. Brill.

Mirecki, Paul, 1994a. 'The Coptic Hoard of Spells from the University of Michigan', 293–310, In *Ancient Christian Magic: Coptic Texts of Ritual Power*, Edited by Marvin Meyer and Richard Smith, San Francisco: Harper Collins.

–, 1994b. 'The Coptic Wizard's Hoard', *HTR* 87: 435–60.

Morgenstern, Julian, 1963. *The Fire upon the Altar*, Leiden: E. J. Brill.

Morray-Jones, C. R. A., 1993. 'Paradise Revisited (2 Cor 12:1–12): The Jewish Mystical Background of Paul's Apostolate', Part 1: 'The Jewish Sources', *HTR* 86: 177–217, Part 2: 'Paul's Heavenly Ascent and its Significance', *HTR* 86: 265–92.

Mortley, Raoul, 1986. *From Word to Silence: The Way of Negation, Christian and Greek*, 2 vols., Theophaneia: Beiträge zur Religions- und Kirchengeschichte des Altertums 30–31, Bonn: Hanstein.

Mowinckel, Sigmund, 1956. *He That Cometh*, Oxford: Basil Blackwell.

Moyise, Steve, 1995. *The Old Testament in the Book of Revelation*, JSNTSup 115, Sheffield: Sheffield Academic Press.

Muffs, Yochanan, 1992. *Love and Joy: Law, Language, and Religion in Ancient Israel*, New York: Jewish Theological Seminary.

Müller, Mogens, 1996a. 'Die Abraham-Gestalt im Jubiläenbuch: Versuch einer Interpretation', *SJOT* 10: 238–57.

–, 1996b. *The First Bible of the Church: A Plea for the Septuagint*, JSOTSup 206, Sheffield: Sheffield Academic Press.

Munzinger, André, 2007. *Discerning the Spirits: Theological and Ethical Hermeneutics in Paul*, SNTSMS 140, Cambridge: Cambridge University Press.

Ness, Lester, 1999. *Written in the Stars: Ancient Zodiac Mosaics*, Marco Polo Monographs 1, Warren Center, PA: Shangri-La.

Neusner, Jacob, 1968. *A History of the Jews in Babylonia*, Vol. 3: *From Shapur I to Shapur II*, StPB 12; Leiden: E. J. Brill.

–, 1970. *A Life of Yohanan ben Zakkai: Ca. 1–80 C.E.*, StPB 6, Leiden: E. J. Brill.

–, 1979–80. 'Map without Territory: Mishnah's System of Sacrifice and Sanctuary', *HR* 19: 103–27.

–, 1993a. *Judaism States its Theology: The Talmudic Re-presentation*, University of South Florida Studies in the History of Judaism 88, Atlanta: Scholars Press.

–, 1993b. 'The Mishna in Philosophical Context and Out of Canonical Bounds', *JBL* 112: 291–304.

Newsom, Carol A., 1987. 'Merkabah Exegesis in the Qumran Sabbath Shirot', *JJS* 38: 11–30.

–, 1990. '"Sectually Explicit" Literature from Qumran', 167–87, In *The Hebrew Bible and Its Interpreters*, Edited by W. H. Propp *et al*, Winona Lake, IN: Eisenbrauns.

–, 1999. 'Introduction', 1-15, In *The Dead Sea Scrolls: Hebrew, Aramaic, and Greek Texts with English Translations*, Vol. 4b: *Angelic Liturgy: Songs of the Sabbath Sacrifice*, Edited by James H. Charlesworth and Carol A. Newsom, Tübingen: Mohr Siebeck.

–, 2000. 'Songs of the Sabbath Sacrifice', 887–89, In *Encyclopedia of the Dead Sea Scrolls*, Edited by Lawrence H. Schiffman and James C. VanderKam, 2 vols., Oxford: Oxford University Press.

Newton, Michael, 1985. *The Concept of Purity at Qumran and in the Letters of Paul*, SNTSMS 53, Cambridge: Cambridge University Press.

Nickelsburg, George W. E. Jr., 1972. *Resurrection, Immortality, and Eternal Life in Intertestamental Judaism*, HTS 26, Cambridge: Harvard University Press.

Niehoff, Maren R., 1995. 'What is in a Name? Philo's Mystical Philosophy of Language', *JSQ* 2: 220–52.

Nitzan, Bilhah, 1994a. 'Harmonic and Mystical Characteristics in Poetic and Liturgical Writings from Qumran', *JQR* 85: 163–83.

–, 1994b. *Qumran Prayer and Religious Poetry*, STDJ 12, Leiden: E. J. Brill.

Nordheim, Eckhard von, 1980. *Die Lehre der Alten*, Vol. 1: *Das Testament als Literaturgattung im Judentum der hellenistisch-römischen Zeit*, ALGHJ 13, Leiden: E. J. Brill.

Norelli, Enrico, 1983. 'Sulla pneumatologia dell'*Ascensione di Isaia*', 211–21, In *Isaia, il diletto e la chiesa: visione ed esegesi profetica cristiano-primitiva nell'*Ascensione di Isaia, Edited by Mauro Pesce, Testi e ricerche di Scienze religiose 20, Brescia: Paideia.

–, 1994. *L'Ascensione di Isaia: studi su un apocrifo al crocevia dei cristianesimi*, Origini [new series] 1, Bologna: Centro Editoriale Dehoniano.

–, 1995. *Ascensio Isaiae: commentarius*, Corpus Christianorum Series Apocryphorum 8, Turnhout: Brepols.

Oberhänsli-Widmer, Gabrielle, 1998. *Biblische Figuren in der rabbinischen Literatur: Gleichnisse und Bilder zu Adam, Noah und Abraham im Midrasch Bereschit Rabba*, Judaica et Christiana 17, Bern: Peter Lang.

Oppenheim, A. Leo, 1949. 'The Golden Garments of the Gods', *JNES* 8: 172–93.

Otto, Rudolf, 1926. *The Idea of the Holy*, New York: Oxford University Press.

Park, Sejin, 2008. *Pentecost and Sinai: The Festival of Weeks as a Celebration of the Sinai Event*, Library of Hebrew Bible/Old Testament Studies 342, New York: T & T Clark.

Parke, Herbert William, 1967. *The Oracles of Zeus: Dodona, Olympia, Ammon*, Cambridge: Harvard University Press.

–, 1988. *Sibyls and Sibylline Prophecy in Classical Antiquity*, London: Routledge.

Parker, Simon B., 2006. 'Divine Intercession in Judah?', *VT* 56: 76–91.

Parmentier, Martin (Martien), 1994. 'Das Zungenreden bei den Kirchenvätern', *Bijdragen* 55: 276–98.

–, 1999. 'The Gifts of the Spirit in Early Christianity', 58–78, In *The Impact of Scripture in Early Christianity*, Edited by J. den Boeft and M. L. van Poll-van de Lisdonk, VCSup 44, Leiden: E. J. Brill.

–, 2004. 'Job the Rebel: From the Rabbis to the Church Fathers', 227–42, In *Saints and Role Models in Judaism and Christianity*, Edited by Marcel Poorthuis and Joshua Schwartz, J&CP 7, Leiden: E. J. Brill.

Paul, André, 1987. 'La Bible grecque d'Aquila et l'idéologie du judaïsme ancien', 221–45, In *Aufstieg und Niedergang der römischen Welt: Religion (Hellenistisches Judentum in römischer Zeit, ausgenommen Philon und Josephus)* II.20.1, Edited by Wolfgang Haase, Berlin: Walter de Gruyter, 1979.

Pearson, Birger A., 1976. 'The Pierpont Morgan Fragments of a Coptic Enoch Apocryphon', 227–83, In *Studies on the Testament of Abraham*, Edited by George W. E. Nickelsburg, SBLSCS 6, Missoula, MT: Scholars Press.

–, 1992. 'Theurgic Tendencies in Gnosticism and Iamblichus's Conception of Theurgy', 253–75, In *Neoplatonism and Gnosticism*, Edited by Richard T. Wallis and Jay Bregman, Albany: State University of New York Press.

Pelikan, Jaroslav, 1989. *The Christian Tradition: A History of the Development of Doctrine*, Vol. 5: *Christian Doctrine and Modern Culture (since 1700)*, Chicago: University of Chicago Press.

Perdrizet, P., 1903. 'ΣΦΡΑΓΙΣ ΣΟΛΟΜΩΝΟΣ', *REG* 16: 42–61.

Perrin, Norman, and Dennis C. Duling, 1984. *The New Testament: An Introduction*, 2nd ed., San Diego: Harcourt Brace Jovanovich.

Petersen, William L., 1994. *Tatian's Diatessaron: Its Creation, Dissemination, Significance, and History in Scholarship*, VCSup 25, Leiden: E. J. Brill.

Peterson, Erik, 1935. *Das Buch von den Engeln: Stellung und Bedeutung der heiligen Engel im Kultus*, Leipzig: Jakob Hegner.

Petuchowski, Jakob J., 1972. *Understanding Jewish Prayer*, New York: Ktav.

Philonenko, Marc, 1958. 'Le *Testament de Job* et les thérapeutes', *Semitica* 8: 41–53.

–, 1985. 'Prière au soleil et liturgie angélique', 221–28, In *La littérature intertestamentaire: colloque de Strasbourg (17–19 octobre 1983)*, Edited by André Caquot, Bibliothèque des Centres d'Études Supérieures Spécialisés, Paris: Presses Universitaires de France.

Philonenko-Sayar, Belkis, and Marc Philonenko, 1982. *Die Apokalypse Abrahams*, JSHRZ 5, Gütersloh: Gerd Mohn.

Poirier, John C., 1999. 'Montanist Pepuza-Jerusalem and the Dwelling Place of Wisdom', *JECS* 7: 491–507.

–, 2002. '4Q464: Not Eschatological', *RevQ* 20: 583–87.

–, 2004a. 'The Montanist Nature of the Nanas Inscription', *Epigraphica Anatolica* 37: 151–59.

–, 2004b. 'The Ouranology of the *Apocalypse of Abraham*', *JSJ* 35: 391–408.

–, 2004c. '"With Stammering Lips and Another Tongue": Isaiah 28:11 in Pre-Pauline Exegesis', paper read at the Society for Pentecostal Studies Annual Meeting, Milwaukee, Wisconsin, March 12, 2004.

–, 2007. 'The Linguistic Situation in Jewish Palestine in Late Antiquity', *Journal of Greco-Roman Christianity and Judaism* 4: 55–134.

–, 2008. 'Judaism, Christianity, and the Hebrew Bible', *JES* 43: 525–36.

Porter, Barbara Nevling, 1993. 'Sacred Trees, Date Palms, and the Royal Persona of Ashurnasirpal II', *JNES* 52: 129–39.

Potin, Jean, 1971. *La fête juive de la pentecôte: étude des textes liturgiques*, 2 vols., Lectio Divina 65a–b; Paris: Cerf.

Price, Robert M., 1997. *The Widow Traditions in Luke-Acts: A Feminist-Critical Scrutiny*, SBLDS 155, Atlanta: Scholars Press.

Puech, Émile, 1991–92. 'Une Apocalypse Messianique *(4Q521)*', *RevQ* 15: 475–522.

Pulleyn, Simon, 1997. *Prayer in Greek Religion*, Oxford: Clarendon.

Quispel, Gilles, 1975. 'Genius and Spirit', 155–69, In *Essays on the Nag Hammadi Texts in Honour of Pahor Labib*, Edited by Martin Krause, NHS 6, Leiden: E. J. Brill.

Rahnenführer, Dankwart, 1971. 'Das Testament des Hiob und das Neue Testament', *ZNW* 62: 68–93.

Rajak, Tessa, 2002. 'Synagogue and Community in the Graeco-Roman Diaspora', 22–38, In *Jews in the Hellenistic and Roman Cities*, Edited by John R. Bartlett, London: Routledge.

Rancillac, Philippe, 1970. *L'Eglise manifestation de l'esprit chez S. Jean Chrysostome, pères et écrivains de l'église d'orient*, Beirut: Dar Al-Kalima.

Raphael, Melissa, 1997. *Rudolf Otto and the Concept of Holiness*, Oxford: Clarendon.

Rebenich, S., 1993. 'Jerome: The "vir trilinguis" and the "Hebraica veritas"', *VC* 47: 50–77.

Recheis, P. Athanas, 1958. *Engel, Tod und Seelenreise: Das Wirken der Geister beim Heimgang des Menschen in der Lehre der alexandrinischen und kappadokischen Väter*, Rome: Edizioni di Storia e Letteratura.

Reeves, John C., 1996. *Heralds of that Good Realm: Syro-Mesopotamian Gnosis and Jewish Traditions*, NHMS 41, Leiden: E. J. Brill.

Regev, Eyal, 2007. *Sectarianism in Qumran: A Cross-Cultural Perspective*, Religion and Society 45, Berlin: Walter de Gruyter.

Reid, Daniel G., 1993. 'Angels, Archangels', 20–23, In *Dictionary of Paul and His Letters*, Edited by Gerald F. Hawthorne, Ralph P. Martin, Daniel G. Reid, Downers Grove, IL: InterVarsity.

Reif, Stefan C., 1993. *Judaism and Hebrew Prayer: New Perspectives on Jewish Liturgical History*, Cambridge: Cambridge University Press.

Reitzenstein, Richard, 1978. *Hellenistic Mystery-Religions: Their Basic Ideas and Significance*, Pittsburgh Theological Monographs 15, Pittsburgh: Pickwick.

Renehan, Robert, 1981. 'The Greek Anthropocentric View of Man', *HSCP* 85: 239–59.

Reventlow, Henning Graf, 1986. *Gebet im Alten Testament*, Stuttgart: W. Kohlhammer.

Reymond, Eric D., 2009. 'Imaginary Texts in Pseudepigraphal Literature: The Angelic Hymns of Job's Daughters in *The Testament of Job*', *Henoch* 31: forthcoming.

Richardson, William, 1986. 'Liturgical Order and Glossolalia in 1 Corinthians 14.26c–33a', *NTS* 32: 144–53.

Richstaetter, Karl, 1936. 'Die Glossolalie im Lichte der Mystik', *Scholastik* 11: 321–45.

Riesemann, Oskar von, 1961. 'Der russische Kirchengesang', 140–8, In *Handbuch der Musikgeschichte*, Edited by Guido Adler, 2 vols., Tutzing: Hans Schneider.

Ringgren, Helmer, 1963. *The Faith of Qumran: Theology of the Dead Sea Scrolls*, Philadelphia: Fortress.

Rist, John M., 1994. *Augustine: Ancient Thought Baptized*, Cambridge: Cambridge University Press.

Ritter, Adolf Martin, 1972. *Charisma im Verständnis des Joannes Chrysostomos und seiner Zeit: Ein Beitrag zur Erforschung der griechisch-orientalischen Ekklesiologie in der Frühzeit der Reichskirche*, Göttingen: Vandenhoeck & Ruprecht.

–, 1987. 'Die Entstehung des neutestamentlichen Kanons: Selbstdurchsetzung oder autoritative Entscheidung?', 93–99, In *Kanon und Zensur: Archäologie der literarischen Kommunikation II*, Edited by Aleida Assmann and Jan Assmann, München: Fink.

Robbins, Vernon K., 2003. 'The Legacy of 2 Corinthians 12:2–4 in the *Apocalypse of Paul*', 327–39, In *Paul and the Corinthians: Studies on a Community in Conflict. Essays in Honour of Margaret Thrall*, Edited by Trevor J. Burke and J. Keith Elliott, Leiden: Brill.

Robeck, Cecil M. Jr., 1992. *Prophecy in Carthage: Perpetua, Tertullian, and Cyprian*, Cleveland: Pilgrim.

Roberts, Louis, 1991. 'The Unutterable Symbols of Ge-Themis Reconsidered', *SBLSP* 30: 207–14.

Robinson, John A. T., 1985. *The Priority of John*, London: SCM.

Robinson, Stephen E., 2000. 'Apocalypse of Zephaniah', 39–40, In *Dictionary of New Testament Background*, Edited by Craig A. Evans and Stanley E. Porter, Downers Grove, IL: InterVarsity.

Rohrbacher-Sticker, Claudia, 1996. 'From Sense to Nonsense, From Incantation Prayer to Magical Spell', *JSQ* 3: 24–46.

Römer, Cornelia, and Heinz J. Thissen, 1989. 'P. Köln Inv. Nr. 3221: Das Testament des Hiob in koptischer Sprache. Ein Vorbericht', 33–41, In *Studies on the Testament of Job*, Edited by Michael A. Knibb and Pieter W. van der Horst, SNTSMS 66, Cambridge: Cambridge University Press.

Rompay, Lucas Van, 1996. 'The Christian Syriac Tradition of Interpretation', 612–41, In *Hebrew Bible/Old Testament: The History of Its Interpretation*, Vol. 1: *From the Beginnings to the Middle Ages (Until 1300)*, Part 1: *Antiquity*, Edited by Magne Sæbø, Göttingen: Vandenhoeck & Ruprecht.

Rosán, Laurence Jay, 1949. *The Philosophy of Proclus: The Final Phase of Ancient Thought*, New York: Cosmos.

Rosen-Ayalon, Myriam, 1989. *The Early Islamic Monuments of Al-Haram Al-Shar§f: An Iconographic Study*, Qedem 28, Jerusalem: Hebrew University.

Roukema, Riemer, 2005. 'Paul's Rapture to Paradise in Early Christian Literature', 267–83, In *The Wisdom of Egypt; Jewish, Early Christian, and Gnostic Essays in Honour of Gerard P. Luttikhuizen*, Edited by Anthony Hilhorst and George H. van Kooten, Ancient Judaism and Early Christianity 59, Leiden: E. J. Brill.

Rowland, Christopher, 1996. 'Apocalyptic, Mysticism, and the New Testament', 405–30, In *Geschichte – Tradition – Reflexion: Festschrift für Martin Hengel zum 70. Geburtstag*, Edited by Hubert Cancik, Hermann Lichtenberger, and Peter Schäfer, 3 vols., Tübingen: Mohr Siebeck.

–, 1999a. 'Apocalyptic: The Disclosure of Heavenly Knowledge', 776–97, In *The Cambridge History of Judaism*, Vol. 3: *The Early Roman Period*, (ed. by William Horbury, W. D. Davies, and John Sturdy) Cambridge: Cambridge University Press.

–, 1999b. 'The Parting of the Ways: The Evidence of Jewish and Christian Apocalyptic and Mystical Material',213–37, In *Jews and Christians: The Parting of the Ways A.D. 70 to 135*, Edited by James D. G. Dunn, Rev. ed.; Grand Rapids: Eerdmans.

Rubenstein, Jeffrey L., 1995. *The History of Sukkot in the Second Temple and Rabbinic Periods*, BJS 302, Atlanta: Scholars Press.

–, 1999. *Talmudic Stories: Narrative Art, Composition, and Culture*, Baltimore: Johns Hopkins University Press.

Rubin, Milka, 1998. 'The Language of Creation or the Primordial Language: A Case of Cultural Polemics in Antiquity', *JJS* 49: 306–33.

Rubinkiewicz, Ryszard, 1979. 'La vision de l'histoire dans l'Apocalypse d'Abraham', 137–51, In *Aufstieg und Niedergang der römischen Welt: Religion (Judentum: Allgemeines, Palästinisches Judentum)* II.19.1, Edited by Wolfgang Haase, Berlin: Walter de Gruyter, 1979.

Rubinstein, Arie, 1953. 'Hebraisms in the Slavonic "Apocalypse of Abraham"', *JJS* 4: 108–15.

–, 1954. 'Hebraisms in the "Apocalypse of Abraham"', *JJS* 5: 132–35.

Rubio, Concepción Gonzalo, 1977. *La angelología en la literatura rabínica y sefardí*, Biblioteca Nueva Sefarad 2, Barcelona: Ameller Ediciones.

Ruderman, David B., 1990. *A Valley of Vision: The Heavenly Journey of Abraham ben Hananiah Yagel*, Philadelphia: University of Pennsylvania Press.

Rudnig, Thilo Alexander, 2000. *Heilig und Profan: Redaktionskritische Studien zu Ez 40–48*, BZAW 287, Berlin: Walter de Gruyter.

Rudolph, Kurt, 1987. *Gnosis: The Nature and History of Gnosticism*, San Francisco: Harper & Row.

Ruiz, Jean-Pierre, 2006. 'Hearing and Seeing but Not Saying: A Rhetoric of Authority in Revelation 10:4 and 2 Corinthians 12:4', 91–111, In *The Reality of the Apocalypse: Rhetoric and Politics in the Book of Revelation*, Edited by David L. Barr, SBL Symposium Series 39, Leiden: E. J. Brill.

Russell, D. S., 1964. *The Method and Message of Jewish Apocalyptic: 200 BC – AD 100*, OTL, Philadelphia: Westminster.

Russell, James R., 1994. 'The *Ascensio Isaiae* and Iran', 63–69, In *Irano-Judaica III: Studies Relating to Jewish Contacts with Persian Culture throughout the Ages*, Edited by Shaul Shaked and Amnon Netzer, Jerusalem: Ben-Zvi Institute.

Russell, Paul S., 2000. 'Ephraem the Syrian on the Utility of Language and the Place of Silence', *JECS* 8: 21–37.

Ruthven, Jon, 1993. *On the Cessation of the Charismata: The Protestant Polemic on Postbiblical Miracles*, JPTSup 3, Sheffield: Sheffield Academic Press.

Saake, Helmut, 1973. 'Paulus als Ekstatiker: Pneumatologische Beobachtungen zu 2 Kor. xii 1–10', *NovT* 15: 153–60.

Sacchi, Paolo, 1990. *Jewish Apocalyptic and its History*, JSPSup 20, Sheffield: Sheffield Academic Press.

Sáenz-Badillos, Angel, 1993. *A History of the Hebrew Language*, Cambridge: Cambridge University Press.

Saffrey, H. D., 1984. 'La dévotion de Proclus au soleil', 73–86, In *Philosophie non chrétiennes et christianisme*, Edited by Jacques Sojcher and Gilbert Hottois, Annales de l'Institut de Philosophie et de Sciences morales; Bruxelles: Université de Bruxelles.

Saggs, H. W. F., 1960. 'The Branch to the Nose', *JTS* 11: 318–29.

Saldarini, Anthony J., 1986. 'Reconstructions of Rabbinic Judaism', 437–77, In *Early Judaism and Its Modern Interpreters*, Edited by Robert A. Kraft and George W. E. Nickelsburg, The Bible and Its Modern Interpreters 2, Philadelphia: Fortress.

–, 1994. *Matthew's Christian-Jewish Community*, Chicago: University of Chicago Press.

Sanders, E. P., 1966. 'Literary Dependence in Colossians', *JBL* 85: 28–45.

–, 1985. 'Taking It All for Gospel" (review essay of Brevard Childs, *The New Testament as Canon: An Introduction*), *Times Literary Supplement* (Dec. 13, 1985): 1431.

Sanders, Jack T., 1966. 'First Corinthians 13: Its Interpretation Since the First World War', *Int* 20: 159–87.

Sandnes, Karl Olav, 1991. *Paul – One of the Prophets? A Contribution to the Apostle's Self Understanding*, WUNT 2.43, Tübingen: Mohr Siebeck.

Sarna, Nahum, 1967. 'Psalm XIX and the Near Eastern Sun-god Literature', 171–75, In *Fourth World Congress of Jewish Studies: Papers*, Vol. 1, Jerusalem: World Union of Jewish Studies.

Sawyer, John F. A., 1999. *Sacred Languages and Sacred Texts*, Religion in the First Christian Centuries, London: Routledge.

Scarborough, John, 1988. 'Hermetic and Related Texts in Classical Antiquity, 19–44, In *Hermeticism and the Renaissance: Intellectual History and the Occult in Early Modern Europe*, Edited by Ingrid Merkel and Allen G. Debus, Washington: Folger Shakespeare Library.

–, 1991. 'The Pharmacology of Sacred Plants, Herbs, and Roots', 138–74, In *Magika Hiera: Ancient Greek Magic and Religion*, Edited by Christopher A. Faraone and Dirk Obbink, New York: Oxford University Press.

Schäfer, Peter, 1975. *Rivalität zwischen Engeln und Menschen: Untersuchungen zur rabbinischen Engelvorstellung*, SJ 8, Berlin: Walter de Gruyter.

Schaller, Berndt, 1979. *Das Testament Hiobs*, JSHRZ 3/3, Gütersloh: Gerd Mohn.

–, 1989. 'Zur Komposition und Konzeption des Testaments Hiobs', 46–92, In *Studies on the Testament of Job*, Edited by Michael A. Knibb and Pieter W. van der Horst, SNTSMS 66, Cambridge: Cambridge University Press.

Schenck, Kenneth L., 2001. 'A Celebration of the Enthroned Son: The Catena of Hebrews 1', *JBL* 120: 469–85.

Schenke, Hans-Martin, 2001. Review of Matthias Westerhoff, *Auferstehung und Jenseits im koptischen "Buch der Auferstehung Jesu Christi, unseres Herrn"*, In *JAC* 44: 237–43.

Schepelern, Wilhelm, 1929. *Der Montanismus und die phrygischen Kulte: Eine religionsgeschichtliche Untersuchung*, Tübingen: Mohr Siebeck.

Schiffman, Lawrence H., 1994. *Reclaiming the Dead Sea Scrolls*, Philadelphia: Jewish Publication Society.

Schimmel, Annemarie, 1988. 'Angel, Islamic', 1.248–49, In *Dictionary of the Middle Ages*, Edited by Joseph R. Strayer, 12 vols.; New York: Charles Scribner's Sons.

Schlier, Heinrich, 1958. *Der Brief an die Epheser: Ein Kommentar*, 2nd ed., Düsseldorf: Patmos-Verlag.

Schmidt, Carl, 1925. 'Der Kolophon des Ms. orient. 7594 des Britischen Museums: Eine Untersuchung zur Elias-Apokalypse', 312–21, In *Sitzungsberichte der Preußischen Akademie der Wissenschaften*, Vol. 1925, Philosophisch-Historische Klasse; Berlin: Akademie der Wissenschaften.

Schmidt, Francis, 2001. *How the Temple Thinks: Identity and Social Cohesion in Ancient Judaism*, The Biblical Seminar 78, Sheffield: Sheffield Academic Press.

Schmidt, Leigh Eric, 2005. *Restless Souls: The Making of American Spirituality*, San Francisco: HarperCollins.

Schmithals, Walter, 1971. *Gnosticism in Corinth*, Nashville: Abingdon.

Schneemelcher, Wilhelm, 1963a. 'Coptic Texts of Bartholomew', 503–8, In Edgar Hennecke, *New Testament Apocrypha*, (ed. Wilhelm Schneemelcher) vol. 1: *Gospels and Related Writings*, Philadelphia: Westminster.

–, 1963b. 'General Introduction', 19–68, In Edgar Hennecke, *New Testament Apocrypha*, (ed. Wilhelm Schneemelcher) vol. 1: *Gospels and Related Writings*, Philadelphia: Westminster.

–, 1965. 'Apocalyptic Prophecy of the Early Church', 684–89, In Edgar Hennecke, *New Testament Apocrypha*, (ed. by Wilhelm Schneemelcher) vol. 2: *Writings Relating to the Apostles; Apocalypses and Related Subjects*, Philadelphia: Westminster.

Schniedewind, William M., 1999. 'Qumran Hebrew as an Antilanguage', *JBL* 118: 235–52.

–, 2000. 'Linguistic Ideology in Qumran Hebrew', 245–55, In *Diggers at the Well: Proceedings of a Third International Symposium on the Hebrew of the Dead Sea Scrolls and Ben Sira*, Edited by Takamitsu Muraoka and John F. Elwolde, STDJ 36, Leiden: E. J. Brill.

Scholem, Gershom G., 1954. *Major Trends in Jewish Mysticism*, 3rd ed., New York: Schocken.

–, 1965. *Jewish Gnosticism, Merkabah Mysticism, and Talmudic Tradition*, 2nd ed., New York: Jewish Theological Seminary of America.

–, 1972. 'The Name of God and the Linguistic Theory of the Kabbala', *Diogenes* 79: 59–80; 80: 164–94.

–, 1974. *Kabbalah*, New York: Quadrangle.

–, 1987. *Origins of the Kabbalah*, Princeton: Princeton University Press.

Schöllgen, Georg, 1999. 'Der Niedergang des Prophetentums in der Alten Kirche', 97–116, In *Prophetie und Charisma*, Edited by Ingo Baldermann *et al*, Jahrbuch für biblische Theologie 14, Neukirchen-Vluyn: Neukirchener Verlag.

Schrenk, Gottlob, and Gottfried Quell, 1964–76. 'πατήρ, πατρῷος, πατριά, ἀπάτωρ, πατρικός', 5.945–1022, In *Theological Dictionary of the New Testament*, Edited by Gerhard Kittel and Gerhard Friedrich, 10 Vols., Grand Rapids: Eerdmans.

Schubert, Kurt, 1992. 'Jewish Pictorial Traditions in Early Christian Art', 139–260, In Heinz Schreckenberg and Kurt Schubert, *Jewish Historiography and Iconography in Early and Medieval Christianity*, CRINT 3/2, Assen: Van Gorcum.

Schürer, Emil, 1909. *Geschichte des jüdischen Volkes im Zeitalter Jesu Christi*, 4th ed., 3 vols., Leipzig: J. C. Hinrichs.

–, 1973–87. *The History of the Jewish People in the Age of Jesus Christ (175 B.C.–A.D. 135)*, (ed. by Geza Vermes and Fergus Millar) rev. ed., 3 vols., Edinburgh: T. & T. Clark.

Schwartz, Seth, 1990. *Josephus and Judean Politics*, Columbia Studies in Classical Tradition 18, Leiden: E. J. Brill.

–, 1995. 'Language, Power and Identity in Ancient Palestine', *P&P* 148: 3–47.

–, 1998a. 'Gamaliel in Aphrodite's Bath: Palestinian Judaism and Urban Culture in the Third and Fourth Centuries', 203–17, In *The Talmud Yerushalmi and Graeco-Roman Culture I*, Edited by Peter Schäfer, TSAJ 71, Tübingen: Mohr Siebeck.

–, 1998b. 'Rabbinization in the Sixth Century', 55–69, In *The Talmud Yerushalmi and Graeco-Roman Culture III*, Edited by Peter Schäfer, TSAJ 93, Tübingen: Mohr Siebeck.

–, 2001. *Imperialism and Jewish Society, 200 B.C.E. to 640 C.E.*, Jews, Christians, and Muslims from the Ancient to the Modern World, Princeton: Princeton University Press.

–, 2002. 'Historiography on the Jews in the "Talmudic Period" (70–640 CE)', 79–114, In *The Oxford Handbook of Jewish Studies*, Edited by Martin Goodman, Oxford: Oxford University Press.

Schwemer, Anna Maria, 1991. 'Gott als König und seine Königsherrschaft in den Sabbatliedern aus Qumran', 45–118, In *Königsherrschaft Gottes und himmlischer Kult im Judentum, Urchristentum und in der hellenistischen Welt*, Edited by Martin Hengel and Anna Maria Schwemer, WUNT 1.55, Tübingen: Mohr Siebeck.

Scott, Alan, 1991. *Origen and the Life of the Stars: A History of an Idea*, Oxford Early Christian Studies, Oxford: Clarendon.

Scott, James M., 1995. *Paul and the Nations: The Old Testament and Jewish Background of Paul's Mission to the Nations with Special Reference to the Destination of Galatians*, WUNT 1.84, Tübingen: Mohr Siebeck.

–, 2002. *Geography in Early Judaism and Christianity: The Book of Jubilees*, SNTSMS 113, Cambridge: Cambridge University Press.

Séd, Nicolas, 1973. 'Les traditions secrètes et les disciples de Rabban Yohanan ben Zakkaï', *RHR* 184: 49–66.

Segal, Alan F., 1986. *Rebecca's Children: Judaism and Christianity in the Roman World*, Cambridge: Harvard University Press.

Segert, Stanislav, 1988. 'Observations on Poetic Structures in the Songs of the Sabbath Sacrifice', *RevQ* 13: 215–23.

Sevenster, J. N., 1968. *Do You Know Greek?: How Much Greek Could the First Jewish Christians Have Known?*, NovTSup 19, Leiden: E. J. Brill.

Shaw, Gregory, 1995. *Theurgy and the Soul: The Neoplatonism of Iamblichus*, University Park, PA: Pennsylvania State University Press.

Sheppard, Anne, 1982. 'Proclus' Attitude to Theurgy', *Clasical Quarterly* 32: 212–24.

Sheres, Ita, and Anne Kohn Blau, 1995. *The Truth about the Virgin: Sex and Ritual in the Dead Sea Scrolls*, New York: Continuum.

Shinan, Avigdor, 1975–76. '"Language of the Temple" in the Aramaic Targums to the Torah', *Beth Mikra* 21: 472–74 (Hebrew).

–, 1977. 'The Form and Content of the Aggadah in the "Palestinian" Targumim on the Pentateuch and its Place within Rabbinic Literature', Ph.D., Hebrew University.

–, 1983. 'The Angelology of the Palestinian Targums on the Pentateuch', *Sefarad* 43: 181–98.

–, 1992. *The Embroidered Targum*, Jerusalem: Magnes.

Shogren, Gary Steven, 1999. 'How did They Suppose "the Perfect" Would Come? 1 Corinthians 13.8–12 in Patristic Exegesis', *Journal of Pentecostal Theology* 16: 99–121.

Sigountos, James G., 1994. 'The Genre of 1 Corinthians 13', *NTS* 40: 246–60.

Siker, Jeffrey S., 1991. *Disinheriting the Jews: Abraham in Early Christian Controversy*, Louisville: Westminster/John Knox.

Simon, Marcel, 1971. 'Remarques sur l'angélolâtrie juive au début de l'ère chrétienne', *CRAI* 115: 120–34.

–, 1984. 'La Bible dans les premières controverses entre juifs et chrétiens', 107–25, In *Bible de tous les temps*, Edited by Claude Mondésert, Vol. 1: *Le monde grec ancien et la Bible*, Paris: Beauchesne.

Simonetti, Manlio, 1983. 'Note sulla cristologia dell'*Ascensione di Isaia*', 185–209, In *Isaia, il diletto e la chiesa: visione ed esegesi profetica cristiano-primitiva nell'*Ascensione di Isaia*: atti del convegno di Roma, 9–10 aprile 1981*, Edited by Mauro Pesce, Testi e ricerche di Scienze religiose 20, Brescia: Paideia.

Sivertsev, Alexei M., 2005. *Households, Sects, and the Origins of Rabbinic Judaism*, JSJSup 102, Leiden: Brill.

Skrobucha, Heinz, 1966. *Sinai*, London: Oxford University Press.

Smart, Ninian, 1972. *The Concept of Worship*, London: Macmillan.

Smit, J. F. M., 1993. 'Two Puzzles: 1 Corinthians 12.31 and 13.3: A Rhetorical Solution', *NTS* 39: 246–64.

Smith, Jonathan Z., 1978. *Map is Not Territory: Studies in the History of Religions*, SJLA 23, Leiden: E. J. Brill.

Smith, Mark S., 1990. *The Early History of God: Yahweh and the Other Deities in Ancient Israel*, San Francisco: Harper & Row.

Smith, Morton, 1976. Review of James D.G. Dunn, *Jesus and the Spirit*, in *JAAR* 44: 726.

–, 1982. 'Helios in Palestine', *ErIsr* 16: 199–214.

–, 1984. 'The Case of the Gilded Staircase: Did the Dead Sea Scroll Sect Worship the Sun?', *BAR* 10/5: 50–55.

–, 1990. 'Ascent to the Heavens and Deification in 4QMᵃ', 181–99, In *Archaeology and History in the Dead Sea Scrolls: The New York University Conference in Memory of Yigael Yadin*, Edited by Lawrence H. Schiffman, JSPSup 8/ASOR Monographs 2, Sheffield: JSOT Press.

Snyder, H. Gregory, 2000. *Teachers and Texts in the Ancient World: Philosophers, Jews and Christians*, Religion in the First Christian Centuries, London: Routledge.

Sonne, Isaiah, 1950–51. 'A Hymn Against Heretics in the Newly Discovered Scrolls', *HUCA* 23: 275–313.

Soury, Guy, 1942. *La démonologie de Plutarque: essai sur les idées religieuses et les mythes d'un platonicien éclectique*, Collection d'Études Anciennes, Paris: Société d'Édition 'Les Belles Lettres'.

Sparks, H. F. D., 1970. 'Jerome as Biblical Scholar', 510–41, In *Cambridge History of the Bible*, Edited by P. R. Ackroyd and C. F. Evans, Vol. 1: *From the Beginnings to Jerome*, Cambridge: Cambridge University Press.

–, 1984. 'Preface', ix–xviii, In *The Apocryphal Old Testament*, Edited by H. F. D. Sparks, Oxford: Clarendon.

Sperber, Daniel, 1994. *Magic and Folklore in Rabbinic Literature*, Bar-Ilan Studies in Near Eastern Languages and Culture, Tel Aviv: Bar-Ilan University Press.

Speyer, W., 1967. In 'Nachträge zum Reallexicon für Antike und Christentum (RAC): Barbar', *JAC* 10: 251–59.

–, 1983. 'Gürtel', *RAC* 12: 1232–66.

Spicq, Ceslaus, 1965. *Agape in the New Testament*, Vol. 2: *Agape in the Epistles of St. Paul, the Acts of the Apostles and the Epistles of St. James, St. Peter, and St. Jude*, St. Louis: Herder.

Spinks, Bryan D., 1991. *The Sanctus in the Eucharistic Prayer*, Cambridge: Cambridge University Press.

Spinoza, Baruch, 1951. *The Chief Works of Benedict de Spinoza*, (ed. and trans. by R. H. M. Elwes) 2 Vols., New York: Dover.

Spittler, Russell P., 2000. 'Testament of Job', 1189–92, In *Dictionary of New Testament Background*, Edited by Craig A. Evans and Stanley E. Porter, Downers Grove, IL: InterVarsity.

Stähli, Hans-Peter, 1985. *Solare Elemente im Jahweglauben des Alten Testaments*, OBO 66, Freiburg: Universitätsverlag.

Standhartinger, Angela, 1995. *Das Frauenbild im Judentum der hellenistischen Zeit: Ein Beitrag anhand von 'Joseph und Aseneth'*, AGJU 26, Leiden: E. J. Brill.

–, 1999. *Studien zur Entstehungsgeschichte und Intention des Kolosserbriefs*, NovTSup 94, Leiden: E. J. Brill.

Stannard, Jerry, 1988. 'Botany', 2.344–49, In *Dictionary of the Middle Ages*, Edited by Joseph R. Strayer, 12 vols., New York: Charles Scribner's Sons.

Stendahl, Krister, 1976. *Paul among Jews and Gentiles and Other Essays*, Philadelphia: Fortress.

Stern, Sacha, 1994. *Jewish Identity in Early Rabbinic Writings*, AGJU 23, Leiden: E. J. Brill.

Stevenson, Gregory M., 1995. 'Conceptual Background to Golden Crown Imagery in the Apocalypse of John (4:4, 10; 14:14)', *JBL* 114: 257–72.

Stone, Michael E., 1990. *Fourth Ezra: A Commentary on the Book of Fourth Ezra*, Hermeneia, Minneapolis: Fortress.

–, 2003. 'A Reconsideration of Apocalyptic Visions', *HTR* 96: 167–80.

Stone, Michael E., and Esther Eshel, 1992. 'An Exposition on the Patriarchs (4Q464) and Two Other Documents (4Q464^a and 4Q464^b)', *Le Muséon* 105: 243–64.

–, 1992–93. 'The Holy Tongue in the Last Days in the Light of a Fragment from Qumran', *Tarbiz* 62: 169–77 (Hebrew).

–, 1995. '4QExposition on the Patriarchs', 215–30, In *Qumran Cave 4*, Vol. 14: *Parabiblical Texts, Part 2*, Edited by Magen Broshi *et al*, DJD 19, Oxford: Clarendon.

Strack, H. L., and G. Stemberger, 1992. *Introduction to the Talmud and Midrash*, Minneapolis: Fortress.

Strobel, August, 1980. *Das heilige Land der Montanisten: Eine religionsgeographische Untersuchung*, Religionsgeschichtliche Versuche und Vorarbeiten 37, Berlin: Walter de Gruyter.

Strothmann, Werner, 1972. *Johannes von Apamea*, Patristische Texte und Studien 11, Berlin: Walter de Gruyter.

Stroumsa, Gedaliahu (Guy) G., 1981. 'Le couple de l'ange et de l'esprit: traditions juives et chrétiennes', *RB* 88: 42–61.

–, 2003. 'Early Christianity – A Religion of the Book?', 153–73, In *Homer, the Bible, and Beyond: Literary and Religious Canons in the Ancient World*, Edited by Margalit Finkelberg and Guy G. Stroumsa, Jerusalem Studies in Religion and Culture 2, Leiden: E. J. Brill.

Strugnell, John, 1960. 'The Angelic Liturgy at Qumrân – 4Q Serek Šîrôt 'Ôlat Haššabāt', 318–45, in *Congress Volume, Oxford 1959*, Edited by G. W. Anderson, VTSup 7, Leiden: E. J. Brill.

Stuckenbruck, Loren T., 1995. *Angel Veneration and Christology*, WUNT 2.70, Tübingen: Mohr Siebeck.

–, 1999. 'Worship and Monotheism in the *Ascension of Isaiah*', 70–89, In *The Jewish Roots of Christological Monotheism: Papers from the St. Andrews Conference on the*

Historical Origins of the Worship of Jesus, Edited by Carey C. Newman, James R.
   Davila, and Gladys S. Lewis, JSJSup 63, Leiden: E. J. Brill.
–, 2004. 'The Holy Spirit in the *Ascension of Isaiah*', 308–20, In *The Holy Spirit and
   Christian Origins: Essays in Honor of James D. G. Dunn*, Edited by Graham N. Stan-
   ton, Bruce W. Longenecker, and Stephen C. Barton, Grand Rapids: Eerdmans.
Stuckrad, Kocku von, 2000. 'Jewish and Christian Astrology in Late Antiquity–A New
   Approach', *Numen* 47: 1–40.
Sullivan, Kevin P., 2004. *Wrestling with Angels: A Study of the Relationship between
   Angels and Humans in Ancient Jewish Literature and the New Testament*, AGJU 55,
   Leiden: E. J. Brill.
Swartz, Michael D., 1994. '"Like the Ministering Angels": Ritual and Purity in Early
   Jewish Mysticism and Magic', *AJS Review* 19: 135–67.
–, 1996. *Scholastic Magic: Ritual and Revelation in Early Jewish Mysticism*, Princeton:
   Princeton University Press.
Sweet, J. P. M., 1966–67. 'A Sign for Unbelievers: Paul's Attitude to Glossolalia', *NTS*
   13: 240–57.
Swiggers, Pierre, 1999. 'Babel and the Confusion of Tongues (Genesis 11:1–9)', 182–95,
   In *Mythos im Alten Testament und seiner Umwelt: Festschrift für Hans-Peter Müller
   zum 65. Geburtstag*, Edited by Armin Lange, Hermann Lichtenberger, and Diethard
   Römheld, BZAW 278, Berlin: Walter de Gruyter.
Szabó, Andor, 1980. 'Die Engelvorstellungen vom Alten Testament bis zur Gnosis',
   143–52, In *Altes Testament – Frühjudentum – Gnosis: Neue Studien zu 'Gnosis und
   Bibel'*, Edited by Karl-Wolfgang Tröger, Gütersloh: Gerd Mohn.
Tabbernee, William, 2007. *Fake Prophecy and Polluted Sacraments: Ecclesiastical and
   Imperial Reactions to Montanism*, VCSup 84, Leiden: E. J. Brill.
Taglicht, J., 1917. 'Die Dattelpalme in Palästina', 403–16, In *Festschrift Adolf Schwarz
   zum siebzigsten Geburtstage, 15. Juli 1916*, Edited by Samuel Krauss, Berlin: R.
   Löwit.
Tantlevskij, Igor R., 1997. 'Elements of Mysticism in the Dead Sea Scrolls (Thanksgiv-
   ing Hymns, War Scroll, Text of Two Columns) and their Parallels and Possible
   Sources', *Qumran Chronicle* 7: 193–213.
Taylor, G., 1993. *YHWH and the Sun: Biblical and Archaeological Evidence for Sun
   Worship in Ancient Israel*, JSOTSup 118, Sheffield: JSOT Press.
Taylor, Joan E., 1990. 'The Phenomenon of Early Jewish-Christianity: Reality or Scho-
   larly Invention?', *VC* 44: 313–34.
–, 1997. *The Immerser: John the Baptist within Second Temple Judaism*, Studying the
   Historical Jesus; Grand Rapids: Eerdmans.
Teicher, J. L., 1951. 'The Dead Sea Scrolls – Documents of the Jewish-Christian Sect of
   Ebionites', *JJS* 2: 67–99.
–, 1953. 'The Teaching of the Pre-Pauline Church in the Dead Sea Scrolls, III', *JJS* 4: 1–
   13.
Theissen, Gerd, 1983. *Psychological Aspects of Pauline Theology*, Philadelphia: Fortress.
Thiselton, A. C., 1979. 'The "Interpretation" of Tongues: A New Suggestion in the Light
   of Greek Usage in Philo and Josephus', *JTS* 30: 15–36.
Thomson, Francis J., 1992. 'SS. Cyril and Methodius and a Mythical Western Heresy:
   Trilinguism: A Contribution to the Study of Patristic and Mediaeval Theories of
   Sacred Languages', *Analecta Bollandiana* 110: 67–122.
Tibbs, Clint, 2007. *Religious Experience of the Pneuma: Communication with the Spirit
   World in 1 Corinthians 12 and 14*, WUNT 2.230; Tübingen: Mohr Siebeck.

Tiede, David Lenz, 1972. *The Charismatic Figure as Miracle Worker*, SBLDS 1, Missoula, MT: Scholars Press.

–, 1980. *Prophecy and History in Luke-Acts*, Philadelphia: Fortress.

Tigchelaar, Eibert J. C., 1996. *Prophets of Old and the Day of the End: Zechariah, the Book of Watchers and Apocalyptic*, OTS 35, Leiden: E. J. Brill.

Tiller, Patrick A., 1997. 'The "Eternal Planting" in the Dead Sea Scrolls', *DSD* 4: 312–35.

Titus, Eric L., 1959. 'Did Paul Write I Corinthians 13?', *JBR* 27: 299–302.

Tomes, Roger, 2007. 'Sing to the Lord a New Song', 237–52, In *Psalms and Prayers: Papers Read at the Joint Meeting of the Society of Old Testament Study and Het Oudtestamentisch Werkgezelschap in Nederland in België, Apeldoorn August 2006*, Edited by Bob Becking and Eric Peels, Oudtestamentische Studien 55, Leiden: E. J. Brill.

Tomson, Peter J., 1990. *Paul and the Jewish Law: Halakha in the Letters of the Apostle to the Gentiles*, CRINT 3/1, Assen: Van Gorcum.

–, 1999. 'Jewish Food Laws in Early Christian Community Discourse', *Semeia* 86: 193–211.

Torjeson, Karen Jo, 1998. 'The Early Christian *Orans*: An Artistic Representation of Women's Liturgical Prayer and Prophecy', 42–56, In *Women Preachers and Prophets through Two Millennia of Christianity*, Edited by Beverly Mayne Kienzle and Pamela J. Walker, Berkeley: University of California Press.

Tov, Emanuel, 2000. 'A Qumran Origin for the Masada Non-Biblical Texts?', *DSD* 7: 57–73.

Trachtenberg, Joshua, 1939. *Jewish Magic and Superstition: A Study in Folk Religion*, New York: Behrman.

Trevett, Christine, 1996. *Montanism: Gender, Authority and the New Prophecy*, Cambridge: Cambridge University Press.

–, 1999. '"Angelic Visitations and Speech She Had": Nanas of Kotiaeion', 259–77, In *Prayer and Spirituality in the Early Church*, Edited by Pauline Allen, Wendy Mayer, and Lawrence Cross, Vol. 2, Brisbane: Centre for Early Christian Studies.

Trigg, Joseph W., 1991. 'The Angel of the Great Counsel: Christ and the Angelic Hierarchy in Origen's Theology', *JTS* 42: 35–51.

Trocmé, Étienne, 1997. 'Le prophétisme chez les premiers chrétiens', 259–70, In *Oracles et prophéties dans l'antiquité: actes du colloque de Strasbourg 15–17 juin 1995*, Edited by Jean-Georges Heintz, Travaux du Centre de Recherche sur le Proche-Orient et la Grèce Antiques 15, Paris: de Boccard.

Tugwell, Simon, 1973. 'The Gift of Tongues in the New Testament', *ExpTim* 84: 137–40.

Turdeanu, Émile, 1981. *Apocryphes slaves et roumains de l'Ancien Testament*, SVTP 5, Leiden: E. J. Brill.

Turner, Max, 1998a. *The Holy Spirit and Spiritual Gifts in the New Testament Church and Today*, Rev. ed., Peabody: Hendrickson.

–, 1998b. 'Tongues: An Experience for All in the Pauline Churches?', *Asian Journal of Pentecostal Studies* 1: 231–53.

Twelftree, Graham H., 2007. *In the Name of Jesus: Exorcism among Early Christians*, Grand Rapids: Baker Academic.

Tyloch, Witold, 1988. 'Quelques remarques sur la provenance essénienne du livre des Jubilés', *RevQ* 13: 347–52.

Ulfgard, Håkan, 1998. *The Story of Sukkot: The Setting, Shaping, and Sequel of the Biblical Feast of Tabernacles*, BGBE 34, Tübingen: Mohr Siebeck.

Van den Broek, Roelof, 1972. *The Myth of the Phoenix: According to Classical and Early Christian Traditions*, EPRO 24, Leiden: E. J. Brill.

Van der Burg, Nicolaas Marius Henricus, 1939. *ΑΠΟΡΡΗΤΑ – ΔΡΩΜΕΝΑ – ΟΡΓΙΑ: Bijdrage tot de Kennis der religieuze Terminologie in het Grieksch*, Amsterdam: H. J. Paris.

Van der Horst, Pieter W., 1989. 'Images of Women in the Testament of Job', 93–116, In *Studies on the Testament of Job*, Edited by Michael A. Knibb and Pieter W. van der Horst, SNTSMS 66, Cambridge: Cambridge University Press.

Van der Woude, Adam S., 1982. 'Fragmente einer Rolle der Lieder für das Sabbatopfer aus Höhle XI von Qumran (11QŠirŠabb)', 311–37, In *Von Kanaan bis Kerala*, Edited by W. C. Delsman *et al*, AOAT 211, Neukirchen-Vluyn: Neukirchener.

–, 1998–9. 'Fifty Years of Qumran Research', 1–45, In *The Dead Sea Scrolls After Fifty Years: A Comprehensive Assessment*, Edited by Peter W. Flint and James C. Vander-Kam, 2 vols., Leiden: E. J. Brill.

Van Henten, Jan Willem, 1995. 'Archangel', Cols. 150–53, In *Dictionary of Deities and Demons in the Bible*, Edited by Karel van der Toorn, Bob Becking, and Pieter W. van der Horst, Leiden: E. J. Brill.

Van Loon, Gertrud J. M., 1999. *The Gate of Heaven: Wall Paintings with Old Testament Scenes in the Altar Room and the Ḫūrus of Coptic Churches*, 158–63, Uitgaven van het Nederlands Historisch-Archaeologisch Instituut te Instanbul 85, Istanbul: Nederlands Historisch-Archaeologisch Instituut.

VanderKam, James C., 1977. *Textual and Historical Studies in the Book of Jubilees*, HSM 14, Missoula, MT: Scholars Press.

–, 1989. *The Book of Jubilees*, CSCO 511, Leuven: Peeters.

–, 1992. 'The Jubilees Fragments from Qumran Cave 4', 2.635–48, In *The Madrid Qumran Congress: Proceedings of the International Congress on the Dead Sea Scrolls, Madrid 18–21 March, 1991*, Edited by J. Trebolle Barrera and L. Vegas Montaner, 2 vols., STDJ 11, Leiden: E. J. Brill.

–, 2004. *From Joshua to Caiaphas: High Priests after the Exile*, Minneapolis: Fortress.

Vermes, Geza, 1983. *Scripture and Tradition in Judaism: Haggadic Studies*, 2nd ed., StPB 4, Leiden: E. J. Brill.

Visotzky, Burton L., 1983. 'Rabbinic *Randglossen* to the Cologne Mani Codex', *ZPE* 52: 295–300.

–, 1994. 'The Conversation of Palm Trees', 205–14, In *Tracing the Threads: Studies in the Vitality of Jewish Pseudepigrapha*, Edited by John C. Reeves, SBLEJL 6, Atlanta: Scholars Press.

–, 2003. *Golden Bells and Pomegranates: Studies in Midrash Leviticus Rabbah*, TSAJ 94, Tübingen: Mohr Siebeck.

Vollenweider, Samuel, 1996. 'Der Geist Gottes als Selbst der Glaubenden: Überlegungen zu einem ontologischen Problem in der paulinischen Anthropologie', *ZTK* 93: 163–92.

Volz, Paul, 1934. *Die Eschatologie der jüdischen Gemeinde im neutestamentlichen Zeitalter nach den Quellen der rabbinischen, apokalyptischen und apokryphen Literatur*, 2nd ed., Tübingen: Mohr Siebeck.

Wacholder, Ben Zion, 1997. 'Jubilees as the Super Canon: Torah-Admonition versus Torah-Commandment', 195–211, In *Legal Texts and Legal Issues: Proceedings of the Second Meeting of the International Organization for Qumran Studies, Cambridge 1995, Published in Honour of Joseph M. Baumgarten*, Edited by Moshe Bernstein, Florentino García Martínez, and John Kampen, STDJ 23; Leiden: E. J. Brill.

Watson, Francis, 1997. *Text and Truth: Redefining Biblical Theology*, Grand Rapids: Eerdmans.

–, 2004. *Paul and the Hermeneutics of Faith*, London: T & T Clark International.

Weinfeld, Moshe, 1995. 'The Angelic Song Over the Luminaries in the Qumran Texts', 131–57, In *Time to Prepare the Way in the Wilderness: Papers on the Qumran Scrolls by Fellows of the Institute for Advanced Studies of the Hebrew University, Jerusalem, 1989–1990*, Edited by Devorah Dimant and Lawrence H. Schiffman, STDJ 16, Leiden: E. J. Brill.

Weitzman, Steven, 1999. 'Why Did the Qumran Community Write in Hebrew?', *JAOS* 119: 35–45.

Werner, Eric, 1945–46. 'The Doxology in Synagogue and Church: A Liturgico-Musical Study', *HUCA* 19: 275–351.

–, 1959. *The Sacred Bridge: The Interdependence of Liturgy and Music in Synagogue and Church during the First Millennium*, London: Dennis Dobson.

–, 1966. 'The Genesis of the Liturgical Sanctus', 19–32, in *Essays Presented to Egon Wellesz*, Edited by Jack Westrup, Oxford: Clarendon.

Westcott, B. F., and F. J. A. Hort, 1882. *Introduction to the New Testament in the Original Greek*, New York: Harper.

Westermann, Claus, 1982. *Elements of Old Testament Theology*, Atlanta: John Knox.

Wick, Peter, 1998. 'There was Silence in Heaven (Revelation 8:1): An Annotation to Israel Knohl's "Between Voice and Silence"', *JBL* 117: 512–14.

Widdicombe, Peter, 2000. *The Fatherhood of God from Origen to Athanasius*, Rev. ed., Oxford Theological Monographs, Oxford: Clarendon.

Wilcox, Max, 1991. '"Silence in Heaven" (Rev 8:1) and Early Jewish Thought', 241–44, In *Mogilany 1989: Papers on the Dead Sea Scrolls Offered in Memory of Jean Carmignac*, Edited by Zdzislaw J. Kapera, Vol. 2, Kraków: Enigma.

Williams, Michael A., 1996. *Rethinking 'Gnosticism': An Argument for Dismantling a Dubious Category*, Princeton: Princeton University Press.

Wills, Lawrence M., 1995. *The Jewish Novel in the Ancient World*, Ithaca: Cornell University Press.

Wingren, Gustaf, 1989. *Creation and Gospel: The New Situation in European Theology*, Toronto Studies in Theology 2, Lewiston, NY: Edwin Mellen.

Wink, Walter, 1984. *Naming the Powers: The Language of Power in the New Testament*, Philadelphia: Fortress.

Winston, David, 1991. 'Aspects of Philo's Linguistic Theory', 109–25, In *Heirs of the Septuagint: Philo, Hellenistic Judaism and Early Christianity: Festschrift for Earle Hilgert* (= *Studia Philonica Annual* 3), Edited by David T. Runia, Atlanta: Scholars Press.

Wiora, Walter, 1962. 'Jubilare sine verbis', 39–65, In *In memoriam Jacques Handschin*, Edited by H. Anglès *et al*, Argentorati: P. H. Heitz.

Wischmeyer, Oda, 1981. *Der höchste Weg: Das 13. Kapitel des 1. Korintherbriefes*, Studien zum Neuen Testament 13, Gütersloh: Gerd Mohn.

Wolfson, Harry, 1979. *Repercussions of the Kalam in Jewish Philosophy*, Cambridge: Harvard University Press.

Wyatt, N., 2007. 'Word of Tree and Whisper of Stone: El's Oracle to King Keret (Kirta), and the Problem of the Mechanics of Its Utterance', *VT* 57: 483–510.

Yadin, Yigael, 1971. *Bar-Kokhba: The Rediscovery of the Legendary Hero of the Last Jewish Revolt against Imperial Rome*, London: Weidenfeld and Nicolson.

Yahalom, Joseph, 1987. '*Piyyût* as Poetry', 111–26, In *The Synagogue in Late Antiquity*, Edited by Lee I. Levine, New York: Jewish Theological Seminary of America.

–, 1996. 'Angels Do Not Understand Aramaic: On the Literary Use of Jewish Palestinian Aramaic in Late Antiquity', *JJS* 47: 33–44.

Yassif, Eli, 2006. 'Jewish Folk Literature in Late Antiquity', 721–48, In *The Cambridge History of Judaism*, Vol. 4: *The Late Roman-Rabbinic Period*, (ed. by Steven T. Katz) Cambridge: Cambridge University Press.

Zaharopoulos, Dimitri Z., 1989. *Theodore of Mopsuestia on the Bible: A Study of his Old Testament Exegesis*, New York: Paulist.

Zimmermann, Johannes, 1998. *Messianische Texte aus Qumran: Königliche, priesterliche und prophetische Messiasvorstellungen in den Schriftfunden von Qumran*, WUNT 2.104, Tübingen: Mohr Siebeck.

Index of Ancient Sources

A. Hebrew Scriptures and Septuagint

B. New Testament

C. Josephus

D. Philo

E. Apocryphal and Pseudepigraphic Sources

F. Dead Sea Scrolls

G. Rabbinic Sources

H. Magical Texts and Hekhalot

I. Patristic Sources

J. Greco-Roman Sources

K. Other

Index of Modern Authors

Index of Subjects

Wissenschaftliche Untersuchungen zum Neuen Testament
Alphabetical Index of the First and Second Series

Bennema, Cornelis: The Power of Saving Wisdom. 2002. *Vol. II/148.*

Bergman, Jan: see *Kieffer, René*

Bergmeier, Roland: Das Gesetz im Römerbrief und andere Studien zum Neuen Testament. 2000. *Vol. 121.*

Bernett, Monika: Der Kaiserkult in Judäa unter den Herodiern und Römern. 2007. *Vol. 203.*

Betz, Otto: Jesus, der Messias Israels. 1987. *Vol. 42.*

– Jesus, der Herr der Kirche. 1990. *Vol. 52.*

Beyschlag, Karlmann: Simon Magus und die christliche Gnosis. 1974. *Vol. 16.*

Bieringer, Reimund: see *Koester, Craig.*

Bittner, Wolfgang J.: Jesu Zeichen im Johannesevangelium. 1987. *Vol. II/26.*

Bjerkelund, Carl J.: Tauta Egeneto. 1987. *Vol. 40.*

Blackburn, Barry Lee: Theios Aner and the Markan Miracle Traditions. 1991. *Vol. II/40.*

Blanton, Thomas R.: Constructing a New Covenant. 2007. *Vol. II/233.*

Bock, Darrell L.: Blasphemy and Exaltation in Judaism and the Final Examination of Jesus. 1998. *Vol. II/106.*

– and *Robert L. Webb* (Ed.): Key Events in the Life of the Historical Jesus. 2009. *Vol. 247.*

Bockmuehl, Markus N.A.: Revelation and Mystery in Ancient Judaism and Pauline Christianity. 1990. *Vol. II/36.*

Bøe, Sverre: Cross-Bearing in Luke. 2010. *Vol. II/278.*

– Gog and Magog. 2001. *Vol. II/135.*

Böhlig, Alexander: Gnosis und Synkretismus. Vol. 1 1989. *Vol. 47.* – Vol. 2 1989. *Vol. 48.*

Böhm, Martina: Samarien und die Samaritai bei Lukas. 1999. *Vol. II/111.*

Börstinghaus, Jens: Sturmfahrt und Schiffbruch. 2010. *Vol. II/274.*

Böttrich, Christfried: Weltweisheit – Menschheitsethik – Urkult. 1992. *Vol. II/50.*

– and *Herzer, Jens* (Ed.): Josephus und das Neue Testament. 2007. *Vol. 209.*

Bolyki, János: Jesu Tischgemeinschaften. 1997. *Vol. II/96.*

Bosman, Philip: Conscience in Philo and Paul. 2003. *Vol. II/166.*

Bovon, François: New Testament and Christian Apocrypha. 2009. *Vol. 237.*

– Studies in Early Christianity. 2003. *Vol. 161.*

Brändl, Martin: Der Agon bei Paulus. 2006. *Vol. II/222.*

Braun, Heike: Geschichte des Gottesvolkes und christliche Identität. 2010. *Vol. II/279.*

Breytenbach, Cilliers: see *Frey, Jörg.*

Brocke, Christoph vom: Thessaloniki – Stadt des Kassander und Gemeinde des Paulus. 2001. *Vol. II/125.*

Brunson, Andrew: Psalm 118 in the Gospel of John. 2003. *Vol. II/158.*

Büchli, Jörg: Der Poimandres – ein paganisiertes Evangelium. 1987. *Vol. II/27.*

Bühner, Jan A.: Der Gesandte und sein Weg im 4. Evangelium. 1977. *Vol. II/2.*

Burchard, Christoph: Untersuchungen zu Joseph und Aseneth. 1965. *Vol. 8.*

– Studien zur Theologie, Sprache und Umwelt des Neuen Testaments. Ed. by D. Sänger. 1998. *Vol. 107.*

Burnett, Richard: Karl Barth's Theological Exegesis. 2001. *Vol. II/145.*

Byron, John: Slavery Metaphors in Early Judaism and Pauline Christianity. 2003. *Vol. II/162.*

Byrskog, Samuel: Story as History – History as Story. 2000. *Vol. 123.*

Cancik, Hubert (Ed.): Markus-Philologie. 1984. *Vol. 33.*

Capes, David B.: Old Testament Yaweh Texts in Paul's Christology. 1992. *Vol. II/47.*

Caragounis, Chrys C.: The Development of Greek and the New Testament. 2004. *Vol. 167.*

– The Son of Man. 1986. *Vol. 38.*

– see *Fridrichsen, Anton.*

Carleton Paget, James: The Epistle of Barnabas. 1994. *Vol. II/64.*

– Jews, Christians and Jewish Christians in Antiquity. 2010. *Vol. 251.*

Carson, D.A., O'Brien, Peter T. and Mark Seifrid (Ed.): Justification and Variegated Nomism.
Vol. 1: The Complexities of Second Temple Judaism. 2001. *Vol. II/140.*
Vol. 2: The Paradoxes of Paul. 2004. *Vol. II/181.*

Chae, Young Sam: Jesus as the Eschatological Davidic Shepherd. 2006. *Vol. II/216.*

Chapman, David W.: Ancient Jewish and Christian Perceptions of Crucifixion. 2008. *Vol. II/244.*

Chester, Andrew: Messiah and Exaltation. 2007. *Vol. 207.*

Chibici-Revneanu, Nicole: Die Herrlichkeit des Verherrlichten. 2007. *Vol. II/231.*

Ciampa, Roy E.: The Presence and Function of Scripture in Galatians 1 and 2. 1998. *Vol. II/102.*

Classen, Carl Joachim: Rhetorical Criticsm of the New Testament. 2000. *Vol. 128.*

Colpe, Carsten: Griechen – Byzantiner – Semiten – Muslime. 2008. *Vol. 221.*

– Iranier – Aramäer – Hebräer – Hellenen. 2003. *Vol. 154.*

Coppins, Wayne: The Interpretation of Freedom in the Letters of Paul. 2009. *Vol. II/261.*

Crump, David: Jesus the Intercessor. 1992. *Vol. II/49.*

Dahl, Nils Alstrup: Studies in Ephesians. 2000. *Vol. 131.*

Daise, Michael A.: Feasts in John. 2007. *Vol. II/229.*

Deines, Roland: Die Gerechtigkeit der Tora im Reich des Messias. 2004. *Vol. 177.*

– Jüdische Steingefäße und pharisäische Frömmigkeit. 1993. *Vol. II/52.*

– Die Pharisäer. 1997. *Vol. 101.*

Deines, Roland and *Karl-Wilhelm Niebuhr* (Ed.): Philo und das Neue Testament. 2004. *Vol. 172.*

Dennis, John A.: Jesus' Death and the Gathering of True Israel. 2006. *Vol. 217.*

Dettwiler, Andreas and *Jean Zumstein* (Ed.): Kreuzestheologie im Neuen Testament. 2002. *Vol. 151.*

Dickson, John P.: Mission-Commitment in Ancient Judaism and in the Pauline Communities. 2003. *Vol. II/159.*

Dietzfelbinger, Christian: Der Abschied des Kommenden. 1997. *Vol. 95.*

Dimitrov, Ivan Z., James D.G. Dunn, Ulrich Luz and *Karl-Wilhelm Niebuhr* (Ed.): Das Alte Testament als christliche Bibel in orthodoxer und westlicher Sicht. 2004. *Vol. 174.*

Dobbeler, Axel von: Glaube als Teilhabe. 1987. *Vol. II/22.*

Docherty, Susan E.: The Use of the Old Testament in Hebrews. 2009. *Vol. II/260.*

Downs, David J.: The Offering of the Gentiles. 2008. *Vol. II/248.*

Dryden, J. de Waal: Theology and Ethics in 1 Peter. 2006. *Vol. II/209.*

Dübbers, Michael: Christologie und Existenz im Kolosserbrief. 2005. *Vol. II/191.*

Dunn, James D.G.: The New Perspective on Paul. 2005. *Vol. 185.*

Dunn , James D.G. (Ed.): Jews and Christians. 1992. *Vol. 66.*

– Paul and the Mosaic Law. 1996. *Vol. 89.*

– see *Dimitrov, Ivan Z.*

–, *Hans Klein, Ulrich Luz,* and *Vasile Mihoc* (Ed.): Auslegung der Bibel in orthodoxer und westlicher Perspektive. 2000. *Vol. 130.*

Ebel, Eva: Die Attraktivität früher christlicher Gemeinden. 2004. *Vol. II/178.*

Ebertz, Michael N.: Das Charisma des Gekreuzigten. 1987. *Vol. 45.*

Eckstein, Hans-Joachim: Der Begriff Syneidesis bei Paulus. 1983. *Vol. II/10.*

– Verheißung und Gesetz. 1996. *Vol. 86.*

Ego, Beate: Im Himmel wie auf Erden. 1989. *Vol. II/34.*

Ego, Beate, Armin Lange and *Peter Pilhofer* (Ed.): Gemeinde ohne Tempel – Community without Temple. 1999. *Vol. 118.*

– and *Helmut Merkel* (Ed.): Religiöses Lernen in der biblischen, frühjüdischen und frühchristlichen Überlieferung. 2005. *Vol. 180.*

Eisen, Ute E.: see *Paulsen, Henning.*

Elledge, C.D.: Life after Death in Early Judaism. 2006. *Vol. II/208.*

Ellis, E. Earle: Prophecy and Hermeneutic in Early Christianity. 1978. *Vol. 18.*

– The Old Testament in Early Christianity. 1991. *Vol. 54.*

Elmer, Ian J.: Paul, Jerusalem and the Judaisers. 2009. *Vol. II/258.*

Endo, Masanobu: Creation and Christology. 2002. *Vol. 149.*

Ennulat, Andreas: Die 'Minor Agreements'. 1994. *Vol. II/62.*

Ensor, Peter W.: Jesus and His 'Works'. 1996. *Vol. II/85.*

Eskola, Timo: Messiah and the Throne. 2001. *Vol. II/142.*

– Theodicy and Predestination in Pauline Soteriology. 1998. *Vol. II/100.*

Fatehi, Mehrdad: The Spirit's Relation to the Risen Lord in Paul. 2000. *Vol. II/128.*

Feldmeier, Reinhard: Die Krisis des Gottessohnes. 1987. *Vol. II/21.*

– Die Christen als Fremde. 1992. *Vol. 64.*

Feldmeier, Reinhard and *Ulrich Heckel* (Ed.): Die Heiden. 1994. *Vol. 70.*

Finnern, Sönke: Narratologie und biblische Exegese. 2010. *Vol. II/285.*

Fletcher-Louis, Crispin H.T.: Luke-Acts: Angels, Christology and Soteriology. 1997. *Vol. II/94.*

Förster, Niclas: Marcus Magus. 1999. *Vol. 114.*

Forbes, Christopher Brian: Prophecy and Inspired Speech in Early Christianity and its Hellenistic Environment. 1995. *Vol. II/75.*

Fornberg, Tord: see *Fridrichsen, Anton.*

Fossum, Jarl E.: The Name of God and the Angel of the Lord. 1985. *Vol. 36.*

Foster, Paul: Community, Law and Mission in Matthew's Gospel. *Vol. II/177.*

Fotopoulos, John: Food Offered to Idols in Roman Corinth. 2003. *Vol. II/151.*

Frank, Nicole: Der Kolosserbrief im Kontext des paulinischen Erbes. 2009. *Vol. II/271.*

Frenschkowski, Marco: Offenbarung und Epiphanie. Vol. 1 1995. *Vol. II/79* – Vol. 2 1997. *Vol. II/80.*

Frey, Jörg: Eugen Drewermann und die biblische Exegese. 1995. *Vol. II/71.*
– Die johanneische Eschatologie. Vol. I. 1997. *Vol. 96.* – Vol. II. 1998. *Vol. 110.* – Vol. III. 2000. *Vol. 117.*
Frey, Jörg and *Cilliers Breytenbach* (Ed.): Aufgabe und Durchführung einer Theologie des Neuen Testaments. 2007. *Vol. 205.*
– *Jens Herzer, Martina Janßen* and *Clare K. Rothschild* (Ed.): Pseudepigraphie und Verfasserfiktion in frühchristlichen Briefen. 2009. *Vol. 246.*
– *Stefan Krauter* and *Hermann Lichtenberger* (Ed.): Heil und Geschichte. 2009. *Vol. 248.*
– and *Udo Schnelle (Ed.):* Kontexte des Johannesevangeliums. 2004. *Vol. 175.*
– and *Jens Schröter* (Ed.): Deutungen des Todes Jesu im Neuen Testament. 2005. *Vol. 181.*
– Jesus in apokryphen Evangelienüberlieferungen. 2010. *Vol. 254.*
–, *Jan G. van der Watt,* and *Ruben Zimmermann* (Ed.): Imagery in the Gospel of John. 2006. *Vol. 200.*
Freyne, Sean: Galilee and Gospel. 2000. *Vol. 125.*
Fridrichsen, Anton: Exegetical Writings. Edited by C.C. Caragounis and T. Fornberg. 1994. *Vol. 76.*
Gadenz, Pablo T.: Called from the Jews and from the Gentiles. 2009. *Vol. II/267.*
Gäbel, Georg: Die Kulttheologie des Hebräerbriefes. 2006. *Vol. II/212.*
Gäckle, Volker: Die Starken und die Schwachen in Korinth und in Rom. 2005. *Vol. 200.*
Garlington, Don B.: 'The Obedience of Faith'. 1991. *Vol. II/38.*
– Faith, Obedience, and Perseverance. 1994. *Vol. 79.*
Garnet, Paul: Salvation and Atonement in the Qumran Scrolls. 1977. *Vol. II/3.*
Gemünden, Petra von (Ed.): see *Weissenrieder, Annette.*
Gese, Michael: Das Vermächtnis des Apostels. 1997. *Vol. II/99.*
Gheorghita, Radu: The Role of the Septuagint in Hebrews. 2003. *Vol. II/160.*
Gordley, Matthew E.: The Colossian Hymn in Context. 2007. *Vol. II/228.*
Gräbe, Petrus J.: The Power of God in Paul's Letters. 2000, ²2008. *Vol. II/123.*
Gräßer, Erich: Der Alte Bund im Neuen. 1985. *Vol. 35.*
– Forschungen zur Apostelgeschichte. 2001. *Vol. 137.*
Grappe, Christian (Ed.): Le Repas de Dieu / Das Mahl Gottes. 2004. *Vol. 169.*

Gray, Timothy C.: The Temple in the Gospel of Mark. 2008. *Vol. II/242.*
Green, Joel B.: The Death of Jesus. 1988. *Vol. II/33.*
Gregg, Brian Han: The Historical Jesus and the Final Judgment Sayings in Q. 2005. *Vol. II/207.*
Gregory, Andrew: The Reception of Luke and Acts in the Period before Irenaeus. 2003. *Vol. II/169.*
Grindheim, Sigurd: The Crux of Election. 2005. *Vol. II/202.*
Gundry, Robert H.: The Old is Better. 2005. *Vol. 178.*
Gundry Volf, Judith M.: Paul and Perseverance. 1990. *Vol. II/37.*
Häußer, Detlef: Christusbekenntnis und Jesusüberlieferung bei Paulus. 2006. *Vol. 210.*
Hafemann, Scott J.: Suffering and the Spirit. 1986. *Vol. II/19.*
– Paul, Moses, and the History of Israel. 1995. *Vol. 81.*
Hahn, Ferdinand: Studien zum Neuen Testament.
Vol. I: Grundsatzfragen, Jesusforschung, Evangelien. 2006. *Vol. 191.*
Vol. II: Bekenntnisbildung und Theologie in urchristlicher Zeit. 2006. *Vol. 192.*
Hahn, Johannes (Ed.): Zerstörungen des Jerusalemer Tempels. 2002. *Vol. 147.*
Hamid-Khani, Saeed: Relevation and Concealment of Christ. 2000. *Vol. II/120.*
Hannah, Darrel D.: Michael and Christ. 1999. *Vol. II/109.*
Hardin, Justin K.: Galatians and the Imperial Cult? 2007. *Vol. II/237.*
Harrison; James R.: Paul's Language of Grace in Its Graeco-Roman Context. 2003. *Vol. II/172.*
Hartman, Lars: Text-Centered New Testament Studies. Ed. von D. Hellholm. 1997. *Vol. 102.*
Hartog, Paul: Polycarp and the New Testament. 2001. *Vol. II/134.*
Hays, Christopher M.: Luke's Wealth Ethics. 2010. *Vol. 275.*
Heckel, Theo K.: Der Innere Mensch. 1993. *Vol. II/53.*
– Vom Evangelium des Markus zum viergestaltigen Evangelium. 1999. *Vol. 120.*
Heckel, Ulrich: Kraft in Schwachheit. 1993. *Vol. II/56.*
– Der Segen im Neuen Testament. 2002. *Vol. 150.*
– see *Feldmeier, Reinhard.*
– see *Hengel, Martin.*

Heemstra, Marius: The Fiscus Judaicus and the Parting of the Ways. 2010. *Vol. II/277.*

Heiligenthal, Roman: Werke als Zeichen. 1983. *Vol. II/9.*

Heininger, Bernhard: Die Inkulturation des Christentums. 2010. *Vol. 255.*

Heliso, Desta: Pistis and the Righteous One. 2007. *Vol. II/235.*

Hellholm, D.: see *Hartman, Lars.*

Hemer, Colin J.: The Book of Acts in the Setting of Hellenistic History. 1989. *Vol. 49.*

Hengel, Martin: Jesus und die Evangelien. Kleine Schriften V. 2007. *Vol. 211.*

– Die johanneische Frage. 1993. *Vol. 67.*

– Judaica et Hellenistica. Kleine Schriften I. 1996. *Vol. 90.*

– Judaica, Hellenistica et Christiana. Kleine Schriften II. 1999. *Vol. 109.*

– Judentum und Hellenismus. 1969, ³1988. *Vol. 10.*

– Paulus und Jakobus. Kleine Schriften III. 2002. *Vol. 141.*

– Studien zur Christologie. Kleine Schriften IV. 2006. *Vol. 201.*

– Studien zum Urchristentum. Kleine Schriften VI. 2008. *Vol. 234.*

– Theologische, historische und biographische Skizzen. Kleine Schriften VII. 2010. *Vol. 253.*

– and *Anna Maria Schwemer:* Paulus zwischen Damaskus und Antiochien. 1998. *Vol. 108.*

– Der messianische Anspruch Jesu und die Anfänge der Christologie. 2001. *Vol. 138.*

– Die vier Evangelien und das eine Evangelium von Jesus Christus. 2008. *Vol. 224.*

Hengel, Martin and *Ulrich Heckel* (Ed.): Paulus und das antike Judentum. 1991. *Vol. 58.*

– and *Hermut Löhr* (Ed.): Schriftauslegung im antiken Judentum und im Urchristentum. 1994. *Vol. 73.*

– and *Anna Maria Schwemer* (Ed.): Königsherrschaft Gottes und himmlischer Kult. 1991. *Vol. 55.*

– Die Septuaginta. 1994. *Vol. 72.*

–, *Siegfried Mittmann* and *Anna Maria Schwemer* (Ed.): La Cité de Dieu / Die Stadt Gottes. 2000. *Vol. 129.*

Hentschel, Anni: Diakonia im Neuen Testament. 2007. *Vol. 226.*

Hernández Jr., Juan: Scribal Habits and Theological Influence in the Apocalypse. 2006. *Vol. II/218.*

Herrenbrück, Fritz: Jesus und die Zöllner. 1990. *Vol. II/41.*

Herzer, Jens: Paulus oder Petrus? 1998. *Vol. 103.*

– see *Böttrich, Christfried.*

– see *Frey, Jörg.*

Hill, Charles E.: From the Lost Teaching of Polycarp. 2005. *Vol. 186.*

Hoegen-Rohls, Christina: Der nachösterliche Johannes. 1996. *Vol. II/84.*

Hoffmann, Matthias Reinhard: The Destroyer and the Lamb. 2005. *Vol. II/203.*

Hofius, Otfried: Katapausis. 1970. *Vol. 11.*

– Der Vorhang vor dem Thron Gottes. 1972. *Vol. 14.*

– Der Christushymnus Philipper 2,6–11. 1976, ²1991. *Vol. 17.*

– Paulusstudien. 1989, ²1994. *Vol. 51.*

– Neutestamentliche Studien. 2000. *Vol. 132.*

– Paulusstudien II. 2002. *Vol. 143.*

– Exegetische Studien. 2008. *Vol. 223.*

– and *Hans-Christian Kammler:* Johannesstudien. 1996. *Vol. 88.*

Holloway, Paul A.: Coping with Prejudice. 2009. *Vol. 244.*

Holmberg, Bengt (Ed.): Exploring Early Christian Identity. 2008. *Vol. 226.*

– and *Mikael Winninge* (Ed.): Identity Formation in the New Testament. 2008. *Vol. 227.*

Holtz, Traugott: Geschichte und Theologie des Urchristentums. 1991. *Vol. 57.*

Hommel, Hildebrecht: Sebasmata. Vol. 1 1983. *Vol. 31.*
Vol. 2 1984. *Vol. 32.*

Horbury, William: Herodian Judaism and New Testament Study. 2006. *Vol. 193.*

Horn, Friedrich Wilhelm and *Ruben Zimmermann* (Ed.): Jenseits von Indikativ und Imperativ. Vol. 1. 2009. *Vol. 238.*

Horst, Pieter W. van der: Jews and Christians in Their Graeco-Roman Context. 2006. *Vol. 196.*

Hultgård, Anders and *Stig Norin* (Ed): Le Jour de Dieu / Der Tag Gottes. 2009. *Vol. 245.*

Hvalvik, Reidar: The Struggle for Scripture and Covenant. 1996. *Vol. II/82.*

Jackson, Ryan: New Creation in Paul's Letters. 2010. *Vol. II/272.*

Janßen, Martina: see *Frey, Jörg.*

Jauhiainen, Marko: The Use of Zechariah in Revelation. 2005. *Vol. II/199.*

Jensen, Morten H.: Herod Antipas in Galilee. 2006; ²2010. *Vol. II/215.*

Johns, Loren L.: The Lamb Christology of the Apocalypse of John. 2003. *Vol. II/167.*

Jossa, Giorgio: Jews or Christians? 2006. *Vol. 202.*

Joubert, Stephan: Paul as Benefactor. 2000. *Vol. II/124.*

Judge, E. A.: The First Christians in the Roman World. 2008. *Vol. 229.*

Lawrence, Louise: An Ethnography of the Gospel of Matthew. 2003. *Vol. II/165.*

Lee, Aquila H.I.: From Messiah to Preexistent Son. 2005. *Vol. II/192.*

Lee, Pilchan: The New Jerusalem in the Book of Relevation. 2000. *Vol. II/129.*

Lee, Sang M.: The Cosmic Drama of Salvation. 2010. *Vol. II/276.*

Lee, Simon S.: Jesus' Transfiguration and the Believers' Transformation. 2009. *Vol. II/265.*

Lichtenberger, Hermann: Das Ich Adams und das Ich der Menschheit. 2004. *Vol. 164.*

– see *Avemarie, Friedrich.*

– see *Frey, Jörg.*

Lierman, John: The New Testament Moses. 2004. *Vol. II/173.*

– (Ed.): Challenging Perspectives on the Gospel of John. 2006. *Vol. II/219.*

Lieu, Samuel N.C.: Manichaeism in the Later Roman Empire and Medieval China. ²1992. *Vol. 63.*

Lindemann, Andreas: Die Evangelien und die Apostelgeschichte. 2009. *Vol. 241.*

Lincicum, David: Paul and the Early Jewish Encounter with Deuteronomy. 2010. *Vol. II/284.*

Lindgård, Fredrik: Paul's Line of Thought in 2 Corinthians 4:16–5:10. 2004. *Vol. II/189.*

Loader, William R.G.: Jesus' Attitude Towards the Law. 1997. *Vol. II/97.*

Löhr, Gebhard: Verherrlichung Gottes durch Philosophie. 1997. *Vol. 97.*

Löhr, Hermut: Studien zum frühchristlichen und frühjüdischen Gebet. 2003. *Vol. 160.*

– see *Hengel, Martin.*

Löhr, Winrich Alfried: Basilides und seine Schule. 1995. *Vol. 83.*

Lorenzen, Stefanie: Das paulinische Eikon-Konzept. 2008. *Vol. II/250.*

Luomanen, Petri: Entering the Kingdom of Heaven. 1998. *Vol. II/101.*

Luz, Ulrich: see *Alexeev, Anatoly A.*

– see *Dunn, James D.G.*

Mackay, Ian D.: John's Raltionship with Mark. 2004. *Vol. II/182.*

Mackie, Scott D.: Eschatology and Exhortation in the Epistle to the Hebrews. 2006. *Vol. II/223.*

Magda, Ksenija: Paul's Territoriality and Mission Strategy. 2009. *Vol. II/266.*

Maier, Gerhard: Mensch und freier Wille. 1971. *Vol. 12.*

– Die Johannesoffenbarung und die Kirche. 1981. *Vol. 25.*

Markschies, Christoph: Valentinus Gnosticus? 1992. *Vol. 65.*

Marshall, Jonathan: Jesus, Patrons, and Benefactors. 2009. *Vol. II/259.*

Marshall, Peter: Enmity in Corinth: Social Conventions in Paul's Relations with the Corinthians. 1987. *Vol. II/23.*

Martin, Dale B.: see *Zangenberg, Jürgen.*

Mayer, Annemarie: Sprache der Einheit im Epheserbrief und in der Ökumene. 2002. *Vol. II/150.*

Mayordomo, Moisés: Argumentiert Paulus logisch? 2005. *Vol. 188.*

McDonough, Sean M.: YHWH at Patmos: Rev. 1:4 in its Hellenistic and Early Jewish Setting. 1999. *Vol. II/107.*

McDowell, Markus: Prayers of Jewish Women. 2006. *Vol. II/211.*

McGlynn, Moyna: Divine Judgement and Divine Benevolence in the Book of Wisdom. 2001. *Vol. II/139.*

Meade, David G.: Pseudonymity and Canon. 1986. *Vol. 39.*

Meadors, Edward P.: Jesus the Messianic Herald of Salvation. 1995. *Vol. II/72.*

Meißner, Stefan: Die Heimholung des Ketzers. 1996. *Vol. II/87.*

Mell, Ulrich: Die „anderen" Winzer. 1994. *Vol. 77.*

– see *Sänger, Dieter.*

Mengel, Berthold: Studien zum Philipperbrief. 1982. *Vol. II/8.*

Merkel, Helmut: Die Widersprüche zwischen den Evangelien. 1971. *Vol. 13.*

– see *Ego, Beate.*

Merklein, Helmut: Studien zu Jesus und Paulus. Vol. 1 1987. *Vol. 43.* – Vol. 2 1998. *Vol. 105.*

Merkt, Andreas: see *Nicklas, Tobias*

Metzdorf, Christina: Die Tempelaktion Jesu. 2003. *Vol. II/168.*

Metzler, Karin: Der griechische Begriff des Verzeihens. 1991. *Vol. II/44.*

Metzner, Rainer: Die Rezeption des Matthäusevangeliums im 1. Petrusbrief. 1995. *Vol. II/74.*

– Das Verständnis der Sünde im Johannesevangelium. 2000. *Vol. 122.*

Mihoc, Vasile: see *Dunn, James D.G.*

– see *Klein, Hans.*

Mineshige, Kiyoshi: Besitzverzicht und Almosen bei Lukas. 2003. *Vol. II/163.*

Mittmann, Siegfried: see *Hengel, Martin.*

Mittmann-Richert, Ulrike: Magnifikat und Benediktus. *1996. Vol. II/90.*

– Der Sühnetod des Gottesknechts. 2008. *Vol. 220.*

Miura, Yuzuru: David in Luke-Acts. 2007. *Vol. II/232.*

Moll, Sebastian: The Arch-Heretic Marcion. 2010. *Vol. 250.*

Morales, Rodrigo J.: The Spirit and the Restorat. 2010. *Vol. 282.*

Mournet, Terence C.: Oral Tradition and Literary Dependency. 2005. *Vol. II/195.*

Mußner, Franz: Jesus von Nazareth im Umfeld Israels und der Urkirche. Ed. von M. Theobald. 1998. *Vol. 111.*

Mutschler, Bernhard: Das Corpus Johanneum bei Irenäus von Lyon. 2005. *Vol. 189.*

– Glaube in den Pastoralbriefen. 2010. *Vol. 256.*

Myers, Susan E.: Spirit Epicleses in the Acts of Thomas. 2010. *Vol. 281.*

Nguyen, V. Henry T.: Christian Identity in Corinth. 2008. *Vol. II/243.*

Nicklas, Tobias, Andreas Merkt und *Joseph Verheyden* (Ed.): Gelitten – Gestorben – Auferstanden. 2010. *Vol. II/273.*

– see *Verheyden, Joseph*

Niebuhr, Karl-Wilhelm: Gesetz and Paränese. 1987. *Vol. II/28.*

– Heidenapostel aus Israel. 1992. *Vol. 62.*

– see *Deines, Roland.*

– see *Dimitrov, Ivan Z.*

– see *Klein, Hans.*

– see *Kraus, Wolfgang.*

Nielsen, Anders E.: "Until it is Fullfilled". 2000. *Vol. II/126.*

Nielsen, Jesper Tang: Die kognitive Dimension des Kreuzes. 2009. *Vol. II/263.*

Nissen, Andreas: Gott und der Nächste im antiken Judentum. 1974. *Vol. 15.*

Noack, Christian: Gottesbewußtsein. 2000. *Vol. II/116.*

Noormann, Rolf: Irenäus als Paulusinterpret. 1994. *Vol. II/66.*

Norin, Stig: see *Hultgård, Anders.*

Novakovic, Lidija: Messiah, the Healer of the Sick. 2003. *Vol. II/170.*

Obermann, Andreas: Die christologische Erfüllung der Schrift im Johannesevangelium. 1996. *Vol. II/83.*

Öhler, Markus: Barnabas. 2003. *Vol. 156.*

– see *Becker, Michael.*

Okure, Teresa: The Johannine Approach to Mission. 1988. *Vol. II/31.*

Onuki, Takashi: Heil und Erlösung. 2004. *Vol. 165.*

Oropeza, B. J.: Paul and Apostasy. 2000. *Vol. II/115.*

Ostmeyer, Karl-Heinrich: Kommunikation mit Gott und Christus. 2006. *Vol. 197.*

– Taufe und Typos. 2000. *Vol. II/118.*

Paulsen, Henning: Studien zur Literatur und Geschichte des frühen Christentums. Ed. von Ute E. Eisen. 1997. *Vol. 99.*

Pao, David W.: Acts and the Isaianic New Exodus. 2000. *Vol. II/130.*

Park, Eung Chun: The Mission Discourse in Matthew's Interpretation. 1995. *Vol. II/81.*

Park, Joseph S.: Conceptions of Afterlife in Jewish Insriptions. 2000. *Vol. II/121.*

Pate, C. Marvin: The Reverse of the Curse. 2000. *Vol. II/114.*

Pearce, Sarah J.K.: The Land of the Body. 2007. *Vol. 208.*

Peres, Imre: Griechische Grabinschriften und neutestamentliche Eschatologie. 2003. *Vol. 157.*

Perry, Peter S.: The Rhetoric of Digressions. 2009. *Vol. II/268.*

Philip, Finny: The Origins of Pauline Pneumatology. 2005. *Vol. II/194.*

Philonenko, Marc (Ed.): Le Trône de Dieu. 1993. *Vol. 69.*

Pilhofer, Peter: Presbyteron Kreitton. 1990. *Vol. II/39.*

– Philippi. Vol. 1 1995. *Vol. 87.* – Vol. 2 ²2009. *Vol. 119.*

– Die frühen Christen und ihre Welt. 2002. *Vol. 145.*

– see *Becker, Eve-Marie.*

– see *Ego, Beate.*

Pitre, Brant: Jesus, the Tribulation, and the End of the Exile. 2005. *Vol. II/204.*

Plümacher, Eckhard: Geschichte und Geschichten. 2004. *Vol. 170.*

Pöhlmann, Wolfgang: Der Verlorene Sohn und das Haus. 1993. *Vol. 68.*

Poirier, John C.: The Tongues of Angels. 2010. *Vol. II/287.*

Pokorný, Petr and *Josef B. Souček:* Bibelauslegung als Theologie. 1997. *Vol. 100.*

– and *Jan Roskovec* (Ed.): Philosophical Hermeneutics and Biblical Exegesis. 2002. *Vol. 153.*

Popkes, Enno Edzard: Das Menschenbild des Thomasevangeliums. 2007. *Vol. 206.*

– Die Theologie der Liebe Gottes in den johanneischen Schriften. 2005. *Vol. II/197.*

Porter, Stanley E.: The Paul of Acts. 1999. *Vol. 115.*

Prieur, Alexander: Die Verkündigung der Gottesherrschaft. 1996. *Vol. II/89.*

Probst, Hermann: Paulus und der Brief. 1991. *Vol. II/45.*

Rabens, Volker: The Holy Spirit and Ethics in Paul. 2010. *Vol. II/283.*

Räisänen, Heikki: Paul and the Law. 1983, ²1987. *Vol. 29.*

Rehkopf, Friedrich: Die lukanische Sonder-
quelle. 1959. *Vol. 5.*
Rein, Matthias: Die Heilung des Blindge-
borenen (Joh 9). 1995. *Vol. II/73.*
Reinmuth, Eckart: Pseudo-Philo und Lukas.
1994. *Vol. 74.*
Reiser, Marius: Bibelkritik und Auslegung der
Heiligen Schrift. 2007. *Vol. 217.*
– Syntax und Stil des Markusevangeliums.
1984. *Vol. II/11.*
Reynolds, Benjamin E.: The Apocalyptic Son of
Man in the Gospel of John. 2008. *Vol. II/249.*
Rhodes, James N.: The Epistle of Barnabas
and the Deuteronomic Tradition. 2004.
Vol. II/188.
Richards, E. Randolph: The Secretary in the
Letters of Paul. 1991. *Vol. II/42.*
Riesner, Rainer: Jesus als Lehrer. 1981, ³1988.
Vol. II/7.
– Die Frühzeit des Apostels Paulus. 1994.
Vol. 71.
Rissi, Mathias: Die Theologie des Hebräer-
briefs. 1987. *Vol. 41.*
Röcker, Fritz W.: Belial und Katechon. 2009.
Vol. II/262.
Röhser, Günter: Metaphorik und Personifikation
der Sünde. 1987. *Vol. II/25.*
Rose, Christian: Theologie als Erzählung im
Markusevangelium. 2007. *Vol. II/236.*
– Die Wolke der Zeugen. 1994. *Vol. II/60.*
Roskovec, Jan: see *Pokorný, Petr.*
Rothschild, Clare K.: Baptist Traditions and Q.
2005. *Vol. 190.*
– Hebrews as Pseudepigraphon. 2009.
Vol. 235.
– Luke Acts and the Rhetoric of History. 2004.
Vol. II/175.
– see *Frey, Jörg.*
Rüegger, Hans-Ulrich: Verstehen, was Markus
erzählt. 2002. *Vol. II/155.*
Rüger, Hans Peter: Die Weisheitsschrift aus der
Kairoer Geniza. 1991. *Vol. 53.*
Sänger, Dieter: Antikes Judentum und die Mys-
terien. 1980. *Vol. II/5.*
– Die Verkündigung des Gekreuzigten und
Israel. 1994. *Vol. 75.*
– see *Burchard, Christoph*
– and *Ulrich Mell* (Ed.): Paulus und Johannes.
2006. *Vol. 198.*
Salier, Willis Hedley: The Rhetorical Impact
of the Semeia in the Gospel of John. 2004.
Vol. II/186.
Salzmann, Jorg Christian: Lehren und Ermah-
nen. 1994. *Vol. II/59.*
Sandnes, Karl Olav: Paul – One of the Proph-
ets? 1991. *Vol. II/43.*
Sato, Migaku: Q und Prophetie. 1988. *Vol. II/29.*

Schäfer, Ruth: Paulus bis zum Apostelkonzil.
2004. *Vol. II/179.*
Schaper, Joachim: Eschatology in the Greek
Psalter. 1995. *Vol. II/76.*
Schimanowski, Gottfried: Die himmlische
Liturgie in der Apokalypse des Johannes.
2002. *Vol. II/154.*
– Weisheit und Messias. 1985. *Vol. II/17.*
Schlichting, Günter: Ein jüdisches Leben Jesu.
1982. *Vol. 24.*
Schließer, Benjamin: Abraham's Faith in
Romans 4. 2007. *Vol. II/224.*
Schnabel, Eckhard J.: Law and Wisdom from
Ben Sira to Paul. 1985. *Vol. II/16.*
Schnelle, Udo: see *Frey, Jörg.*
Schröter, Jens: Von Jesus zum Neuen Testa-
ment. 2007. *Vol. 204.*
– see *Frey, Jörg.*
Schutter, William L.: Hermeneutic and Compo-
sition in I Peter. 1989. *Vol. II/30.*
Schwartz, Daniel R.: Studies in the Jewish
Background of Christianity. 1992. *Vol. 60.*
Schwemer, Anna Maria: see *Hengel, Martin*
Scott, Ian W.: Implicit Epistemology in the Let-
ters of Paul. 2005. *Vol. II/205.*
Scott, James M.: Adoption as Sons of God.
1992. *Vol. II/48.*
– Paul and the Nations. 1995. *Vol. 84.*
Shi, Wenhua: Paul's Message of the Cross as
Body Language. 2008. *Vol. II/254.*
Shum, Shiu-Lun: Paul's Use of Isaiah in
Romans. 2002. *Vol. II/156.*
Siegert, Folker: Drei hellenistisch-jüdische
Predigten. Teil I 1980. *Vol. 20* – Teil II 1992.
Vol. 61.
– Nag-Hammadi-Register. 1982. *Vol. 26.*
– Argumentation bei Paulus. 1985. *Vol. 34.*
– Philon von Alexandrien. 1988. *Vol. 46.*
Simon, Marcel: Le christianisme antique et son
contexte religieux I/II. 1981. *Vol. 23.*
Smit, Peter-Ben: Fellowship and Food in the
Kingdom. 2008. *Vol. II/234.*
Snodgrass, Klyne: The Parable of the Wicked
Tenants. 1983. *Vol. 27.*
Söding, Thomas: Das Wort vom Kreuz. 1997.
Vol. 93.
– see *Thüsing, Wilhelm.*
Sommer, Urs: Die Passionsgeschichte des
Markusevangeliums. 1993. *Vol. II/58.*
Sorensen, Eric: Possession and Exorcism in the
New Testament and Early Christianity. 2002.
Vol. II/157.
Souček, Josef B.: see *Pokorný, Petr.*
Southall, David J.: Rediscovering Righteous-
ness in Romans. 2008. *Vol. 240.*
Spangenberg, Volker: Herrlichkeit des Neuen
Bundes. 1993. *Vol. II/55.*

Spanje, T.E. van: Inconsistency in Paul? 1999. *Vol. II/110.*
Speyer, Wolfgang: Frühes Christentum im antiken Strahlungsfeld. Vol. I: 1989. *Vol. 50.*
- Vol. II: 1999. *Vol. 116.*
- Vol. III: 2007. *Vol. 213.*
Spittler, Janet E.: Animals in the Apocryphal Acts of the Apostles. 2008. *Vol. II/247.*
Sprinkle, Preston: Law and Life. 2008. *Vol. II/241.*
Stadelmann, Helge: Ben Sira als Schriftgelehrter. 1980. *Vol. II/6.*
Stein, Hans Joachim: Frühchristliche Mahlfeiern. 2008. *Vol. II/255.*
Stenschke, Christoph W.: Luke's Portrait of Gentiles Prior to Their Coming to Faith. *Vol. II/108.*
Sterck-Degueldre, Jean-Pierre: Eine Frau namens Lydia. 2004. *Vol. II/176.*
Stettler, Christian: Der Kolosserhymnus. 2000. *Vol. II/131.*
Stettler, Hanna: Die Christologie der Pastoralbriefe. 1998. *Vol. II/105.*
Stökl Ben Ezra, Daniel: The Impact of Yom Kippur on Early Christianity. 2003. *Vol. 163.*
Strobel, August: Die Stunde der Wahrheit. 1980. *Vol. 21.*
Stroumsa, Guy G.: Barbarian Philosophy. 1999. *Vol. 112.*
Stuckenbruck, Loren T.: Angel Veneration and Christology. 1995. *Vol. II/70.*
-, *Stephen C. Barton* and *Benjamin G. Wold* (Ed.): Memory in the Bible and Antiquity. 2007. *Vol. 212.*
Stuhlmacher, Peter (Ed.): Das Evangelium und die Evangelien. 1983. *Vol. 28.*
- Biblische Theologie und Evangelium. 2002. *Vol. 146.*
Sung, Chong-Hyon: Vergebung der Sünden. 1993. *Vol. II/57.*
Svendsen, Stefan N.: Allegory Transformed. 2009. *Vol. II/269.*
Tajra, Harry W.: The Trial of St. Paul. 1989. *Vol. II/35.*
- The Martyrdom of St.Paul. 1994. *Vol. II/67.*
Tellbe, Mikael: Christ-Believers in Ephesus. 2009. *Vol. 242.*
Theißen, Gerd: Studien zur Soziologie des Urchristentums. 1979, ³1989. *Vol. 19.*
Theobald, Michael: Studien zum Römerbrief. 2001. *Vol. 136.*
Theobald, Michael: see *Mußner, Franz.*
Thornton, Claus-Jürgen: Der Zeuge des Zeugen. 1991. *Vol. 56.*
Thüsing, Wilhelm: Studien zur neutestamentlichen Theologie. Ed. von Thomas Söding. 1995. *Vol. 82.*

Thurén, Lauri: Derhethorizing Paul. 2000. *Vol. 124.*
Thyen, Hartwig: Studien zum Corpus Iohanneum. 2007. *Vol. 214.*
Tibbs, Clint: Religious Experience of the Pneuma. 2007. *Vol. II/230.*
Toit, David S. du: Theios Anthropos. 1997. *Vol. II/91.*
Tolmie, D. Francois: Persuading the Galatians. 2005. *Vol. II/190.*
Tomson, Peter J. and *Doris Lambers-Petry* (Ed.): The Image of the Judaeo-Christians in Ancient Jewish and Christian Literature. 2003. *Vol. 158.*
Toney, Carl N.: Paul's Inclusive Ethic. 2008. *Vol. II/252.*
Trebilco, Paul: The Early Christians in Ephesus from Paul to Ignatius. 2004. *Vol. 166.*
Treloar, Geoffrey R.: Lightfoot the Historian. 1998. *Vol. II/103.*
Troftgruben, Troy M.: A Conclusion Unhindered. 2010. *Vol. II/280.*
Tsuji, Manabu: Glaube zwischen Vollkommenheit und Verweltlichung. 1997. *Vol. II/93.*
Twelftree, Graham H.: Jesus the Exorcist. 1993. *Vol. II/54.*
Ulrichs, Karl Friedrich: Christusglaube. 2007. *Vol. II/227.*
Urban, Christina: Das Menschenbild nach dem Johannesevangelium. 2001. *Vol. II/137.*
Vahrenhorst, Martin: Kultische Sprache in den Paulusbriefen. 2008. *Vol. 230.*
Vegge, Ivar: 2 Corinthians – a Letter about Reconciliation. 2008. *Vol. II/239.*
Verheyden, Joseph, Korinna Zamfir and *Tobias Nicklas* (Ed.): Prophets and Prophecy in Jewish and Early Christian Literature. 2010. *Vol. II/286.*
- see *Nicklas, Tobias*
Visotzky, Burton L.: Fathers of the World. 1995. *Vol. 80.*
Vollenweider, Samuel: Horizonte neutestamentlicher Christologie. 2002. *Vol. 144.*
Vos, Johan S.: Die Kunst der Argumentation bei Paulus. 2002. *Vol. 149.*
Waaler, Erik: The Shema and The First Commandment in First Corinthians. 2008. *Vol. II/253.*
Wagener, Ulrike: Die Ordnung des „Hauses Gottes". 1994. *Vol. II/65.*
Wagner, J. Ross: see *Wilk, Florian.*
Wahlen, Clinton: Jesus and the Impurity of Spirits in the Synoptic Gospels. 2004. *Vol. II/185.*
Walker, Donald D.: Paul's Offer of Leniency (2 Cor 10:1). 2002. *Vol. II/152.*

Walter, Nikolaus: Praeparatio Evangelica. Ed. von Wolfgang Kraus und Florian Wilk. 1997. *Vol. 98.*

Wander, Bernd: Gottesfürchtige und Sympathisanten. 1998. *Vol. 104.*

Wasserman, Emma: The Death of the Soul in Romans 7. 2008. *Vol. 256.*

Waters, Guy: The End of Deuteronomy in the Epistles of Paul. 2006. *Vol. 221.*

Watt, Jan G. van der: see *Frey, Jörg*

Watts, Rikki: Isaiah's New Exodus and Mark. 1997. *Vol. II/88.*

Webb, Robert L.: see *Bock, Darrell L.*

Wedderburn, A.J.M.: Baptism and Resurrection. 1987. *Vol. 44.*

Wegner, Uwe: Der Hauptmann von Kafarnaum. 1985. *Vol. II/14.*

Weiß, Hans-Friedrich: Frühes Christentum und Gnosis. 2008. *Vol. 225.*

Weissenrieder, Annette: Images of Illness in the Gospel of Luke. 2003. Vol. II/164.

–, *Friederike Wendt* and *Petra von Gemünden* (Ed.): Picturing the New Testament. 2005. *Vol. II/193.*

Welck, Christian: Erzählte ‚Zeichen'. 1994. *Vol. II/69.*

Wendt, Friederike (Ed.): see *Weissenrieder, Annette.*

Wiarda, Timothy: Peter in the Gospels. 2000. *Vol. II/127.*

Wifstrand, Albert: Epochs and Styles. 2005. *Vol. 179.*

Wilk, Florian and *J. Ross Wagner* (Ed.): Between Gospel and Election. 2010. *Vol. 257.*

– see *Walter, Nikolaus.*

Williams, Catrin H.: I am He. 2000. *Vol. II/113.*

Wilson, Todd A.: The Curse of the Law and the Crisis in Galatia. 2007. *Vol. II/225.*

Wilson, Walter T.: Love without Pretense. 1991. *Vol. II/46.*

Winn, Adam: The Purpose of Mark's Gospel. 2008. *Vol. II/245.*

Winninge, Mikael: see *Holmberg, Bengt.*

Wischmeyer, Oda: Von Ben Sira zu Paulus. 2004. *Vol. 173.*

Wisdom, Jeffrey: Blessing for the Nations and the Curse of the Law. 2001. *Vol. II/133.*

Witmer, Stephen E.: Divine Instruction in Early Christianity. 2008. *Vol. II/246.*

Wold, Benjamin G.: Women, Men, and Angels. 2005. *Vol. II/2001.*

Wolter, Michael: Theologie und Ethos im frühen Christentum. 2009. *Vol. 236.*

– see *Stuckenbruck, Loren T.*

Wright, Archie T.: The Origin of Evil Spirits. 2005. *Vol. II/198.*

Wucherpfennig, Ansgar: Heracleon Philologus. 2002. *Vol. 142.*

Yates, John W.: The Spirit and Creation in Paul. 2008. *Vol. II/251.*

Yeung, Maureen: Faith in Jesus and Paul. 2002. *Vol. II/147.*

Zamfir, Corinna: see *Verheyden, Joseph*

Zangenberg, Jürgen, Harold W. Attridge and *Dale B. Martin* (Ed.): Religion, Ethnicity and Identity in Ancient Galilee. 2007. *Vol. 210.*

Zimmermann, Alfred E.: Die urchristlichen Lehrer. 1984, ²1988. *Vol. II/12.*

Zimmermann, Johannes: Messianische Texte aus Qumran. 1998. *Vol. II/104.*

Zimmermann, Ruben: Christologie der Bilder im Johannesevangelium. 2004. *Vol. 171.*

– Geschlechtermetaphorik und Gottesverhältnis. 2001. *Vol. II/122.*

– (Ed.): Hermeneutik der Gleichnisse Jesu. 2008. *Vol. 231.*

– see *Frey, Jörg.*

– see *Horn, Friedrich Wilhelm.*

Zugmann, Michael: „Hellenisten" in der Apostelgeschichte. 2009. *Vol. II/264.*

Zumstein, Jean: see *Dettwiler, Andreas*

Zwiep, Arie W.: Judas and the Choice of Matthias. 2004. *Vol. II/187.*

For a complete catalogue please write to the publisher
Mohr Siebeck • P.O. Box 2030 • D–72010 Tübingen/Germany
Up-to-date information on the internet at www.mohr.de